THE SELECTED LETTERS OF JUANITA BROOKS

Juanita Brooks in 1979. Photo courtesy of Willa Derrick.

THE SELECTED LETTERS OF JUANITA BROOKS

Edited by Craig S. Smith

THE UNIVERSITY OF UTAH PRESS
Salt Lake City

The Defiance House Man colophon is a registered trademark of The University of Utah Press. It is based on a four-foot-tall Ancient Puebloan pictograph (late PIII) near Glen Canyon, Utah.

Library of Congress Cataloging-in-Publication Data
Names: Brooks, Juanita, 1898-1989, author. | Smith, Craig S., 1967– editor.
Title: The selected letters of Juanita Brooks / edited by Craig S. Smith.
Description: Salt Lake City : The University of Utah Press, [2018] | Includes bibliographical references and index.
Identifiers: LCCN 2019009207 (print) | LCCN 2019010684 (ebook) | ISBN 9781607816485 () | ISBN 9781607816478 (cloth : alk. paper)
Subjects: LCSH: Brooks, Juanita, 1898-1989—Correspondence. | Women historians—Utah—Correspondence. | Women historians—Utah—Biography. | Utah—Biography. | Mormons—Utah—Historiography. | Utah—Historiography.
Classification: LCC F826.B877 (ebook) | LCC F826.B877 A4 2018 (print) | DDC 979.2/03092 [B] —dc23
LC record available at https://lccn.loc.gov/2019009207

Errata and further information on this and other titles available online at UofUpress.com

Printed and bound in the United States of America.

Contents

Editorial Procedures

The purpose of this volume is to present a selection of Juanita Brooks's letters to the reader interested in the history of Utah and the Mormons. The selected letters are a window into her life and priorities in her own voice, allowing for an intimate encounter with a person who has become an icon. These letters are more than just a collection of historical documents, they are a biography of her interactions with her contemporaries and her efforts to influence how Mormon history is presented and written. While Levi Peterson's award-winning biography,[1] employing excerpts from some letters, details major events in her life, this broader selection of letters provides a fresh perspective on her personality and her growth as a scholar. The letters afford an important glimpse into her struggles, concerns, and interests. They also trace her development from her days learning the trade as a historian to when she was a well-known and well-loved speaker and recognized authority. The compiled letters function like a diary that she only briefly kept.

This volume includes 222 letters selected from the more than nine hundred extant letters written to her colleagues and friends. The selected letters are reproduced in their entirety so that readers have the opportunity to experience her thoughts in context. She often mingled the business at hand with quaint stories of her roots in the deserts of southern Nevada and Utah, making these letters a joy to receive and read. They are arranged chronologically, starting in 1941, the year of her first letters to her mentor Dale Morgan, when she started to focus seriously on historical writing, through 1978, the final extant correspondence, which was composed while she was struggling with her declining mental health. Not incorporated in the selection are a few earlier letters, from the 1930s, which concerned her collecting and copying of pioneer diaries and her duties as LDS Church St. George Stake Relief Society president.

The selections focus on letters to colleagues and friends, dealing primarily with her professional activities, and only a couple of letters to her family are included. I selected the letters for inclusion to provide as wide a cross section of recipients as possible while presenting a broad sampling of her thoughts and concerns through time. Letters detailing important events in her life, such as her encounter with Apostle Delbert Stapley in 1961 and the death of her husband in 1970, were also chosen.

The letters highlight the range of her correspondents, comprising individuals with a wide spectrum of opinions and beliefs, from faithful Latter-day Saints to those who rejected the faith, from LDS general authorities to outspoken opponents of the Mormon Church. She befriended everyone regardless of their opinion and was always willing to listen and communicate. She graciously defended herself to those who disagreed with her and allowed them their views, though she always strongly advocated open and unbiased writing of Mormon history. Among the historians and authors with whom she maintained correspondence were Dale Morgan, Charles Kelly, Fawn Brodie, Leonard Arrington, Wallace Stegner, Samuel Taylor, Harold Schindler, Gustive Larson, LeRoy Hafen, Richard Anderson, Claudia and Richard Bushman, Klaus Hansen, Rodello Hunter, and Virginia Sorensen. She also communicated with general authorities of the LDS Church, including George Albert Smith, Stephen Richards, Harold B. Lee, and LeGrand Richards, and government officials such as Secretary of the Interior Stewart Udall and Utah governor Calvin Rampton. Some of her friends included Alfred Bush, Ettie Lee, Albert Lambert, Stanley Ivins, Winifred (Peg) Gregory, Grace Woodbury, and J. Wesley Williamson.[2]

Most of her letters are housed at the Utah State Historical Society in the Juanita Brooks Papers, MSS B103. The collection is in the form of typed carbons of the originals that she mailed to her correspondents. Interlaid with the carbons are many of the original responding letters. She carefully saved much of this correspondence, though not all, as a record of her activities in place of a diary. The reproduced letters are from this collection, unless otherwise noted at the bottom of each. A number of her letters, especially those from the 1970s, not in the Juanita Brooks Papers are instead located in the Levi Peterson Collection of Juanita Brooks Papers, MSS B 1221 at the Utah State Historical Society. It is unclear why much of her later correspondence is in this separate collection.

Additional known letters are in the collections of her recipients. The Dale L. Morgan Papers, BANC MSS 71/161 c, at the Bancroft Library, University of California, Berkeley contains the original of many of her letters from the early 1940s to Dale Morgan that were not saved as carbons in her collection. The Special Collections at the Marriott Library, University of Utah, holds her letters in the files of several correspondents, including Charles Kelly, Fawn Brodie, A. Russell Mortensen, and Lowry Nelson. Copies of most of her known letters made by Levi Peterson during his research for Brooks's biography are located in the Levi S. Peterson Collection, WSUS 05-02-001, Archives, Stewart Library, Weber State University.

Brooks typed all her letters except in rare cases when her typewriter was not available or when she wrote short note cards. She was an excellent typist, seldom making typos or overstrikes, even though she would at times criticize her typing skills. The occasional typos have been corrected in the reproduced letters without comment. Otherwise, Brooks's wording and punctuation in the letters have been maintained. This practice was followed even where modern orthographical or typographical practice would deem Brooks's way of writing incorrect or unusual. In a few letters, a portion of the carbon was unclear or part of the letter was missing. These cases are noted in the reproduced letters with brackets.

When possible, a short biographical note and birth and death dates are given in footnotes for the correspondents, as well as for the individuals mentioned in the letters. This information was obtained from online obituaries and genealogical information.

In citing manuscript collections in which the letters in this volume are found, shortened titles have generally been used. Collections frequently cited have been identified by the following abbreviations:

Dale L. Morgan Papers	Dale L. Morgan Papers, BANC MSS 71/161 c, The Bancroft Library, University of California, Berkeley.
Institutional Archives	Institutional Archives, Huntington Library.
Juanita Brooks Papers	Juanita Brooks Papers, MSS B103, Utah State Historical Society.

Levi Peterson's Collection	Levi Peterson's Collection of Juanita Brooks Papers, MSS B 1221, Utah State Historical Society.
Marriott Library Special Collections	Special Collections, J. Willard Marriott Library, University of Utah.
WSU Levi Peterson Collection	Levi S. Peterson Collection, WSUS 05-02-001, Archives, Stewart Library, Weber State University.

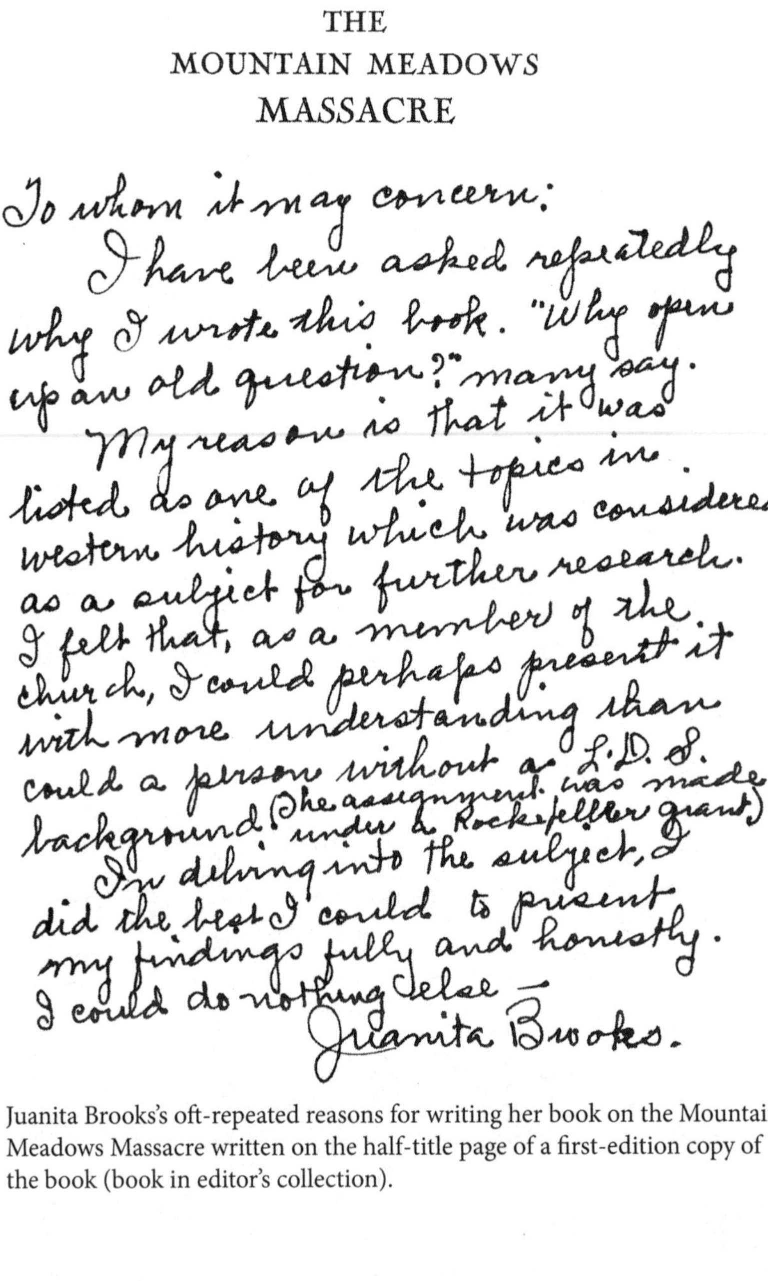

THE
MOUNTAIN MEADOWS
MASSACRE

To whom it may concern:

I have been asked repeatedly why I wrote this book. "Why open up an old question?" many say.

My reason is that it was listed as one of the topics in western history which was considered as a subject for further research. I felt that, as a member of the church, I could perhaps present it with more understanding than could a person without a L.D.S. background. (The assignment was made under a Rockefeller grant.)

In delving into the subject, I did the best I could to present my findings fully and honestly. I could do nothing else—

Juanita Brooks.

Juanita Brooks's oft-repeated reasons for writing her book on the Mountain Meadows Massacre written on the half-title page of a first-edition copy of the book (book in editor's collection).

Introduction

"To whom it may concern:

I have been asked repeatedly why I wrote this book. 'Why open up an old question' many say." Juanita Brooks then goes on to give her reasons for writing the book and that she provided her results as fully and honestly as she could.

She wrote this message on the half-title page of a first-edition copy of her book *The Mountain Meadows Massacre*,[1] the copy that was inscribed and presented to Apostle Delbert L. Stapley of the Quorum of Twelve Apostles of the LDS Church. Though the inscription is undated, the book was probably presented to him at the time of their meeting on June 13, 1961, in which he insisted that in her biography of John D. Lee she not include the notice of Lee's reinstatement to his former blessings and membership in the LDS Church.[2] The quote gives her often-repeated reasoning for writing her groundbreaking book, which was her most significant work. It also highlights her lifelong quest for truth and honesty in the writing of Mormon history.

The publication of her landmark book in 1950, which recounted the terrible 1857 tragedy in southern Utah, served as a bridge to the new, more progressive era in which Mormon history was studied and written, often called the New Mormon History. Prior to her book, Mormon history within the faithful Mormon community was typically projected as faith promoting where controversial issues and sensitive evidence were not tackled and the historical actors were portrayed without fault or well-rounded human character. The authorities in the LDS Church were concerned that any discussion of provocative topics in Mormon history would destroy faith and damage the church's public relations, especially given the historically negative public views of Mormonism. LDS leaders strongly advised against exploring anything controversial and argued that avoidance of such subjects was best for the church.

Within this climate, Brooks courageously wrote and published her book *The Mountain Meadows Massacre*, at that time one of the more forbidden subjects in LDS Church history. She approached her study as comprehensively as possible and presented her research as objectively and honestly as she could. She followed all the evidence available to her regardless of the resulting conclusions, and her principal goal was to determine and relate what actually transpired without a hidden agenda. The result was a scholarly work received with high praise by both non-Mormons and many Mormons.

Brooks was born on January 15, 1898, and raised in Bunkerville, Nevada, a remote agricultural village on the fringes of the Mormon frontier in the desert region known as Dixie, which encompassed southeastern Nevada and southwestern Utah. After graduating high school and attending a year of normal school in Bunkerville, she taught school and eventually married Leonard Ernest Pulsipher in 1919. He died of a malignant tumor after less than a year and a half of marriage, but not before producing a son, Ernest. She then continued her education, completing an undergraduate degree at Brigham Young University, and returned to Dixie to teach English at Dixie College in St. George, Utah, where she later also served as Dean of Women. She also spent a sabbatical year at Columbia University where she received a master's degree.

In 1933, Brooks married the well-known and well-liked Washington County sheriff, Will Brooks. He had four sons from a previous marriage and they added an additional daughter and three sons, so, along with her son, her household contained at times nine dependents under her care. Even with the large family, she took on the organization and supervision of a staff of women in collecting and copying in typescript form early Mormon diaries and journals in 1934 under the Federal Emergency Relief Administration and later the Historical Records Survey. During this time, she also commenced her long career of researching and writing by submitting manuscripts for publication in magazines, always with the support of her husband. In addition to the Mountain Meadows Massacre book, over the years she wrote several books and family histories, edited a number of pioneer diaries, and contributed numerous articles and essays to magazines and journals on the history of Dixie.

She spent most of her adult life in St. George, except for a couple of interludes in Salt Lake City in the early 1960s and 1970s. She and her husband lived in Salt Lake City from 1960 to 1963 while she was employed by the Utah State Historical Society to edit the Hosea Stout diaries. She returned to Salt Lake City after the passing of Will Brooks in 1970. As her mental health declined, she moved back to St. George for the final time in early 1977. She traveled extensively throughout Utah and the region during her career, often taking the night bus, giving frequent speeches and attending meetings, especially those for the Utah State Historical Society of which she was a board member for twenty-four years. She died of Alzheimer's disease on August 26, 1989.[3]

Brooks was an active member of the LDS Church and stayed anchored to her roots in Dixie. She raised a family of mostly faithful members of the LDS Church and often stressed to them the importance of church attendance. She did not allow her own membership, though, to constrain her intellectual independence and found it impossible to yield unquestioning obedience. Prior to the issuance of her Mountain Meadows Massacre book, Brooks responded to her Stanford University Press publisher's concerns over what repercussions its publication might have on her personally from her fellow Mormons, declaring, "I do not want to be excommunicated from my church for many reasons, but if that is the price that I must pay for intellectual honesty, I shall pay it—I hope without bitterness."[4]

Her unwavering commitment to honest scholarship effected gradual change in the way Mormons presented their history because of her determination to remain part of the LDS community, in contrast to her contemporaries historians Fawn Brodie and Dale Morgan. After tackling Mormon subjects early in their career, these scholars left the culture and region of their birth and switched to other topics of research, reducing their impact on the way Mormons related their history. Brooks knew if she abandoned her Mormon faith she would be labeled an apostate and her efforts discounted in Mormon circles. In this context she often used an analogy from her rural upbringing: "the best way to turn a herd of cattle is not to ride directly counter to them, but to travel with them and turn them gradually."[5]

Among Brooks's major contributions was her steadfastness that historical documents be presented unaltered regardless of the light they shed on early Mormons. A common practice at the time was to edit pioneer journals to eliminate any passages deemed offensive or that had the potential to discredit the pioneer author or the LDS Church. Brooks continually expressed alarm at this practice and contended that the only real way to honor early Mormons was to reproduce their writings in full, unexpurgated. Her feeling throughout her letters was that "'Saints are People' steeped in the concepts of their time."[6] She rejected the overeagerness of many to make pioneers demigods and considered their human side important to the understanding of their history.

Following the publication of *The Mountain Meadows Massacre*, she consistently maintained that she had done a great service for the church she loved and encouraged those disagreeing with her open approach to await the passage of time before deciding whether it was good for the LDS Church. During correspondence in late 1955, with LeGrand Richards of the Quorum of Twelve Apostles, who questioned her loyalty for broaching the subject of the Mountain Meadows Massacre, she noted that five years had passed since publication of the book and he should wait five more years to evaluate whether her actions were a disservice to the church. Her forecast proved correct in that the book as well as her other efforts became a catalyst for constructive change in how Mormons examined and wrote about their history. Over time, more classes at the LDS Church's Brigham Young University discussed her book, and even the church-owned bookstore, Deseret Book, eventually offered it for sale, in 1963, thus legitimizing her work among Latter-day Saints.

After opening the door to a more truthful portrayal of Mormon history, other historians followed her lead. Leonard Arrington, an early proponent of the New Mormon History, recognized her important role when he thanked her "for the high integrity and intellectual probity which you have demonstrated again and again. You are a model for us all."[7] She continued to receive honors for her pioneering activities throughout her career, including an honorary Doctorate of Letters from Utah State University in 1964; other honorary degrees from the College of Southern Utah in 1969 and the University of Utah in 1973; the Distinguished Service Award in Letters from the Utah Academy of Sciences, Arts, and Letters in 1958; the Brigham Young University Alumni Association Emeritus

Club Award in 1981; and membership in the Beehive Hall of Fame in 1985. The citation for the Emeritus Club award read: "Her commitment to probe and inquire in order to tell the truth, to narrate and interpret history honestly made it easier for fellow Mormon scholars to pursue church-related history more objectively."[8]

Brooks bravely took the leap of publishing her book on the Mountain Meadows Massacre without knowing how its publication would affect her membership in the LDS Church, which she greatly valued. Following publication, her worst fears did not materialize as she was not excommunicated, disfellowshipped, or excluded from the LDS Church, as is often rumored in Utah.[9] She probably felt disgraced and ostracized immediately following publication, with some individuals shunning her and her family. She received a couple of negative reviews of the book from Latter-day Saints, though most of the reviews were positive. A few on the Brigham Young University faculty appear to have considered her an apostate, which required some of her children to defend her in classes, as she later noted to a faculty member who requested a copy of her book in 1974.[10] The book was mostly received with silence within the Mormon community following publication. LDS Church authorities avoided reference to it. As time passed, the local LDS Church leaders in St. George came to "treat me very well" she asserted. Many of the authorities had not read the book.[11] She was presenting Relief Society talks at her ward by at least 1953.[12]

By the 1960s she was even more welcome in the mainstream Mormon community, being invited to present talks to many LDS Church groups including at Brigham Young University and church institute classes.[13] For example, she traveled to Southern California in 1962 to speak before an LDS institute class. In 1963, she wrote that she was happy to see her book on display at the LDS Church–owned Deseret Book, a store that had refused to carry it earlier.[14] Marion Hanks, a general authority of the LDS Church, invited her to serve on the advisory council of the Friends of the BYU Library organization in 1965. Brooks declined the offer and Hanks responded by thanking her and appreciating her "courage and your solid brand of faith."[15] She also edited her LDS ward's "Biographies: Federal Heights Ward" in 1963 and was even asked to speak on John D. Lee in LDS ward Sunday sacrament meetings. Though she kept busy speaking before many LDS Church groups, the official church magazines apparently would still not consider publishing one of her articles. In 1962, Juanita asked Marba C. Josephson, editor of *Improvement Era*, "Or could you consider such an article—done by me? I don't really expect an affirmative answer; I just asked." Evidently the answer was negative.[16]

In 1970, she wrote the bishop of her LDS ward in Salt Lake City listing reasons why she could not assume an official assignment or "calling" in the ward, demonstrating that at least by that time she was an accepted member as callings in the ward are typically only given to active Latter-day Saints. In this letter she also listed her busy schedule, including speaking at LDS Church teenage group meetings, talking to youth groups at Brigham Young University, and lecturing the Lady Faculty of Brigham Young University, all activities that only LDS members in good standing would be asked to perform.[17]

Through the years her stature and influence continued to grow as the result of not only her written corpus, but also her unceasing public speaking. She was always in great demand to speak to academic groups at all the Utah universities and to LDS Church youth groups, among others. This wide range of audiences allowed her to inspire her contemporaries, as well as the younger generation, with her insistence on the truthful portrayal of Utah and Mormon history. Her prominence among the general Utah and Mormon public was greater than if she was a university professor lecturing only to her students and writing for the academic profession. She was respected for her integrity and honesty, which added to her standing, resulting in her becoming an honored pillar of the community. As Melvin Johnson noted in a review article, her unyielding dedication to truthfulness led her to establish "a standard of integrity that is the basic requirement that all writers of Mormon history must meet."[18] Speaking at her funeral in 1989, Levi Peterson, her biographer, claimed that her venture into the history of the Mountain Meadows Massacre and John D. Lee "made her into, not merely a respected historian, but an authentic Utah hero." He concluded his talk by predicting, "Unquestionably, Juanita Brooks will remain famous as one of the foremost champions of free inquiry and open debate in the history of Mormonism."[19]

Adding to her reputation and charm was her background as a homemaker in the arid southern regions of Utah and Nevada. She often laced her writings and speeches with stories from her upbringing, roots she never really left throughout her life. Her letters exemplify this attachment to the desert and her past. She felt "it is the desert that is important—and the isolation."[20] Her stories ranged from relating her experience with someone possessed by the Devil while growing up to mentioning, upon receiving a gift of almonds, that they were her favorite nut because she had helped harvest almonds from the LDS Relief Society–owned trees in Bunkerville and had been given some for her work. Another time she thanked Ettie Lee for a monetary Christmas gift by reciting a story of her excitement when she received her first quarter from her father when she was a child. She wrote, "I spent that money a hundred different ways as I rode along. I do not know now what I got with it; I remember only the joy I had in contemplating the things which I might get."[21] She ended the story, as she often did, with "Forgive these silly musings." In many letters she would slip in sayings from her past on the farm, such as "saving my 'Sunday Eggs,'" when she needed to save some extra money, for which in this case she then apologized by writing, "I forgot that I was not still down on the farm. Excuse the slip."[22]

Brooks has become part of the fabric of the history of Utah and the Mormons over the years since the end of her career. She is consistently listed with other notable historians such as Leonard Arrington, Dale Morgan, and Fawn Brodie as making a lasting influence on Mormon history. Her biography is included as one of the bridge historians along with Bernard Devoto, Fawn Brodie, and Dale Morgan in Bitton and Arrington's *Mormons and Their Historians*. She is again considered with the same cast of historians along with novelist Wallace Stegner in Gary Topping's review of Utah historians.[23] Speaking of the New Mormon History, Topping concluded, "The critical spirit that Juanita Brooks brought to the writing of Mormon history has long been recognized as the fountainhead of the movement."[24] She also appeared with the likes of Emmeline B. Wells and Eliza Roxcy Snow in the chapter entitled "Women of Letters" in Scott and Thatcher's volume *Women in Utah History*.[25] Another short biography of Brooks, written by Douglas D. Alder, was included as an introduction to the compilation of the first thirty lectures given at Dixie State University in the annual lecture series named in her honor.[26] She was also the topic, along with Dale L. Morgan, of eminent historian Patty Limerick's keynote address to the Utah State Historical Society Conference in 2016. Limerick explored, "How can the work, conduct, and character of those two close friends guide us today in the strenuous work of applying historical perspective to the dilemmas of the contemporary West?"[27]

Part of her relevance today is the inspiration she still provides to those laboring with producing objective history of Utah and the Mormons. The instances are numerous of individuals who knew her or her writings that speak her praises. One such person is Melvin Johnson, a former student at what is now Dixie State University. In a review article, he wrote that Juanita Brooks and her cousin, Professor Pansy Hardy, had personally inspired him to become a historian.[28] Historian Will Bagley venerated Brooks and her influence by devoting a chapter to her in his study of the Mountain Meadows Massacre.[29] Another important example is that of Richard E. Turley Jr., the former LDS Church Assistant Historian and Recorder and coauthor of the LDS Church–sponsored book on the Mountain Meadows Massacre.[30] In his talk in honor of Juanita Brooks given at the historic Alta Club in Salt Lake City in 2017, he maintained that her Mountain Meadows Massacre book is "a very fine book indeed, one that has moved generations of readers, yours truly among them, and remains in print today, a classic of Utah and Mormon history." He goes on to say that today "we find ourselves in a Renaissance of Mountain Meadows study, a renaissance started by her."[31] Thus, in the approximately sixty-five years since the appearance of her book, she has made a full circle from being shunned by the leading authorities of the LDS Church to being embraced by at least some of the leaders of their historical department. This acceptance is further validation of her prediction that her book would be considered a service to her church given the passage of time. It must be remembered, however, that she was always fearlessly independent, always questioning and pushing for truthful history, even in the face of the powerful. She avoided any sponsorship that had any possible appearance of dictating her conclusions. For this integrity, she remains important today.

She is also remembered for rescuing pioneer diaries and placing copies of them in libraries so this wealth of information is readily available to current researchers and future generations. Researchers make pilgrimages to places such as the Huntington Library because of her efforts. Many of her best works, including the book on the Mountain Meadows Massacre, her biography of John D. Lee, and her autobiography, *Quicksand and Cactus*, remain in print and are read and discussed today, maintaining her significance.[32] Her stories have been reprinted in major anthologies including *Great Western Short Stories* and *Westward the Women*, where she joins some of the greats.[33] Her stories also appear in regional collections such as *A Dixie Christmas* and *A Believing People: Literature of the Latter-Day Saints*.[34] Her works continue to be reprinted in volume collections such as the recent *A Zion Canyon Reader*.[35]

Chapter 1

1941–1943

Mentoring under Dale Morgan

This chapter begins with the first extant letter to Dale Morgan dating to February 23, 1941. In this letter, Brooks thanked Morgan, then working for the Historical Records Survey (HRS) and Utah Writers' Project, for materials and summarized her progress in collecting diaries to be copied by the HRS. Though she had resigned from the HRS in 1937, she was still actively searching out pioneer diaries. Their correspondence blossomed into a close friendship in which she revealed her desires and ambitions. She later described him as her "pen pal" and often mentioned to him, "I tell you everything." Juanita wrote him almost sixty letters between 1941 and 1943, with only about five of her existing letters from these years not directed to him. The early letters were addressed to "Mr. Morgan," but by November 1941 they dropped formalities and were on a first-name basis.

Dale Morgan was one of the preeminent historians of the West, a careful and prolific researcher, and the author of many books and articles. He wrote or edited about two dozen books focusing primarily on the American fur trade, but also authored on Mormon subjects among others. Morgan would often spend his lunch hour creating typescripts of records in the LDS Church Historian's Office, making some of these copies without permission. He would share his efforts with Brooks with the condition that she be discrete and vague on the source of the materials. He remained with the HRS and Utah Writers' Project until October 1942 when he resigned and moved to Washington, DC, eventually taking an editorial position at the Office of Price Administration in December 1942.

These early letters to Morgan portray an assertive woman from a small Mormon town with the ambition and passion to write. In the first letters she admitted this desire and requested Morgan's assistance in applying for an Alfred A. Knopf fellowship to produce a biography of Jacob Hamblin, mentioning that she lacked confidence. She felt that if she could obtain some financial support and assurance of publication, she could then write "openly and unashamedly" and hire someone to help with her household duties. Because having these aspirations was outside the norm for a woman in a small Utah town, she concealed her goals from her friends, even to the point of leaving her ironing board out so she could switch from the typewriter to her wash whenever visitors appeared. The Knopf fellowship never materialized, but she persistently continued to work on the manuscript, even with the uncertainty of getting it published. It was not completed, though a partly fictionalized biography on Jacob Hamblin based on her 1952 movie script was published in 1980.

In several of these letters Brooks detailed her pioneer diary collecting and copying efforts, even typing for hours in a cold room on a document an owner had refused to let out of the house. In another case she described how she painstakingly steamed and scraped off papers that had been pasted over the pages of an early journal. Brooks often supplied Morgan with copies of these labors. She also inserted gossip into her letters, such as recounting her frequent interactions with novelist and St. George resident, at the time, Maurine Whipple, a friendship of which Whipple continually took advantage.

At Morgan's suggestion, Brooks initiated a lively discussion in 1941 with Charles Kelly, author and editor of several books including a selection of John D. Lee's diaries and the first superintendent of Capitol Reef National Monument. At the time, he was rumored to have been writing a book on the Mountain Meadows Massacre, a book that never appeared. These letters centered on the Mountain Meadows Massacre and Jacob Hamblin's role. Brooks strongly disagreed with Kelly's insistence that Hamblin was involved in the massacre and maintained that she just followed the evidence and had no other motive to clear Hamblin's name. She also questioned some of the folklore repeated by Kelly that swirled around the Mountain Meadows Massacre, demanding his sources and documentation for the stories, a demand she often repeated whenever someone presented her with undocumented stories. She emphasized in her first letter that someone in good standing within the LDS Church should tell the story of the massacre, so that it would not be so easily discounted.

~

To *Dale Morgan*,[1] February 23, 1941

St. George, Utah
Sunday morning, Feb 23, 1941

Dear Mr. Morgan:

This isn't a very good time for me to stop to write a letter, but I don't want to wait a day before I thank you for the copy of "Inventory of State Archives"[2] which I received just yesterday. I spent half the night with it last night, and was more and more delighted. It's a splendid piece of work. Wish I had anything half as good to my credit.

I think I shall send it, after a week or so, to my brother, Francis H. Leavitt, who is working toward his PHD at Berkeley. He is making his Thesis topic "The Mormon Settlement in Nevada." Since all of Nevada was included in the original state of Deseret, he should find this most interesting.

I'm on the scent of other manuscripts for you to copy. In fact, I know of another set of line-a-day diaries that I think I can get, if you want them. There are two more volumes of Lang material,[3] too, which I have here at the house.

Thanks again for the book. It was so kind of you to send it.

Sincerely,

Source: Dale L. Morgan Papers.

To *Dale Morgan*, August 14, 1941

St. George, Utah
August 14, 1941

Dear Mr. Morgan:

Your kind letter of August 12 has given me nerve enough to tell you some things which I might not otherwise have done.

For a long time now I have tried to screw up courage enough to make application for the Knopf Fellowship in Biography. They give an advance on the work, which would enable me to do the necessary research, and would give me help in my home so that I might have time to write.

But I have lacked confidence. I have not felt that I could do anything that they might consider worthy. Now I do want to do a biography of Jacob Hamblin[4] (who, by the way, is not my grandfather, but who married my grandfather's sister), I should like to make him the focal point around which to weave the fascinating history of this Southwest.

One of the requirements for the fellowship is that I have letters from people who know me regarding my ability to do research and the value of the work I am interested in. Do you think you would be willing to write such a letter for me? If so, address The Alfred A. Knopf Literary Fellowships, 501 Madison Avenue, New York City. Since the letter should accompany my material when it goes in, perhaps you should send it to me, though that seems hardly fair to you. If you prefer to write directly to them, mail it about Sept. 1, as that is when I want to get my material out.[5]

Do you have any first-hand information on the visit of Brigham Young,[6] Heber C. Kimball,[7] Parley P. Pratt[8] and others to Harmony in May 1854? I do not have any reports concerning it.

I know it is an imposition because of the number of people who write and ask me to do their research for them. If you do not have time for this, let it go. Perhaps I can find something on it from the files of the Deseret News.—though, come to think of it, I have only the years 1856–1859.

There should be letters, too, from Jacob to the first Presidency. I know of some of John D. Lee[9] describing this country before the mission was established.—If I could get this fellowship, wouldn't I have a good time! I can think of no keener pleasure than to be able to devote my time to this, my hobby.

Even with all the support that I may get from others, I dare not hope that I can win this Fellowship. Yet I suppose I should be cowardly not to try, at least. I have everything to gain and nothing to lose. With that in mind, I'm going to give them the best I have. If it is not good enough, or if they like someone else's better—that's still all right.

Sincerely,

Source: Dale L. Morgan Papers.

To *Dale Morgan*, August 27, 1941

St. George, Utah
August 27, 1941

Dear Mr. Morgan:

I'd be glad to get the material as soon as you have time to sort it out. And I most certainly will not let anyone else see it. I've told no one that I am making application for this fellowship except the few people I have asked to do letters for me. I figure that if I should get it, it will be time enough to tell people about it then, and if I should not, no one need be the wiser. Anyway, the fact that I have material of yours is not a point of discussion with me.

My husband is sympathetic with my ambitions, but most of my neighbors think I'm a little "teched" (or is it "pixilated"?) because I will write when I could just as well be darning socks or playing bridge. Even with Maurine Whipple[10] I do not discuss my work. We talk only of hers. Since I gave her freely of material that I had for her first volume, I think I don't owe her more. Anyway, her present volume deals with a contemporary theme, I understand.—All this by way of gossip, and just to show you that I would not mention to anyone the fact that I have the material in my possession.

Thank you for the suggestion about Charles Kelly.[11] I shall write to him today. I had assumed that because Hamblin was not in the county at the time of the M.M.M. he could not have been directly connected with it. He was on his way to Salt Lake to marry his third wife, Priscilla Leavitt, my grandfather's sister, when it happened. Reports that he passed the company at Corn Creek, twelve miles south of Fillmore that they inquired of him about the road and wrote down the information he gave them. His family record says he was married to Priscilla Sept 11, 1857.—I have wondered if his being absent could have made any difference. He was so opposed to bloodshed all his life.

That Hamblin found out the details on his return, there can be little doubt. That Brother Brigham found them, too, there can likewise be no doubt. Legend here has it that Hamblin's Indian boy, Albert, witnessed it all from a tree. But he died in a few years, before anything was ever done about it.

I had hoped to get my material in to Knopf by the middle of Sept. if possible. I want to do a good job of it, but I understand that I need not have all the research done. I know nothing of Hamblin's life prior to 1850 except what he tells in his book, and it is too sketchy to be of much use. I want to go to Mesa, where members of the family have his letters and a great deal of personal material, but that, too, would have to wait on the chance of the Fellowship. I don't know when I could do it otherwise.

Now I think that I should be able to do well as I can in another month of work, so far as the sample chapters are concerned. I have been at it some time now.

Will look forward to getting the material and will refund postage. Thanks.

Source: Dale L. Morgan Papers.

To *Charles Kelly*, August 27, 1941

St. George, Utah
August 27, 1941

Mr. Charles Kelly
1349 South 5 East
Salt Lake City, Utah

Dear Mr. Kelly:

I am writing to you because of our common interest in the Mountain Meadows Massacre, and because Mr. Dale Morgan told me that you plan to do a book on that subject. I am interested in a biography of Jacob Hamblin. Mr. Morgan says that, according to you, Jacob was directly mixed with that affair. As a prospective biographer, I am naturally interested.

Perhaps I should make myself clear on my own opinions as to it. I think the whites were responsible—the <u>local</u> church leaders planned and determined upon it, I think. (How I would like to get hold of some documentary evidence as to what went on in their council meeting!) John D. Lee was more a victim of circumstance than any man I know. I have positive proof that he protested, not once, but two or three times, to carrying out orders.

For more than seven years now I have held material—This sounds silly, I know—waiting for three old people to die. Remaining sons and a daughter who would be terribly hurt by what I could tell. They are all gone now, but one.—Grandchildren don't care so much, and I don't care if they do.

Then I am a member of the Mormon Church in good standing, I hope, and wishing to remain connected, even though I'm not too orthodox. But I think that story should come from within the Church, by a member in good standing, so that it will not be discounted because people think, "Oh, well, she's an apostate, anyway." I think it is so silly to keep trying all the time to build defenses that we are forced to abandon. I act on the theory that the best way to turn a herd of cattle is not to ride directly counter to them, but to travel with them and turn them gradually—I draw my figure from my own early experiences.

Well, I think that the people on the southern frontier (76 families south of Cedar City—or was it 79? I have the figures somewhere) inflamed by George A. Smith's[12] fiery speeches and suggestions that they might "again have to take their wives and children and flee to these crags and rock for protection"—and interpreting some of Brother Brigham's bluster about "holding the Indians by the wrist any longer" decided to put it into practice. Do I just imagine it, or did Brigham quiet down in his talks after the M.M.M.

Many things no doubt entered into the decision—revenge, blood atonement, the zeal of the reformation—but chief of all the hysteria of an approaching army bent on their annihilation. Of course it was not—but they thought it was, so for all intents and purposes it was the same.

A ghastly, cowardly deed, not in any way to be condoned. But it should be seen in relation to its peculiar circumstances. Other companies had been attacked before; a few small groups had been killed. Mormons piloted others safely across, both before and after this affair, many of them. I have heard my own grandfather tell how he rode night and day to overtake a large group camped at the Muddy crossing—How he found them surrounded by Indians, how he compromised with the natives, helping them stampede the loose stock and not trouble the teams or the people. And then later how he rode the range three weeks to gather the remnant of the herds together to deliver to the company's agent sent back from California—all without reward, and not because he wanted to, but because he was sent.—There are other such stories, as typical of the times as the Meadows one.

As to Jacob's connection with it. He says that he was on his way to Salt Lake; that he met the company at Corn Creek, twelve miles south of Fillmore, that they asked his advice about the roads and wrote down what he told them. The Hamblin record shows that he married Priscilla Leavitt as his third wife on Sept 11, 1857 in the Endowment House at Salt Lake City.[13]—That seems to let him out of the actual murder. How could he have been in on the planning of it, unless he knew the company was on its way? That is a possibility I had not thought of before.

That he found out all about it after his return, there can be no doubt, just as there can be no doubt that Brother Brigham found out all about it. The men involved were even warned by runners from the north whenever officials headed south—but I suppose you knew all this. That is, for a few years, at least, they were.

Legend here has it that Jacob Hamblin's Indian boy, Albert,[14] was a spectator and told him all about it. Members of the Haight[15] family have told me how Brother Brigham held council with their father all forenoon in a white-topped buggy, and how, at the end the men shook hands. But then Haight might not have told the truth. Another old lady told me of how Brigham came to Kanab and had brought in, one at a time, every man who was supposed to have had any connection with it. Still another told me of the council meeting which lasted all night long before the act was consummated.

Well, I have two accounts written by participants and I think I know where others are. I am using a long round-about method of getting them, but I haven't given up. I'm sure I could never secure them by bluntly asking for them—I must build up confidence over a period of time and I must, If I can, get the family indebted to me in some way. It's a great game.

I'm sorry if I have imposed on you. I'd like to hear your opinion on Jacob's relation to that affair, if you care to give it.

Thanks. Sincerely,

Source: MS 100, Marriott Library Special Collections.

To *Charles Kelly*, September 4, 1941

St. George, Utah
Sept. 4, 1941

Dear Mr. Kelly:

Thank you for your letter on the Mountain Meadows Massacre. The idea of Jacob Hamblin's being present is entirely new to me. I assumed from what he said that he was married Sept.11—which would not give him time to be back to the meadows even by the 18th. By the way, doesn't Roberts give the date as Sept 16?[16] That is the date I have always thought it was. I expect to follow your suggestion and find out, however.

As to Hamblin being a relative—he isn't, except that his third wife was my grandfather's sister. And if he were, it would make no difference to me, my grandfather, Dudley Leavitt lived at Santa Clara[17] at the time, so I would rather expect that he was present, though he always said he was not—or the family always said he was not. I've heard several reasons. One was that he started for the place with Samuel Knight[18] and his brother Lemuel, and then turned back and refused to go on. I doubt this very much. Another was that he was out after a load of wood when the messenger came and did not get back in time. This seems more likely. But I would not be surprised to hear that he was present, though one of the most vivid memories of my childhood centers around the time when, letting his cane fall back against his body, he stretched his hands toward the fire and said, "I thank God that these old hands have never been stained by human blood." Still, he could have been there, and been one of those who shot into the air.

I know that he was present when Brigham Young had the first monument destroyed. I have heard him tell it. Not long ago my father repeated the story, and last week, an uncle from Provo told it again almost verbatim—except that he used "Judgment is mine, saith the Lord," etc. instead of vengeance. And he said, just as Grandpa did that Brother Brigham did not order the monument torn down, but he gave them to understand that it should not be there. Grandpa's words were, "He didn't give an command, he didn't say a word. He just lifted his arm like this, and we knew what he meant. In a few minutes there wasn't one stone left upon another."—That is as I remember it.[19]

Now as to Jacob's being in it. I shall look in the records of the old Endowment House and find the date of his marriage to Priscilla. His family record gives it Sept. 11, but I shall try to go behind that. More important still, I think that if he had been there, I would have heard of it. I have interviewed dozens of people here, and knowing that I am a church member and friendly, they have talked very freely. They blame Haight . . . [Missing]

Source: MS 100, Marriott Library Special Collections.

To *Dale Morgan*, September 10, 1941

St. George, Utah
Sept 10, 1941

Dear Mr. Morgan:

I don't know how to say "Thank you" for the material I have received. That doesn't, somehow, seem adequate. I hope that I may get you something that will seem of value to you, or that I may do something that will show you, how truly I do appreciate this. You are more than generous with me.

I think I can get the volumes of the Journal of Discourses[20] that you lack. I am sure they were all in the library of the late Judge David H. Morris,[21] but I have not yet found what disposition was made of them at his death. I shall let you know.

I know that the material you have sent does not cover the whole field of my research, but it does go a great way toward it. I can find good related material from some of the records of contemporary writers.

The James G. Bleak[22] records are all in the Church Historians office, I am sorry to say. I have had access to them before, but did not copy entries pertaining to Hamblin, though I do remember of having read some. I don't know whether or not I could get access to them now.
I shall be glad to see a copy of Mr. Reid's[23] work. He has it here, but seems reluctant to let people see it.

Later—

I was interrupted in the middle of this. I spent most of the night and all of the day that I could steal from my work to go through this. I'm delighted. I don't know when anything has given me keener pleasure. And I, too, find some questions raised as to the standard story of Jacob's where-abouts in September 1857. I must get the diary I told you of—or was it Charles Kelly that I told?—which is said to have been kept by one of Lee's hired men, and which covers the dates in question. If only I had time and means to go as I would like! I'd leave this afternoon for it.

Your comment on Maurine Whipple's explanation of circumstances surrounding the MMM interested me. It is true that I talked this thing over with her by the hour. I read every line of her book before it went in the first time, and then again went over the printer's dummy with her.[24] I knew of some historical discrepancies which I could not get her to change. I found many things which she did modify or cut, and I gave her an abundance of local items and folk-lore. I am not trying to take credit for her book—it is distinctly hers. But on the question of the MMM she did accept my interpretation literally. I may modify my views, but I will not until I find other and conclusive proof.

Hamblin's little Autobiography[25] does not check with some of the material which you sent me in regard to dates. Some of the letters which he quotes are "pruned", also.

Well, if I get this off today, I must stop. And it must go, tardy as it is, or you will think I am ungrateful (Just had visitors come in, which makes it hard for me to write)

Thanks again. I am taking the best of care of this, and will get through it as soon as I can.

Sincerely,

Source: Dale L. Morgan Papers.

To *Dale Morgan*, October 28, 1941

St. George, Utah
Oct. 28, 1941

Dear Mr. Morgan:

Was I thrilled to get that material! It was like finding a gold mine for me. I'm doubly appreciative because I know that I could never have secured it myself.

I decided it was time I got busy and tried to get something that you would like. I have located some Journals of Discourses but none that are for sale as yet. So I went after the Proceedings of the Bishop's Courts. It's a good thing I did, too. The lady who had the one copy (all the others have gone in with the records of the St. George Stake) said that she had been advised to send it in too. She was reluctant to let me see it—did not want it taken from the home. Well, I wanted to be on the level with her, but I wanted a copy of that material, too, so I phoned home and had them bring my typewriter out. I was by myself in a cold room, but I worked like fury and got it all—Took from 4 to 10:30 p.m.

While I was about it I made carbon copies, so you may keep this. She wasn't too pleased when she knew I had copied it, but I visited with her a long time and I think she felt better when I left. She is so afraid some one will get it and use it to hold our people up to ridicule. Better keep it in your personal files for the present.

This seems to be all the cases that came before the court during the period from Jan 2, 1883 to August 2, 1888. Each case is different, but on the whole I think they are typical of the work the Bishop's courts did in this part of the state.

Now about Jacob. . . . I certainly appreciated your word about DeVoto.[26] I read his material in Harper's, but do not know him, and had no idea that he would know of me. I am going after the Knopf Fellowship with the best I have, of course, but I know that there will be hundreds of applicants whose work will be as good or better than mine.

I ran into a couple of interesting things this week. Mr. Chesley from Short Creek[27] says he is a son of Jacob Hamblin's favorite daughter by his favorite wife, (I have written to have him identify them). He insists that Jacob was called to Australia on a mission, and that he disappeared and a search failed to find him. I wrote sending him an account of the death at Pleasantville N.M. Aug. 1886—Then Dr. Joseph Walker[28] of Los Angeles insists that he cut a skin cancer out of Jacob's face, while they were at the Pulsipher ranch. Said he used a razor and sewed it up with good old O.N.T. sewing thread. Said the old Indian fighter stood it fine. When I protested that Jacob was dead years before, he came back with the statement that it was Jacob, anyway, he knew and you couldn't fool him.

Well, a thousand thanks. I can hardly understand anyone as accommodating as you are. I shall get it copied and back right away . . . Also the other material.

Gratefully,

Source: Dale L. Morgan Papers.

To *Dale Morgan*, April 5 [1942]

St. George, Utah
Sunday afternoon, April 5

Dear Dale:

Poor Richard's Almanac said, "Who rises late must trot all day and can scarce overtake his business by night". I should paraphrase it to read "Who takes a week-end away must gallop from Monday through all the next seven to catch up by Sunday."—It isn't literary, but it's true. Finally, by Easter afternoon I can get breathing time to sit and visit on my typewriter.

I did enjoy my stay in Salt Lake, and appreciated more than I can say your kindness.[29] I'd really like to settle down for several weeks in the various depositories there and get acquainted with some of material. And if you can ever come down here, how I'd like to take you to some of the points of interest. Did you see the Jacob Hamblin house while you were here? Or go into the Brigham Young home? What you would like best would be to look through this collection of old books the Carter sisters have—If I can only get them to loosen up a little. We might even go out to the Meadows. I'd welcome a chance to go around a bit with you.

I think I'll have to use you as a sort of safety-valve on some things that trouble me. For example, I'm annoyed by the fact that our leaders are clamping down on church activities at a time when people are crying for spiritual guidance. I sometimes wonder why they don't just dissolve the church entirely—for the duration. I don't want to be sarcastic, but this matter of keeping the tabernacle locked and doing away with the Stake Boards and the Auxiliary groups where all our young, vigorous leaders were given a chance, sort of gets under my skin. It seems that they have been just marking time for so long, or as my Dad would say "treading water", that they spend all their time and energy emphasizing the DON'TS that they have no time for vital, forward-looking Christianity.

This morning I went to a sun-rise Easter service put on by the college students here, freshmen and sophomores, that was really stimulating and gave evidence that our young people will forge ahead in spite of their leaders—I mean the way-uppers. I think the hope of the institution lies in its young seminary teachers—if they are not stifled to death—and in our young bishops and local leaders.

I retain my fellowship in the church because I like it and I need it and I want my children to have its benefits, but I refuse to surrender my intellectual independence to it. I'm amazed with the things I can get away with, with the fact that they have me teach a Sunday School class—students in their early twenties—and we do not follow the lesson outline. Neither do we always present the orthodox point of view. Do I sound on the verge of apostasy? Some would say so. Perhaps if I ever finish this work on Jacob they'll be more convinced than ever.—Enough of this. I've had to get it out of my system and I felt that you would appreciate my point of view.

How about you. Did you maintain your city chess championship? And why didn't I see some of your pictures, and some of your creations in clay? I'd have liked to, really.

Thank you for the material from The Heritage of the Valley.[30] I don't see how you take so much time for others and still get anything done for yourself. I've never met such unselfishness before, and I hardly know how to react to it. I'm certainly grateful enough, though that doesn't seem sufficient.

Now that this bit of a biography of my grandfather is about off my hands, I can turn back to Jacob seriously again.[31] I've sort of waited to hear from Knopf. Now that I have quite reconciled myself to the idea that I have no chance for the Fellowship, I begin to figure ways and means by which I can go on anyway. I am sure that I must, if I am to have any peace with myself. Only it will be much harder than it might have been if I could have attacked it with the assurance that it would be published when it is done.—I do wish they'd let me know before too long.

The Fish[32] material that you asked about seems to be pretty well scattered. He was a voluminous writer, but his family evidently did not take it very seriously. His son Semour B. may have some of it. Will may make a trip out to Enterprise soon, in which case I may stow-away and go along. If there's anything still there I can smell it out. It will take a personal trip, though I am sure.

Well, with Easter baskets and colored eggs and lunches behind me, and my work at school in the black again, I can go through this MMM stuff leisurely enough to really form some opinions. The matter of the date intrigues me more and more. I believe I can find convincing clues in the Harmony records at Cedar City—Oh, for the money and time to go! I don't really care whether that tragedy occurred on the 11th or the 18th or the 16th—But I would like to know beyond a doubt just when it did occur, because of the implications. I don't want to shield Jacob if he were involved; I just want to get the facts and adjust my thinking to them. The fact that Dudley Leavitt and Samuel Knights, his two counselors at Santa Clara are mentioned so specifically and that in our family (which was connected by marriage, through Priscilla, the third wife) the story has always been that he did not get back from his wedding trip in time makes it hard for me to re-adjust all my premises unless I need to.

The cubs storm in. They've been to see Walt Disney's Dumbo this afternoon (in direct defiance to counsel, because I wanted them to see it and because I wanted the two hours of quiet while they were gone) Now I must hear their excited versions of it.

Hope your office problems have ironed themselves out by now.

Best wishes,

Source: Dale L. Morgan Papers.

To *Dale Morgan*, September 6, 1942

St. George, Utah
Sunday, Sept. 6, 1942

Dear Dale:

For more than two weeks now I've thought I could take time out and write you. There were so many things that I needed to talk to you about. Now I have waited until I'm sure you will not have time to visit because you will be in the midst of your last-minute preparations for leaving. I will wait until you get settled in your new location and work before I trouble you again, though, I'm sure you'll keep yourself equally busy no matter where you are.[33]

I've had a hectic time lately—a sister-in-law brought here from the hospital to convalesce, her tiny, premature, four-pound baby to feed every two hours, the company and family and relatives that naturally came to visit. Then this week I had a wedding group. The boy is in the service in California, the girl in defense work in Provo and they met here to be married in the temple. His parents came, and her mother, and stayed through the three-day leave which constituted the honeymoon. Don't mis-understand me. I was thrilled to have them and glad to be able to help make the occasion one they would like to remember—only it did play havoc with my writing. Add to that the fact that I've put out more than four hundred quarts of fruit in two weeks, and you know why I've thought about my friends instead of writing them.

Mr. Poulsen[34] spent one day last week here. He suggested that you wanted incidents connected with the collection of the diaries for your article in the Rocky Mountain Review.[35] I think I told you about the Farmer[36] journal, didn't I? How we found it scattered in an old cellar and gathered up the loose leaves—and then spent three weeks putting it together. How the lady told us that she couldn't read it and we were welcome to it, and then later wrote telling how she prized it? And how they were tearing out the pages of the Myron Abbott[37] one to start fires in the kitchen stove? I think the most interesting one was the Henry Bigler[38] ledger which was turned into a scrap book and pasted over every page with recipes and sentimental stories and love poems. It was literally a case of reading a sealed book. Night after night we worked at it, steaming each page off carefully with hot towels and scraping away the paper with safety razor blades. The purple ink came out clear and legible, and we eagerly read the entries before we started on the next. It was the nearest I ever came to digging out material from the printed page. Then there was the Levi M. Savage[39] one, with its long religious dedication wherein he prayed God that nothing but the truth should ever be recorded on these pages and that this book should never fall into the hands of the ungodly . . . It began in the fine Spenserian hand of the young college man and traced his life through to the wavering strokes of one grown old and finally released from his mission to Arizona. When he recorded the death of his boyhood sweetheart his hand trembled so that the writing was all wobbly.... I've probably told you this before, or maybe you know it already, but when Mr. Poulsen spoke of it, I thought I'd see if this is the sort of thing you want ... I can multiply incidents if it would help. Not so many were apologetic for the records they had. "Oh it doesn't say much. Every entry starts by saying 'I take my pen in hand'—or "'It can't be much. It's only daily happenings, and little unimportant things."

What I wanted to talk to you about was Jacob. I struggled with the chapter on the MMM, and have about decided that perhaps I had better do an article on it—that is, the bit of new material I have on it, for a historical magazine, say the Utah Quarterly or the Mississippi Valley Historical Review, and then make it more incidental in the Biography. It seems too obviously dragged in if I make too much of it in the book; at least if I try to bring in the Nephi Johnson[40] account. I wish I had sent you what I wrote on it back in 1935 and put away to wait until President Grant[41] and a few others of the older generation pass on—But I knew that you are swamped with your own work and worries and I hadn't the heart to trouble you with mine. If you ever get to where you have time, I'd like to send it to you and indicate changes and additions, etc. to see what you think about it. I would never submit it to anybody until you do see it.

As to Jacob, I am going on with him because I must, I can do a great deal more on the 1854–1874 period with what I have now, and I'm going to assume that I'll get in contact with his family before snow flies, by making a trip into Arizona if necessary. I can interview a number of people here that remember him, too. I'm going to work on the theory that if I once get it finished in a shape to satisfy myself—or if I could possibly make you feel that it would do—some publisher will take a chance on it. My chief business now is to settle down to systematic work. With my cellar full and my children in school, I should be able to manage better, unless some other member of the family gets sick and I need to run a combined hospital-hotel again.

I'm afraid you will have gone before this reaches you. I hope not. You have no idea what a hole you will leave in Utah for me. Just knowing you are there and I can get in touch with you when I need to has been a real help. I know that letters will reach you in the East, but it will somehow seem different. I hope you are happy in your new location. I'm sure you will find plenty to do and will form a lot of stimulating new contacts. And in the end, you'll turn out the most significant piece of work to be done on Utah and the Mormons.

The best of luck to you. Whenever you can, drop me a line. I'll be interested to know of your whereabouts and your doings.

Sincerely,

Source: Dale L. Morgan Papers.

To *Dale Morgan*, December 16, 1942

St. George, Utah
Dec. 16, 1942

Dear Dale:

A few days ago I wrote you a letter in the midst of a radio blaring ragtime, children playing marbles, and a few other distractions, with the net result that it was pretty incoherent. Don't remember now what I did tell you . . . Doesn't matter much, anyway.

Since that time I have been pretty much occupied with Christmas boxes to the boy in the army, the one in the navy, the mother of little foster children who is in the hospital, etc.etc. A tiny one found its way in your direction, and since you may not know what to do with it, I hasten to offer some explanations.

The pine and the berries were just added thoughts. The Brigham tea[42] comes with Will's compliments. It has the same value in his mind that lobelia had in Priddy Meeks.[43] He considers it delicious to the taste, a tonic, a blood purifier, a general pepper-upper. There is enough for a great many "drawings" in the little bundle if you don't like it any better than I do. The beaded book cover is the work of local Indians and may be put on any book that seems appropriate. Since you are batching, I enclosed the hot-pot holder. (No, I didn't do the crocheting. It's out of my line.) The cookies will probably be reduced to crumbs. At least they'll prove my good intentions and poor cooking. The material in the bottom is designed for a Dixie salad, if you will do the work. You'll have to furnish your own apples, too.

The pomegranates are small, but they are the only kind that are left. They don't keep very well, you know. Dig out the blossom end with a knife and peel back the skin before you break them. They are messy; they stain your hands. You'll swear a dozen times that they aren't worth the trouble. They're not, either. But go ahead and shell them. Crack the almonds and crush with a rolling pin or pound with the bottom of a milk bottle to break the nut. Dice two or three apples, add a half cup of raisins over which boiling water has been poured (Drain off the water, of course) Mix the pomegranates apples, raisins, and nuts, and serve with whipped cream. It's our standard Dixie salad. I wish I could send along some of our sunshine. The days are so clear and bright that children play out of doors without wraps.

I told you that I spent a day in Cedar City with William R. Palmer.[44] He was most cordial. Showed me all his Indian collection, and his originals from that section, which are most interesting. He has somehow contrived to work both for the State and the church. Anyway he has an order from the first Presidency asking all people in charge of church records to give him free access to them (something like the passes they used to issue the emigrants in 1857). Well, he says he will look up the date of Jacob's sealing to the Indian girls. If he only will!

My enforced vacation from writing this week—I have to help at the Post Office—only makes me more eager to be at it again. Best wishes for the holiday season. I hope that it is happy for you, and that the New Year will bring the satisfaction of added achievement.

Source: Dale L. Morgan Papers.

To *Dale Morgan*, February 21 [1943]

St. George, Utah
Sunday afternoon, Feb. 21

Dear Dale:

If Fate is kind I may get this finished before someone comes to call or the youngsters storm in from the show, or my good husband wakes up. Anyway, here goes for a start.

I've had the Devil's own time getting to do anything this last week. Seems like everything has combined to scatter my wits—croup, and talk of trading off our home, and visitors—mostly visitors! I long ago hit upon the expedient of keeping my ironing set-up out with everything ready, so that as soon as there was a knock I could plug in the iron on my way to answer the door. Then it would be easy to say, "Excuse me, please, my iron is burning" or "Come on in. I'm ironing." Then as soon as they left I'd pull out the plug. It isn't economical, I know, and it kept the clothes lying dampened too long sometimes. My next neighbor to the south has a habit of running in every morning about 11 o'clock and she finally said, "My, you must have big ironings. You have been at it for three mornings now."—

I didn't tell her, but I should have, that all the ironing I had done she had watched me do. Once that is out of the way for a week, I keep the most urgent of the mending in a neat pile on the table, with a threaded needle stuck into it, so that I can shift to that when I am interrupted, but as soon as she gets what she wants, I go immediately back to the typewriter without taking another stitch. The trouble is, I get more ironing and mending done than I do writing.

Then there's this business of trading our home off. It's disturbing. A Mr. Adams, a photographer, wants the house we live in, and wants to give us in exchange a fruit farm in Hurricane,[45] 35 acres of land, 10 in bearing fruit trees, a good home, barns, corrals, chicken houses, etc.etc, which the County Agent and the Ag. teacher and all the others who ought to know tell us is far too good a bargain for us to turn down.[46]

Well, I've tried to stay out of it, for after all, I want only peace, and quiet. Will's son who is the athletic coach at the Hurricane high school would move on the place and manage it, while we will move into one of the little houses we own on the hill north of town—just under the Sugar Loaf. It's the one Will was born in—red rock, with an enormous fireplace, and a big kitchen, and one tiny bedroom . . . All of which adds up to our having to finish the big basement room for the boys, put in shower & bath, new floors, closets, porches, etc.etc.[47]

Once we are actually in it, there will be many advantages, chief of which will be my inaccessibility (now we're a convenient stop-over for shoppers and people coming to the hospital and folks wanting to phone from the Morgue across the street, and folks wanting something from the Post Office after hours) As I started to say, I'll like the hill once I am up there and have solved the problem of how to compress this crowd into that house and what to do with the surplus furniture.

This sounds awful, I know. I don't mean it that way. I love my friends and I really do rather enjoy living in a house by the side of the road, and so on. Fae Ollerton used to often say to me, "You'll never get any writing done. You like people too well. You're too social." And 'Rene says again and again, "I tell you, Nita, you've GOT to learn to say No! You've got to be ruthless! You just can't stop to talk to every Tom, Dick, and Harry that comes along", and so on ad infinitum—

Now that the trade is about made—all but signing up the papers, and the carpenters and plasterers have spent the required time looking over the little house, there will be a lull of a month or so before the actual upheaval begins. During that time will I have to make the dust fly—I'll really get in and scratch—or rather peck at this.

I'm still living with Jacob, though I don't seem able to manage him well. If ever I get that date of his Endowment to the Indian girls—Bro Palmer has promised to get it, since he has one of the sacred Passes—I'll be glad. I don't count on it too strong, for he may not even be able to get it. And I'm still going to Mesa and Phoenix if I have to steal the money. I'll not have to though—I'll find a way. I want to send you a bundle of stuff within the next week, and then take off for a few days. By traveling the bus at night I find that I don't have to waste so much time. I'll go via Kanab and call on Walt Hamblin.

The thing for me to be concerned about, I know, is not anything that Corbett or anyone else may do, but what I may NOT get done. Corbett's thesis is in to the B.Y.U., but is not even typewritten yet, I understand, and it must be passed on by several people after it is.[48] Then the Church has promised to select parts of it for another Faith Promoting book, all of which is O.K. so far as I am concerned. My worry is only that perhaps, after all my bother, I'll have something on my hands that will never get printed. If I could have any assurance of publication, I could go after it for all I am worth, but with such uncertainly as I feel, I catch myself wondering if maybe I'm not as crazy as the neighbors think I am after all.

Oh, I'll stay with it. And I'll finish it. And by the Eternal, I'll get it printed. It's got to be! There are plenty of books all bound and sold that won't be any better—

Well, here I go on talking to you as if you were God. In a way, you are better, because your answers are more intelligible. Don't take any of this too seriously, it's an attempt to let off steam to keep from an explosion.... I'll steal a couple hours or so, & get you an oose root,[49] or part of one, which you must shampoo your hair in. And later, maybe, I can send a sample of the bloom. "The candles of the Lord", the natives call them.

It's spring here. Almond trees are in bloom, and bees are beginning to buzz around the cottonwood behind the house. It's in my blood, too. Isn't it grand that for a while each year a fellow feels as if he could literally turn the world over?

I'll send you a bit of stuff soon, so brace yourself, and regardless of set-backs, I think I'll gather myself together and go at it again.

I forgot to say, but I do hope things are well with you, and that your new job has turned out to be the answer to your prayer. I'm not really as self-centered as this sounds.

Adios,

Source: Dale L. Morgan Papers.

To *Dale Morgan*, March 9, 1943

St. George, Utah
March 9, 1943

Dear Dale:

I've been so low this week that the under side of a snake's belly would look like a strip of the milkyway. It's been a good week to write, with the rain shutting me in and others out (the children aren't much of a distraction; I'm used to them), but I've just seemed barren, somehow. I've helped Maurine through the Slough of Despond[50] so often that I swore that once I got in myself I'd wallow my way out—and I will. I'll be going strong again before long. But I do get disgusted at myself when I let a perfectly good forenoon pass and I just fritter about manufacturing things to do because I don't want to set myself down and stay there.

Of course there is the matter of the little house to fix up—things to decide like whether to put the bath tub cross-wise or the long way of the room and should the laundry room be in the basement or on the back porch—and ought we to line the fire-place with fire-brick or put in a circulator, and so on endlessly. But once they are decided I can pigeon-hole them in the back of my mind, and forget them. It's just that I can't seem to get the faculties going on Jacob as I thought I would.

I've had a few good conversations with relatives this week who remember him and the family, and have struck some interesting legends. For example I had always wondered who the nine people were who came across the plains with him in the one little wagon, drawn by a yoke of oxen and two cows. Mrs. Beeler had told me that Rachel[51] had married a Mr. Henderson at Winter Quarters—his wife had died, leaving him with two small boys. Then in just a few months he died, leaving her with the orphan children. Jacob had four by his first wife, who had decided not to come on west. So that made six youngsters, and his father. . . .

Now another legend, accredited to Ben Hamblin, is that Rachel Judd's oldest sister[52] had married John E. Page.[53] Rachel went to stay with her during a confinement. It was the time when Plurality was first being practiced, and Mr. Page explained it to her, telling her that there need be no ceremony, but only a secret agreement between them. She accepted the idea and lived in that relationship with him for some time. Then when he was cut off the church she came on west to Winter Quarters. . . . After he was left alone with the children, Jacob was so worried about what to do that he made it a matter of fasting and prayer. One night he dreamed that he saw a lumber house, and he was impressed that the woman who would be his wife was in that house. Some time after, he passed a house that he recognized as the one of his dream. He went to the door, but found the latch-string drawn in, so had to knock. Inside, Rachel was spinning, and had a thread the length of the room. She called out for him to wait a minute and she would open the door. When he came in, he explained that he had come here in search of a woman who was to be his wife (One thinks of Priddy Meeks) Rachel was all prepared for this but in her conversation she told him that in fairness he should know that she would probably never bear a child. She was now twenty-nine years old and thought that had she been going to have children, she would have done earlier during her life with John E. Page. "You shall not only have a child, but you shall have a number of children, and your sons shall be Joseph and Benjamin", Jacob promised her.

I ran across a number of Joel E. Johnson[54] descendants, and learned some about him and about Nephi Johnson, and the Indians that were killed at Pipe Springs—innocent Paiutes.[55] The talk naturally drifted to the MMM and Nephi's part in it, when Bro. Shumway told me this.

"You know that Nephi was in hiding for twenty years over that affair. Well, during the John D. Lee trial, Brigham Young wrote him a letter telling him to go in to Beaver and testify. He wrote to one of his friends that he was coming.

"One day this friend was talking to the U.S. Marshal, and told him that I expected Johnson in town that day to testify, but the Marshal did not believe that he would come. While they were talking, Nephi rode up on a horse. When they were introduced, the Marshal looked at him closely and said, 'I don't think I have ever seen you before.' 'I know you haven't', Nephi answered, 'but I've seen you many, many times.'"

That was the point of the story for him, but for me it was the fact that Brigham Young wrote ordering him to go in and testify. How I'd like to get hold of that letter! It would really be something, wouldn't it?

Will came in bringing my poor little Indian Article with your red-pencilings.[56] Thank you so much for the time and trouble you take with me. I'll get back at it again as soon as I can, and you may have to worry through it again. It's something if you think it is improved.

About Jacob—I'm about to assume that my readers will have to believe that I know what I am talking about without the proof on every page. I think foot-notes frighten the average person, and references confuse them. Besides Corbett says that his will be printed without question, and then they would be too much the same . . . What do you think?

This is an example of how much easier it is to visit than it is to work. Already I feel better with myself.

Adiooooo

A note from the editor of Arizona Highways asks if I can do a 3500 word piece on Jacob for their magazine.[57] Can I!—

Source: Dale L. Morgan Papers.

To *Dale Morgan*, April 6, 1943

St. George, Utah
Tuesday, April 6 1943

Dear Dale:

I was glad to get your letter—glad especially to hear of the progress of your book[58] and the prospects you have for publishing many, many more. Looks as if you have a full life's work all cut out before you, a genuine contribution to American culture. It seems that you have laid the foundation for a Tabernacle—while I've been trying to pitch a pup-tent. That's a homely comparison—new-carved, too, with my dull tools—but I think it fits. And I'm proud of you.

Guess you think I'll never get you oose root. I haven't forgotten; I just haven't got that far out into the hills. My Dad's birthday is April 18, and according to custom, we all gather in on that day—that is as many of the ten and their families as are able to come. So I had planned to get some oose root then. We always stop to let the children run and so that Will can gather some of his precious Brigham tea, and we'll just combine my errands with it. The desert should be in bloom by that time, too, so who knows what other interesting things we may find at the same time. I promise not to include any horned toads or turtles, though.

I've done precious little toward writing for the last little while. I make trips daily to the hill to check on the progress of the old house; I try to maintain the routine here. Those things I can fit in. It's these other unexpected ones that destroy me—Like the fact that the 19 year-old son of the neighbor just to the north shot himself last Saturday rather than go into the war, and that our closest friends had word that their boy was killed in action today. And Mother and Dad and the grandson (the baby I had until Christmas) have spent the last three days here.

I think maybe Rene is right—I get too tangled up in the process of living to write systematically.

Yet, in spite of it all, I'm mailing the article to Arizona Highways today. It's nothing new; nothing that hasn't been told before. The editor insisted that he must have something that the Mormons would like—"Don't apologize for Jacob's Prayers", he told me, "and don't try to explain them away. Show him as missionary first and explorer second." So, though I know I'm not adding anything new to the historian, maybe I can make a few people acquainted with Jacob in a sketchy sort of way.

As to the Utah Historical piece[59]—I'm waiting to get in touch with Brother Palmer this week, he is in Salt Lake City to conference, and has promised to look up some dates in the record book at the temple. If I get them, I will have to slant the part dealing with Jacob somewhat differently.

Thanks for telling me about the Lillard book.[60] I've seen some advertising for it, but haven't had hold of the book yet. And is the one you mention by DeVoto "The Year of Decision"[61] which was used in the Atlantic Monthly—that is, some chapters of it? I read them with great delight. I'd like to see the volume.

This Hamblin-Lee feud[62] was most interesting to me, too; I met it in so many places.[63] Dudley Hamblin began by telling some terrible tales as to how Lee and others (Lee at the head) had been hatching this plot for months ahead, of Lee's bestial treatment of some of the girls of the company, and of how it was his father's testimony that convicted him.

Well, I didn't care to say too much, but I told him that I didn't think John D. was as black as some would paint him, with all his evils, and I always believe in giving even the Devil his due. He blew up completely, so we agreed that it was a subject which we would not discuss—Then I met an old Brother Jarvis who started on John D. out of a blue sky, but I had learned my lesson, so I didn't commit myself, but sort of gathered his opinion.—The same day Bro. LeSuer told me that the descendants of John D., some of them, had wanted to do his work in the temple, but that they had instructions that that could <u>never</u> be done. He told me that the difficulties that had begun with the naming of the bridge had almost disrupted some of the Stakes there.[64]

Most interesting of all, I got acquainted with a Mrs Lee who was a daughter of William Hamblin and had married a son of John D. She told of the wide-spread quarrel, and of the efforts of the Lee family to show that Jacob lied at the trial to convict him. She gave me copies of two of Lee's Patriarchal Blessings, one given by Isaac Morley[65] in 1838 and one by Hyrum Smith[66] in 1842. I think there was a third given after he was in Harmony, so I'm writing and sending another dollar for a copy of it. She also sent a copy of his last entry in his Journal, March 13, 1877. I think Kelly had it published—at least I've read it somewhere before.

All of which added up to the impression that the MMM needs to be written more for the membership of the church than for the world at large, for they are the ones who are most interested in it, and who really know little of the facts.

Well, you'll probably get the third draft of that Indian piece to worry through again before long. That is, if things work out at all as I plan. I'd like to clear it off my hands.

Just noticed that the clock says mid-night—straight up. No wonder I have seemed heavy-headed. Good-night. It's time decent folk were a-bed. (my Dad says)

Source: Dale L. Morgan Papers.

To *Dale Morgan*, July 25, 1943

St. George, Utah
July 25, 1943

Dear Dale:

I have had a good chuckle over your wrath at Maurine.[67] I'm tempted to go you one better and tell you of similar tricks she has played on me, for if I'd start "I could a tale unfold". But I Guess I'd better not. I've been so roaring mad at her a few times that I have told her off in no uncertain terms, but she always comes back with "But, after all, Nita, what difference will it make? The way I will use it would not be like you would", etc. etc. Two or three times in the writing of the <u>Giant Joshua</u>, I told her things and let her know of incidents which I thought I might use myself some day, with the understanding that she leave them alone. Without exception she used them. I just had to learn not to say a word that I didn't want her to use.

Only last week she said to me, "You've got to help me with this or I'll never get it done"—speaking of her projected sequel to <u>Joshua</u> "You know I can't do it if you don't."—and so on. Well, I swore a mighty swear that I was through with helping her, and I am.

She would be the last to ever admit that she is unethical. According to her ideas, all information and material is for the fellow who can use it first, and the method of securing it is secondary. Her standards certainly aren't yours, or mine—I hope. The fact is, she is ingrown. She sees everything only in its relation to herself and without any thought for anyone or anything else.

Right now she is riding the crest of the wave regarding her picture book.[68] While she was in Salt Lake she secured the support of the Chamber of Commerce and some influential individuals, and got pictures from a number of sources, so that she really has a lot of good ones. Then she says that Z.C.M.I.[69] and the Chamber of Commerce and a man (I've forgotten the name—Was it Plumhoff?) each guarantee that they will take 5,000 copies. Knopf now has the first two chapters, and she is waiting impatiently for them to accept. Privately, I think that if they do take the book—and they probably will—she'll have a great deal more work to do on it. She figures on making a mint of money with a minimum of effort.

So I agree that Maurine is a dirty doublecrosser—and I have plenty of proof besides this. I've often said of her that she's not immoral; she's just un-moral. She has no standards. Yet I haven't condemned her for using my material because she did at least get it in print, which is something I should probably never have done. She does write very much better than I ever can and I've decided that there is no reason why I should be a dog in the manger and try to hold onto things that I can't use myself. (This doesn't apply to your picture project; that's a different matter)—I've tried to be as charitable as I can toward her. Only I just don't help her any more. See?
Source: Dale L. Morgan Papers.

Chapter 2

1944–1946

Laboring with *Quicksand and Cactus*

At the beginning of these years, Brooks continued her extensive correspondence with Morgan, writing thirty letters in 1944, twenty-three in 1945, and ten in 1946, but dropping to only eight letters for the rest of the decade. In a number of these letters she inserted stories of her growing up in the desert of the southern frontier, motivating Morgan to suggest she write of her childhood in Bunkerville. This request in January 1944 was the commencement of a two-year persistent struggle to produce and publish these frontier narratives that she ultimately titled *Quicksand and Cactus*. She wrote and rewrote a series of drafts, submitting them, using Morgan as a literary agent, to one publisher after another, only to receive rejections. Her letters to Morgan during this time often focused on these labors and disappointments, though she also filled them with quotes and discussions of pioneer journals and her daily life experiences as a woman in St. George. By early 1946 she finally shelved the undertaking, as the Mountain Meadows Massacre loomed as the more viable writing venture. The Bunkerville stories were ultimately included as part of her autobiographical writings in 1982.

One of their more dynamic exchanges followed Brooks's disclosure of her faith after she had read Morgan's review of Fawn Brodie's biography of Joseph Smith. She concurred that Brodie's book was a scholarly and literary production but disagreed that Joseph Smith was a "conscious fraud and imposter." Based on her experiences, supernatural manifestations were real and could not be easily discounted. She then recounted one of these incidences, one she considered almost sacred. When she was living in Salt Lake City with her first husband, Ernest Pulsipher, who was almost at the point of death, a stranger appeared at their door at just the right moment to provide the desperate couple relief. Morgan responded to her letter saying that they were on opposite sides of the "Great Divide" in terms of their belief in God. To which, Brooks wrote that their disparity in belief would result in different approaches to Mormon history, not that she agreed with all the practices of her church.

In addition to Morgan, she initiated a lucrative association that lasted for many years with a letter innocently addressed to "Director, Huntington Library" in February 1944 requesting information and possibly photostats of the testimonies given at the John D. Lee trials in Beaver, Utah, one of the holdings of the library. This appeal led to a long relationship with the Huntington, resulting in her collecting diaries and reminiscences of early Mormon pioneers for photostating by the library, receiving a Rockefeller Foundation grant to write her Mountain Meadows Massacre book, and collaborating with Robert G. Cleland, Huntington Library research associate, to produce a two-volume edition of a selection of the John D. Lee diaries.

Much of the Huntington Library correspondence during this period, written as formal reports to librarian Leslie E. Bliss, summarized her untiring and often extensive collecting pursuits for the library. Brooks's early letters to Cleland demonstrate her strong negotiation skills, often used with her publishers and others throughout her career. When offered a Rockefeller Foundation grant to write the Mountain Meadows Massacre book without an increase in her fifty-dollar-per-month stipend for diary collection, she countered that she must have misunderstood as she thought the grant to write would include a monetary consideration and that she could not do justice to both activities at fifty dollars per month. Cleland quickly replied with a one-hundred-dollar-per-month offer.

A paramount concern of hers during preparation and following publication of her Mountain Meadows Massacre book was its reception by the principal leaders of the LDS Church. She communicated with a number of them in a futile attempt to achieve acceptance of the work, as well as an opportunity to examine the Mountain Meadows Massacre affidavits from the Judge David H. Morris collection in the hands of the LDS Church pertinent to her study. Her first contact with these authorities involved writing George Albert Smith, president of the LDS

Church, in October 1945 requesting an audience with him to discuss the project and obtain the affidavits. President Smith graciously replied and Brooks met with him, though he knew nothing about the affidavits and recommended that she visit with David O. McKay of the First Presidency. He concluded the interview saying, "The Lord bless you, Sister Brooks, I hope you are happy—permanently happy—about what you do." After several persistent attempts to see McKay, she got only as far as Joseph Anderson, the general secretary to the First Presidency, who during one meeting sat across a table from her holding an envelope containing the affidavits, but not allowing her to view them.

She also launched in 1946 an intermittent correspondence with Fawn Brodie, author of the biography of Joseph Smith, *No Man Knows My History.* In this first letter, she discussed how her friend in Salt Lake City, Vesta P. Crawford, was facing strong negative repercussions from being acknowledged in Brodie's book, while Brooks, who was also listed as contributing information, had not received a word. She explained this contrast by observing that they probably "consider me lost already."

Another significant lifetime friendship, launched with an introductory letter in late 1946, was with the wealthy Ettie Lee, a granddaughter of John D. Lee and founder of the Ettie Lee Youth and Family Services in California. Lee ensured the Stanford University Press publication of the Mountain Meadows Massacre book in 1950 by guaranteeing the purchase of a thousand copies of the book with a prepublication payment of $3,000 to the press. Lee and Brooks conducted mostly friendly and supportive correspondence throughout their lives, into the 1970s.

Near the end of 1946, she also wrote Hugh Nibley, a prolific Mormon author and professor at Brigham Young University, a scathing letter concerning his review of Fawn Brodie's biography of Joseph Smith. She questioned his assertion that the gospel as presented by Joseph Smith has not been changed in any way. She felt that Fawn Brodie was entitled to her opinion and Joseph Smith remained "untouched by Mrs. Brodie's attack as his monument does by the pecking of sparrows."[1]

~

To *Dale Morgan*, January 7, 1944

St. George, Utah
Jan 7, 1944—4 p.m.

Dear Dale:

Let's visit a while, shall we?

I was so happy for the Ms material which you sent me. I think I realize the value of these things, and the fact that you would take time to copy them for me makes them all the more valuable. I have read the Brimhall[2] narrative aloud the last two nights, and believe me, I've had a great wallop out of it. I was interested in his account of Walker[3] at Parowan,[4] and even more interested in his account of the exploration of the Colorado. There he was speaking my language, for I know that country—its heat waves and floods and hot, barren wastes. How well I know it! The St. Thomas[5] people were our neighbors, only forty miles away, and the nearest settlement to our two on opposite sides of the Virgin River.

Which makes me think of your statement that the frontier is right inside me.[6] Well, that southern desert frontier is. It is a fact of which I have never been very proud, and which has sometimes caused me some embarrassment—like the time in New York City once when I gave myself away by saying "Whoa!" out of turn. But I know about cattle dying of thirst, and people getting near the dying point, too. I was my father's boy for years while he ran the mail across that desert—so I know horses (cared for twelve head almost entirely) and cows and out door life. I know the frontier dances with only an accordion for music, or at best a harmonica and organ, or a fiddle. I've had a lot of fun in my time at such hoe-downs. And home theaters! the only kind we ever had. Believe it or not, I've actually had my turn acting in them. . . . In the same way, I assisted whenever there was a death, and know the problems attending keeping a body presentable until the second day, while some of the good sisters sewed all night to get the clothing ready. And the frontier remedies. They are legionary. The superstitions are even more numerous.

What made me get off on this line, anyway? I was just saying how precious the Brimhall story is to me, because I understand it. The account of the peace parley I think is a gem. I'll get busy reading the other two pieces right away. Late at night when I am too weary to do anything else, I can refresh myself at that.

Speaking of Christmas—your tiny gift is still here. Maybe you'll get it by next Christmas. One of our neighbors amuses himself with such little bits of hand-work, so I told him to make me one. He didn't get it to me until late, and during the last two weeks before Christmas I was putting in from six to eight hours a day at the office, besides trying to manage the home, with the net result that every night I was completely exhausted. My reserve was low, anyway. Then on Sunday night, after I had lain around all day, I had a telephone call from my sister in Phoenix. Her husband was going down from Boulder City on Tuesday, alone, and would be glad for company, and Clara Hamblin, who stayed two months with me during the summer and was now in Phoenix for the holidays, would be coming back on Saturday. Why didn't I come down? Well, Will urged it, so I washed and baked and got the children's clothes ready to leave, got a teen-age girl to stay with them, caught the bus to Las Vegas at 3 p.m. Monday and was off. Landed in Phoenix early Tuesday evening and back home Saturday. Incidentally, I had a long visit with two of Jacob's older girls, who talked quite freely of their father and home life.

Last night I got another old ledger, one kept by William P McIntire[7] and dating back to Nauvoo, 1840. I am a little disappointed in it; I thought the account of Joseph's suits gave his measurements and more of significant detail. I'll copy what little there is for Fawn,[8] and give you a carbon, though, as I said, it has little value. I'm sure that there are some other Nauvoo items in town, if I can get around to locating them for her.

Maurine Whipple has called several times today for me to come down and visit her. She evidently has something on her mind. She has had a dose of flu, which means that she will not get her picture book done on time and since she has chiseled some money out of the state (their letter said $1500.00 with $100. for secretarial aid for her, and she says $2000.), Plumhoff is getting nervous about her not getting it done. She called for your address yesterday and asked if I thought she should send her Ms to you. Remembering one letter that you wrote, I advised against it. This morning when I talked to her, she told me that she had decided not to trouble you at all, which probably means that she sent her first chapters. I know that this sounds catty—I don't mean it that way. I have only learned that when she says one thing she often means another. I get so disgusted and out-of-patience with her at times, and at the same time I do feel sorry for her. She's so shut-in and completely self-centered. Nothing except her own immediate desire amounts to a tinker's dam with her. She can write, though.

My brother, Francis Leavitt of whom I have spoken to you several times, writes that he comes up for induction on Jan. 10 and expects to leave for the service on about Feb. 1. And here he was to come up for his finals for his PhD in March! Oh, well, it's one of those things over which we seem to have little control.

I must stop. I've been taking one meal a day to a little old lady across the street, and it's far past her dinner time. I'll probably write within a few days again, when I get this stuff copied.

I've had it in my mind to send you a box of stuff from my cellar, thinking it might save you time and food stamps. I have so much more than we will ever use. I've already traded two dozen full bottles for two dozen empty ones to one sister-in-law and one dozen to another. I'd never miss a bottle or two of chicken or venison or corn or apricot marmalade or apple butter or fig preserves. It's been only a matter of getting a suitable box for packing and taking time to do it Then there was the feeling that maybe you'd have no place to put it, or would rather not be bothered.

Did I ever tell you that I finally got positive proof of Jacob's marriage to the Indian girl, Eliza?[9] From the Endowment house records. So that need no longer be a matter of argument. I sent it to Miss Sinclair[10] when I first got it, early in December, but have had no word from her.[11]

Source: Dale L. Morgan Papers.

To *Dale Morgan*, February 2, 1944

St. George, Utah
Feb. 2, 1944

Dear Dale:

A letter from you always does for me about what a toddy used to do for Old Windy Bill, one of the characters of Bunkerville.[12] It gets me all hepped up. Your suggestion that I make my frontier life the subject of serious consideration teases me. How I would like to! And yet it really seems pretty unimportant.

But I'll try to answer your letter in part first, and then we'll talk about this other.

With regard to Maurine. I think your guess was right. She was evidently sending out a trial balloon to sort of get the lay of the land. Since she accomplished nothing, your guess as to the next procedure will be as good as mine.

The news that the transcripts of the John D. Lee trial are in the Huntington library[13] are cheering indeed. That is, if they are accessible. I can manage a trip down there—I don't know how, but I can manage—if I could have any assurance that I might see them when I arrive. I'll watch with interest for further information.

About your friend of the poor sick heart[14]—I can find out about accommodations in Phoenix, I'm sure. But it has just occurred to me that nowhere in the world is the weather finer than it is right here during March and April and May. The sun in May is plenty warm, but not so hot as in Phoenix. And there are some good, homey places with gardens and sun and friendliness and quiet. The only hitch is that she would have come by car from Cedar City—about 50 miles. If she could stand that, I think she could find other accommodations satisfactory—both as to price and quality. At least I'd be thrilled to help her get located. If this is out of the question, I'll still write to some of the people I know in Phoenix about her. Talk it over with her and let me know.

An old lady across the street has been trying to die for nearly two weeks now, and tonight has about decided that she will postpone it for a while. Since she is childless and friendless and so feeble, I've spent more time there than I could afford. I went once and found her on her back on the floor, not able to turn over or get up. I lifted her to the bed, sent for the doctor, and got some help, with the net result that she may last months yet . . . or years. She is nearly eighty-five. Oh, well, now that she is getting around her little house again, I think she will not be such a care.

Now as to your suggestions about a book—I've jotted down a few things in the shape of possible chapters.[15] I don't think of a title that would do at all, and the chapter suggestions are probably not in a good order. And I've had such fun reminiscing on paper. While I had the time of my young life writing some of these sketches, now that they are beginning to cool, they don't sound so good. In fact, I wonder if they'll "jell" at all . . . But you asked for it, and here it is. If in the meantime you see the error of your first assumptions, I hope you know me will enough to say you were mistaken. Even so, I've had the fun of this much of it. To tell you the truth, I doubt that any publisher would find in my experiences material for a book.

When you read these scraps, remember that they have been dashed off and need revision. They are often too expository; they are too sketchy. They lack the physical quality which you spoke of. If they have any virtue at all, I hope you can find it.

Here I am even finishing a sentence several days later. I'll send this just as it is. Red-pencil it to your heart's content and send it back—unless you think it better to do away with it right there.

Source: Dale L. Morgan Papers.

To *Director of Huntington Library*,[16] February 16, 1944

St. George, Utah
Feb. 16, 1944

Director
Huntington Library
San Marino, Calif.

Dear Sir:

I have just learned that you have the originals of the testimony given at the John D. Lee trials in Beaver, Utah.[17] Does this cover one or both trials?

May access be granted to these records? What use can be made of them?

For more than ten years now I have been doing research on the Mountain Meadows Massacre, with the intent to do a monograph on the subject, and have been able to secure some very valuable records, including the testimony of two participants. I am a member of the

Utah Historical Society, and will present letters of reference from that society, also character references from other sources.

Would it be possible to get photostats or microfilms of this material?

I would appreciate any information that you may give me.

Sincerely,

Source: Institutional Archives.

To *L. E. Bliss*,[18] July 11, 1944

St. George, Utah
July 11, 1944

Mr. L.E. Bliss, Librarian
Henry E. Huntington Library
San Marino, California

Dear Mr. Bliss:

Here are two early day newspapers from St. George. The hand-written one was made up by four young men before there was a printing press in the country, and was done more for their own edification and training than for anything else.[19]

The owners of both of these were very reluctant to let them go out of their hands, but I have assured them that the copies will be well cared for and returned in about two weeks. You have permission to Photostat them if you consider them important enough.

Mrs. Miles, the lady who owns the hand-written paper, has also an eleven-volume diary of her father—signed in the paper as Mark Whiz[20]—which I think I can get when this is returned. It was not copied under our WPA project, but I have read from it extensively and consider it one of the best I have seen. It gives such a clear picture of social conditions, celebrations, public activities, polygamy raids by the United States Marshalls, etc. She has an idea that you would not go to the expense of photographing all of it because it is so long. The volumes are not very large, however. You might let me know if you will be interested, so that I shall have some evidence to offer her.

I wish you would tell me which of the Millennial Stars[21] you do not have, also the Journal of Discourses, and about what they will be worth to you. I have located two other families who have some copies, but until I can be sure which you are anxious to get, I have done nothing about them. I understand that you have some of both of these.

I am all excited about a John D. Lee diary which is supposed to be in hiding in one of the little towns up the river. I dare to hope that the report is true, and yet I must follow it up to be sure. It would be almost too good to discover one of those missing ones, wouldn't it?

Mr. Louis B. Wright might be interested in those newspapers. I shall write him more in detail about their backgrounds later.

In the meantime, wish me luck! I'll need it.

Sincerely,

Source: Juanita Brooks Papers, MSS B103, Utah State Historical Society.[22]

To *Dale Morgan*, August 7 [1944]

St. George, Utah
Monday Morning, Aug 7

Dear Dale:

Your letter of August 4 came yesterday, and I find myself almost believing that you may place "Quicksand and Cactus" in time..... I went to Mesquite in the afternoon to attend the funeral of Ernest's father[23]—young Ern's grandfather—and it was almost like turning the clock back twenty-three years. There were the same sheet-draped chairs, the same wilted oleanders and zinnias and asparagus sprays. Instead of the paper flowers for the casket there were some flowers which we took down from here, in all four regular pieces. There was even the same smell of mortified human flesh—there is not another odor in all the world like it—and it made me so sick. There was one difference. The casket was not opened at the close of the service for the audience to walk past single file and look at the remains. In that heat, even an hour would have made such a difference in the smell.

He was a fine old man, and I am glad for him that it is over and that he is through with the business of living. He must have had diabetes, for his one foot and leg was black and mortified before he died. His last months were pure torture.

I was reminded of other things—some youngsters were trying to make chewing gum by burning the oozings from green pine boards, just as we used to. They got the sticky, clear drops on a wire and held a burning match under it until it melted and fell in black circles into a dish of water. Such bitter, black gum! Not so bitter as sunflower gum, but with a different bitterness. We also had milkweed[24] gum, besides the regular pine gum, which was good once you got it past the crumbly stage and worked into a plastic mass. Mothers always had to chew the gum up first for the children. Best of all was the squaw-bush[25] gum, though we had none of that on the Virgin River. Sometimes, coming from St. George, we would camp on the Santa Clara Creek for noon, and gather a chew. We considered it a great delicacy.

Then there were words and phrases peculiar to our town. A man was said to be "spreading the Gospel", by which I knew that he was hauling manure onto his field. Barnyard fertilizer was always called "Gospel"; we always hauled gospel or spread it, etc. when one of my brothers-in-law spoke of "Chuck-ne-bucks", which made me remember how George Leavitt, by us all called Chuck, used to tell tall tales, jokes, adventures, and so on, which earned the title of "Chuck-ne-bucks" to distinguish them from stories which one was supposed to believe.

The women all looked so brown, their hair so dried and sort of bleached, so many of them shapeless and heavy. Yet they had been so kind, so willing to stay up nights during the sickness, ready with a lunch of sandwiches and water melon after the burial. Anyway, I kept wondering if it is not different to die and be buried there than it would be in Washington D.C. or New York City.

Another Californian came to try to buy our place! We turn away several every week, it seems. So now I've lost what I was going to write about.

Source: Dale L. Morgan Papers.

To *Dale Morgan*, August 13 [1944]

St. George, Utah
Sunday morning, August 13

Dear Dale:

I have the family all off to Sunday School, and though the dishes are still in the sink and my weekly letters to the soldier lads have not been written, I'm going to drop things and follow the impulse I have had for days to visit with you. If I hurry, I can get it done and still have the dishes washed and dinner on when the crowd troops in at twelve o'clock.

First, about "Quicksand and Cactus". I have an idea that you will find it hard going to make a sale of it or to get any chance for publication in its present form. I have wondered if maybe it would be better to re-write it in the third person—it has always seemed to me that books do not go so well unless the author is a person already known. If I had a good book or two or a half dozen before my name, or if I had been outstanding in any field, then perhaps an autobiographical work would go. And perhaps I had better make it a children's book—or at least end with adolescence and about my high school time. I spent some time with Harper's "find"—Ma Counted Six—the other day, and decided that while my material is different, perhaps it could be made as interesting.

I had as well confess what is wrong with me. I've had doubts all along that this would be published unless I could in some way inject more interest into it, unless I could make my manner of telling more than I seem to be able to. Last night I listened with a group to Maurine's script for her picture book.[26] She is trying to conjure up $1500. for colored plates and the local clubs would not cooperate unless a group decided that her script was worthy. Well, of course she had not done it as I would have done it, she has brought in some things which seem to me trivial and has omitted others which seem more important, she has emphasized some most controversial issues—but, boy how she does write in some places! It is lovely. It is the best writing that she has ever done, I think, and I have always been a booster for "Joshua". It makes me feel that I lack the spark, somehow, or the touch which distinguishes between just writing and art. I have always said that a quail has its place as well as a canary, but I feel like a quail. Perhaps I should stay with the one thing which I have been able to do—collect material for others to work into best selling novels.

Oh, yes, I must report my finds at the temple. President Harold Snow[27] was very kind to me, took me to the record room upstairs and left me for an hour and a half, came back and helped me go through what is left of the records up there. We found a petition signed by many people to have John M. Higbee[28] acquitted and re-instated into society,[29] a paper written by Higbee stating his part in the MMM, that he went to the place to burn the dead and without an idea of what was before him, etc.etc. Then there was a statement from Joel White[30] to the effect that he had never accused Higbee of being responsible for the disaster. And that was all. I found letters of instruction to Jacob Hamblin, and letters regarding the Powell[31] party, along with bishop's court records, High Council minutes, etc.

Then I told President Snow what I think I told you, about the fact that there are at least eight sworn affidavits[32] from participants from this section in the hands of the General Authorities. They were given to David O. McKay[33]—I'm sure I told you the details long ago, for I tell you everything. Well, I have not had courage to go and call Brother McKay's hand. I could not out and ask for the material unless I could say why and when I was to use it and what for; I was afraid that if I did, I would have the wrath of the leaders upon me before they understood that, after all, I AM a good member of the church and not an apostate—President Snow suggests that I do not wait for President Grant to die, but that I go before the general shake-up which is bound to follow that event, and get the things before Joseph Fielding Smith[34] gets them, if he has not already. He offers to write a letter to Brother McKay for me if I think that will help. Well, I am going back to Huntington next Saturday, along with Will—or would it be more accurate to say that he is going with me—anyway, there is a conference there on Tuesday, Aug.22, which I want to attend. After I get back perhaps I shall know more definitely how to proceed to get that MMM material from Salt Lake. If the people at Huntington—Dr. Cleland[35] and Mr. Bliss—will let me announce about the Lee journals it might be a good pry with which to get this other.

I think that I told you about the show <u>Buffalo Bill</u> which I saw some time ago, and how I felt about it. It seemed to me that Jacob's association with the Indians would make a better picture, more dramatic in spots, and more in keeping with the present government policy with the Indians. I thought that if I could just write the story, assuming that I have the material and not stopping to prove every point, bringing in the human interest angle, that it would make a picture and a good one.[36] Kanab, for years Jacob's taking off place, has gone in for the movies whole-heartedly, and the Parry boys would back the project because they are in the business.[37] It would have to appear as a book first, though, I think, and be protected by a copyright. Only I have an idea that it is going to be done, and that I will have done all this research for years and then someone else will reap the benefits.

Then, one thing more. Both the Era[38] and the Relief Society Magazine[39] asked me to do articles for them. I told Mrs. Josephson[40] that she could not use what I would write, but she insists that I try to slant it for them and give them a chance. She suggested anything in line with the early history of this section, and I have thought that T.D. Brown's[41] account could be made the basis for one, Thales Haskell,[42] George W. Brimhall, or Levi M. Savage others. I'd like to keep the good will of these people, but I made no promises.[43]

From all this you can see how dissipated or scattered my interests are. The point is, I would like to be able to write, openly and unashamedly, to hire some one to come in and take over much of the routine of my home and set up where I could make a business of writing. But I can't do it on just the chance that I MIGHT sell something; I must be quite sure that eventually what I am doing will see print whether it makes anything or not. Of all things, I would prefer to settle down and give myself completely to "Quicksand and Cactus" and let fruit and garden and mending and washing and ironing go for a few months. Or if it would seem more likely that Jacob Hamblin might ever amount to anything, do him, for I have done a lot of work there, as you know.

I'll be glad to follow your suggestions and work over "Quicksand and Cactus." I can see myself a great many ways in which it can be improved, and I have thought of a number of incidents which I want to include. The first chapters I can scrap and work into a chronological pattern; I can give myself some name and write in the third person. I can leave off or condense the later part if you think I should. I am at last ready for work. I want your direction.

Well, between this and three telephone calls, my hour is up. I must be about my family's business and get things moving in the kitchen. You'll hear from me as I can find time to write, and you feel free to answer or not as you, too, have time

Source: Dale L. Morgan Papers.

To *Marba C. Josephson*, September 20, 1944

St. George, Utah
Sept. 20, 1944

Mrs. Marba C. Josephson
Improvement Era
50 North Main Street
Salt Lake City, Utah

Dear Sister Josephson:

Here is the enlarged version of the Southern Indian Mission.[44] Though it is three times the length of the first, it still is very brief. I have about decided that the story of the Southern Indian Mission is enough for a book, especially if one were to include the material on the group at Santa Clara, the one at the Muddy, and the Las Vegas mission, with some reference to the men who devoted most of their lives to the work among the natives . . . But that is another problem.

I've had my troubles, in that my typewriter chose to get distemper just when I needed it most, and I have had to borrow a machine. Never an expert typist, this has been confusing, so that there are many more than my usual errors—spaces that just happened in the middle of words, letters transposed, capitals that did not register. I have corrected it, but it looks patched.

There were many quotations which I might have used, but didn't—little things like: "Bro. Robinson of American Fork had sent some good beer to R. Harrison which we enjoyed very much, and spoke our good feelings &c., freely." "I again resolved to quit smoking because it does me harm. I tremble all over as if my nerves were let loose, and my head shakes often as if I had palsy. Tobacco I believe is the cause." Or in describing the Indians: "Oh! how she feared to approach us when we kindly asked some shutcup—holding out a basket of berries at full arms length yet some feet off from where we could reach, we approached a little near; she trembled and sweat and held her limbs together as if required to keep her reins steady that there should be no apparent leakage; such was her fear." Or "All seem to remember keenly the oppression of the Authorities." "Government so absolute, power so despotic, I have not witnessed in the Kingdom of God! How long will the people endure, or be suffered to be humbugged?" This last in reference to local authorities. To me they only show the humanness of the men, but I felt that they would be inappropriate for The Era.

I enclose two or three pictures. If I can get to Salt Lake, I should like to get a scene from the city in 1854 to illustrate Part 1, or perhaps the picture of Parley P. Pratt's home, or of the Captain, Rufus C. Allen[45]—yes, or of Brother Brown himself. These Indian pictures I thought might be good in Part 2.

I shall wait a little before I start on either of the other titles suggested: Jacob Hamblin's explorations of the Virgin and the Colorado, or George W. Brimhall's Journal.[46] I have the material, and can do either if and when you want them.

I hope that you like this story better. I myself think it is improved, though, as I said, there is material here for a book.

Sincerely,

To *Robert G. Cleland*, May 28, 1945

St. George, Utah
May 28, 1945

Dr. Robert G. Cleland
Henry E. Huntington Library
San Marino 15, California

Dear Dr. Cleland:

Thank you for your letter of May 24 and your generous appreciation of my attempts to gather material for the library.[47] I have honestly tried to make myself worth the grant which you gave me for that purpose. By doing all my traveling at night, I have been able to cut expense for you and time and expense for me—this last in hiring a woman to come into my home in my absence. When Mr. Bliss said that you both wished me to continue the work, I assumed that I should go on about as I have done.

I am sorry that I mis-interpreted the term Grant-in-aid. I had assumed that there was something standard about it, that the people who were doing research on Imperial Valley, or the Government's Indian policy in the Southwest, or the Salt Lake–San Bernardino Trail, or any of the other subjects, received more than an official nod of approval or a sort of "green light" signal. I thought that you considered the Mountain Meadows Massacre a subject upon which research should be done. While I have spent some time and money in this, I have by no means exhausted the field. There are other California newspapers which I must consult, there are reports and letters and papers in the national archives which I must obtain, besides the very important papers which I have already talked to you about.

Perhaps I was foolish to assume that I might be given an assignment such as the others had, since I am not now connected with any educational institution. Yet since I left the teaching profession I have been quite consistent in going on with my research. Dr. Hafen[48] will tell you that the material which he secured from my files saved him months of time in research.

I am interested in the preservation of history, for I have seen how easily originals are lost or misplaced or just disappear. I think that I can obtain enough of these to make it worth while for you. But for fifty dollars a month I cannot afford to take the necessary trips and also work at writing, because I cannot afford to hire the necessary help to relieve me of my routine of home work.

I hope that this does now sound unappreciative. I am glad for the privilege I have had of working with you and Mr. Bliss during the past year. But I do feel I should be enabled to devote more time to this work if I am to do justice to both projects, which means that the grant should be increased. Otherwise I should prefer to devote myself to one or the other of the two assignments.

With kindest personal regards, I am

Very sincerely,

To *Robert G. Cleland*, June 5, 1945

St. George, Utah
June 5, 1945

Dr. Robert G. Cleland
Henry E. Huntington Library|
San Marino 15, California

Dear Dr. Cleland:

The arrangement which you suggest in your letter of May 31 will be entirely satisfactory to me.[49] You may be sure that I will make every effort to merit your confidence.

As to the collecting of material for the library, I have listed seven originals which I can secure, I think, for very little cost. I am anxious to fill in the set of the Millennial Star and the Journals of Discourses, but have not located others, though I have some leads. Perhaps by planning what trips I do take more carefully and writing ahead, I hope to make them more profitable and perhaps less expensive.

With regard to the study of the Mountain Meadows Massacre: I think I did not tell you that I tried to get an interview with Pres. David O. McKay, but could not get past his secretary. After I had given her a full account of my mission, she said she had been employed there for the past ten years and had never received such papers nor seen them and therefore was sure that they had never been brought in. It made me realize a little more what I am up against.

I am getting a letter from Mrs. Hafen[50] who took the affidavits in and also one from my Stake President. This time I shall go directly to the president of the church, George Albert Smith,[51] and I feel sure that I shall meet a more tolerant and understanding attitude. Which brings me to my reason for all this explanation.

Would it be out of order to ask you to write me another letter, naming me as working under a grant from the Rockefeller Foundation rather than the Huntington Library? This is a minor point, I know, and may sound silly, but with the cards stacked as they are, I cannot afford to fail this time, and I believe that such a letter would help. In Utah, California is considered just another state and there is a hint of rivalry or jealousy toward her, while the Rockefeller Foundation carries a commutation of national importance. It is only a detail, as I said before, but in this particular undertaking every detail is important. And I MUST get those accounts written by men who actually participated in that thing

Under separate cover I am mailing the last issue of the Utah State Historical Quarterly, which carries a little study of mine written over a year ago.[52] While it is not very pretentious, I did try to give an overall picture and to describe rather minutely a particular area, both:

in subject and geography. The Thales Haskell journal was photostated by your library.

I thank you again for the opportunity you are giving me to follow this piece of research and for your cooperation. I look forward to a visit with you when I am down in August, and hope to be able to stay at the library for some research along this line.

Very sincerely,

To *Dale Morgan*, August 15, 1945

St. George, Utah
August 15, 1945

Dear Dale,

It came at last, the word we have waited so long to hear. I was sitting at the typewriter when my neighbor over the fence called, "It's coming! It's on right now!" Since we can't get reception on our radio during the day, I ran over. Afraid lest the whole town might not be hearing the news, she took down the receiver and told the operator to set the fire sirens going. The operator replied that she couldn't without orders, so she called the mayor and said, "Why in the name of heaven, don't you set the fire siren going, so that people can know what is going on?" Almost the same instant the tabernacle bell began to ring. We learned that President Glenn E. Snow[53] of the college was listening, too, and decided he could spread the good news quicker by running to ring the bell himself than by sending someone.

Well, we got into our little one-seated car with all our kids and our neighbors in the back, and went down town. Everybody was out. The fire engine with two big flags led the line of cars—we were in the middle of it—all honking and clattering, around and around the town. Kids on bicycles ran in groups, with bunches of tin cans tied to their fenders. War widows collected and laughed and cried and hugged each other.

We let our youngsters go to the show, while we came home to get out notes to our boys. I had their envelopes addressed since last Friday, but didn't want to write until I KNEW. Our last word from our youngest was dated July 11, and said that he was going out again where he could not write nor get letters, so we hope for him especially that he got the good news—and is still whole when he gets it.

This morning at nine the noise-makers started again, the college band and the martial band were both out, and people gathered at the tabernacle for a public meeting of thanksgiving. My first impulse when the word came was to sit right down and bawl. It seems that the combined joy and gratitude are almost more than I can contain, certainly more than I can express—at least by any noise making devices that I know. I think that the combined prayers of gratefulness of all the mothers of the earth must rock the throne of heaven.

Your letter of August 10 reached me yesterday. True to form, we have written each other on the same day, or nearly the same again. There's something almost uncanny about how we do that, isn't there? I was glad for it and hope that your plans to bring Darrel and Anna[54] and their kids out to Utah can materialize. You tell them for me, that we'd like to entertain them at The Mansion; my youngsters would have the time of their lives showing theirs around.

You were right in your placement of the tabernacle and the general locations in St. George. As you can see from the map I sent, we live near the top of Main Street. I'll hope to get one of the place now, if ever we can get film again.

I take the Saturday Review, so shall look with much interest for your review of Scowcroft's book.[55] I wish you would tell me the publisher, so that I may order a copy—but never mind, for it will be in the review. I'm eager to see it.

About Q&C—I hesitate to send these first fifteen chapters to you again when I know how over worked you are on your own projects, and how positively nauseated you must be with the repeated re-reading of them. I'm sick of them myself. I've rewritten them and modified them somewhat and think that I should probably let Knopf see them—Brother Alfred A. can say <u>No</u> as well to fifteen chapters as to twenty five. Or shall I send it all to you, the chapters that are practically done and these last nine or ten that must be worked over after you see them?

I wish I could shake off this feeling that the whole thing is a farce. I write a chapter and then I think, <u>So What</u>? What difference does it make? Who am I that I should be written about? What is Bunkerville that the General public should be troubled to read about it? If I followed my impulse, I would have boxed the whole thing up, tied it securely, and stored it in the back of the basement closet.

I must finish it, of course, if it kills me. And I must not take too much longer doing it if I fill my obligations on the MMM. My trips everywhere are canceled until I get into the mail either to you or to Knopf, this draft, done after a fashion to the end.

Don't get too disgusted with me. Perhaps in time I can regain what little self confidence I had, or develop some new. In the meantime, I'll plug along and write whenever I have the impulse—which means, or seems to mean, whenever you sit down to write to me

Source: Dale L. Morgan Papers.

To *Dale Morgan*, October 3, 1945

St. George, Utah, Oct. 3, 1945

Dear Dale,

Let's sit us down for a little visit, shall we? The family is all at school, the kitchen floor wiped up, Q & C started on its way yesterday, no fruit on hand that is going to spoil, so why not?

I sent the Ms. direct to Knopf and asked them to mail it to you when they had finished with it. I shall send postage to you for its final return to me, and also for whatever other excursion it shall need to make, if any. The two chapters dealing with the high school and normal training years will have to be re-worked, either amplified or perhaps cut, and one or two of the others may need modification in the interest of coherence. But they can get an idea of what it will be like anyway.

Now for the MMM. Mrs. Hafen finally came in for the winter and I had a long talk with her. She will write a letter for me regarding the affidavits which she handed in, and will even go up with me if I want her to.[56] I hope to be in Salt Lake City a week from today, if the bus strike does not spread too hopelessly. I felt that I should not expect to get audience with President Smith until after the October conference; he has been pretty well occupied with temple dedications and other activities lately, and I didn't want to go without the letter from Mrs. Hafen. In the meantime, I have plenty to do here in the way of organizing material and going through some which I have not to date given careful attention.

Looks as if all three of our boys might home by the first of the year. Bob writes from Berlin for us to save him some Thanksgiving turkey; Ernest has been in two years and has enough points for release from the navy; Clair said he didn't know when he could come, but the radio and also the Tribune reported that the 31st army would sail from Manila on the last day of October. We think that means him.

Now as to a little friendly gossip—Have you heard anything of Maurine's arrival in the east? I wondered how much of a ripple she caused in the general surface of things. Again she has shaken the dust of Utah from her feet and resolved never to set foot upon it again. As for me, I don't take her seriously at all, for I have heard her swear so many times that she would never, never, NEVER come back to St. George again, and then within two or three weeks return to say with equal emphasis that she simply cannot work anywhere else, that she MUST come here for getting her batteries re-charged, etc.etc. This time she made her promise never to return to the department of publicity in Salt Lake.

As you can guess, there is something behind it all. It's a long story, but I think I'll give it to you anyway, as nearly as I can, for I've had to refuse to be implicated in any way myself.

It seems that along about the first of September Maurine was going up town when she met two of our young women, one the wife of a service man and the other a teacher. The little wife was pulling her two-year-old son in a cart and weeping as they went. Maurine inquired the trouble and found that the girl's husband was due home on a 30-day leave enroute from Europe to the Pacific: and she had been trying to find an apartment where they might have some privacy during his visit. She thought she had one engaged, but the landlady had a chance to rent it to permanent tenants, and had let it go. Hence the tears.

Well, Maurine thought she should roll up her sleeves and do something about this discrimination against the wife of a man who had been over-seas, so she piloted the group to the office of the local paper and asked what they could do about it. The editor said he knew that there was a definite housing shortage here, and he didn't know that there was anything he could do. The attitude of his wife infuriated

Maurine, so she went home and wrote letters to the Tribune and the Deseret News setting forth the situation as she saw it and asking them to expose the condition. The Trib bit, and ran an editorial in which they mentioned St. George definitely as a place where service men were getting no consideration. It appeared in the issue of Thursday, Sept. 6. If I can locate it, I'll mail it in.

Naturally when people here read the piece they were pretty much stirred up. Some thought that the correspondent, Mabel Jarvis,[57] had written it. The Rotary Club, the Lions, and other organizations had it up for discussion and indignation was pretty wide-spread. When they found that Maurine had written it, things did begin to happen! Here was a person for whom they had raised $500. in hard cash to help her publicize St. George in her book, and then she gives them this sort of publicity!

Maurine was angry at Mabel, thinking that she had stirred up the furor and Mabel was angry at Maurine because people had blamed her. There followed angry telephone calls, and Maurine finally wrote a vitriolic letter which Mabel showed to all and sundry—all of which added up to Maurine's sudden decision to leave and go East. Knowing that she will be there and have dealings with Knopf has made me wish that my Ms. had either arrived much earlier or much later. I'm afraid if she knows any such thing is brewing, she will bungle things for me. She won't help, I'm sure, but I'll just have to let things take their course.

As far as the personal quarrel was concerned, I managed to stay clear. Mabel has been a friend of long standing, and I have had fairly congenial relations with Maurine in spite of Will's intense dislike for her. I couldn't justify the Tribune article at all, for it was misrepresented from start to finish. Just as an example:

1—It said the wife had came into the County seat to find a place to live, when she has been here with her mother all the time and has a comfortable room in the home.

2—that the boy was coming here to attend the Dixie college, when he was only on 30-day leave.

3—That he had been overseas for four years, when it was only 18 months.

4—that he had a son whom he had never seen. Since the child is only two years old, some folks wondered whose baby it is! As a matter of fact, his wife and baby were with him several months before his departure.

5—that she was refused a place to live because she had a child. She found two places where she could have got in, but they were not nice enough, she thought. The one she wanted was leased to a long-time tenant.

And so on and on. I think that the Tribune is still hearing about that editorial. I have taken no part in the discussion, figuring that the least said the soonest mended. Maurine came up to talk it over, but I was out, and I haven't seen Mabel. It has been a tempest in a teapot, though, for sure.

Now to change the subject, and for some more gossip. Jonreed[58] tells me that Verda is "expecting" and hence will have to leave her school at Christmas. She doesn't come down because she is self-conscious about meeting folks generally. That means that he will have to heave to and support the flock for a few months at least. Sometimes it seems just too bad, the impositions we would-be writers inflict upon those who love us.

Well, this has spun out long enough, don't you think? And it's time to shuck the corn and put it on for lunch. The pack are simply ravenous when they get to the top of the hill.

Source: Dale L. Morgan Papers.

To *George Albert Smith*, October 9, 1945

St. George, Utah
October 9, 1945

President George Albert Smith
L.D.S. Church Office Building
Salt Lake City, Utah

Dear President Smith:

I would be more reluctant to write this letter if it were not for my close association with your cousin, Mrs. Zora Jarvis,[59] and my uncle, Dr. LeRoy R. Hafen, who have both assured me that you might take time to give me a brief audience. Sister Jarvis was my counselor in the Stake Relief Society for the seven years which I served, and Dr. Hafen has been a close friend as well as a relative, since we are both interested in history.

There are two things which I should like to talk over with you. The first is the matter of the naming of the city of St. George, which I understand Zora has already written you about. I have promised to do a brief statement to go with a picture to be hung at the Dixie College. I had also talked over with Sister Josephson the possibility of an article, in two or three installments, on your grandfather George A. Smith, for the Improvement Era.

The second item which I need to talk over with you is my study of the Mountain Meadows Massacre. I have been given a Fellowship from the Rockefeller Institute through the Huntington Library at San Marino, California, to do this piece of work. You remember that Dr. Hafen is making a similar study on the Salt Lake–San Bernardino trail.

I felt that since it was to be done, it had best be done by a member of the church, someone with an L.D.S. background and an understanding of our people. I am sure that I can do it better than some who might have been selected. I think, too, that it should come from someone not officially connected with the Church Historian's office. I know that there is now one book on the subject almost ready for publication by a rabid anti-Mormon,[60] and I believe that it would be to the interest of the church to have my study come out first. As in anything else, it is good to get there with the first blow; an "answer" is never so effective.

Since I first became interested in this subject, some ten years ago, I have had offers from publishers in the East to do it for them. I have always refused, feeling that they would want something sensational, something upon which to capitalize, but when I was offered this fellowship for the purpose of making a complete and impartial study, I accepted. I think that the time has come when the church can be benefited by such a study.

I should like very much to have a chance to talk with you. I had expected to come into Salt Lake City next week or the end of this, and to be there for two or three days. If you would give me a little time, I shall make my trip to suit your convenience, as I can leave here in a few hours' notice.[61]

May I hope to hear from you? Thank you.

Sincerely,

To *Dale Morgan*, December 9, 1945

St. George, Utah
Dec. 9, 1945

Dear Dale,

I wonder if I will really be able to stay with this long enough to accomplish anything. I have just finished reading your good review of Fawn's book in the SRL,[62] and I feel in the mood to talk about it a little. I haven't organized my ideas or even crystallized them well, but will jot some thoughts down at random.

I agree wholeheartedly with you in saying that this book needed to be done. I think it is scholarly; I think it is literary. I think that it sets up new points from which to judge Joseph Smith. It certainly shows careful and patient research. I like especially her work on backgrounds and social conditions and current interests. (I remember, for example, that it was something of a shock to me when I first learned that there were active temperance societies in Joseph's day, that some doctors were coming out against the use of tobacco and liquor. I had been taught the revelation on the use of these things had come unheralded and entirely new to the world rather than as a conclusion to a discussed and debated subject.)

Joseph's youthful diggings for gold and Indian mounds, even his first court experiences, seem but the normal activities of a growing boy. I remember that one writer, I've forgotten who or where, made a point of his later mention of early indiscretions to try to prove that he was a homo-sexual. To me, the admission meant only that he might have been indolent, perhaps raided a melon patch or a hen-roost with his friends, or teased and annoyed some old parson. What got me started on that? Oh, yes, I began to say that different people put entirely different interpretations even on simple statements. So with some of Fawn's material, I didn't always arrive at the same conclusions from her evidence that she did. Nor do I think that it is humanly possible for anyone to collect all the evidence; and all the written evidence must be, at best, only a fragment of a human life.

I do not agree that he was a conscious fraud and imposter. The things that were real to him may not seem so to her nor to you or to most other people, but I think they must have been to him. I have felt that it was his own deep and sincere convictions that attracted and held his following. For a fraud, he inspired loyalties too deep in too many. Certainly he had SOMETHING. Men, catching their spark from him, were willing to sacrifice too much to further his cause. Consider the Pratts, and John Taylor, Willard Richards, Wilford Woodruff,[63] and the others. They were normal men, interested in families and homes, and yet they dropped everything to spend years in spreading what they thought was the Truth—as he taught it. And their loyalty remained after his death—to him and his cause, and to Brigham Young only because the mantle of Joseph fell upon him. It would be an interesting thing to know how many man-years of missionary work was done at his instigation, even during his lifetime.

Was it Carlyle[64] who said that an institution is but the lengthened shadow of a man? Anyway, the Mormon church of today, for all its wanderings and perversions, for all the imprints that have been left upon it by his various successors, still carries the shadow of Joseph Smith.

As I remember, you both seem to feel that he wrote much without revealing much about himself. I felt that the Doctrine & Covenants give a good cross section of his interests and studies and conclusions. And for all its chaff and verbiage, I find some illuminating passages in it. He puts a "Thus saith the Lord" to preface a request for money or a rebuke or a commandment, but you may be sure that the Lord spoke only after Joseph had pondered and studied, and whether we accept the reality of God's voice or not, we still know something of the working of Joseph's mind, which is himself.

As to polygamy, the church has always maintained that he lived it. True, Fawn has found some extra wives. I doubt that there were children for this reason: during the period when women were anxious to be known as the wives of Joseph, any one who had borne him a child would have been only too glad to have given the fact full publicity. It would have been a most coveted honor, one she would have been too eager to claim. Zina D. and Eliza R. Snow Young[65] used to make public statements before groups of women throughout the church that they had been wives of the prophet. I have found records of it in minutes and I have had too many elderly women tell me about it. A son of the prophet would not have been a thing to hush up—except for

Emma[66]—but to announce proudly, especially among the saints in the mountains. It is O.K. to suggest the possibility, but to me the probability is not great . . . not that I would care at all.

My whole background makes me slow to think that I can analyze Joseph Smith. My Grandpa Dudley used to speak of him as "The Prophet of the Living God" in a tone and with an expression that made me quiver inside. To him, Joseph was second only to Christ himself, and a close second, at that. Though he was only a boy, Grandpa had been impressed with the character of this man. His followers paid allegiance to Brigham because God had shown them in a miracle that Brigham was to carry on. Then my reading has been too much from the writings of those who were his ardent disciples; the journals and diaries that I have found certainly give respect for a man who could inspire such devotion and loyalty. To me he seems to have a dimension that is quite un-get-at-able.

There are those who do not believe in visions or supernatural manifestations, hence decide that Joseph could not have had any. A few experiences which I have had personally make me slow to try to judge whether a person has really had an experience with spiritual significance, or whether he was suffering from indigestion. These are hard things to write about—to try to put on paper. But during the year of Ernest's sickness, when we were so determined that "I, the Lord, am bound, when you do what I say,"—so determined that Ernest should live because he thought God had promised him that he should live, there were happenings which were to me the essence of reality, a luminous, certain reality, that I could not deny. There was the time, for instance, when I was alone in Salt Lake with him, only a child myself, never away from Bunkerville so far before, and him desperately ill, suffering beyond imagination. We lived up on 9th avenue, not far from the L.D.S. hospital and west of the Ensign Ward chapel. Across a deep gully to the west was the State Capitol Building. How was it that one night, when I felt that I MUST have help, that unless I did have it—well, anyway, there was a knock, and when I answered the door a man asked, "Is there any trouble in this house?" I could not answer; could only point to the man on the bed. Without preliminaries, I got the oil, he administered to Ern and as he did, Ernest fell asleep. Afterwards he visited a while with me—now he was NOT one of the three Nephites.[67]

But he told me a story as incredible as any I have ever heard. He was a slight man, around 50, I'd say, with thick hair parted in the middle, with one bad eye, and with a decided foreign brogue. He told me that he lived in the southern part of town, that he had been impressed to go uptown, that he had come to the center of town, had transferred to a 9th ave. car, had got off at our stop, walked up past the other four or five doors to our place. He was a recent convert to the church, he said, and he had been promised that his bad eye would be restored. (I doubted that, as it looked utterly shrunken and gone to me). Anyway, I went to bed that night, the first in many, and slept until the sun wakened me in the morning, because Ernest slept, too. An incredible story? Yes, I can hardly believe it myself. Yet at the time it was real. I wrote home about it. I made a note of it in a little record book.[68]

Nor was it more remarkable than was the birth of little Ernest, nor than the restoration of Dudley's sight. Nor, for that matter, than the miraculous way in which my Grandma Hafen, now seriously ill, gets instant relief at the administration of the elders—so great is her own faith in that ordinance.

What I am trying to say is this: I believe that it is possible for human beings to tap the great source of all good—to contact God direct, if you will. I believe that there were times, rare, perhaps, when Joseph Smith did that. I believe that it was those times that held his people to him in spite of all his human blunderings and frailties and mistakes....

Well, I really didn't set out to bear my testimony. I have always been intrigued by Joseph Smith, and Fawn's book only whets my interest. I think I can learn much more about him, and then not know it all. I think he is hard to fit into a pigeonhole. I think, strip him of the encrustations as we may (and should) there remains something more than remarkable left.

I doubt that this book will seriously affect the church. (I'd like to see Milton Hunter[69] try to do something about it. They make such a point of parading his PhD. and I thought his research on Brigham Young was pretty flimsy indeed. He certainly did not find what he did not want to find; he seemed never to go back of the "right" sources.) But I started out to say that I am afraid not many people will read it. We have become so accustomed to having people either "fur or a gin" us that many will read only to the statement that the church was founded on a fable in the preface, and go no further. Just another anti, they will say. I have offered my copy to several, but no one seemed to have time for it. Something like Maurine's is easier to read and pleasanter and less disturbing.

But if Mormon laity will not read it, Mormon scholars should. Some of them will. And the book cannot but have its effect, and in the long run, a very profound effect.

Well, well, here a whole Sunday afternoon is gone. It's nearly dark outside; the boys have come in from their hike up on the Sugar Loaf. Supper time.

As I look back over these pages, I see even more mistakes than usual. The machine is skipping cogs oftener. My fingers have not been sure, maybe because my head is still hardly clear from a dose of flu, which I had felt so sure that I could avoid entirely, and which I didn't escape after all. I could do a better letter if I'd leave this and re-write and compose it. But when would I get the time? I should have made and sent it to Fawn. I guess—though I doubt that I have said anything that would matter to her.

I'll get into gear on the MMM later. It's too late tonight.

To *Dale Morgan*, December 13, 1945

St. George, Utah
Dec. 13, 1945

Dear Dale:

You should see our land of sunshine and roses today. We've had a real snow storm, one that covers the ground and bends down the bushes. You never saw youngsters more thrilled than mine, either. They want to be out in it all the time, rolling snow men and pelting each other with snow balls. I could be more thrilled myself if the kitchen floor didn't get such a mess.

Just finished Scowcroft's "Children of the Covenant" and enjoyed it very much. He really writes well; makes it come alive. I thought his drawing of Esther and Caroline were marvelously done, but somehow couldn't make Burton ring true. He should not have been a moron, exactly, I thought, and yet he acted like one from first to last—a spineless nit-wit who would lie around three months without doing one earthly thing, nothing but eat his three meals and lie and try vacantly to think or try to decide whether or not he should smoke a cigarette. Perhaps instead of criticizing him, I'd rather just say that I've never seen a boy like him.

If these are at all typical Mormons, we're of a pretty low grade, aren't we—from Albert and the Johnson girl up and down. I know mothers who are just as dramatic on the question of smoking; I know the church under Presidents Grant and J. Reuben Clark[70] have made the use of tobacco one of the major sins. I hope for a more tolerant regime from here on for a while—except, of course, for Joseph Fielding and a few of the other good stand-patters.

I've wondered about me. The year I was in New York my best friend there was a girl who was born and raised in Mesquite, who graduated from our little high school a year after I did, who went through the U[71] under about the same conditions that I got through the Y,[72] and then went to New York and did social work. She had been promoted until she was head of a district with about 14 workers under her. Well, we spent quite a bit of time together, and I have a genuine admiration for her, as I always had. She had taken up tobacco with an emphasis—smoked constantly, even drizzled ashes in her cooking. She insisted that I should learn, that I should try, at least. Sometimes now I wonder why I didn't. I have never liked the smell of tobacco, so I had no desire to taste it, just as I have never liked the smell of garlic and hence had never eaten it. I had an idea that it would make me sick, and I don't like to be sick. I could have taken a calomel course with as much logic. But she had an idea that if I would seriously try, I could learn to like it, and then I could show my independence and intellectual honesty by coming back here to teach in the Dixie College. By her arguments, such a course would be a courageous thing to do.

Perhaps it would have been, at that. But I figured that I could see no point in deliberately cultivating a habit that I had no inclination toward, a habit that would ruin my prestige among both students and teachers among whom I must work. I explained my stand to her by using the comparison which I have often used since: When a cowboy wants to turn a herd of stampeding cattle, he doesn't run directly counter to them. If he did he'd be run over. He rides with them, and turns them gradually. So if I don't like the stand of the church, I can do more about it by staying in.

It was the same thing with wines. Her husband was a connoisseur of wines; they had a big room full. They kept insisting that I might be right cute or clever or entertaining if I would unbend enough to get right good and drunk once. Well, I was plain cowardly about it. I argued that there are some experiences that are not worth having, and for me, that was one. The few drunken women I had seen were so sloppily nasty that I had no desire to imitate them. I would as soon have tried marijuana or opium.

Well, anyway, I've wondered that the church will let me teach a Sunday School class when they know that I say repeatedly to the students that it is not a matter of being just good, but good for something, that negations never lead to positive righteousness, that I would rather have a smoker and a drinker who is fundamentally and aggressively Christian than a man who boasts that he has never tasted either liquor or tobacco, and at the same time has never done anything worth while in his life. I get so tired of our "Thou Shalt Not's." I'd like us to put our emphasis on some good, positive "Thou Shalt."

Now I wanted to talk about the MMM, and that man Burton in the book got me off on this tirade. Excuse it, please.

I've spent a little time on J.H. Beadle's "Western Wilds."[73] The report of his conversation with Lee at the ferry in 1872 sounds genuine, Lee's explanation of the "why" of it, the current stories of the emigrants, the type of men who were present—"Those men were God-fearing men. Their motives were pure. They knelt down and prayed to be guided in council. But they was full of zeal. Their zeal was greater than their knowledge." . . . and later on "It is told for a fact that I could tell great confessions, and bring in Brigham Young and the heads of the church. But if I was to take forty confessions, I could not bring in Brigham Young. His counsel was: 'Spare them, by all means.'" Though the book was not published until 1878,[74] the author said that here he has set down but a small part of the conversation "only such as I could remember beyond doubt and jot down at my first halting place the next day."

Later in the book he tells how Rachel Hamblin told him: "A Mormon woman, far advanced in pregnancy, was at Hamblins; her husband was driving one of the wagons containing the wounded.... When the massacre began this man took a fit, and soon died of excitement or fright. When the bloody wagon, containing children and the dead body of her husband, was brought to Hamblin's, this woman went into a spasm, prematurely gave birth to a child, then became insane, and lingered twelve years a raving maniac."

Now this is clearly a piece of fiction, whether Rachel Hamblin told it or not. The woman was the wife of Samuel Knight;[75] he lived to testify against John D., and for many years after, and his wife bore him a number of children after that event. I can get dates on all this, and will do it soon.

Both Beadle and Lyford[76] tell the story of the wounded emigrant men and the paper which was written telling of the plight of the company and listing the names of the people. I cannot make up my mind whether each man secured his information independently from Jacob Hamblin, or whether one borrowed it directly from the other.

In the story of the trial Beadle gives some space to the testimony and appearance of Klingensmith.[77] This I have seen nowhere else. I wonder what happened to the written account by this man.

I think it was Maurine in Joshua who intimated that Hickman and other destroying angels were present.

The more I think of it, the more I am convinced that Beadle and Lyford got their information independently, that each must have talked to Hamblin. Their story is essentially the same, but where Beadle names the Indian chief definitely as Jackson and John D. Lee as the man who tore up the paper, while Lyford speaks of "my informant" as the honest old Mormon, says he had a ranch near the scene of the tragedy, and otherwise identifies Jacob; but does not directly name either the Indian who found the paper nor the man who destroyed it.

I cannot understand how Kelly can be so persistent in his statements that Hamblin was present. The conversation of Beadle and Lee referred to earlier says also that Jacob was in the north.

In Gove's "The Utah Expedition" I found for the first time the story of Milo Andrus[78] cutting his third wife's throat,[79] the first time I have seen it in print except in Kelly's "Holy Murder."[80] I wonder if that is where he got the story. I don't have his book, so cannot check direct.

Do you have Bill Hickman's[81] book? I'd like to see it, or to buy a copy. I think I told you that the Gilson sisters say that it was written on their kitchen table. They said first that they had the original, but later did not let me see any of their material.

Our court reporter Keller, I think his name is, has told us of one Cook[82] who claims to have been a clerk at the Lee trial and to have his original notes and the transcriptions. He says that the Church has wanted to purchase them, but Cook will not sell to the church. I'm writing Cook to learn what I can learn. From Albert E. Miller,[83] who is something of an historian on Southern Utah, I first heard of Cook and his claims. He must be extremely old by now. I'll let you know developments.

To *Dale Morgan*, December 28, 1945

St. George, Utah
Dec. 28, 1945

Dear Dale,

At the end of this long spring day I'm going to steal time for a short visit. For several days now it has been warm, but today it has been really growing weather, with all the children in their shirt sleeves raking leaves and playing marbles. The kind of weather St. George should capitalize on.

Your letter of December 15 was most interesting to me, though the thought that maybe your spanking will reform Maurine makes me grin.[84] She can't be reformed; she can't see that she has anything to reform in. She severed diplomatic relations with me when your review first came out. She came here full of accusations and complaints; she just couldn't understand why you should have it in for her; goodness knows, she had tried hard enough to be friendly to you. I couldn't agree with all her line, so she left in a miff and has never been back nor spoken to me since. I don't mind, really. I know that when she needs something that I can help her with she will come, soon enough. She has not mentioned your letter, nor will she, I imagine. And she will still insist that she has not "borrowed" anything. Knowing her, I just accept her as she is and find her interesting and stimulating at times, even though her facts are colored to distortion by her current emotional tempo—when she's high, she's high, and when she's low, how low she can be! She talks only in superlatives, and in one extreme or the other.

But it is your discussion of Fawn's book that interests me most. Your question "What is Truth?" is one that I have puzzled over before, one, in fact, that this MMM business makes me face with new seriousness. If I could feel that I really deserved your complimentary paragraph, I'd not be as disturbed about getting at the TRUTH of this matter as I am.

But the fact that we are on opposite sides of what you choose to call "The Great Divide" with regard to the question of the reality of God, does indeed make our whole approach to all the history of the Mormons different. As you say, I could be a good Catholic or Methodist or Mormon, having this fundamental belief. I am in fact in a state of apostasy, perhaps, with many of the practices and teachings of our church. I simply cannot accept them and retain my intellectual independence, which I do try to maintain. And yet, I am loyal to it. I think it is as much my church as it is J. Reuben Clark's or anyone else's.

But back again to the book: I think I told you that B.H. Roberts had done some good independent thinking on the origins of the Book of Mormon. (Did I ever send you the parallel which he worked out between it and the Smith book?[85] Seems that I did.)

On the matter of polygamy, you must remember that the church has taken a complete right about face on this subject during the last administration. Now the matter of extra children would be most embarrassing, but the time was when any women who had borne a son to the prophet would have wanted to shout it from the house-tops. Being a Prophet, he could do no wrong; to bear him a son would have placed a woman in a most strategic position. (I get my tenses mixed, but you get the idea.) Did you hear of the speech of President Grant wherein he himself announced that he was a son of the prophet? His family were horrified, I understand, and those next to him were much disturbed by his speech and took it as a definite sign that, he was in his dotage. Time was when the church generally would have been cheered and happy about it.

I was much interested in your remarks about J. Reuben Clark and his speech at the Y.[86] I understand that the faculty there resented it quite bitterly—that is, many of them did, bet a penny that I can guess who her anonymous friend is. Brother Clark certainly does have a capacity for making enemies. I've heard even good Republicans say that it is hard to tell when Bro. Clark is speaking in the name of the Lord and when he is speaking in the name of the Republican Party.

I felt like adding sometime, "or the name of the big money interests." But the fact that so many of the professors at the Y are not in sympathy with such statements as you quoted is for me a cheering thing.

Last night I went, by special invitation, to Santa Clara to a program honoring the pioneers of that settlement, and especially Samuel Stucki,[87] my great grandfather. I couldn't help thinking how hard it would be to understand this man, the force which brought him from the green Alps to this dry, red land, the power that sustained him and kept him happy and forward-looking in spite of everything without taking God into the picture. I know that analogies are often dangerous, but it occurred to me that a deaf person could as well criticize a grand opera from what he could get of the actions of the characters and without hearing the music that was basic to it all as for a person to whom there is no God, could evaluate the life of a man like Samuel Stucki. To you, God is not; to him, He was very real and very near; an ever-ready help in time of trouble.

I respect your views. I have boundless admiration for your intellect and for your fairness. I like you as a person more than almost anyone else that I know. But I suppose that we shall have to stay each on our own side of the Great Divide, and each make our judgments in the light of that position. I hope that mine can be as fair in my way as I know that yours will be in your way.

Did I tell you that Jonreed's wife presented him with a pair of twin boys on December 12th? I knew that Verda was hardly prepared for one baby, to say nothing of two, so I sent some little shirts, stockings, and other essentials. This morning I had a letter from them both . . . I believe that the experience has been a most wholesome one for him, because he has had to face realities and assume his responsibility. Then, too, he has received $500. for an article on Las Vegas, and that has given his morale a good boost. How I would like to see him succeed with this next book! He deserves to, but more than that, his wife deserves to have him. Succeed, I mean.

Maurine is setting herself up in Salt Lake City, I hear, where she can have some social life at the same time that she works at her next book. I think I told you that Simon & Schuster are giving her an advance of $1800—or $150, a month for a year—on it. I don't know the name of the work, but it is to be a sequel to GIANT JOSHUA.[88]

Well, I've about decided that for Dutton's, too, it is to be thumbs down.[89] I had never had any hope of Knopf but I have let myself think that MAYBE Duttons—Oh, well—

One more thing to illustrate the Mormon attitude toward Fawn's book. I handed it to my mother with the suggestion that she read it, but after glancing through it briefly and reading the preface, she handed it back, "I don't have time for things like that," she said, "What time I can spend reading I want to spend to better advantage. Do you remember how Pa always said that he would as soon expose the bodies of his children to a contagious disease as to expose their minds to that bitter, anti-Mormon stuff?" Yes, I do remember, and I remember how that only made me more eager to hear the other side of the story.

Now that the Christmas rush is over at the office and at home, the tree taken out and the gifts put away, perhaps I can get back to some consistent work again. I must tackle good Brother David O. once more. I think that he should talk to me, at least. Perhaps he wants to prevent my errors, lest I should not correct them while my soul and body are still together. But I think each person should have a right to make his own mistakes and to make his own particular kind of a fool of himself in his own way.

Source: Dale L. Morgan Papers.

To *Dale Morgan*, May 19, 1946

St. George, Utah
May 19, 1946

Dear Dale,

You have no idea how good it was to hear from you after your long silence. I'd hate to confess how many times I have had the impulse to write; but knowing under what pressure you are working, I did not, for I did not want to distract you even to the extent of reading a letter, much less answering it. So now, while I feel like it, I'll write, and you set it aside until you feel that you have the time to answer.—I mean to bother to read it, even.

First, as to Fawn's book. I have heard of the pamphlet which you mention—"No, Ma'am, that's NOT History,"[90] but have not seen it yet. I did see the article in the Sunday issue of the Deseret News, "Appraisal of the SO CALLED Brodie Book,"[91] and it makes me embarrassed and ashamed. I have no idea who the author is—some say Bowen, some Joseph Fielding Smith, some say Henry Smith, some Widtsoe[92]—but whoever it is, he makes it very hard for a person who would like to be loyal to the church. It begins with a vitriolic attack upon Father Dwyer. It seems that the good father has made some remarks that draw blood, but the answer is below the dignity of any Christian. The inference seems to be that if my church is a hoax yours is also, and we are both hard put to keep the laity from getting wise to us. There follows two full pages of fine print, picking at errors . . . Well, I didn't even read it all, but I am sure that it defeats its own ends.

Yesterday afternoon I had a most stimulating two hours with Daryl Chase,[93] the first time I have ever met him. To me, he represents the type of person on whom the fate of this institution must hang. Perhaps you know him, but if you don't, here's what I gathered: He has been in the Seminary systems of the church, taught in Arizona—Tucson—and was director of the Institute at Logan, then resigned to accept a position in the USAC.[94] Was put in the Stake Presidency in Logan, but resigned because he couldn't be so confined in his thinking. He was here to give the Baccalaureate address to the graduates. Well, he says that he has reviewed Fawn's book twelve times in Logan. Without giving too many of his conclusions, he told me that he always prefaced his reviews with the statement that here was absolute sincerity. People wonder why she wrote it. He is convinced that it was not for money and not for fame, but because she honestly and sincerely believed that this is a hoax and she had to get the idea out of her system before she could rest. He pays high tribute to her skill as a writer; he thinks her use of the English language is most remarkable. He feels that she will be an even better novelist, I mean, that she is a biographer. He thinks that, standing as she does on the opposite side of what you called The Great Divide in thinking, our people who accept God as a reality and believe that he does work through men cannot accept her first and major premise, hence cannot follow her logic. But he knows, as we all do, that she has material which will be a burr under the collar of the church for a long time to come.

And before I forget it, here is something else. He asked about you and your work. Then he said he knew a person with whom you should become acquainted if you have not already. He is one Earl Arrington or he was not sure but there was an initial first.[95] He thought perhaps it was J. Earl Arrington. He didn't know the address, except that it is New York City. But his point was that he had met this man and found him to have the most amazing collection of Mormonia. Hence, his eagerness to have you contact Mr. Arrington.

Another thing: While I was in Salt Lake City in April I talked with Marguerite over the phone, and she told me they had the Tracy Journal almost ready for the publisher.[96] Then she added in a most confidential tone that they were cutting all personal references to Brigham Young, nothing, you understand that would affect the story any, but then you know how it is, we just can't afford to offend our readers.[97] I told her that the John D. Lee he mentioned was really one John Dailey as per your letter, and she was much disturbed. When I got back I copied your comments on the matter and mailed them to her along with the most vigorous protest that I could compose against her cutting a single word from the ms. I tried to impress her with the fact that we are not so thin-skinned as all that; that the writer could hardly be expected to praise Brigham and that what he said about him is what he felt and that it should be left in; that as soon as you begin to tamper with an original you throw suspicion on all that you do, unless you state definitely that this is a precis or a digest, etc. etc. I doubt that the protest did any good, but I wanted it on record, anyway.

Now as to my own experience there—I did secure seven volumes of the Samuel Richards[98] records at Ogden, scattered books, and not the ones which Claire Noel[99] had borrowed and returned. They seem to be lost temporarily. The ones I got are dated 1846, 1849–50, 1856, 1866, 1867–8–9–71, 1877, 1887, and one small book of poems and songs. I also secured another Bigler record,[100] but one which had been copied and condensed from the small day-books. I borrowed a copy of the record of the 2nd Brigade 1st Division record of the Nauvoo Legion presided over by F.D. Richards[101] and beginning Aug. 6, 1857—for my MMM study a helpful document.

But so far as getting to see McKay, the trip was a total flop.[102] I told you before of my earlier attempts to get to him. Well, this time I thought I would use better strategy. I felt that Joseph Anderson,[103] the general secretary to the First Presidency was an ally, so I telephoned him long distance to be sure that Pres. McKay would be in the office.

Then I called the secretary to make an appointment. Over the phone she was very cordial. My name had evidently not registered enough to make her remember it after a year, but it was evident as soon as she saw me that I was a red flag.

She must know "precisely what it was that I wish to talk to Brother McKay about." I think that if it had been about the weather she would have shown me in without hesitation. But something really important he must not be troubled with. So again I was permitted to see Joseph Anderson. That is what has bothered me all along—not that I do not enjoy talking with Brother Anderson, but that I must NOT talk to David O—It would have saved time for us all and been better all around.

I was forced to stay over another day during which time Bro. Anderson would present my case for me to the brethren. When I came back the next day for the verdict, we sat on opposite sides of the table and he held in his hand a large brown envelope, so old that it was cracking and full of folded papers. Around it was an elastic band. He cleared his throat and began

"Well, Sister Brooks, I took the matter up with the Brethren last night, and one of them sat down with me and we went over all this material very carefully. I am . . ."

"Specifically, which one of the Brethren?"

"Brother Clark. We went over the material carefully and I am instructed to tell you that there is nothing here that you do not already have, nothing that will do you any good . . ."

"So the answer is no?"

"Well, it adds to that, yes."

Naturally I should like to have a chance to decide for myself whether or not the material would be of any value to me, and I think he honestly would like to have permitted me to see it.

"Tell me, Brother Anderson," I said, "Is the material in that package handwritten or is it type written?"

"It is typed, but it is signed and it is notarized."

"And in that package there is a telegram from the First Presidency authorizing David H. Morris to get these statements from the participants."[104]

He hesitated just a little, I thought, and then he said, "Yes, the telegram is here."

How I wanted the date of that telegram! I'd have given anything to have it. But he didn't remember and he didn't dare take the material from the envelope. He did say that there were only three affidavits, though—two by Nephi Johnson (one of which I have already) and one by Samuel Knight.[105] I doubted his word just a little on that for those who had handled the material said there were several. The other papers were affidavits, he said, regarding some of the wives of Joseph Smith (More material that Fawn should have had.)

Well, I told him that I should not trouble him or the Brethren again, but that I wish he would tell David O. McKay that some day I expected to actually talk directly to him.... Now I am almost glad that I couldn't. I think perhaps I shall be more free to say what I want to say than I would had they taken me in and wanted to cooperate. They would then have been in a position to ask to see my ms.... And I shall certainly make a point of the fact that for fifty years they have known the truth and that Joseph Fielding as late as 1945 still insists in the face of all the material which he has to the contrary, evidence unmistakable, that "it was the work of one man and one only."

So much for that. I have not been able to work as I have wanted for several reasons. My eyes are giving me some trouble; I have headaches which keep me awake at night. I am practicing typing blind and keeping them closed, with the thought that I can have final drafts copied for me. And I find that being a Grandmother is much more complicated than being a mother. Like an old mule who has just used to the fit of the saddle, I had adjusted my life with Will and the four younger ones. Now with Clair back and Ern and his wife just over the fence, and Walt's wife having her teeth out and sending me three extras, a boy of six and twin girls of four, every morning at 7:30 to stay all day until that time at night, and last day of school programs and costumes, and Primary Conference with all of them to take part in, and Mother's Day program which featured three of them—well, it is a perfect merry-go-round.

Now it's over. School, I mean, and I'll have to make further adjustments. I shall do it, though.

As for Q & C, I have my hands plenty full for the time being without that, so take your time about it. I know that your last weeks now will be pretty hectic ...

I'll watch for Virginia Sorenson's book[106] as soon as it is off the press. Didn't read Lillian McQuarrie's[107] yet, either, but have reviewed "Children of the Covenant" three times. I've been asked to do Fawn's but didn't feel that I could put enough time on it to do it justice. These book reviews are distracting things at best. I'll get at hers yet, I expect, but not until next fall.

This visit has run into lengths, hasn't it? And after it is gone, I'll think of a dozen other things I wanted to talk over. In the meantime, luck to you—

To *Charles Kelly*, August 2, 1946

St. George, Utah
August 2, 1946

Dear Mr. Kelly,

Just finished reading your story in the last Desert Magazine on Lee's Lost Gold Mine, and enjoyed it very much.[108] But where do you get the story that he was held captive by the Indians for two years? That was new to me. I'm not a particular student of John D. Lee, but I've kept my eyes and ears open for material about him, and it's the first time I ever heard that suggested.

Later I'll take some pains to follow him through these years, but I think you'll find he was hiding in the mountains near Harmony during the spring and summer of 1859. The Haight Journal tells how on April 29, 1859 a messenger came to warn them of the approach of Judge Cradlebaugh,[109] and of the hide-out of a whole group of those implicated in the MMM. They called their camp Balleguard and stayed there until June 3rd. On August 7th they were warned again, and this time were out until Sept.4. On Sunday Dec.14, 1859, Haight had a dinner for the men who had been in hiding, and their wives. He does not name the men, but I had assumed that John D. was probably one of them.

You no doubt have the notation from the Bleak Record book A[110] that on the 6th of June 1859 the County court refused to honor the accounts of John D. Lee for road work. The same book tells how on Dec. 22, 1861 the saints met in John D. Lee's family hall at Harmony and organized a branch of the church with John D. Lee as presiding elder.... and on Dec. 25 Lee gave a public dinner and social party at his family hall. In Feb. following, a part of the wall at fort Harmony caved in as a result of the rains and flood and winds, and John D. was reported not to have been undressed for several nights as he was battling with the elements trying to save their possessions. Later (March 5, 1864) "Elder John D. Lee, on suggestion that he do so, resigned his position as presiding elder of Harmony Branch ..."

Well, I haven't gone through it too carefully, but I believe he can be accounted for during all those two years. I'm sure the court records mention him several times—the records were taken from him that year (1859) and the court moved to Washington. At the March term 1860 John D. Lee was appointed Road Supervisor at Harmony.

John D. had a conference with Forney[111]—I don't have the date handy, but the Jl. History[112] of May 4, 1859 says, "C.E. Bolton reports that Forney was somewhat favorable impressed with J.D. Lee's statement of the massacre at the Mountain Meadows." On June 3, 1859 Jacob Hamblin made an affidavit to the effect that about the first of May previous the Marshall Rogers[113] had asked him to help take Lee, or to direct the Indians to go get Lee, and he had refused to do it, giving as his reason that it was contrary to his instructions from Dr. Forney, his superior. He knew where Lee was in hiding and how he was armed.

Wm Rogers report of his trip south published in the Valley Tan[114] for Feb. 29, 1860, tells how in April 1859 Forney called on John D. Lee at Harmony and talked with him concerning the property of the emigrants. "The day after this conversation with Lee, we started for Cedar City; Bishop Lee also set out with us" ... but he rode ahead horseback and they did not see him again.

Well, these are pretty hit-and-miss. Never having heard it suggested before that Lee was captured by the Indians and held during those years, I have never taken the trouble to follow him carefully—Perhaps some day I will, but not now.

My study of the MMM proceeds more slowly than I would wish. If you would like to review the ms before it goes to press, I'd be glad to have you do it. In view of your own future plans, you may not care to, and I will understand and respect this attitude if that is how you feel. I may have material which you would like to check; my interpretations will likely not be just like yours in all cases. But that is a writer's right, I presume. So be frank to say what you think ... Maybe I'm a little previous, for it is not ready yet, and the Appendix is growing at a rate which would make it seem a case of the tail wagging the dog. However, I'll likely cut some of it. I just thought that folks who would like to go back of my opinions and make their own on the basis of the evidence might like to, though I know most would rather have their opinions neatly packaged and labeled and handed out . . Or am I wrong on that?

Time to go back to work. Thanks for the visit.

Source: MS 100, Marriott Library Special Collections.

To *Fawn M. Brodie*, September 25, 1946

St. George, Utah
September 25, 1946

Mrs. Fawn M. Brodie
46 Hilltop Place
New Haven 15, Conn.

Dear Fawn,

A letter from Dale today tells of your visit in Washington D.C. and that you look "wonderful"—all of which I am glad to hear. He tells me also that the U finally got permission to microfilm the Mayer[115] record which Mrs. Grace Calderwood had. I am glad that is done by someone as it seems a safeguard to insure the permanence of the record. Under their arrangement for the exchange of records, it may be possible for the Huntington Library to get a copy also.

Dale says that with regard to the Peck Ms,[116] you consider having it reproduced before you present the original to some institution. I should be glad if you would allow Huntington to photostat it, as in that form it is so much more easily read.[117] Often the photostat is clearer than the original, and they sometimes lift the writing if it is small. I have not found it so easy to use the microfilm—perhaps because I have not had a good "lifter."

I'd be glad to have you send the ms. to me or direct to the library in care of

Leslie E. Bliss, Librarian
Henry E. Huntington Library
San Marino 15, California

When I was in Salt Lake City last I had a good visit with Vesta.[118] She says that the repercussion for having her name in your book had been pretty strong—at least fifty phone calls of protest, and some of them bitter.[119] As for me, not one person has ever said a word. I think they consider me lost already. At any rate, I'll not be surprised to be cut off right below the ears when this MMM thing is finished.

I was happy to hear of the arrival of the new son—again via Dale. I specialize in boys, as you know. Though I have given birth to only four, I've raised, in part at least, eight—not to mention two brothers whom I engineered through high school and college. So I think I'm something of an authority on boys. I like em!

If you consider sending the Peck Ms., send it by first class mail, registered, and we will refund the postage—I will if you send it here, and pass the bill on to the library, or they will from there. The only reason I'd like it to come to me is that I'd have the fun of browsing through it a bit myself without taking time to go to California to do it.

I've felt that Utah records should be kept in Utah, but it is a fact that no institution that I know has the facilities for keeping them properly that Huntington has. And they're accessible to students—that is, the photostats are. I think they would be at the U, and at present the policy at the Y is liberal, but we know nothing of when some one will come into authority who will squelch it all there. The State Historical Society is a pretty good bet, too, but with all the Utah Institutions, there is the danger always of the pertinent material just not being found when it is wanted. Once the photostat is made and the negatives kept on file, the original is safe—I mean the content of the record is permanent.

I suppose that you already have a full typescript. Would you consider letting the Y copy it for their files after it is photographed at Huntington? The procedure I have followed is this: I send the original to Huntington for photostating, which takes about three weeks; then they forward it to The B.Y.U. Library in care of Prof. N.I. Butt,[120] who is in charge of the copying. Here it is typed, indexed as to contents, and a name list prepared of all persons mentioned in the text, and bound. The original together with a bound volume is then given to me to be returned to the owner. This last service takes from one to several months, depending upon the length of the manuscript.

Well, think it over, and if you care to, send it along.

Good luck to you, and continued success.

Sincerely,

Source: MS 360, Marriott Library Special Collections.

To *Hugh Nibley*,[121] November 7, 1946

St. George, Utah
Nov. 7, 1946

Mr. Hugh Nibley
B.Y.U., Provo, Utah

Dear Mr. Nibley,

I have just finished reading your No, Ma'am, That's Not History, and while I think that a part of your discussion is good, I should like to ask some questions on other statements.

I should probably make clear the fact that I think I am a good member of the church. I want to be, I am not defending Mrs. Brodie's book; in fact, I think we have been entirely too hysterical about it and have given it an importance greater than it deserves. She has approached a study of the prophet from a different angle than I would or than you would, but what of it? She is entitled to her opinions. Why should we be so disturbed about them? We read of this man from equally authentic original sources and arrive at entirely different opinions, sometimes from the same documents.

I think her book is good for the church and good for us all, if only to stimulate further study of this man who was the founder of our faith. Probably we have built up a set of traditions about him that tend to deify him and have rather forgotten some of his fine human qualities. From the very beginning her approach is not ours, because behind her interpretations is the conviction that there is not a God. Assuming that, how could any man have a revelation? For those of us to whom God is a reality, there is no common ground in all her study. We cannot accept her major premise, hence cannot follow her logic.

As for your writing—Has there really never been a Mormon scholar? To me that would be a reflection on our church, if during all our existence we have never had a scholar. I had thought of the

Pratt brothers, of B.H. Roberts,[122] and others as quite fine students, at least.

"There has never been a council or synod to alter or <u>even discuss</u> any matter of doctrine." I wonder. Seems to me that our doctrine might well be discussed with profit, and I thought that the Quorum of Twelve did not shun it.

"The Saints have always had more than their share of crack-pots," is an admission I would hesitate to make, even if it were true. We have had plenty, perhaps, but so has every other sect, and it seems a reflection either on our materials or our methods if we have attracted too large a proportion of crack-pots.

"The gospel as the Mormons know it sprang full grown from the words of Joseph Smith. It has never been worked over or touched up in any way, and is free of revisions and alterations," What a delight that should be to the Fundamentalists! If it is true, my study of Church History has been faulty indeed. I have had some pride in feeling that there had been changes and alterations. How do you ACCOUNT for such changes as the ones that have taken place with regard to: 1—The law of consecration? Have you seen many of the old deeds turning over all of the property to the church? I have. I'd like to show you some, and some of the discussions which make it clear that this principle was a burning one for a time.

2—Polygamy . . . Has there not only been a change, but a complete reversal here? I know a number of the adherents who live in this vicinity, and they seem to think so.

3—The United Order.[123] Perhaps that was only postponed as impractical.

Perhaps it is, in part, a change of emphasis. The location of the Ten Tribes and the time and manner of their return, does not concern my children with the same intensity that it did my grandfather. The imminent return to Jackson County to build up Zion is another point that is not given the emphasis that it was formerly—in fact, Anthony W. Ivins[124] actually preached that we might not return as a group.
Or wasn't he a Mormon scholar? He tried to explain the resemblance between the temple ceremonies and the rites of Free Masonry . . .

I may be wrong. I often am. But it seems to me that in our zeal to answer Mrs. Brodie, we make some statements almost as far fetched as hers.

I think Joseph Smith stands as untouched by Mrs. Brodie's attack as his monument does by the pecking of sparrows. I think I see in our church evidence of change—even since President Smith has come into the head of it—that are wholesome and healthy and a good reason for alert and progressive People to have faith in it. I can think of nothing more terrible than one that was immune to revisions or alterations, one that could not claim continuous revelation.

I hope that I have not misinterpreted you. I purchased your book because of a discussion I heard of it by a fine group who were much stronger in its condemnation than I have been.

Sincerely,

To *Ettie Lee*,[125] November 28, 1946

St. George, Utah
Nov. 28, 1946

Miss Ettie Lee
661 Shatto Place
Los Angeles 5, Calif.

Dear Miss Lee,

I was very happy to get your letter today.

It is true that I am making a study of the Mountain Meadows Massacre for the Huntington Library, and since no study of that tragic event can be made without some reference to John D. Lee, I have spent considerable time in research about him. If you have any material about him, I am only too eager to have access to it, especially any documentary evidence.

I have long ago decided that John D. Lee has been greatly wronged, and that his families have borne an undue burden. His letters and records, of which I have seen many, are evidence that he was a man of superior intelligence and of unquestioning loyalty to the church. That he took part in that unfortunate affair he never denied; that he was only one, and that he acted in a subordinate position and under orders seems quite evident when one goes into the matter.

My own grandfather was on the ground or in the vicinity at the time, as were many other good men, so that whatever is true of any of the participants is true in a measure of him. It seems to me entirely impossible to single out any single man and say that he was the ONE responsible, for so many things entered into the creating of the war hysteria which stirred the entire southern settlements,

I shall be very glad to hear from you again. If you can trust me enough to let me see your material, I shall be glad. If you could send it here, I will guarantee to pay insured postage both ways and return it to you intact. If you feel that risk too great, I shall try to come there and meet you in person, though it is hard for me to leave my family.

Hoping to hear from you soon, I am

Very sincerely,

Chapter 3

1947–1950

Publishing *Mountain Meadows Massacre*

Brooks' major effort in the years of 1947–1950 was the writing and eventual publication of her Mountain Meadows Massacre book. She wrote several drafts of the manuscript including addressing at least two sets of comments from Morgan. Again, as with the *Quicksand and Cactus* manuscript, she was faced with finding a publisher. The Huntington Library was the expected choice as they, through the Rockefeller Foundation grant, had funded the writing of the book with the assumption they would publish it. After a frustrating experience submitting drafts to Robert Cleland at the Huntington Library and waiting for some response and review, the library finally released any claim to the manuscript and recommended she find a publisher.

At this point Morgan stepped in and connected Brooks with Wallace Stegner, novelist and creative writing teacher at Stanford University, who facilitated Stanford University Press's acceptance of her work. This contact with Stegner initiated another valuable relationship, and they corresponded periodically over the years.

Donald Bean, director of the press, ultimately accepted her study in March 1949 with the stipulation that Brooks guarantee the purchase of a thousand copies. Ettie Lee had agreed to buy these copies. Several frantic letters between Brooks and Bean and Brooks and Lee finally resolved Lee's $3,000 payment schedule for the thousand copies, thereby allowing publication to proceed. As the manuscript was being prepared for publication, Brooks, in a letter to the assistant editor at Stanford University Press, Pamela Faust, insisted that the pages comparing the Mormons of

1857 to American World War II soldiers not be cut as Faust insisted. She also responded to Faust's letter received just under the wire in October 1950 saying that Brooks was responsible for the index, an index that she thought the press was completing. After all these efforts, in December 1950 she had the pleasure to write Bean thanking him for a job well done after reviewing the finished book.

Brooks considered mob psychology resulting in good people doing bad things as a critical cause of the massacre. In an April 1947 letter to Morgan, she described a minor example of mob dynamics in her backyard in St. George permitting her to better understand the Mountain Meadows Massacre. During a strike and picketing by the local telephone operators, some of the businessmen got upset and angry, obtained the city fire engine, and started spraying high-pressure water at the young women, first at their feet and then at their faces. Once they realized what they had done, all the participants quickly disappeared with no one taking responsibility.

As the final terms of publication were being debated, Donald Bean, in a letter dated July 8, 1949, questioned how the book would affect her relationship among the Mormons. In response, Brooks recited how she became involved with the subject of the massacre by repeating the often-told story of her sitting at the deathbed of Nephi Johnson, a participant in the massacre, as her first introduction to the terrible event. She summarized her diary collection and copying activities of the 1930s and her meeting with LDS Church president George Albert Smith and her failed attempts at meeting David O. McKay. In conclusion, she clearly declared, "I do not want to be excommunicated from my church for many reasons, but if that is the price that I must pay for intellectual honesty, I shall pay it—I hope without bitterness."[1] But she felt that most would consider it was time for the incident to be fully investigated.

One of her major crusades throughout her career was to insist that pioneer diaries and other documents be rendered unaltered regardless of how the early Mormons were portrayed. She strongly asserted this position in a paper she read before the Arts and Letters section of the Utah Academy at the University of Utah in early May 1947. In this paper, she lambasted the editorial procedures of the Daughters of Utah Pioneers under the direction of Kate Carter, whose policy encouraged the removal from edited diaries of anything considered provocative. Carter, in response to Brooks's outspokenness, urged her members not to turn over pioneer diaries to out-of-state institutions, an affront to Brooks who was working for the Huntington Library. In an attempt to obtain more cooperation in their collecting activities, Brooks wrote Carter in May 1947, after failing to meet with her, suggesting that the Daughters of Utah Pioneers and the Huntington Library trade photostats of materials held by each institution.

On January 18, 1949, Brooks wrote a three-page letter to Stanton Schmutz, a missionary she had taught in Sunday School, addressing his Christmas card request for information on John D. Lee. She reviewed Lee's achievements and failings, especially his role in the Mountain Meadows Massacre, stressing he was taking orders from others and was not the only one to blame. She emphasized that it was the human side that made mistakes, not the divine, and to "accept truth wherever we find it."[2]

She forwarded a copy of the letter the next day to LDS Church apostle Harold B. Lee seeking approval. Lee quickly replied saying that he was not a John D. Lee descendent and that her conclusions of what happened at Mountain Meadows were "obtained from hearsay and rumor rather than from any historical source."[3] He also questioned her inference that John D. Lee was given all the blame to "close the incident once and for all" and told her that it would be best to avoid any unnecessary discussion of the subject.

~

To *Dale Morgan*, April 25, 1947

Friday morning, April 25

Dear Dale,

Tony is singing, so I've decided that if Tony can sing, I can finally write to you. You see, I've had a bad time with Tony for the last little while. He has always been frail, and perhaps during the week of our Centennial Celebration, April 9–15, I neglected him a little. The Larsens[4] were staying here and I had some responsibilities with regard to the programs. Maybe he just got a germ that was particularly malignant. Anyway, just two weeks ago today he took down with a head infection, high fever, and pain in his ears. The doctor prescribed sulfa, but after two tablets he broke out in a solid scarlet rash. Fearing that it might be a reaction to the medicine, we stopped that, but when after four more days of fever and earache, the rash cleared away, we started again. This time I gave, under the doctor's orders, five more tablets. Well, it seemed to help the infection, though now his temperature was below normal. Then, just a week ago, he woke up with one side of his face paralyzed!

For me that was a blow in the solar plexus. In all my experience, nothing has simply got me worse. His funny little face, so peaked and pale anyway, now dead on one side. When he would laugh or cry it was positively sickening. I insisted all the time that it must be temporary. It HAD to be. But I was beset by such heavy fears. He had been almost stone deaf from the beginning, now the one ear was positively out. I kept my controls before him and before the other children, but my nights were sleepless and miserable. I used hot packs and massage, and poured him full of orange juice and vitamins, and read him stories and books and entertained him without making him conscious of how he looked. Yesterday I knew definitely that he is better. This morning he can smile a little with both sides of his face, and his eye will blink more instead of that fixed, wide-open stare. And now he is singing a full review of all the songs he has learned in school this winter, and my own load is lifted so that I can turn my thoughts to things that have had to be suspended for a while.

First, of course, is "The Great Salt Lake."[5] There is no way to thank you for it, or for the generous note in it. I had got well into it before things closed in on me too much, and between times it has been a saving diversion. It's superb how you have managed to give the impression of all your great research and your rich background without making the book heavy with it. And how I like your gentle irony, your little thrusts that make the reader pause to see if they might be sincerity or sarcasm. Vesta Crawford wrote that she enjoyed it all very much, but hardly agreed with parts of the last chapter.[6] Well, I agree with them. I like them. I think they might be put even more strongly, if that happened to be the chief purpose of the writer. But for a book primarily about the Lake, you have been more than skillful with the people on its shores—and generous.

When I had the Laub[7] journal a while ago, I read his account of the grave robber, and the furor that the discovery caused. Now I can hardly wait to get my hands on the volume again to follow up and find if he gave details of the disposal of the man. It is now being copied at the Y.

I've noticed a review or two of it (your book, of course.) In case you don't have them, I'll slip them in. As I come back to this after a day full of other things, I see evidence of haste in it and a little confusion, maybe. Tony has had a good day and is now abed and asleep; Willa has gone forth to the show all thrilled with her first date; Will and the two other boys are deep in a game of checkers on the floor. Oh, yes, and Bob set out for Las Vegas for a plane ride back to Arlington. He has been here for the past ten days on a leave before going over-seas to Europe. What I am trying to say is that unless there is an unexpected visitor, I'll have a chance to visit.

One thing I have wanted to ask about in regard to the Parley P. Pratt death[8] and the MMM. Both Roberts[9] and Neff[10] insist that word of the death could not have reached the southern towns, so that revenge of him could not have figured in the massacre. Methinks they protest too much—anyway, I am suspicious. I noticed where John Stillman Woodbury[11] heard the news in some detail on July 2 way out in Carson Valley. I saw where Andrew Sprowl, near Iowa City, recorded that Bros Snow and Little had visited their company and among other things "Bro. Snow tells me P.P. Pratt is in trouble and that McLean has got him prisoner also woman and children. God Deliver him if this is true."[12] Snow and Little arrived in Salt Lake City on August 7 but since they had stayed to see all the emigration companies on the road, my guess is that word had reached Salt Lake City in June. It's something to probe a little further.

The recent telephone difficulties here have made me understand the MMM better. I don't know that you heard of the incident, though it was broadcast on the radio. When the local girls joined the strike, business men were much upset. They called a meeting and then met with the girls, trying to persuade them to go back to work. Some became a little warm and said they had better go back—"or else." When service was still suspended and girls were out picketing the next morning, a group of men met—among them the two McGregor doctors, one lawyer, merchants and service station men—and decided to force the girls to leave the sidewalk. Members of the volunteer fire department were in the crowd, and some city officers. Anyway, while they were planning it, they were excited and almost hilarious, a little angry too of course. But everybody was in it and everybody was encouraging everybody else. They got the city fire engine and drove down. When they ordered the girls to go, they were met with a silent refusal. One man got the hose, another turned the water on full force, and the first fellow directed it at the walk and the girls' feet. When they still would not go, another man, a married man with daughters and granddaughters of his own, seized the hose and gave it to them full in the face. When the girls stood and took their drenching, some of the men in the crowd reacted against the whole thing, and when they learned that one was a GI's wife nearly five months pregnant, they all left the scene hurriedly. When there was danger that the union would sue them, there was no one who wanted to assume any responsibility whatever. No one gave them the keys to the building, no firemen were involved, the city officials knew nothing about it. It happened that the girls who were picketing were from out of town, or new comers, one from Enterprise, one from LaVerkin, and one from Hurricane,[13] so they could not call the men by name, though they would know them when they saw them. Now, though they did not approve of the doing, witnesses will not testify in court. On a small and unimportant scale, it's a dead-ringer for the thing that went on at the Meadows.

My MMM ms, has gone to Huntington for a preliminary reading there. I may go down early in May and talk it through with them and check again on some quotes from their material. While there are still some things to be done to it, I hope that the basic work is done.

Tell Darel when you see him that I'll get a note to him also before long. In more than two weeks I have hardly looked toward the typewriter, but if Tony keeps improving—as he must—I'll get things organized and ready to take a shift at work.

I felt good about our Centennial activities.[14] The pageant was so much better than I had hoped for, the music score simply super, the 300-odd characters all local people. Anyway, it was honest, an outgrowth of the culture of this section, and our tribute to the founders of the Cotton Mission. And I'm glad it is done.

Better stop for now. By morning I'll think of other things I should have told you.

To *Ettie Lee*, November 28, 1947

St. George, Utah
Nov. 28, 1947

My dear Miss Lee,

Such a surprise! Such a thrill! I think I have never felt more excited and elated about a gift since the time—long, long ago—when my father unexpectedly gave me my first 25¢ piece. Though I was ten years old, I had never had more than a dime of my own to spend before. Father ran the mail across the 40-mile desert to the rail-road, leaving home on alternate days at about four o'clock in the morning. Once at 2 a.m. he roused me to say that one of the ponies was lame and I must go to the field after another to make the run. It was pitch dark and the field was two miles away, and I would have to walk. It was one of the hardest assignments of my life, but I conquered my fear, walked to the field, caught the horse, and met father out on the road on the bare hills. After he had changed horses and put me on the lame animal, he slipped into my hand this shining piece of silver. Croesus[15] never felt as rich, I know. The east was getting red with the coming morning as I rode the limping horse toward it in my hand this precious quarter and in my heart a song. I spent that money a hundred different ways as I rode along. I do not know now what I got with it; I remember only the joy I had in contemplating the things which I might get.

Forgive these silly musings. I'm only trying to say that I was surprised and thrilled and humbled to think you would even remember me, and opened your letter with something of the same feeling that came to me that morning long ago. I haven't decided yet whether to be perfectly selfish and get something for myself that I could not afford otherwise, or whether to be more sensible and make it cover a gift for each of the young children. Whatever it is to be, accept my thanks, my most sincere gratitude.

By a coincidence, Brother Palmer came to my home on the very day your letter arrived. He had already invited me to come to Cedar City and give a report of my research on the Mountain Meadow Massacre two weeks ago. Did I tell you? They invited in about 65 people, members of the college faculty and prominent towns-folk, and gave me an hour, after which they asked questions and had an open discussion. They were very liberal in their attitude, and are going to welcome my contribution.

Brother Palmer told me the other day that at the Church Historian's Office in Salt Lake City there are 26 volumes of the diaries of John D. Lee: He says that he has seen and read them all.

This greatly interests me because now I think we should have access to them before any biography of the man is done. In fact, I think it is hard for anyone to write as eloquently for John D. Lee as he writes for himself. But how to get at them? I think that if we move carefully, it can be done. First, is there a descendant in some of the Arizona wards or stakes in a prominent position, who might approach President George A. Smith with a request to see and read these records? I think that is the first move. Once a member of the family has actually handled the records and gone through them and knows exactly how many and which ones are there, we can begin negotiations for having them copied, or preferably photographed. For the family of Jesse N. Smith,[16] the Church Historian's Office gave a typed copy of his record in exchange for the original; for the descendants of George A. Smith I know they did the same. Of these, however, a photostat would be much better, and Henry B. Huntington would do it free of charge.

If other attempts did not succeed, the family as a group or organization, once they are properly organized, could demand the books, I think, since they were private records and should be owned by the family organization. Rather than risk any legal tangle, I think the church would give them up, or give permission to have them reproduced. Anyway, it is something to think about and work on.

Brother LeRoi C. Snow[17] wrote me yesterday urging me to come in to his office at once—he wants me to do the biography of Eliza R. Snow. I have made him no commitments, however. I am just saying that once I go in, I shall find if there is any chance for me to see the books myself. Wouldn't I like to!

Thank you again and sincere good wishes for a happy Christmas season,

To *Dale Morgan*, January 6, 1948

St. George, Utah
Jan. 6, 1948 Tuesday afternoon

Dear Dale,

I've heard it said "when angry, count a hundred," and I've always tried to live by the adage "when disturbed, do not write." Fact is, I'm a little disturbed about this MMM business, and since I must not talk about it, I'll just have to blew off steam to you. So skip this page, if you want to.

I think maybe I told you that the people at the Library seemed in no hurry to have the project completed.[18] Mr. Bliss suggested a number of times that I "take my time." Without discussing the matter, I assumed that they felt it would be the tact not to have it appear during the Centennial Celebration. I, myself, felt that we might be wise to wait until the party was over and we all began to deflate just a little. Then I knew they wanted (The Library) photostats of newspapers and magazines from the Church—in short, the Church is a big organization and they don't want to incur its displeasure. I could be wrong on all this, of course; I'm just saying how it seemed to me.

Well, I sent the ms in—Oh, how long ago—and they kept it endlessly. When I was down near the end of June, I brought it back with me. In a conversation with Dr. Cleland I suggested that I had understood that they meant to handle it, either as an addition to their file or to be printed by them, but he felt that it could be done commercially to my advantage. He was very fine about it all. Finally he said, "We will assume full responsibility of publication. If it seems best to have a commercial house do it, we will do that; or if it is better to have a University Press handle it, we may do that. Or we can publish it ourselves." He had already pointed out that where they might sell 100 copies a University press would sell 500 and a commercial house several thousand.

So we left it at that—I thought. I took the ms. back, after working at it during the summer, in October, but Dr. Cleland was away and Mr. Bliss urged me to bring it home with me until later. I rewrote several chapters and added some new material, and sent it in again in early December.

Now today I get a note written Jan. 2, to say that he has had no time to look at it, but should like to hold it until he returns from the East and ends with the statement that "I hope I made clear to you that the Library has no claim of any kind upon the manuscript, nor any authority to tell you by whom it is to be published. Whatever royalties it may bring also belong to you. I shall of course be glad to serve in an advisory capacity but beyond that the Library has neither responsibility nor authority."

So that's that. Will says it is O.K., but I feel a little like I'd been slapped, and can't tell why. He admits that he has not looked at the ms.

I have felt that someone will publish it, but I dread to start the merry-go-round of finding who. Mr. Selby asked about it in November, and seemed eager to see it, but that means nothing. I think libraries or schools who teach western history might be interested; within this state and in Arizona some copies would be sold. But it will not be of wide general interest, I'm sure.

When you finally get to Huntington, do you think you can take time to look at it? I don't want to lean too heavily on you, but I would appreciate your suggestions. I might even run down for a day or two while you are there.

I'm a little ashamed to trouble you with all this in the midst of your busy life. The way you are able to work is a constant source of wonder to me. About the Ginn ms.[19]—I quoted only very briefly from it in my chapter which dealt with that trip, but I planned to include an extract in the Appendix. Which brings up another worry: what about quoting the Johnson affidavit, the Higbee account, the Jacob Hamblin journal,[20] and other originals, copies of which have come into my possession from one or another. Do I again run into danger of legal complications? Must I get permission from families, members of which do not even know of the existence of this material, before I dare to use it? With some of these polygamist groups, that would be a colossal undertaking.

Thanks for the Eliza R. Snow letter. She runs on at some length doesn't she. I had my doubts about doing anything about her, but a note from LeRoi C. the other day made up my mind. "I am sure my Aunt Eliza is anxious for us to get to work on a fine biography of her life, and thousands of people are as anxious to have it in their homes for reading." Well, I can't write to please dead Aunt Eliza nor her living nephew, and I had as well save time and trouble for us all.

I shall look forward to seeing you sometime this spring, and hope that you can accept the hospitality of our little place. You'll find us primitive, but perhaps you can put up with it for a while. We'd like to take you to Mountain Meadows and to other points of interest, and to help you get access to some books here.

Oh, Oh—the boys just came with a swarm of neighbor [missing]

To *Kate Carter*,[21] May 20, 1948

St. George, Utah
May 20, 1948

Mrs. Kate Carter
D.U.P. Captain
State Capitol Building
Salt Lake City, Utah

Dear Mrs. Carter,

I had hoped to see you when I was in your city last Monday, but found that you were busy all day. When I talked to Mrs. Leah Cheever a little later, she said she would take the three volumes of her grandfather's record[22] and let you look at them. Since you and I have similar interests, I had hoped to get acquainted with you personally.

For three years I have worked with the Henry E. Huntington Library at San Marino, California, under a grant from the Rockefeller Foundation which was given for the collecting of the history of the south west. This included only Utah, Arizona, New Mexico, Colorado, Nevada, and the southern half of California. My business has been to find any authentic history, either in printed books or papers, or in handwritten diaries and records of the early days.

When I first started, I made it plain that I would not buy for them any diaries of our pioneers. I would borrow the originals and return them to the owners after they were photographed. The B.Y.U. have made copies of many of these, when the owner wished it done, and have given a free typed copy, indexed and bound, back to the owner along with his original. When the owner did not wish this service, his original was returned direct to him.

I have worked in this way because it seemed the fairest way to work. The University of Utah—or Mr. Hector Lee,[23] rather—tried to get me to bring originals to him; the B.Y.U also hoped to collect originals, and the Utah State Historical Society. The Church Historians Office has instructed us that they should be brought there. So rather than affiliate myself with any of these, I took the book back to the owner and suggested that sooner or later they put it in a public depository for safe keeping, whichever they cared to. Almost without exception they preferred to keep it themselves.

When I first began, the Huntington Mormon collection consisted of a few items, almost every one anti-Mormon. I told Mr. Bliss that they could never really study Mormon history until they read what the people themselves wrote, and feel the spirit of devotion and sincerity of their diaries. He said that was exactly what they wanted. Now I am sure that every member of the church wishing to do research can be proud of the Mormon collection in the Huntington Library. I have sent in the neighborhood of 150 original, handwritten diaries and biographies, every one of which has been photostated—some of the Mormon Battalion march, many of the trips across the plains, more of the stories of the settlement of parts of the west.

I have been pleased to learn that the prize-winning Centennial Play[24] was written upon the basis of material which I had collected, as was also the novel "Sweet Love Remembered."[25] Both authors did their research largely at Huntington Library. Mabel Harmer's "Story of the Mormon Pioneers"[26] came also from the first collection I made under the W.P.A.[27] in southern Utah. That, as I see it, is the reason for this work—to preserve these precious diaries in the first place and to make them available to reputable scholars in the second. It makes me just heartsick to see how many handwritten originals have been lost or disappeared between 1936 when I left the HRS,[28] and 1945 when I began again to collect.

As I see it, the state of Utah is much richer for the work I have done. They have all their records back in the state, in addition to the fact that our people in California have access to many of them, and the B.Y.U. have built a fine library of typed copies, which students there may have access to.

The thing that has happened in the case of Mrs. Cheever's family has been repeated many times. One volume of this diary came from St. Anthony, Idaho, one from Reno, Nevada, and one from Mrs. Cheever. But for this project, they might never have been brought together in one complete life. Now they will be available to descendants for generations to come, all in a unit. And we never know which one of the great-grand-children will be the one to take an interest in these things.

Now as to what I had hoped we could work out: I should like to give you these three Photostats for your permanent files in exchange for permission to Photostat three of the originals which you have already used in your publications. These would be out of your files about three weeks, and would be returned direct to you. For every original which you will allow the Huntington to photograph, you may have a photostatic copy of another original which you do not have. In this way you can also build up your own collection at the same time that you keep all you have.

You will see by looking through the Laub journals that they are very good, and could be the basis of fine articles for you or for lesson outlines. There are others equally good—one of 23 volumes has been done; one of 12, and a number of two, three, or four volumes, besides some single volumes.

Well, I did not mean to write at such length. I have been much interested in your work, and have admired very much the things which you have been able to accomplish. I think this whole business should not be a matter of competition, but of cooperation. Whatever any of us is able to find and preserve from destruction is for the good of us all, and of those who will follow after us.

The story of the Mormon conquest of the desert is an epic which will grow in importance with the years, and the spirit in which they worked cannot but impress every fair-minded student.

I should like to talk to you in person if you have time when I am up. If you do not care to discuss with me, I can pick up the Photostats from Mrs. Cheever or from the office.

Sincere good wishes,

To *Wallace Stegner*,[29] September 24, 1948

St. George, Utah
Sept. 24, 1948

Dear Wallace Stegner,

Thank you for your letter of September 16. I shall be glad to send this Mountain Meadows Massacre study to you—could have mailed it at once except that Dale brought several new items which he thought should go into the bibliography, and which will necessitate re-typing a number of pages.

He was here for a few days on some road mapping business. Yesterday we went out to the Mountain Meadows to see the "large and handsome monument" of which Mr. Palmer speaks with such pride, but found ourselves shut out of the field. Leaving the car, we hiked for more than an hour, through something less than a thousand miles of sage, and could not find it. Today Mr. Brooks is going back with us. Tomorrow we examine the Virgin Narrows and cover the road south to the Nevada line; Sunday we explore on the Arizona Strip with a look in at Jonreed and Verda.

By Tuesday at the latest, this ms. should be on its way to you, and I hope that it can arrive before you leave for the east.

Sincerely,

To *Ettie Lee*, November 12, 1948

St. George, Utah
November 12, 1948

My dear Miss Lee,

I arrived home from Salt Lake City at five o'clock this morning after a full night on the bus (the heating system went out and we nearly froze—sat in the cold more than an hour while they fixed it.) but I am so pleased with what happened that I must tell you.

At Provo I called Mrs. Henrie[30] and she went over with me. About a year ago Brother Myers, who is in the genealogical library had showed her the record book of the first quorum of Seventies, of which her grandfather was secretary. We went first to see that, followed it through two offices, the archives in the basement, and then over to the Seventies headquarters. There we found it, a very large, heavy ledger bound in red leather. It had not only the minutes of the Seventies' meetings, but records of all the work done in the Nauvoo temple, general church history items, etc., and was beautifully done.[31]

After an hour or so with it, we went up to the Historian's Office, and asked for permission to use the diaries of John D. Lee. The young man at the desk was very new at the business, and the name meant no more to him than if we had asked for John Doe. He asked which diary we wanted, and we said, the first.[32]

I tried hard to conceal my excitement, signed the card in her name, and hurried to the table near the large window in the other room. The library number of the book was 14A. On the fly leaf was written, "John D. Lee's Journal bought in St. Louis, May 29, 1844. No. 4." (So there must be three earlier ones than this.) Daily entries begin on Tuesday, May 28, 1844, as he is boarding a ship on the Mississippi River to go on a mission for the church. It is written in a fine, small hand, decorated in some places with geometric drawings, has several embellished acrostics, and stops to go back and list his sealings and adoptions in the temple—Nancy Bean, Feb. 5, 1844, Louisa Free, April 19; Caroline Williams, Abigal Woolsey and Rachel her daughter[33]—and so on. He told of Rigdon's[34] bid for the presidency. How I should like to have copied every word! There was a blank space, after which the last 1/3 of the book was an account, day by day, of his mission to get the Battalion money for Pres. Young.

The last date in this book was Nov. 18,1846.

The fly leaf of the second book was arranged something like this, only of course, in handwriting:

JOHN D. LEE RECORD
A
BOOK
Containing an Inventory of
All the Camps of the Saints!
Also the circumstances connected with the
Exodus from Nauvoo
The City of Joseph
West through the Wilderness in search of
Home and Place of Rest
by
John D. Lee Young. 1846

I haven't it spaced exactly right, and the hand writing makes it look different, but that is the general idea. It held lists of the men composing the various companies, minutes of meetings where plans were made as to outfits and loads. I noticed, for example, that on Feb. 1st, A.D. 1846, Brigham Young ordered the captains to take a complete inventory of all persons and property in each company, and especially to determine how much cloth was in camp that was suitable for wagon covers. Then they were to collect money from their people to give to J.D. Lee to take to Missouri to purchase this material, since he could buy in bulk to advantage, and could make a better deal for the whole camp.

This book was 14B.

The third volume, 13C, was the Journal of the Iron Mission 1850–2. This is a lovely thing, especially, in the beginning. (With so short a time you can guess that I could not read it all.) He tells how President Young called at his home and asked him to go south with George A. Smith—how he tried to protest, saying that he would rather donate $2000. and be permitted to stay, but Brother Brigham would not be put off. He was building a new home, and left it without a roof; B.Y. took his city lot to sell for $600. to pay one debt for material, he fitted out two wagons with four yoke of oxen each, and one carriage, listed his load of flour, bacon, beans, kraut, pickles, etc. etc.—took Mary & Lovinia,[35] his wives, with Hyrum Wooley[36] as teamster. I loved this: "Let the writer here remark the tender regard, the kind, liberal, & affectionate feelings manifested on the part of Mrs Lee towards her husband with reference to this mission." He left her and at least two other wives behind, and spoke of what a test of faith this call was to him, just getting established well after so many years of camping. How I wish I could have taken it all down, for I have seen nothing finer.

None of these were large books, and they were not in a set. We asked for others, telling him that there should be 26 volumes, but he insisted that only these three were upstairs. Of course I knew that many of the most precious records have been transferred to the new vaults in the basement.

While we were examining the last two volumes, we heard Brother Lund[37] begin to scold him loudly and angrily, asking if he did not know that NO ONE should see these except after permission from Bro. Joseph Fielding. I sat quietly and read as fast as I could, determined to get all that I could before I was literally kicked out, while Mrs. Henrie went in to explain that she had meant to break no rules, she thought she had a right to see the records of her grandfather. "How do I know that you are his grand-daughter?" Brother Lund demanded, and she quietly unrolled her long sheet of genealogical research. He finally quieted down, and we stayed until quitting time.

The next day was Armistice, and the offices were closed, so she went back to Provo and I went about other business. But I was happy to know of the existence of these, and to examine them. I could see nothing in them to prevent the church proudly showing them, even printing them, in fact. And I believe that family members may be given permission to see them later, but feel sure that they may not be taken from the building.

Before I forget it—I am much impressed by the work that is being done by Mrs. Henrie. She has certainly put in years of time and study in an effort to complete the genealogy, both in attempting to link the family with the Lees of Virginia, and in collecting the full posterity of John D. Lee. She is in very moderate circumstances, and says that, besides $20. contributed by Wilford Lee of St. George, she has had little or no help. I am sure she is a relative of whom you can be proud when you meet her.

Well, I didn't expect to write at such length. I was so pleased and happy to have made this little spearhead into the archives that I had to tell you.

Sincerely and affectionately,

To *Stanton Schmutz*,[38] January 18, 1949

St. George, Utah
Jan. 18, 1949

Dear Stanton,

Ever since Christmas I have promised that I would take time out and write to you, but crowds and colds and things have interfered. Then Sunday when I saw Joyce at conference (over a week ago) I resolved again that I would go home and write.

I didn't get to speak to Joyce.[39] She sat in the body of the hall, on a chair in the aisle, and I was in the north gallery. She looked so like a pale Madonna to me that I could hardly keep my eyes off her—her skin—so clear that it was almost transparent and her hair so lovely in the light of the sun from the south window. She held her head high, and wore such a serene, quietly happy expression. As I said, I tried to get down in time to talk to her, but I was on the wrong side of the house for one thing, and those in the aisles were asked to go out first, and I was way up the side with so many people before me (we had a jammed-in conference and many had to be turned away.) It was snowing outside, too, so that folks didn't stand around and visit as they usually do in Dixie. I just thought to myself, "If Stanton could see her now, he'd know better than he ever has before what a brick she is, and what a fundamentally wholesome and lovely personality."

I appreciated your Christmas card so much, and especially the note in it. We have let this business of Christmas cards become so commercialized that unless there is a personal note, they don't mean a great deal. And yours was so full of the spirit of your work that I was thrilled with it.

You asked about John D. Lee. I have spent four or five years in research about southern Utah, and Lee and Hamblin in particular. This is how I see John D. Lee: He was one of the most devoted members of the church. He was a personal guard and friend of the Prophet Joseph Smith, and in his dying hour he bore testimony to the divinity of the mission of Joseph Smith. He was also very close to Brigham Young. In the Nauvoo Temple he was adopted to President Young as a son, in the ceremonies which have since been discarded by the church. I have the date and full information on that. He always wrote to Brigham Young and signed himself "your son and brother."

I have read the minutes of the meetings of the first counsel of the Seventies, and John D. Lee was trusted with the most important and dangerous missions. For example—when they were fitting out to leave Nauvoo, he was given money from all the companies to go back and buy wagon covers or material to make them for the whole group, because they could trust him with their money, and because they felt that he could buy in wholesale to an advantage, and because they knew he would make a good bargain. At Winter Quarters he was sent to collect the wages of the Mormon Battalion—and with Howard Egan[40] he crossed the rest of the continent and came up with the Battalion at San Diego, got the money—$8000, I think—I should take time to look this up—but he brought it back to President Young to help fit out companies to cross the plains.[41] (This last money was used to buy the townsite of Ogden, Money from Fort Leavenworth did the other) He wanted to go with the first company of pioneers to the west, but President Young asked him to stay behind and help with caring for the main body of the saints. In Utah (he did not come until 1850) he was just getting settled when he was called to come south with the first company to Parowan. He was clerk of the company, and I have read his records and many of the letters he wrote to Brigham Young. If I had time, I'd copy off a few for you, because I have never read letters so full of devotion and of loyalty to the church. In 1852, in the fall, he was sent on to Harmony to build a fort and start another colony. He was living there, but had another home and a farm at Washington also, at the time of the massacre in 1857.

He was in the massacre. He took part in it, and killed at least 2 people. He never denied that, and he paid for it with his life. But he was not the most responsible for it, nor was he the leader. He was killed because he was the one that happened to get caught.

When the plan was first originated, he was in Harmony. He was NOT at the meeting where the fate of the emigrants was discussed. He came to Cedar City because he was sent for and ordered to come. He went out and took charge of Indians because he was the Indian Farmer for the government and had more influence with the natives than anyone else. There were 52 white men who took part in that, most of them members of the militia at Cedar City who had been sent out by a higher officer than Lee, and who were under another officer, still higher than he was. He carried out orders which he received from others. His business was to get the emigrants out of their fortification. He did that. He loaded the children and the guns into one wagon and sent it ahead. He put the wounded emigrants into another wagon which followed. He walked on foot between the two wagons. Some distance behind came the women and older children, and a half mile behind them, the men marched single file with an armed Mormon man beside each. At a signal, the Mormon men each shot the man at his side (that is, most of them did) the Indians rushed out of ambush and killed the women and children, and Lee and the driver killed the three or four wounded men in the wagon.

It was a horrible thing. A thing which we cannot justify or excuse, but neither can we go forward laying the full blame to John D. Lee. We have tried that silly expedient long enough now. Lee's descendants now number well into the hundreds, and are among the leaders in the church, and perhaps the most prominent family, as a whole, in Arizona—legislators, teachers, bankers, community leaders, yes, even stake presidents are found among his descendants. As a group they measure up well, to those of any other leader—including Brigham Young. At the time of Lee's death it seemed the best thing to do, the easiest way to quiet all the stir, to just let him take all the blame and close the incident once and for all. Since that time our writers have tried to leave his name out of any of the accomplishments of the church, and smear it with only this one incident. Well, that too must finally come to an end as the truth more and more becomes generally known. Anyone who takes time and trouble to go into the life and activities of Lee will find a loyal member of the church, devout, prayerful, generous, hospitable, a good, keen mind—a great man.

Well Stanton, I did not mean to go on at such length as this. I think as young members of the church who love it and are loyal to it and willing to work for it and sacrifice for it, we can serve better by knowing the truth than by kidding ourselves. We will have to accept the Mountain Meadows Massacre as a blot upon our history, which we can understand in the light of the persecutions our people had endured and the hysteria of war that grew out of an invading army that they thought was coming to drive them from their homes. Any fellow that saw action in the last war will understand well how such thing might be done by good people under the pressures of hate and revenge and fear, and the assurance that they were helping to "avenge the blood of the prophets." So don't let it disturb your faith in the church—it is not, the church of Brigham Young or even Joseph Smith, and if in human weakness mistakes were made, they were the human side and not the divine, and we must accept both, striving always for the guidance of the latter. Ours is the Church of Jesus Christ, and in His name and as His children, it is our business not to be content with error, but to accept truth wherever we find it.

The Lord bless you, Stanton, as He has already, and help you to get the most good out of this wonderful opportunity and to serve well your wonderful church.

Love,

Do write me again.

To *Harold B. Lee*, January 19, 1949

St. George, Utah
Jan. 19, 1949

Apostle Harold B. Lee
L.D.S Church Office Building
Salt Lake City, Utah

Dear Brother Lee,

At Christmas time I received a long letter with my Christmas card from Elder Stanton Schmutz, and in it he asked me what I knew about John D. Lee. I wrote back freely and rather fully, without making a carbon. Then I decided that perhaps I should have an exact copy in my possession, in case it opened any question or discussion.

I made this copy and a carbon which I keep for my files. I send this to you, not to have it open any discussion or be circulated necessarily, but in the hope that you will read it and file it where it will be accessible later if the question ever comes up. It is my opinion, which I can support with ample evidence if I need to, but which as a Sunday School teacher and a friend of the young Elder and his lovely girl-wife, I wrote of spontaneously in answer to his question.

When I am in Salt Lake City some time, as I am very often, I should be happy indeed if you would have time to talk to me upon this problem. I am in touch with many of the Lee descendants and find them people of extra-ordinary ability and of firm faith in the gospel—but with the feeling that they have suffered a grave injustice and have carried a heavy load through three generations.[42]

Sincere good wishes,

To *Lowry Nelson*,[43] January 25, 1949

St. George, Utah
January 25, 1949

Dr. Lowry Nelson
University of Minnesota
Department of Agriculture
University Farm, St. Paul 8
Minnesota

Dear Lowry,

Thank you so much for your note about my little contribution to the Utah Academy.[44] I think perhaps the most "remarkable" thing about it was that I was permitted to go through it to the end—or that it should finally be published. I honestly didn't think they would use it.

As you have perhaps guessed, it was done while I was at hands-grips with the Centennial celebration here in our county. I was on the central committee, and was perhaps too close to it for proper perspective.

To change the subject—I have heard of your own correspondence with the Brethren on the negro problem, and have been promised a copy.[45] As yet I have not received it—but I shall. I think I shall quote a bit from a letter I received from Gustav Larson[46] of Cedar City regarding it. He has probably written you also.

"You mentioned the Lowry Nelson correspondence on the negro problem. By interesting coincidence I received copies of it from George Boyd, Institute Director at Berkeley. Virginia and I sat on the floor by my desk until 1:30 a.m. while she read the letters between Lowry and the Brethren. We were entertained, amused, delighted and disappointed alternately. I admire Lowry's frankness and envy him his relative position of freedom. Sometime I'd like to show you some of my own written expressions on the subject as a result of inquiry from the Brethren. So far, I'm still employed!"

And then as a footnote he adds: "I was shocked to see the Brethren take such a definite stand on something I had hoped we were outgrowing. I find myself in a peculiar position as a teacher in the LDS system."

So you see there is yeast at work. Success to you.

Source: MS 0115, Marriott Library Special Collections.

To *Donald P. Bean*,[47] March 14, 1949

St. George, Utah
March 14, 1949

Mr. Donald P. Bean
Stanford University Press
Stanford, California

Dear Mr. Bean:

I had no idea you were waiting to hear from me, or you'd received a letter early last November. I waited for you to acknowledge receipt of the ms. for the first month, and then just assumed that it was probably going the rounds of readers.

Now that the ice is broken, perhaps we can go into some detail. I should have been more than happy to discuss points in the actual writing, though as I told you, I sense myself many of the weak spots. I really mailed it a little before I was ready in order to meet Mr. Stegner's wish to take it with him.

As to your questions—I have no authority, of course, to speak for the Lee family.[48] They have told me repeatedly that they were sure they could use a thousand copies. Now, without knowing the price of the book, I shall find it a little awkward to deal with them. Could you give me approximate cost? And if they were to take the 1000 copies in bulk, should they not have some concession as to price? To me, that would seem fair. Did your statement about finance infer that you would want some money in advance, as a guarantee that they would actually take the stipulated number of copies? If so, how much would you expect?

They had hoped for a family reunion early in the summer. Last November they talked in terms of this coming April, but when I could only report that I had no word from you, they have left their date undecided. They would definitely like it by September 1st, however, as it would be much harder for them to gather after school begins.

As you may guess, I am new at this business. I have done a piece of work which I would like to have published. But I do not know how to bargain about it. I had just assumed that publishers had perhaps some standard procedure into which I should fit.

Please be frank in writing me. Let me know the approximate cost per copy of the manuscript, with 20 additional pages of bibliography.

I should like it cloth bound, also, and on a good paper. If I know this, I can talk to members of the Lee family organization to better purpose. And if there could be any possibility of having the book out by September 1, let me know that too, for it may make some difference in their eagerness for the copies. They want a reunion and figured that it would be much easier to dispose of many of the books at that time.

I do not want any delay on my account. As soon as we can come to an understanding, I shall be glad to get the manuscript in shape, taking into account the suggestions and questions of your readers—and to do it promptly.

I look forward to hearing from you again.

Sincerely,

To *Ettie Lee*, June 19, 1949

St. George, Utah
Sunday morning
June 19, 1949

My dear Miss Lee,

Your letter was here when we returned last night. As before, I deposited the check in the Lee account to be used as we need it.[49]

Our trip was a happy one. Will was made vice-president of the State Association of Postmasters, and the convention for next year was scheduled for St. George. My responsibility in the Era convention[50] went off very well, I believe—I hope—At any rate, I did meet many new friends and many old ones, and for me it was all a very pleasant and profitable experience.

I was delighted that Mrs. Bickley[51] had the other John D. Lee missionary diary for 1842–3. It had come into her hands in such a way that it seemed providential, and actually without the knowledge of the sister who had owned it. As I understood it, things happened about like this: Mrs. Bickley had written, pleading with her sister to either bring or send the book in, so that she might make a copy. On Sunday before Decoration Day,[52] she did come, and brought with her all the material she had. But something evidently happened to sour her again, for she refused to even let the family see or examine the material. After she had gone home, this was found on Mrs. Bickley's bed, but she did not know how it came to be there.[53]

At first she had been torn between the thought of sending it back to Panguitch,[54] but her brother advised her to have it photostated first, so that she could make copies from the photostat if the sister demanded the original. I sent it to Mr. Bliss with this explanation, asking him please to rush the original back to her, just in case the sister returned for it. When I saw Mrs. Bickley again and suggested that you would like to examine the book, she said to ask Mr. Bliss, the librarian, to hold it a few days. I wrote him this morning to that effect, so if you care to telephone him, and if you have time, I feel sure that you can see the diary.

Because the book is 106 years old, it is very frail. When I got it, it was turned inside out and the pages were all mixed up, as the sewing is gone and many of the page numbers torn off. I spent a full day going through it, getting the pages in order, and reading it. It seems to me more interesting than the one we had copied before; there are several remarkable healings recorded, all the baptisms he performed, and some good leads for genealogy. He told of visiting his family, his Uncle James Connor, and gave the names of other relatives, so that perhaps we can get some leads from the records in that vicinity.

I hope that the book is not yet returned, as I should like very much to have you see it. I think it would be a wholesome contact for you to make also, to become better acquainted with Mr. Bliss or rather, to have him become acquainted with you.

Sunday morning is a busy time for me, so you will excuse the haste of this. My little second boy, Kay, is to be ordained a deacon this morning and he is all thrilled about it—Father's Day, besides—and not all our things unpacked and put into place yet. By getting up a little extra early I could get off these two letters.

If I am too late, I shall see that you do get to examine this when you come up to Salt Lake, for I shall go with you.

Affectionately,

To *Donald P. Bean*, July 11, 1949

St. George, Utah
July 11, 1949

Mr. Donald P. Bean, Director
Stanford University Press
Stanford, California

Dear Mr. Bean:

Your letter of July 8 was a blow right between the eyes, for your demand for the full $3000. in advance may cancel our arrangements entirely.[55] At best, it will delay matters.

I have no authority to speak for the Lee family. As I told you before, they came into the picture last year, after most of my research was done and the ms. in its present form. I did not think they would accept your first proposition of 1,000 books for $3,000, with the implication, as I read it then, that they would make a sufficient down payment to protect you, with the balance when the books were delivered, or soon thereafter.

Now paying $3,000 in advance for a book that is not even under way at the press may look like a very different matter to them, especially when not one of them has ever seen the ms. or any part of it. They may not be willing to accept your terms, in which case, I assume, our negotiations will automatically be at an end.

It would seem good business practice, and a good guarantee to you of their intent to complete the contract, if they sent half the amount in advance, with the balance upon delivery of the book at the same time that it would assure them of your good faith.

I shall forward your letter to Miss Ettie Lee, acting representative for the family, today, and await her answer, or suggest that she deal directly with you.

I had hoped to do an independent piece of work, as scholarly and impartial as I can make it. I am as reluctant to have an implication that it is sponsored by the Lee family as I would be to have it sponsored by the Mormon Church on one hand or the Catholic Church or any other organization on the other. I had hoped that the time has finally come when this could be treated as any other historical incident, calmly and objectively.

Because of the uncertainty which surrounds the whole arrangement, I shall answer only one point in your letter, and if we continue on this project together—which I sincerely hope we shall—I shall be glad to discuss other points in detail. With regard to what the publication of this study may do to me among the Mormons, let me first give a little background:

My first interest in this subject came when, as a girl of 18, I sat at the death bed of Nephi Johnson, a participant who, by his own admission, managed the Indians. He died hard, and his last hours were haunted by that scene. At one time, with a profound shudder, he said "Blood! Blood! Blood!" in a voice that would have chilled a stone. At that time, I knew nothing of the affair; our people had lived by the counsel of silence on the subject.

In the spring of 1933 I left my position as a teacher in the Dixie College to get married; that summer, with the encouragement of Mr. Nels Anderson,[56] I initiated a project in our county under WPA for the collection and copying of pioneer diaries. For more than four years, I supervised this, and because of my interest in this subject, I collected every reference I could about the massacre.

When I became connected with the Henry E. Huntington Library five years ago, I suggested this subject as one upon which I should like to do research, and was given a grant under the Rockefeller Foundation to carry on.

Knowing the extreme sensitivity of some of our church leaders upon the subject, I worked quietly until after President George A. Smith came into office. Then I wrote him of my assignment and asked to talk it over with him. He received me cordially and, after an hour's conference, shook my hand and told me he hoped that I would be happy with my work and that I would get permanent satisfaction from it. I answered that I did not want to write anything that in twenty years from now I would need to be ashamed of.

With the other two members of the First Presidency I was not so fortunate. President David O. McKay's office girl refused me audience when she knew what I wanted to discuss—though I had made an appointment and come a long distance to keep it. President Clark did not see me, either, but sent word by the secretary that the material which I wanted to see would not be made available. I have asked no favors of any of the other General Authorities.

I do not know what this publication will do to me personally. Among my many friends I find the following predictions: (1) that the book will be ignored, in accordance with the general policy of silence upon the subject; (2) that I will be openly condemned as an apostate, and the book discounted because of that; (3) that I will be cut off the church immediately; (4) that I should hold the ms. until after I am dead before it is published. This last I consider silly and cowardly.

I do not want to be excommunicated from my church for many reasons, but if that is the price that I must pay for intellectual honesty, I shall pay it—I hope without bitterness. Is that the statement you wanted? I hold no one but myself responsible for my research or conclusions.

The most encouraging thing that I have found is the wide spread feeling among our people that it is time for this incident to be investigated and the real story told. Particularly among the teachers of the state, the professors of our major universities, have I met help and encouragement, and expressions of confidence. The people of southern Utah generally know the facts already, and are tired of the empty story that "this is the crime of an individual" etc. They know too well that it was the crime of a group, acting under stress of war hysteria, revenge, religious fanaticism, and lust for property.

I apologize for going on at such length. I did not intend to when I began. I shall send your letter on and wait for word from Miss Lee, and shall also hope for further word from you.

Very sincerely,

Source: Operational Files, Stanford University Press.

To *Ettie Lee*, July 12, 1949

St. George, Utah
July 12, 1949

My dear Miss Lee,

The enclosed letter came yesterday, and I was so disturbed about it that I hardly slept last night. Before morning I felt reassured and calmed, until now I feel that things will eventually work out for us.

The demand for $3000 in advance seemed to me unfair and uncalled for. It may be that Mr. Bean is like the old-fashioned horse traders, bidding for more than he thinks he can get, but willing to come down if he has to. At any rate I had thought that an advance of one half the full price would be too much—plenty, anyway.

I wrote him briefly this morning saying that I was surprised and somewhat taken back by this demand, that I had no authority to speak for the Lee family, but would send the letter on to you and await your decision. Since the later paragraphs of his letter indicated that he is troubled about what the attitude of the church is to be, I gave him a brief statement of my stand: that I am a good member, I hope; that I had a long, friendly talk with President George A. Smith in which I told him in detail of the undertaking; that I hope I shall not be cut off the church for this—I think I will not be—but if I am I shall be willing to pay even that price without bitterness for this attempt to set forth the truth about this one blot on our history. Also that I and I alone am responsible for the research, which I have tried to make extensive, and for the conclusions arrived at as a result.

Since we have both felt so certain of publication here, and I have told all my friends who have asked that Stanford Press is handling this, and you have acted in good faith in advertising the fact among the family, I feel that they do owe us some consideration—I should hate to change now if we can avoid it.

The ms has not arrived. I had asked him to return it some time ago, because there were a few revisions, chiefly of form, that I wanted to make. As soon as it comes, I shall devote full time to it again, putting every page in final form and finishing off the bibliography. That will take a month or six weeks. September lst should see it all ready to set up. If they would take their part of the business as seriously as they do ours, they could have it off by Thanksgiving . . . What I Mean is—if they demand the full payment in advance, we should be able to expect that they act promptly and efficiently once the manuscript and the money are there.

As to the money—I have here on deposit the $600. you have sent since April 30, and can put $400. of my own with it to make up one thousand. If you think you can get another thousand by September 1st, I shall try to sell a piece of land that we have considered disposing of and get another thousand as down payment. Then we could make up a tentative contract to effect that the $3000 will be paid on or before September 1st, and that upon receipt of it, they shall proceed at once toward publication.

Or if you think that is too soon, let us set a later date, but get their name on the dotted line.

If you feel about it as I did yesterday and last night—that you do not want to deal with them at all on such terms,—we might make a counter-proposal to the effect that $1500 would be paid in advance, and the balance on or before final date of publication.

I have a feeling that pressure is being brought to bear on them to persuade them not to undertake this project by the same forces that have fought open discussion of this subject for more than ninety years, and I hate to be beaten by them.

There is the possibility of talking the matter over with Mr. Arthur H. Clark[57] there in Pasadena before we make any final commitment. He wrote me the second time to say that, if things did not work out with Stanford, he would like to consider publication. He is a reputable publisher of historical books, and with a guaranteed sale of a thousand copies, he might give us some good terms. I could come to Los Angeles and bring the Ms. and talk it over with him, if you think it might be better.

As you can see I am trying to think myself clear on the whole matter. Somehow, in the early morning, I had the assurance that my first business is to get that Ms. go through it very carefully again, add such items as I have secured since I sent in to them last October, and finish the bibliography, and if I do my part as well as I can, things will smooth out for us. I hope I am not wrong.

I hate to add this to all the other worries and concerns which I am sure that you have, but I know of no other way. Let us both take time to give it full consideration, and if you would like to withdraw from the venture entirely, I shall feel that is best, and shall offer the work to the Princeton University Press instead. I have some reason to believe they will take it.

God's choicest blessings
be on you,

To *Donald Bean*, July 16, 1949

St. George, Utah
July 16, 1949

Mr. Donald P. Bean, Director
Stanford University Press
Stanford, California

Dear Mr. Bean:

This morning's mail brought a letter from Miss Ettie Lee, in which she expresses her willingness to go along, as far as she can, with your demands for payment in advance. She enclosed $1,000 (to my great surprise) which she asked me to send as soon as some definite agreement can be made up. She says she can pay a second $1,000 by September 15, or perhaps Sept. 1st.

I would prefer to be left out of this part of the deal, but it seems that it will expedite matters if I do not. From my point of view, an advance of $2,000 before any work on your part is begun should be evidence enough of her good faith in completing the contract. It occurs to me, too, that it will take until almost September 1st for me to get the ms, and the bibliography back to you, so that we might write into the agreement a clause to the effect that the second $1,000 shall precede the shipment of the ms.—so that you have $2,000 before you even have to lift a hand yourself.

In this, it seems to me, the Lee family are the ones who are taking the chance. They are gambling $3,000 on a book without knowing the quality of paper, whether it is to be paper or cloth bound, whether it is a full length book or just an enlarged pamphlet, what it contains. Their faith in both of us surprises—and humbles me. Many of them, I know, will be disappointed in my treatment, for their chief wish is to have their grandfather vindicated, as he cannot be. Of course, Miss Lee figures that any impartial study will be to their advantage, and in this she is right.

While Miss Lee probably can, and if forced to, will pay the remaining $1,000 before the book is completed, I think she should not be asked to, as a matter of good business relations. I do not yet know how she plans to dispose of all this 1,000 books, but my guess is that she will ship several hundred to each of several different members of the family in scattered localities in Utah and Arizona and have them distributed in that way. She may wish to stipulate names and numbers of books to you and have them go direct to these people from your office—in lots of 100 or more. It would simplify matters for her, and does not seem to be asking too much of you in view of her willingness to cooperate so far.

I am enclosing a tentative agreement. If you cannot accept it, please make another yourself. If you can, return it to me and I will mail this $1,000 immediately. (I'll be glad to get it out of my hands!) Then just as soon as the ms. arrives, I shall set to work to put it in final shape, and shall see that you get the second $1,000 by the time you get the script to work on. The third $1,000 will be ready by the time the book is off the press.

I hope that you are able to persuade the "authorities" of whom you speak that this course is fair to all concerned.

Sincerely,

P.S. I find that I know little indeed about making up agreements. I should like to send this $1,000 now and get it off my hands, but dare not until you accept these terms or write others. I have made this up in triplicate, so if you OK it, return it and I'll send the money and all three copies for you to sign.

If you prefer to write one of your own, send triplicate copies to me and if Miss Lee will sign them, I shall return them, with the initial payment of $1,000.

Since the ms. has not arrived, I wonder if it is coming by mail or express. I shall try to get it back to you before September 1st, with the second $1,000.

To *Pamela Faust,*[58] November 11, 1949

St. George, Utah
November 11, 1949

Mrs. Pamela Faust
Assistant to the Editor
Stanford University Press
Stanford, California

Dear Mrs. Faust:

Thank you for your letter of November 2. I appreciate your interest in my study of what went on at the Mountain Meadows in September, 1857, and your desire to help improve the manuscript.[59]

I wish that I could accept your first suggestion with better grace, for I too, feel very strongly on this subject. What I was trying to say is that in any age war is hell, that it releases the beast in man, and that in spite of our so-called civilization, we have not changed essentially. It is easy to point out the atrocities of our enemies, but we should realize that our own men react in a similar manner to the emotions engendered by war.

I wrote those two or three pages because I particularly wanted them to go into the book. We had four sons in the last war; two of them saw combat in all its most horrible aspects. One lived through the Battle of the Bulge in the European theater; the other was for months in the jungles of a Pacific Island, where it was at some times a close-up, hand-to-hand affair, and at others a business of crawling, under low fire, over the bodies of dying and dead Japanese. I see no reason why I should be less realistic in writing of the experiences of my sons that I would be in discussing the actions of their ancestors.

Because I am so new at this, I am not sure whose book this is to be. If, in spite of any protest of mine this section is to be cut, I shall try to accept it without too much heat or fuss, but if by making a protest, I can save it and keep it in, I shall protest, of course.

I think your second point is well taken, and I should insert a summary paragraph, though I wonder if it could not better come on page 103, at end of the Klingensmith affidavit and before the final generalization. What would you think of something like this?

"Perhaps at this point we should recapitulate briefly in order to note variations in the different accounts. While both Higbee and Macfarlane[60] emphasize the threat of the Indians and insist that the final massacre was carried out in order to appease them, Klingensmith pictures it as strictly a military affair, conducted by the officials of Cedar City under orders from William H. Dame[61] of Parowan. Nephi Johnson likewise places the blame upon the Mormon military leaders, but admits that the Indians were getting out of hand and he was called to help manage them. Lee's statement that the original plan was to stir up the Indians to the attack seems to be true, with the Mormons brought in later when it became evident that the Indians alone could not commit the crime. Certainly the final responsibility must rest squarely upon the Mormons, William H. Dame as commander and those under him who helped to form the policy and to carry out the orders."

It seems to me that such a summary as this would come more naturally here, after all the contemporary evidence has been presented. If you still prefer it, we can also insert a short paragraph at the end of the Affidavit.

Please excuse this last error. They just brought in my 14-year-old with an injury from a foot ball game—unofficial and junior-high. I think it cannot be too serious, though he is pale and shaken. Rather than wait until I can re-write this in better fashion, I shall mail it now, and perhaps be able to go through the next bit of correspondence uninterrupted—I hope.

Thank you again. I do sincerely want to cooperate in this, believe me.

To *Pamela Faust*, October 4, 1950

St. George, Utah
October 4, 1950

Mrs. Pamela Faust
Assistant to the Editor
Stanford University Press
Stanford, California

Dear Mrs. Faust:

Is my face red! I know how utterly stupid this will sound to you, but I'll tell you, anyway.[62]

Last spring, before I had received the first galley of this MOUNTAIN MEADOWS MASSACRE book, Dr. Herbert E. Gregory[63] was visiting at my home. In our conversation about it, I said I was concerned about the index.

"Oh, don't worry about that," he said. "They have a staff to take care of that. They feel that their experts can do a better job of indexing than the author. Most of the University Presses do."

He seemed so assured and definite on the matter that it was easy for me to accept the suggestion again in June when I was at the University of Utah and the subject came up, with one of the group assuring me that I had no worry about the index.

I was wrong, of course. Being undecided myself I should have written you direct and asked for suggestions on the matter. As it was, I interpreted the "Index to Cum" as to come from you to me, and I waited with some little impatience for it.

When your letter arrived on Friday evening, September 30, I locked myself up over the week-end and hardly came out for air. It has taken until now to get it into this state—this type of thing would move faster, I imagine, with more than one to work at the checking end. Perhaps I should hold it for another week, give my eyes a chance to rest, and go over it all again. I think I shall not, though. I have written some notes and questions about it on another sheet—things which you there must decide for me.

Since one can hardly apologize for stupidity, I'll not try to further. If there is anything else that I can do, let me know. Or if I should start back over this again at once, wire me collect. I promise to not let the grass grow under my feet.

Sincerely,

To *Donald P. Bean*, November 13, 1950

St. George, Utah
November 13, 1950

Mr. Donald P. Bean, Director
Stanford University Press
Stanford, California

Dear Mr. Bean:

Thank you for your kind letter and for the finished MOUNTAIN MEADOWS MASSACRE. I am very pleased with the make-up, and especially glad for the change in the jacket. If there is any wish that it were different, it is with my own writing. Don't misunderstand—I am not apologizing for my research or my conclusions, but for the literary style of some passages. Now to brace for the consequences!

I am writing this morning to Miss Ettie Lee, with the hope that she will deal directly with you in the final arrangements for distributing her copies. If she does not, I'll write again as soon as I hear from her.

I know well of course, that I have not said the last word on this subject. I'm sure this will call out other material of which I knew nothing. If I had only been able to get access to the few things I did know about—the affidavits in the LDS Church office, the James H. Martineau[64] diaries, and the Wilden[65] records! I doubt that they would have changed any conclusions, but they would have given the points of view of at least six additional participants.

Thank you again and all the staff who have worked so carefully and patiently to make this the fine book that it is.

Sincerely,

To *Levi S. Udall,*[66] December 28, 1950

St. George, Utah
Dec. 28, 1950

Judge Levi S. Udall
Supreme Court, State of Arizona
Phoenix, Arizona

Dear Judge Udall:

Thank you so much for your letter of December 17. I appreciate it very much—because it came from you, in the first place, and because you did not hesitate to express an opinion, in the second. So many of our fine people here are waiting for some pronouncement from the leaders of the Church before they dare to make up their minds as to whether or not this work is justified. I had hoped that they would read the book and judge it upon its merits rather than condemn or praise it unread because someone else passed judgment.

I felt that, since I was writing for an audience of both church members and non-members, I must be careful to maintain an objective attitude myself. I am pleased with the number of letters that have come from those not of our faith, every one accepting my explanation of why and how that tragedy could happen. If, even after years, my own people can accept it also, I shall feel justified in whatever censure I may have to take now.

I take it as a hopeful sign that neither of our state papers nor the ERA[67] has mentioned it as yet. Some friends are impatient that they have not, but I cannot hope for a friendly review and would naturally prefer none at all than a bitter, vindictive one. Two or three of my friends who are on the staff at the University of Utah think I am to be called in and examined or tried for my fellowship in the church. I hope I may escape that.

Perhaps I should not have launched upon this discussion here, but I felt such a warmth and friendliness in your letter that I could not resist. Thank you again

Sincerely,

Chapter 4

1951–1952

Aftermath of *Mountain Meadows Massacre*

Upon the release of her book, Brooks received a steady stream of encouraging letters from both Mormons and non-Mormons congratulating her for her efforts. She answered a number of them, saying she was pleased with the positive attention from so many, though disappointed that none in the leadership of the LDS Church had commented. One letter to Robert Cleland of the Huntington Library dated April 29, 1951, summarized the reception of the book to that date. Of all the numerous letters received, only one had been bitter, and even those from members in good standing in the LDS Church thought a telling of the massacre was long past due. All the letters from non-Mormons had been quite supportive, as well as those from faculty members of the three universities in Utah. The book had even been reviewed positively sixteen times in towns near St. George including Cedar City, Enterprise, Hurricane, Veyo, and Zion Park. She concluded this letter by suggesting for the first time that all of the John D. Lee diaries be published together, a goal she continually pursued throughout her career but which never materialized.[1]

Her most critical review, one of only a couple of negative responses, came, through her sister, from Albert Lyman, an author in Blanding, Utah, who exclaimed that her book "is the most vicious thing published against the church since the days of John C. Benned [*sic*], William Laws, and the men who contrived at and finally accomplished the death of Joseph Smith" and then went on to rebuke, "I am disgusted and shocked with the unwarranted aspersions cast by this book on the prophet of the Lord."[2] Brooks, respecting his opinion, in a reply affirmed her testimony of the gospel and declared, "You think I have done an evil thing; I believe sincerely that I have done a wholesome thing and done the church I love a service."[3]

Brooks often lamented in her replies the total lack of any mention of her book from the general authorities of the LDS Church and a complete silence from all church publications. Though she regretted the evasion, it was also a relief that her work was not publicly denounced. She noted in a letter to Charles Kelly of January 5, 1952, that she had heard "not a word anywhere. My local people, the bishop and the president of the Stake, and all the authorities have never referred to the book—they evade it with the delicacy and solicitude they might show to a mother who has given birth to a monster child."[4] Morgan in an April 1951 letter compares the LDS Church's avoidance of the troublesome issue to rituals of primitive peoples such as the mother-in-law taboo.[5]

A minor controversy swirled around a request by Frank H. Jonas, associate professor of political science at the University of Utah, for reviews of the book and responses from LDS Church leaders and scholars Joseph Fielding Smith, Preston Nibley, Levi Edgar Young, and Milton R. Hunter. None of them or their associates admitted reading the book, though some such as Joseph Fielding Smith offered an opinion that the book could "be placed in the class with Fisher's, Whipple's, and Brodie's production."[6] Milton Hunter claimed that most of the church authorities he knew had received their negative judgment of the book from Judge William H. Reeder of Ogden and that he personally practiced a policy encouraged by Herbert Bolton, the history professor at the University of California under whom Hunter had received his PhD, to stay away from such minor incidents and that "they were parts of history that should be forgotten."[7] Brooks wrote several letters concerning these reviews and even tracked down Reeder and confronted him. When shown a copy of her book, he admitted that he had never seen it and did not recognize the cover.

In the fall of 1951, she met with Stephen L. Richards, first counselor in the First Presidency, in an unsuccessful attempt to obtain acceptance of her book by at least one of the leaders of the LDS Church. After the meeting she mailed him a copy of the book and he responded without reading the book with a letter admonishing her for digging up "such a sad chapter in the history of southern Utah."[8] She shot back asserting that the terrible incident "had never been out of public attention, especially since President Grant [Heber J. Grant of the LDS Church] went before the Arizona legislature and protested the naming of the Lee's Ferry Bridge [which was eventually renamed the Navajo Bridge]."[9]

Also in the fall of 1951 she heard unexpected and exciting news of a possible Mountain Meadows Massacre movie deal with Warner Brothers. As told to Dale Morgan in her enthralling storytelling style, immediately after taking the call from Warner Brothers on a Friday evening, she was on a night bus to Salt Lake City to make contact with LDS Church authorities to obtain their blessing for the project. She first called and met with Judge Reeder and then proceeded to call a number of the church leaders including Joseph Fielding Smith upon arrival Saturday morning, finally reaching Stephen L. Richards at home on the phone, who courteously informed her that the LDS Church could not provide a formal approval without seeing the final product. She eventually declined the movie proposal partly because of the small amount of money offered and also due to the sensational quality of the script.

Will Brooks retired as St. George postmaster in May 1951 and they spent that summer at their Hurricane orchard farm about fifteen miles northeast of St. George. At the beginning of 1952, they accepted Ettie Lee's offer to manage a hotel, renamed the Lee Hotel, that she had recently bought and settled at 420 East St. George Boulevard, the main highway through town.

~

To *Irvin Mcquarrie*,[10] January 6, 1951

St. George, Utah
January 6, 1951

Dr. Irvin McQuarrie
Department of Pediatrics
University of Minnesota
Minneapolis, Minn.

Dear Doctor McQuarrie,

Saint Josef[11] of the Desert, as he jokingly calls himself, sent me a check for which I was to forward to you a copy of my little book,

The Mountain Meadows Massacre. While he may be over-enthusiastic about this piece of work, I am still glad to send it to you.

He has told you that I was a student of yours the year you taught in Bunkerville. As I remember it now, I was in the seventh grade. If you remember me at all, I am sure it will be as a skinny child with too much nose and protruding teeth, and a flair for speaking up out of turn. My piano teacher that year told me I had a "swill-pail" complexion.

I remember you chiefly because you were my idea of what the perfect prince charming should be—tall, black, curly hair, brown eyes, a quiet voice, an engaging smile. It was a longtime before I gave up that hope that maybe someday I would meet some one who fit the same description. But then I needn't tell you how silly and sentimental a 13-year-old girl can be.

I have followed your career with some interest as far as I could from the occasional newspaper comments, and have been proud that you had once been my teacher.

My own pattern has been checkered: teaching in the grades, a wife, a mother of a son, a widow in one year; finishing college and teaching here at Dixie; a Master's from Columbia University; more teaching; marriage to a fine man (and a family); another family of 4 coming close on each other's heels; connection with the Henry E. Huntington Library; now back again at the teaching game. That brings us up to date, I think.

St. Joe suggests that perhaps you helped to make me a "naughty" girl. You did help to establish in me an independence of thought, I am sure.

Sincere good wishes,

To *Michael Harrison*,[12] January 23, 1951

St. George, Utah
January 23, 1951

Mr. Micheal Harrison
3183 Carly Way
Sacramento, California

Dear Mr. Harrison:

Thank you so much for your letter of January 7, forwarded to me by Stanford University Press. It is cheering to get a word of appreciation from one who knows the essentials of that most unfortunate happening in Utah history.

I am pleased with the reactions which have come to me about the book. Though no word has been said by anyone in authority in the L.D.S. Church, many good members have commended me in about the same tone which you used. It is all that I hoped for—to present a story truly and fully and without bias.

I understand that the Huntington Library has been at work on the Lee journals for some time now. I shall be very glad when they are published. The descendants have also copied three original diaries that are in the LDS archives, and hope to make them available also, within the next year or so.

Thank you again for your kind letter. I shall let you know if I learn anything definite about the Lee material.

Sincerely,

P.S. The publishers would like to know if you have any objection to their quoting from your letter. Do you?

To *LeRoy and Ann Hafen*, February 11, 1951

St. George, Utah
Sunday morning, Feb, 11, 1951

Dear Roy & Ann:

One of my real problems this winter is getting letters answered. I manage to keep so entangled in so many things—everything from school kids struggling with a debate problem that is too big for the best minds of the nation or trying to inflate a 60-word vocabulary to make something that will sound like an oration, or their idea of one, to scout circuses or Gleaner Comraderies in formal dress or weekly washings and ironings. At least there's never a dull moment.

I did appreciate your letter, though, Roy. I'm surprised at the number of letters I have received and at the willingness of folks to accept my effort at face value. Even Charles Kelly, violent anti-Mormon that he is, complained only at the fact that there were no pictures. He offered me refuge in a cave on the Colorado in case I should be run out of the state. There has been absolutely no comment from any of the Brethren, and total silence on the part of all church publications. I did have a review in the Provo Herald[13] which stirred enough interest that I had 13 copies of it sent to me by different people. I'll enclose one for you. Western Humanities is to run a panel on it, I understand.[14]

As for me, I long ago determined that I would say as little as I could—nothing, in fact, except under pressure.

It seems that Dale Morgan had seen the work of the Wisconsin Historical Society on the Lienhard ms.[15] His own is now ready for publication in the Utah Historical Quarterly, a part of an article he has completed in tribute to his friend Rod Korns, who died last year.[16] Which reminds me—he is about to apply for a Rockefeller grant to study on some topic (seems that I've left his letter in my desk at school) and he wonders about the amount that is usually given in such cases. My guess would be $2000, to perhaps $2500. From what these two young men from Harvard said who came West on fellowship grants. They have spent the winter in New Mexico, one at Gallup and one at Ramah. Both stopped over here a day or two enroute.[17] Would you know, or could you learn if that is about right?

Things here go about as usual, except that it is too warm and too dry. We've had neither winter nor storm this season—which is wonderful Chamber of Commerce stuff, but bad for the farmer and cattlemen.

I might have told you before that Will has now had official notice that he will be allowed to stay in the office only until the end of the month in which his birthday comes—which means that on April 30 we will be off that.[18] All of which adds up to some major family adjustments. We've known all along that it must come; it's just that we're never quite ready, I guess.

Well, it's nearly time for the family to storm in from Sunday School.

I'll hope to see you before you go back to Denver. I had thought I might get that way later this spring, but it's hard to make definite plans.

Goodbye for now, and good luck. You make me break the Tenth Commandment.[19]

Love,

To *Albert R. Lyman*,[20] February 12, 1951

St. George, Utah
Feb. 12, 1951

Mr. Albert R. Lyman
Blanding, Utah

Dear Brother Lyman:

Charity[21] sent me your criticism of my book, The Mountain Meadows Massacre. I thank you for your frankness, though it did seem a little tinged with bitterness, I thought. I respect your opinion, too, and honor your right to express it.

I was much interested in your statement that Procter Robinson[22] died from poison which this company had put into a spring. I have searched for any name of any person who did die of poison, but failed to find any, either in reports or letters or Deseret News items or the Journal History of the Church. Our people have always kept such careful records that I thought names and dates should appear somewhere. Since this is the first I have seen, I should certainly be glad for further evidence.

I need not say to you that I was writing as an historian, in an attempt to see this tragedy and the events which led up to it. It was an assignment which, if I had not taken it, someone else would have done. I feel that it is a good thing to "come clean" on once and for all.

I doubt that the book will ever win favor with the world, because most of the world is not interested in the matter, in the first place. I am cheered and warmed by the many letters I have had from our own people, not apostates and not jack-Mormons, but folks active in the church, who commend my effort. I have had some very good letters from non-Mormons, too, who had never had any idea of the relation of the massacre to the approach of Johnston's[23] army. Only two of more than fifty letters received have been critical—one by an anti-Mormon who thinks I tried to "whitewash" the affair to shield our leaders, and you who write in disgust and anger. I am keeping them all.

It seems idle for me to recount to you my activities in the church, or the activities of my children. My testimony of the Gospel is dear to me and very real, but it does not rest upon any man, or group of men alone. I love and honor our leaders, not because they are perfect, but because they are human. This includes Brigham Young, who could not help being affected by the things which had happened to him in Missouri and Nauvoo and which later developed in Utah. I wonder how much of the correspondence between him and John D. Lee you have read, or how conscious you have been of the deep affection between the two men.

Well, Brother Lyman, do not judge me too harshly now. I have only followed my light and my conscience as you follow yours. You think I have done an evil thing; I believe sincerely that I have done a wholesome thing and done the church I love a service. It will do no good to argue with each other, much less to hold hard feelings. I certainly have none. And let's wait a few years before the judgment is final.

My sincere good wishes to you and all your family, in which my fine husband joins.

To *Robert Cleland*, April 29, 1951

St. George, Utah
April 29, 1951

Dr. Robert G. Cleland
Henry E. Huntington Library
San Marino 15, California

Dear Dr. Cleland:

I have waited to acknowledge your letter of January 2, thinking that perhaps I should have some official reaction to my book. As yet there has been only silence, so far as the Authorities are concerned. I'm very much relieved, for I had feared that they might publicly denounce my work.

Of all the letters I have received, only one has been bitter. It came from Albert R. Lyman, of Blanding, Utah. He called the book "the most vicious thing published against the Church since the days of John C. Bennet, William Laws, and all the men who contrived at and finally accomplished the death of Joseph Smith."

On the other hand, many members of equally good standing say that it is long past due, and seem relieved to have the whole thing told at last. Non-members, without exception, have been very kind to me. Of course, I know there are many things to criticize, perhaps, but I have appreciated the reception it has received—especially among the teachers of the three major universities of the state.

It has been reviewed 16 times now in this area, including Cedar City, Enterprise, Hurricane, Veyo, and Zion Park, with a very good reception at each.

But I did not set out just to write about this. I learn from members of the Lee family that they plan to publish the three diaries which they copied at the office of the Church Historian. They are the 1844, 1846, and 1850–52 ones. I believe they will include also the two small missionary diaries of 1841 and 1842, copies of which are in your library.

I have wondered if it might not be well to fit these into the ones which you have there and have them all done together. Then perhaps we could get photostats of the three long ones to add to the collection there.

I hope to come to Los Angeles this week-end to take care of some other items of business, so I wondered if perhaps I should not ask your opinion about this before I talk to Miss Lee.

Will you be in on Saturday? If so, would you have time to talk to me?[24]

Sincerely,

To *Dale Morgan*, June 10, 1951

Hurricane, Utah
Sunday, June 10, 1951

Dear Dale,

I've spent the whole day with John D. Lee, so I may not be able to talk in the present tense for a while. Will & the boys went to St. George about 8:30 this morning to go to meetings there—it is now 3:30, and I have hardly moved out of the kitchen, where I am temporarily set up.[25]

Since the early diaries have not come—those that Manetta Henrie copied out of the Church archives—I've been browsing through those from Huntington.

I was interested in the date of his excommunication, since some members of the family have been pressing A. Will Lund about it, and have been told that nothing was recorded. Now I find under date of Nov. 17, 1870—just after Lee has accompanied the Brigham Young group out to the Colorado River and has made detailed record of each day's travel and of his many friendly talks with Brother Brigham—"I was also informed that myself, I C Haight & Geo Wood had been expelled from the Church, but for what cause it was not stated. My conscience being clear & that I had not done anything knowingly or designedly wrong I borrowed no trouble about the matter." Then the next day he records: "From them I received quite a No of letters one of them from A. Carrington notifying me of the action of the 12 &c but did not state the cause . . ." Still later: "Rachel Andora received the intelligence of my expulsion from the church with firmness & reminded me of a Dream or night vision that I had related to her about the time about the 8 of Oct 1870, which was the date of my being dropped from the Church."[26]

Anyway, now this Kathleen girl who is descended from both Lee and Young, and claims Lee in Arizona and Young in Salt Lake, can use her one grandfather's name to get information about the other—can take this date and let A. Will Lund see what he can find. At least it will satisfy her.

Clearly Lee had access to this volume when he was writing, for he quotes from it in several places. The one 1873–4 is full of the conflicts and differences with Hamblin.

I notice this item, for instance, entered Aug. 24, 1873: "As Elder H. C. Kimball once said at Winter Quarters, when he Prophesied in the Name of Israel God that I would walk my enemies under foot in time & in eternity. & the prediction was endorsed by Prest B. Young in 1848."

In the light of the present drought, when that area has had the combined weight of the Indian rain dances, the Mormon fasts, and the commercial rain makers, I've had to smile at this entry: "Mowebba Frid. Aug 29, 1873. . . . Reports are that Pres B Young, Prophet & leader of the Latterday Saints, declared that the clouds & rain shall be taken from the gentiles *&* delivered to the Saints commencing with the present season."

But enough of John D. Let him rest in peace or fry in hell . . .

I'm almost set up for the summer, I guess. My little room under the porch is all plastered & ceiled, with only some painting to be done before I can move into it. In the meantime, this isn't bad. Will goes with the boys into the orchard—our cherries have been especially nice—and for a few hours each day, I can work here in the kitchen. The telephone never rings, and I haven't made one call out myself. Willa is fully occupied at Zion Park, seems to be enjoying it, and earning her way besides.

We didn't get to go to the Postmasters Convention, after all. The cherry crop was just at its height; we had a crew of about 10 pickers, and just had to stay and see the fruit delivered—and collected for. Now that the thing will be over in three or four days, I may slip out by bus if Will can't get away to take me. I do want to follow a few good leads in the Salt Lake Area, & maybe go out toward Escalante.[27] Later in the summer we want to go toward Arizona & New Mexico. I must get some records to justify the Library in reactivating me for the summer.

These folks from the University of Chicago and the young man from the University of Paris (did I tell you about them?) are coming over later this evening again.[28] I tell them we'll have to take time out on this end to analyze the Annalists. He—Prof. Ed. Banfield—is doing a book-length study of Washington County. I'll see that you get a copy if and when it is published. In the meantime, I find them a very interesting, stimulating group. We plan a camping trip with them to Tuweep[29] this week-end. Will stop at Tumurru[30] with Jonreed & Verde one way.

I hear via the Grapevine that I am being severely condemned by some in the S.L. area, but my Bishop still puts his arm around me, so I'm not crossing any bridges.

Oh-Oh Gotta stop.

To *Dale Morgan*, June 20, 1951

Hurricane, Utah
June 20. 1951

Dear Dale,

I'm officially installed in this basement room, so by way of celebration, I'll warm up by a letter to you. Our last passed each other again characteristically. Maybe this will start another on its way.

Just after I mailed the last, I wish that I had waited to include another item which should have gone into my book. Lee gives a detailed account of the visit of President Young south in 1861—Here are two or three short cuts:

> "Washington May 29th 1861 . . . at 12 noon I met the Co near my mill—on meeting Prest BY he greeted me with a hearty Welcome took me up into his carriage and drove to my House & corrallid near my dwelling 23 carriages & 70 persons of the 1st Presdency . . . (he goes on to name them and to discuss the sermon, etc. Lee went with the party to Toquerville, Grafton & Pocketville then rode horseback all night to make preparations to entertain them at Harmony—butchered a beef and two sheep. Etc.)
>
> "Thursday May 31st 1861 at 30 m. to l p.m. the Prest & suite hove in sight. I hoisted a Flag in token of their reception they marched into the fort at 1 p.m. Pres & the leading men sat down to a sumptuous dinner I feasted about 125 persons three meals each Dinner super & Brakefast. I never saw Pres BY feed better. . . . After meeting I had some private conversation with him he advised me relative to my future location . . . Pres Young said that the company that was used up at the Mountain Meadows were the fathers, mothers, Bros sisters & connections of those that Muerders the Prophcts, they merritd their fate,, & the only thing that ever troubled him was the lives of the Women & children but that under the circumstances could not be avoided, although there had been that—wanted to betrayud the Brethrn into the hands of their Enemies for that thing will be Damned & go down to Hell I would be glad to see one of those traitors, though I suppose that there is any here now, they have ran away & when he came to the monument that contained their Bones, he made this remark, vengeance is mine saith the Lord, & I have taken a litle of it. . . ."

Well, this is not at all what I had in mind when I came down here. I began looking for information about the cannon barrel that decorates(?) the front of the Information Building at the temple. Jonreed stopped in a while ago to ask about it, saying that he had a wonderful title for an article NAPOLEON HELPS TO BUILD THE MORMON TEMPLE. He went on with the story about Napoleon being forced to leave his cannon when he gave up the siege of Moscow, how two of those were carried either across Siberia, over the Bering Strait, and along the coast south to Sutter's Fort or had been taken south to make the trip around the world by water. Then the Mormon Battalion men accepted two for pay, dragged them to Salt Lake City, thence south to Parowan, on to Dixie, Etc. etc. What did I know about it?

Well, I told him I thought it was a wonderful story, but not true. I heard Homer Durham[31] tell it, but when I asked for documentary evidence, he said he had none; He had heard it from Howard R. Driggs.[32] I examined the cannon, and decided, first of all, that it was not a BRASS cannon, as those were supposed to be. Miller[33] says that it came from San Diego over the Old Spanish Trail, and was brought in by Jesse W. Crosby,[34] but again he has no real evidence, or if he has, will not say so. That would seem the more likely story, though.

I know about the brass cannon that was used at Provo, the one that exploded prematurely, killing one man and taking off George W. Bean's[35] hand; I know that PPPratt brought a brass cannon south on his exploring expedition,[36] and that there was one at Parowan, though I'm not sure that it was left on the site or brought down again.... But none of these seem to be the one at our temple.

It's not important, I know. More like a tempest in a teapot. But Jonreed said that he was going to tell the story anyway, true or not. IF he does, after I've told him enough to make him want to verify it one way or the other, I'll be tempted to do an article myself and name it THE MANUFACTURE AND MARKETING OF HISTORY or HISTORY IN THE MAKING or something else. It seems to me to illustrate the too common attitude of passing on not only half-truths but actual fabrications.

I had a long letter from Nels Anderson the other day. He is now in Germany, but says he spent the war years in Iran, Iraq, Egypt, India, and other countries, working for the War Shipping Administration. Now he is working on a book on American community life designed for use as college text in Sociology. He seems to feel that eventually he must get back into university work.

Levi Edgar[37] wrote me, too. I'm not sure just what he is getting at, but it makes me grin. Think I'll enclose it for your Urim & Thummim.[38] Just toss it into a waste basket when you've read it.

I learn that I am to be in SLC on June 25 & 26, so other trips will have to be temporarily cancelled. I'll combine some record hunting with the Institute of Higher Education. Will ride up with Lee Hafen & Matthew Bentley.

Looks as if I've forgotten to thank you for the notes for my book work file, and for the lead on a Warren Foote[39] diary. I am careless, but I do appreciate them very, very much.

Time to start lunch. Looking this over, see that my fingers have gone hay-wire this morning. Perhaps it's the experience of starting out in this new room . . .

To *Dale Morgan*, September 9, 1951

Hurricane, Utah
Sunday afternoon, Sept 9

Dear Dale,

This isn't an answer to the letters I owe. I promise that I WILL get at them early this week. This is just a little letting off of steam.

I've been crowded lately, what with trying to read and absorb all this Lee stuff, taking the family on a 12-day trip into Idaho diary hunting. But I've told you that I got all the Elias Smith[40] journals, haven't I? Then catching up after I get back, acting as secretary to a 2-day Institute of Higher Education panel at Cedar City, fruit, visitors, etc.etc.

Well, the climax came about 7 p.m. Friday when one of the boys came out to call me to the phone. "Long distance from Hollywood." It was a man who said his name was Brian Foy,[41] production manager of Warner Brothers. He wants to do a movie with the MMM as a side issue, with Hamblin, Lee, Haslam,[42] Haight, and other local characters involved. How had my book been received? Was I a member of the church in good standing? Could I get a go-ahead sign from some of the Brethren? They would not portray either Joseph Smith or Brigham Young; they would try to make it not objectionable to the Church. Would I go to Salt Lake City at once and talk to some of the higher ups? What was I planning to do this winter, or for the next few months? Could I get a leave of absence from school and help work the thing out on location?

Naturally, I was floored. No, I didn't have a literary manager... They didn't ask, but I couldn't have told the terms of my contract regarding movie rights, so little had I ever imagined there would be any need to know.

I caught the 10 o'clock bus to SLC. As early as I decently could, I called Bro. Reeder[43] and asked for an interview. He didn't seem at all anxious, but finally granted it. When I arrived, he was extremely cold and short and unfriendly. I hardly knew how to begin, but told him that I had the letters written to Dr. Jonas[44] in answer to his inquiry from 4 of the higherups and that each man had said that he had not read the book himself, but had condemned it on the basis that Bro Reeder had made an unfavorable report. Mr. Reeder hadn't the slightest idea what I was talking about. He had made no report. He did not have any book there, and had no memory of reading anything of mine. When I pulled my work copy out of the brief case he examined it carefully, and said he had never seen this book before; the one he had read was much smaller, hardly half as thick and was put out by Caxton Printers,[45] he thought... He was so frustrated that I almost felt sorry for him. His only knowledge of the MMM he had from talking to Bro Palmer of Cedar City, a man whose historical background was not to be questioned. I told him that Palmer had heard me review my book twice, had been to the site with a group from the U and AC only the day before when I had reviewed it again, he had told me that he agreed with my interpretation whole-heartedly.

He suggested that I go to Joseph Fielding, as he was the man in charge of that type of thing. Being Saturday, the offices were all closed, so I called the Smith home. Apostle Smith himself answered the phone. He was leaving for a stake conference and would not be back in town before Wednesday; didn't know when after that date he could get time to talk to me. I should get in touch with Will Lund, and present my problem to him.

Mr. Lund has no telephone, evidently, at least not in his own name. Widtsoe, Kimball, Stapley, and Lee were all out of town.[46] Stephen L. Richards[47] was in, and I talked to him on the phone. He said that there is no monopoly on history; any movie company may use any historical incident as basis for a show. If I felt that the presentation was to be historical and fair, I should not hesitate to cooperate in such an activity. But the Church would not give a formal consent or approval to any such activity. They would not approve a magazine article before it was written; they would not give a go-head signal to a movie company. IF the movie people wanted help or suggestions or approval AFTER the scenario was prepared, they had people whom they would recommend to go over it. Altogether, his stand seemed fair enough to me.

Now I am to call this Mr. Foy tomorrow. In the meantime, I'll go home, dig out the contract with Stanford, and see what the score is with them. I have not breathed a word of this outside the family, not to Willa at all (she is still at Zion) and hardly to the boys, except that big-eared little Tony stood around while I talked to Mr. Foy. Somehow I think nothing will come of it, and I'll have fewer questions to answer in that event.

After all Maurine's frantic efforts to hit the movies and Jonreed's long stays in Hollywood trying to sell his books, I can't help being just a little inflated at even receiving a telephone call. But there are too many "if's" to say anything yet.

Enough for now. I'm expecting my sister Mary[48] and a part of her family any minute. They're bringing their boy down to Dixie—he's the all-American high school center of last year. And I'm reviewing briefly, Sam Taylor's "Family Kingdom"[49] at a fireside in St. George this evening. First faculty meeting at 8:30 a.m. tomorrow. I'll wait until after it is out to call this man at Hollywood.

Keep your fingers crossed for me. I frankly don't know what I do want to happen. I've had my mind all set to have a bang-up year teaching this winter, have kept clippings for my American Problem classes, and gone through texts, etc. for my others. I don't have an idea what this other would involve at all—if it should materialize. Seems that I can only stand still and stay quiet and let things happen. Any suggestions will he greatly appreciated.

To *Brian Foy*, September 10, 1951

St. George, Utah
Sept. 10, 1951

Mr. Brian Foy, Production Manager
Warner Brothers Studio
Hollywood, California

Dear Mr. Foy:

This is a preliminary report of the telephone call which I expect to make later this forenoon, so that you may have it for the record.

Less than three hours after I talked to you last Friday evening, I was on the bus enroute to Salt Lake City. I knew that all Church offices of the L.D.S. church were closed on Saturday, but I figured that I might contact some of the higher-ups officially at their homes.

Perhaps I should back up a little and give you what I know of the action behind the scene. As you know, the whole subject of the Mountain Meadows Massacre has been taboo in the Mormon church; people have repeatedly been forbidden to talk about it even. I was in Salt Lake City for two weeks early in June before the book appeared in November. Olive Woolley Burt,[50] the Magazine Editor of the Deseret News, and a good friend of mine, told me then that she had received the page proofs and had read them, but knowing the attitude of the leaders, had passed them on to Mark Peterson,[51] editor and an Apostle in the church. Via the grapevine, I heard that the matter was up for discussion at summer gatherings before the book ever came out.

When I book did appear, there was no comment. Again via the grapevine, I learned that it was to be given the silent treatment, that it should not be mentioned in any publication in the state without which the church had anything to do. Dr. Frank Jonas of the Political Science department of the University of Utah wrote a form letter to four of the Authorities most interested in western history, in which he asked each if he had read my book and, if so what was the reaction. He sent the four replies to me: Apostle Joseph Fielding Smith, Levi Edgar Young and Milton R. Hunter of the Council of Seventy, and Preston Nibley,[52] writer for the church. Every one of them said that he had not read the book himself; every one condemned it on the basis of a report by Brother William H Reeder who said it was "vicious."

That will explain why the first person that I went to see was this man Reeder. He treated me coldly at first, insisted that he had never made any report on my book. When I handed him a [missing] I had along in which Lee himself, after he had been dropped from the church, said that Brigham Young did not order the massacre and knew nothing of it until after it had happened. Since the only concern seems to be to keep the skirts of B.Y. clear, Reeder was won at once.

I next called Stephen L. Richards, first counselor in the First Presidency. I chose him because Pres. McKay was just being released from the hospital, and Richards is next in authority. I explained that you wanted to do a western in the setting of 1857 in Southern Utah, that you did not plan to portray either Joseph Smith or Brigham Young on the screen, but that you would use such characters as Jacob Hamblin, John D. Lee, Ira Hatch, Thales Haskell, James Haslam and other local people. He replied that he could see no reason why such a show should not be made, and no reason why I as a "good" member of the church, should not identify myself with it and assist in the production.

But when it came to giving a written approval from them, or a written statement of any kind, that was out of the question.

"We do not approve magazine articles before they are written," he said. "We could not approve a moving picture without going over the scenario carefully, or having someone competent go over it. If, when it is ready, the company wish us to do that, we shall be glad to do it, but advance approval is out of the question. I see no reason why such a show should not be done, or why you should not help if you wish, provided the intent is to be historically accurate and to picture the conditions as they actually were."

From my point of view, that is as good as you could expect or want. Certainly you do not want the restrictions which their official "approval" would entail.

As to my cooperation, I do feel that I am in a position to be helpful in such an undertaking. In the first place, I had done extensive research on Jacob Hamblin and had a book on him almost done when Paul Bailey[53] came out with his. I have articles on the setting in the *Pacific Spectator* and the *Utah State Historical Quarterly*; I have the only copy of a number of very important documents—the only available copy. I grew up on the frontier; my grandfather was an Indian missionary of the first group in the south. My husband kept a trading post for years at Mexican Hat[54] and understands and speaks Navajo. I have made no comment to the President of Dixie College about this yet, because I did not want to start talk anywhere until I knew something definite.

In looking up my contract, I find that you will have to deal with Stanford Press for movie rights to the book. I had thought the chance of a moving picture company's being interested was so [missing]

To *Finlay McDermid*,[55] October 22, 1951

St. George, Utah
October 22, 1951

Mr. Finlay McDermid
Warner Brothers Studios
4000 Olive Avenue
Burbank, California

Dear Mr. McDermid:

As soon as I received your letter yesterday, I called Mr. Bean of Stanford Press by telephone. He says that he has not received a check in payment for moving picture rights on my book. Perhaps it is better that way, because, I have decided not to take your offer, you may be able to cancel that transaction without loss.

As you know, I am without experience in this business. I have had only Mr. Foy's telephone conversation to go by. Now, from my point of view, this is the proposition: My contract with Stanford Press promises me 1/2 the "net" returns on a sale to the moving pictures. The gross to me on your offer would be $1750.00; what the "net" might be, I do not know. Weighed against my years of research, it means little.

Then I am assured "250.00 a week for a guaranteed period of four weeks" from you—again a gross of $1,000, which after my expenses here for a substitute teacher, extra help in my home, and my living expenses there would net me little over my experience.

Most important of all to me, in the eyes of my community and of my people generally, I would be held responsible for the finished product—a responsibility which I certainly do not want to assume under the present arrangements. Since this is only history, and hence anyone's province, I suggest that you go ahead without me. I am happy here in my work, and the distraction and disruption and responsibility would not be worth it.

Thank you for your consideration of my book. I think I shall let it stand as my contribution to history, and you may do as you wish with your interpretation of it.

Sincerely,

Source: MS 112, Marriott Library Special Collections.

To *Charles Kelly*, January 5, 1952

St. George, Utah
January 5, 1952

Dear Charles Kelly,

In going through some of my things today, trying to get them into some kind of order after our move, I came across a letter from you written just a year ago.[56] On the envelope I have made no notation as to whether or not I have answered it but my guess is that I have not. With those that I answered, it was my habit to write the date on the envelope, so that when I handled it again I could have a clear conscience. I'm surprised at myself that this should have been unanswered—if it has. At any rate, I'll write again just to make sure.

I certainly did appreciate your evaluation of my book—people who write books are the only ones who have any idea of what actually goes into one. I was glad, too, that you felt I have made some little contribution to the cause of history. Maybe I was too kind to Brother Brigham—I'm almost inclined to think I was myself, especially since I spent all summer reading Lee material. I think I came out of it with a clearer idea of how, with his background, his unquestioning loyalty to Brigham Young, Lee could have been expected to take the part he did in it all.

You asked how it has been received. Well, by silence, total and absolute. Not a word anywhere. My local people, the bishop and the president of the Stake, and all the authorities have never referred to the book—they evade it with the delicacy and solicitude they might show to a mother who has given birth to a monster child. No one among the higher ups will admit that he has read it—as near as I can tell, few have. At any rate, no official action has been taken, which must mean that I have a few friends in camp.

This bid of Warner Brothers was exciting while it lasted. Brian Foy was hot after it, wanted to get at it at once—within two or three weeks—and would do nothing without my full sanction and cooperation. By the time they had stalled along with Stanford Press and I had got into the midst of school teaching, and I found that their scenario man had been at work on it for a month, I had cooled off a bit myself. Then when the General Authorities made a formal protest, it was dropped. I could have used the money, of course, but I can also get along without it. So in the end nothing was accomplished except the fact that they had to admit that such a book had been written. I assume that nothing will be done further.

As I indicated at first, we have moved. Perhaps I should say we are moving, for it seems never to be quite finished. Mr. Brooks was retired from the post office last spring, and now has taken over the management of the Lyn-Mor motel which Miss Ettie Lee has recently purchased. So here I am, set up in one of the cabins, trying to arrange and rearrange this accumulation—and here I have stopped in the middle of it to say hello to you and thanks for the letter. When you come to Dixie, if you ever do, be sure to look in. I thought I might get out your way this summer, but didn't make it. It would be fun to sort of compare notes.

Good Luck!

To *Stephen L. Richards*, January 15, 1952

St. George, Utah
January 15, 1952

President Stephen L. Richards
47 East South Temple
Salt Lake City, Utah

Dear President Richards:

Thank you for your kind letter of January 7. I appreciate it very much.

Since you referred to our visit in your office, I should like to tell you of my interview with President Smith. As I told you, he was very kind to give me more than an hour of his time.

When I told him of my assignment, he said, in effect, "I don't know what good it will do. The men who took part in that terrible affair were among the finest in the church. To open this up again could only bring sorrow to many of our people."

I explained that, since the assignment was to be made, I felt that it would be to the advantage of the church to have it done by a member who had some understanding of our backgrounds, and some appreciation for our people.

When the interview closed, he shook hands with me and said, "The Lord bless you, Sister Brooks. I hope that you will be happy—permanently happy—with what you do."

"Thank you, President Smith," I said. "I would hate to do something that I would be ashamed of ten years from now."

He walked down the hall with me and shook hands with me again and said, "The Lord bless you." I have no words to say how moved and grateful I was.

You speak of my calling the unfortunate affair again to public attention. I did not think it had ever been out of public attention, especially since President Grant went before the Arizona legislature and protested the naming of the Lee's Ferry Bridge.[57] That really broke it wide open, this time within the Church, among the many friends and descendants of John D. Lee.

I wish you had time to read the reviews the book has had from across the nation, and the many letters I have received from active members of the church. Here is Southern Utah, where the essentials of the story have always been known, the reaction is always, "Why hasn't this been done before?"

Dear Brother Richards, do not judge me too harshly before all the evidence is in, or before you have examined what you have.

My sincere good wishes to you,

Source: WSU Levi Peterson Collection.

To *William R. Palmer*, August 14, 1952

St. George, Utah
August 14, 1952

Dear Brother Palmer:

Your letter just came and I was glad to get it, for it fills a gap in my pattern, like a missing piece of the puzzle. I'll have to explain more fully, I guess.

I knew that you had refused to review my book for the <u>Western Humanities</u>. So many others did, too, that they almost decided they could not get a panel. Stanley Ivins thought I leaned over backwards trying to be good to our people; I should have called them the robbers and murderers he thought they were. Maybe that last is too severe, but he told me and he told the group to whom he gave his review that. I understand that Mr. Kirkpatrick[58] of the University had the same feeling. Russell Swensen[59] also refused to write a review. I hold nothing against any of them for this. There is no reason why they should "stick out their necks" for me.

About the time he wrote you, Mr. Jonas wrote me also, asking about the same questions. I answered, maybe a little sharply, that the book would have to be its own defense, and suggested that he read it for the answers to his inquiry. He became acquainted with Ralph Hafen,[60] a former student of mine, and Ralph took me to his home for a visit. He had written letters almost like yours except for the first line, to Apostle Joseph Fielding Smith, Pres. Levi Edgar Young, Milton R. Hunter, and Preston Nibley. He gave me the form letter and all four of their answers.

Without going into detail, each one said that he had <u>Not</u> read my book. Milton R. Hunter went into most detail. Among other things he said:.... "Judge Reader from Ogden, Utah, talked to me rather in detail regarding this book about two weeks ago ... He is greatly disappointed regarding her approach and what she had published in the book. In fact, he was really stirred up over the matter. I ask all the members of the First Council of the Seventy in our meeting yesterday if any of them had read the book, and found that none of them had. I did find, however, that the majority of them had the same experience that I had the other day with Judge Reader." (This was under date of Feb. 2, 1951)

Preston Nibley said "It might surprise you to tell you that I cannot find anyone in this office or building who has read this book . . ."

Well, I could understand that. They are all busy, and many books are being written. Naturally they could not read them all. I had already learned that the page proofs were sent to Olive Wooley Burt months before, and that she had passed on to Brother Mark Peterson, but that Brother Reeder was assigned to make an evaluation and report.

Well, when the Warner Brothers manager telephoned and asked about making a moving picture, I went to Salt Lake City to consult with anyone who would talk to me. Naturally, I went first to Brother Reeder. He insisted that he knew nothing of any report that he did not know what I was talking about. I took a copy of the book from my brief case and handed it to him. He examined it carefully and said, "I have never seen this book." I did not press the matter too much, but I had a copy of Lee's diary covering the years of his excommunication from the church, and I read from it, in two or three places, Lee's defense of President Young and his firm declaration that the president DID NOT order the massacre and knew nothing about it until it was over. He seemed much impressed by the material I had, and finally said, "What I know about this subject I got from Brother Palmer of Cedar City." I told him that not two weeks before you had stood directly in front of me at the monument while we discussed it, and you had led me to think that you did not differ materially with my conclusions. This was in September following the visit from Cedar City.[61]

I thought then that I would come and talk to you but when I saw the scenario the movie people were preparing, no money in the world would have tempted me to be part of the undertaking. I had already told them that before the protests from Salt Lake City convinced them not to go on with the production.

Now as to your letter: The George Wood story I gave just as it was told to me. This I should not have done. I should at least have looked up the court case and trial. So your point there is well taken and the criticism is deserved. In the next edition I shall either omit or modify this footnote.[62]

The Bull Valley Snort story[63] was in the files at the Utah State Historical Society for years before I used it. The family had loaned it to me on the promise that I would keep it secret. Then I found it there, I was much surprised and asked how they got it. One said he thought you brought it in; another thought it came through Charles Kelly.

Without going into your letter point by point, I concede you the right to your opinion and judgment, even as you do me to mine. I did the best I could; I used the best judgment I had; I tried to be objective and honest, for I had no personal ax to grind. I know there are faults of one kind and another, but your own concluding paragraph is a very good summary of the thing I tried to put over—the attempt to see the deed against its background.

If I can get time, I may copy an excerpt or two from the Lee Journals to illustrate his attitude.

Thank you again for sending this to me.

Sincerely,

Source: WSU Levi Peterson Collection.

Chapter 5

1953–1956

Editing the John D. Lee Diaries

As the flurry surrounding the publication of *The Mountain Meadows Massacre* subsided to a degree, Juanita Brooks focused her attention on her next major project—the editing of the John D. Lee diaries. She met with Robert Cleland of the Huntington Library in January 1953 when he proposed that they collaborate on editing the five Lee diaries held by the library. He offered her a stipend of $150 per month for twenty-four months to edit four of the diaries. He would do the final one. She quickly accepted the offer and went immediately to work submitting manuscripts of two of the edited diaries by early 1954 and completing the final two in the summer of 1954. The diaries finally were published in two volumes in November 1955.[1] During the process, she again pressed for edited volumes of all the John D. Lee diaries and not just the ones housed at the Huntington Library. Her many letters concerning this editing effort reveal her persistent and untiring research methods in tracking down and comparing information to fill in missing details in Lee's life or to uncover one of his missing wives, a determination she employed in all her studies. Some of these letters vividly depict her adventures in searching out the principal locales associated with Lee, including the desolate and isolated sites of Lee's Ferry, where he sought seclusion in the face of possible arrest.

Brooks's letters exhibit her compassion and her inclusiveness with people from all sorts of backgrounds. One example arose from her indignation concerning the Short Creek raids on the polygamists in July 1953. Though not in agreement with their beliefs, she condemned the way the Arizona authorities raided the town, confiscated their property, and separated children from their mothers. She also strongly protested the attempt of the Utah authorities to separate polygamist Vera Black from her children, which led her to write critical letters to the editors of several Utah newspapers in 1956 denouncing that approach.

Her diverse friendships included the one she developed with J. Kenner Fancher, president of the Richard Fancher Society of America, the family whose members were among the victims of the Mountain Meadows Massacre. They first met in September 1955 when Brooks traveled to Harrison, Arkansas, and delivered a consolatory speech concerning the massacre at the dedication of a monument to the victims. Fancher wrote Brooks soon after that her "coming has done much to establish a spirit of love and forgiveness. The Mormon Church owes you much because now the people in this section feel much better toward the Mormon people."[2] They continued their friendly correspondence concerning the Mountain Meadows Massacre site and Arkansas history into the 1960s.

She often conveyed in her letters her sensitivities to the hand of Providence in her life and work. One such incident was her near-death experience in 1930, which she carefully detailed in several letters, including one to her sister Charity Rowley in 1953. She wrote that she had just lain down on a bed in her house in St. George when she became completely detached from her body. After a moment she was in her parents' house in Bunkerville observing her father and mother in their living room. Then she was back home and awake. She traveled to Bunkerville for Sunday dinner the next day and confirmed everything she had seen. She figured that her heart had stopped beating for a few seconds. An outside power she also attributed to guiding and facilitating her research; on many occasions she considered the discovery of some vital document or the delay in publication of her work until important information came to light the result of divine intervention. She felt, for example, that these intercessions postponed her Mountain Meadows Massacre book until new critical records were available.

The final interaction with a leading authority of the LDS Church over her Mountain Meadows Massacre book involved an exchange of letters with LeGrand Richards of the Quorum of Twelve Apostles in late 1955. As with the other authorities, Richards cautioned it would have been in the church's interest not to bring attention to the tragic history, even if her statements were correct. She responded that when the book first came out she predicted time would tell if her book was in the best interests of the church and to give it ten years. She noted that five years had passed since that prediction and recommended waiting the additional five to evaluate what she had done. Richards replied that he had defended the church all his life and would rather the topic would just die, but did agree to read the book. Richards's final letter to Brooks negatively reviewed her book, questioning her deductions and advising she should have followed repeated counsel to keep it quiet.

Among the historians and authors with whom she commenced an amiable interaction during this period were Mormon historian Leonard Arrington and novelist Virginia Sorensen. Arrington and Brooks wrote and commented on each other's studies, with Arrington always being particularly supportive of her efforts. After the appearance of the John D. Lee diary volumes, Arrington offered Brooks some comments and reflected that the diaries portray the "seamy side of humanity."[3] She replied saying that she grew up in a small town where "bickerings, fights over the water turn, quarrels about whose washing was whitest" were common and part of the "daily trivialities that fill many of our lives."[4] Writing to Sorensen, Brooks repeatedly congratulated her on her most recent novels, noting which ones she especially enjoyed and comparing them to her own early upbringing on the Mormon frontier.

In January 1956, Anthony Bentley, a BYU religion professor, sent Brooks a questionnaire requesting her opinion on "the place of creative thinking in the Church" for a discussion group he was heading.[5] She addressed many of the questions, revealing her thoughts on a number of topics. She argued, "We should bring the best we have to the consideration of every problem and accept what seems truth to us regardless of dictums from any authority."[6] Among her statements were that the church should encourage creative thinking, Mormons should accept friendly criticism of each other's opinion, and she always uses her American right and speaks her mind.

Brooks had the exciting opportunity to discuss the John D. Lee diaries on a Los Angeles television program, *Cavalcade of Books*, in February 1956. This appearance spotlighted her and brought a number of requests for literary submittals. Even the interviewer on the show, Turnley Walker, proposed working with her on a movie script for the Mountain Meadows Massacre. She responded that the copyright for the book still resided with

Stanford University Press and recommended not asking permission from the LDS Church. The project never materialized.

~

To *Robert G. Cleland*, January 19, 1953

St. George, Utah
January 19, 1953

Robert G. Cleland
Henry E. Huntington Library
San Marino 9, California

Dear Dr. Cleland:

Thank you for your letter of January 15. Naturally, I was pleased that the Trustees had approved the grant, and since it makes no difference to you, I think I should prefer the checks monthly.[7]

It is a relief to learn that the final draft of the diaries will likely be made there in the office. With that reassurance, I can go right ahead.

Will it be better to just indicate points where I must refer to the photostats, and after I have finished a volume, spend a few days there doing it, or would it be possible for me to have one photostat here while I work on the typescript, and refer to it as I go along? If you could consent to the latter, I am now on the 1857–1861 one. Unless you think I should send it in smaller units, I shall finish this before mailing it in. I mean, of course, I shall finish the initial draft.

Perhaps you should return the unit I mailed in, if you have time to look it over a bit and offer suggestions to guide me from here on. Otherwise, I shall keep working along until I do hear from you.

Sincere good wishes

To *Dale Morgan*, August 3, 1953

August 3, 1953

Dear Dale,

With our uncanny way of writing to each other about the same time, I had a letter to you in the machine when Will brought yours in with the mail. If I can put my hand on it in this week-end's accumulation, I'll include it.

Sorry you didn't make it this way. I had looked forward to a visit with you here. Maybe I'd have persuaded you to stop long enough to go out to Short Creek. But I mustn't get started on that, I get too angry at the methods of those Arizona officials.[8] Imagine bringing a convoy of 110 armed men—and I mean armed—with a unit of the National Guard and a whole gang of others out to take a group that would have been taken as easily by 3 or 4 or at most a half dozen. I doubt that there was a single gun in all Short Creek. All the rest of the great state of Arizona was certainly left wide open for criminals and gangsters!

How disappointed they must have been not to be able to go into the homes and yank the folks out of bed and frighten the children to death. To come in with all the array of battle and find their victims all out, gathered around the flag pole! What a let down to the publicity stunt!

Will had some dealings with these folks at the Hurricane Coop, and he developed a great respect for their honesty and industry. Their purchasing agent bought in bulk from him—flour, rice, beans, soap—all the staples. Of course they are fanatical on this matter of the plural family, and I don't want to preach the doctrine or live it myself. But I think this way of robbing them entirely of the fruits of more than 20 years work, and just as they are beginning to prosper a little. They have got some big equipment, taken some large road and lumber contracts, built at least 8 modern homes with electricity and water systems—Now the boast is that the fine will be so heavy that the state will confiscate the property of the entire village. Worst of all, they have taken the children away from the mothers to put them in an institution or to give then to foster parents . . . But why go on? Will suggests that they drown the younger ones as they would excess litters of cats, if they are so determined to manage families. . . .

But to something more pleasant—I did have a good visit with Fawn and her family. I like her husband very much. And aren't her kiddies grand? And last night Sterling McMurrin[9] and his were here enroute to Los Angeles, where he is to teach a short course at a summer school. I begin to see the advantages of living at a motel.

I am sending the part of Bleak Book B that is copied—approximately 60%. This is to be my copy when it is finished and bound, so feel free to annotate it as you wish.

Pearson Corbett lives at 149 East 300 South. He is at work on another biography, I understand. Don't know whose.[10]
Source: Dale L. Morgan Papers.

To *Charity Rowley*, September 29, 1953

Dear Charity,

I hardly know how to write the experience that I had for two reasons: it happened so long ago, and 2nd—I don't think I have ever told it again since I talked to you.[11] Still it is quite clear in my mind, and I'll do my best to tell it just as it was.

When you look at it one way, it really must not have been much. I'm sure it did not take more than a half-minute in time; it was just that things all seemed so clear, or my mental scope seemed so broad that it was as if in a flash I KNEW many things that it now takes time to tell.

It was in the spring of 1930 soon after I bought the house on the hill. On a Friday night, after a strenuous week, I walked up, arriving just after sunset. I was warm and a little tired and breathless, so I went into the tiny west bedroom and stretched out and relaxed completely. Then suddenly it was as if I were out of my body—I don't know whether above or beside or what, but detached completely so that I knew that I was there and my body was there on the bed, the mouth slightly open and the eyes not quite closed. My only sensation was one of wonder and surprise, as if I would say, "Well, so this is what it is like to be dead! I had no idea it would be like this! Now isn't this strange!"

In the same thought was that Francis would soon be there, I seemed to know he was even then coming up the hill, and how surprised he would be to find me thus. And would they hold two funerals, one at St. George and one at Bunkerville? And then bury me at Mesquite beside Ernest?

I don't know how to explain other than that I felt no worry about it, or sorrow, or trouble. I didn't seem to really care. This was what had happened; this was how it was; and other developments did not seem to matter a great deal.

Then in a flash I was at home in the front room. In the same instantaneous way I seemed to think of this big house once so full now all included in one room. The lamp wick was crooked, and the chimney a bit blacked on one side. Mother was stirring Lumpy-Dick[12] in a skillet on some coals pulled out to the edge of the fireplace; Daddy was shaking some cream in a 2-quart jar. It was just dusk outside, and again it seemed that I knew of their sorrow when they should hear about me. But at the instant Daddy said, "The Old Bitch would have killed her if I hadn't got there in time."

Then without knowing why or how, I was back, the heart had evidently picked up its beat and I took a deep breath and sat up on the edge of the bed. Just then I heard Francis come in at the front door and through the house to the bedroom. He took one look at me and said, "For heaven's sake, what is the matter?" "I've been dead," I said, and described the incident as fully as I could.

We both chalked it up against a strange experience, and thought little of it. The next evening Stan Pulsipher and several others called to visit a bit, and asked if we'd like to ride home with them to spend Sunday. The car was so crowded that Francis had to hold me on his lap all the way. I don't remember that this was mentioned at all on the way down, but when I went into the house, I said, "Well, mother, I see you haven't washed the lamp chimney since last night." Then I told her and Daddy about it, and learned that what Pa was talking about was that one horse had another against the manger and was kicking it, until he went out and separated them, and that things there were just as I had seen them.

I tried to figure this out, but can only conclude that for a few seconds my heart stopped beating, and then in the normal course of things began again. There was nothing more spectacular than that—no "Guardian Angel" or other personage, no being carried to another world, not any wish to go or to stay—Only a sense of wonder and surprise that this is how it is, only a feeling that to the spirit, which is fully alive and conscious, space is nothing, and a feeling in seeing things in an over-all, instant, inclusive way, such as is not possible in life. A seeing with the understanding rather than with the physical sight of the eyes, if you get what I mean.

I should have written this down immediately. At the time, I told a few people, and I never go into the presence of death since without a different attitude. Now, after all these years, I begin to wonder about details—I feel sure that it was Francis rather than Dudley who was with me, then when I begin to figure, I'll have to look up some record to be exactly certain. I do know that it was in the spring of 1930, though, for that is when I bought the place on the hill . . .

Source: WSU Levi Peterson Collection.

To *A. Russell Mortensen*,[13] December 14, 1953

St. George, Utah
December 14, 1953

Dear Dr. Mortensen:

I write for several reasons, which I'll try to stay with, rather than to enter into any discussion of our local school prospects, etc., in which I am currently so interested.

First, here's a picture and a brief sketch of Thomas D. Brown, sent from George A. Brown, 2222 North, 13 Street, Phoenix. He is very much interested in having the "Journal" published, and thinks that Mrs Fonnesbeck or some others of the family can fill in further information.

Second, I am mailing the first installment of Evans Coleman's (Box 113, Thatcher, Arizona) Missionary Reminiscences.[14] While not history in a technical sense, this represents an interesting and different approach to that phase of Mormon culture. If you do not feel that it is worth copying for our files, ship it back to me and I'll see if I can't get it done here. He wants a copy.

Third, Regarding this "Branch of the Historical Society"—I've talked to Albert Miller, H.L. Reid, and Karl Larson,[15] all of whom think it would be an interesting thing to do, but none of whom want to lead out and spear-head it. Perhaps after the first of the year I can do something about it myself in a more active way. I'm a little behind in my Huntington assignment, enough so that I'm burning the before-daylight oil consistently. I am scheduled to go down to the Library either during the holiday season or immediately following it.

As I see it, I must either do something about this or resign from the Board—neither of which I want to do. Unless I can have something started before the next meeting, I'll write in my resignation.

This Lee material grows more and more interesting. My first duty, I think, is to have it done on schedule, so that it may get into print about a year from now. I find that the time slips along, and one little distraction today which does not seem so very important, leads to a whole brood of them tomorrow and the next week, until finally they swarm around my head like angry bees each demanding attention. I mean things like giving a Literary Lesson in Relief Society, with all its attendant meetings, an Extension class from the University to teach, a club committee, Etc. Sometimes I feel that one more complication & I'll do like the old Tramp who lay sleeping under the tree who patiently permitted the gnats and flies and ants to explore his face until, a bee lit on his nose and stung it. "Now just for that, you'll all have to move," he said, and with one angry swoop cleared out the whole outfit. . . .

Good luck and good wishes. I'm constantly more happy that you are where you are.

To *Robert G. Cleland*, February 16, 1954

St. George, Utah
February 16, 1954

Dr. Robert G. Cleland
Henry E. Huntington Library
San Marino 9, California

Dear Dr. Cleland:

Since my return home, I have been spending some time on the John D. Lee materials which the Lee family have copied from the L.D.S. Church Archives. They are very interesting, I think, and would make a decided addition to what we have. Our problem is one of getting consent to use them of course.

While Mrs. Henrie insists that Bro. Joseph Fielding Smith released them to her with the comment that the family might print them if they cared to, I doubt that he would ever give permission in writing. One or two alternatives suggest themselves:

1—Ignore them, and let the Lee family publish them if and when they wish.

2—Persuade the Lee families to get a microfilm, which they would certainly give to us.

3—Let Mr. Bliss ask for a microfilm of these in exchange for some of the material there that Mr. Preston Nibley or others may want.

In the meantime, here is a summary of what they are:

1—Lee's first Mission January 31, 1841, to July 18, 1841, a copy of which you have there.[16]

2—Lee's Second Mission May 28, 1844 to August 20, 1844.[17] This is some 50 typed pages long, with a summary of six pages which brings him up to November 1844.

3—Camp of Israel Journal, with a note on the fly-leaf: A book containing Plan and Inventory of All the camp of the Saints Also the circumstances connected with Exodus from Nauvoo the City of Joseph West through the wilderness in search of home and place of rest.
By John D. Lee[18]
This consists of 110 typed pages and covers the period from February 1, 1846 to August 28, 1846, and gives an excellent picture of the methods of organizing the people and the problems attending the mass move.

3—Mormon Battalion Journal August 20, 1846 to Nov. 19, 1846, a day-by-day account of his trip to Santa Fe for the Mormon Battalion money.[19] (Incidentally, the Kelly excerpt[20] begins on Nov. 21, just two days later, and goes until July 23, 1847, with a 6-months lapse before our first one begins Feb 1848)

Whether we publish them or not, I intend to study them carefully and refer to them in footnotes. By using date reference instead of page, I can do that.

It was good to visit the Library again and to go over some of this material with you. I'd like to see it shape up for publication as soon as possible, and shall work to that end.

I include my expense account on this same page.

Thank you so much for your kindness to me.

Sincerely,

To *Robert G. Cleland*, June 12, 1954

St. George, Utah
June 12, 1954

Dr. Robert G. Cleland
Henry E. Huntington Library
San Marino, California

Dear Dr. Cleland:

This week I have been to Lee's Ferry and the Lonely Dell. I was asked to speak of his experiences there to a group of some 200 of his descendants who had gathered there for family reunion.[21] The meeting was held in the trees just south of the house now occupied by Mr. and Mrs. Griffen, the owners of the ranch.[22]

At this place two log cabins still stand which were built by John D. Lee. There is an outline of a rock foundation of another house said to have been his, and the rock cellar still in use. Whether the home occupied by Griffens was built around a one-room place of his, no one seems to know. It was either built or remodeled by the Johnson family[23] who ran the ferry after Lee's death.

Some two and a half miles from the Dell are the rock houses; two or three that look as if they had been homes are falling into decay, as is the rock fort built in 1874 by men sent out by Brigham Young to protect the crossing at that place. Above them are three or four modern houses occupied by people who are employed to make recordings of the river. We saw one man and his wife, but did not talk to them, and the sign on the gate GOVERNMENT PROPERTY KEEP OUT was not inviting.

The pagination of my Confessions[24] is not the same as yours, so I have not located the exact quote you use. I wonder if he refers to the time in 1848, when a number of his wives and adopted sons left him … During his time in prison he keeps in touch with Rachel, Sarah Caroline, Emma, Polly and Lavina—he even records writing one letter to Terressa.[25] Anne left him immediately after his excommunication … But we can go through most of these things together when I come down.

I have the footnoting almost finished. Sometime within the next week or so I'd like to check some items in Provo and Salt Lake City, and then perhaps we can get down to the business of seeing what to do with fill-in material, etc. My problem is chiefly to know what to do with these footnotes—how much to include and what to leave out. If I'm not careful, I'll have the tail wagging the dog …

It's good to be back at it in earnest again and to see that making some headway.

Sincere good wishes,

Source: Juanita Brooks Papers.

To *Dale Morgan*, August 11, 1954

St. George, Utah
Wednesday. Aug 11, 1954

Dear Dale:

Move over and get yourself comfortable. I'm in the mood to visit. To your question, how am I doing with the John D. Lee annotation, I must say that for this short 1873–1874 Diary when he is across the Colorado among the Navajo's, living at what he calls Mow E abba, I can do little. The Indians appear on every page; Old Mr. Windburn who has a malignant foot infection which stinks; Jacob Hamblin, who is the villain, and occasional prospectors are all the humans who cross his pages. Oh, yes, Rachel does come and brings with her six small children and he builds a rock house 34 by 17 feet. Come to think of it. Quite a few interesting things happen in the 10 months that he lives there—with a couple of visits back to the Dell and on into the settlements.

The Lee–Hamblin–Indian incidents are not as they are told in Little's book[26] exactly. In fact, so disgusted did Lee become with Hamblin that he wrote a long letter to Brigham Young setting forth the facts as he saw them. Said letter was dated March 15, 1874. How I'd like to see the original! Would it be in the letter books of B.Y., I wonder? And if so, who can I get to spirit out a copy?

Lee keeps in touch with B.Y. by way of A.F. MacDonald,[27] the clerk at St. George. His last personal visit—at least that I have record of—was made on April 5, 1874, before he was taken prisoner the next November 7. Of it, he says, "washed & shaved, then roade horse back to Prest B Y at home—who received me with kindness of a Father, introduced me to the company & had his wives & Family come & shake hands with me; ordered my Horse put up on the Barn & fed & had me partake of a splendid supper with him as the guest. The table was furnished with everything that the country could afford, from oyster soup down to hull corn & milk, or Mormon rice . . ." Lee drew out the route to the San Juan and advised the president as to the settlement of Arizona, etc., then went with the group the next day as far as Belleview.[28] Oh, yes, and on his way in he had preached to the saints at the Pahreah settlement[29] . . .

I've had a good time trying to straighten out some of the marriages. Have about decided that I do as well to follow my own intuition. For example: I was interested in what happened to his wife Martha Berry.[30] While he mentioned often his son William Orson and always added, "by my wife, Martha Berry," and occasionally his daughters Harriet Josephine and Thurza,[31] whom he identified in the same way, he made no reference to their mother. He stopped at the home of Mother Berry at Kanarra and also of William Berry.[32] Martha's elder brother. So I reasoned that she must have left him for another man. Then once he mentioned an Elder Dennis Dority,[33] who had said that he (Lee) had always treated him like a gentleman. That is the man I said to myself.

In the paper I saw that one Aunt Vina Berry had just celebrated her 100th birthday, so I called on her. She sat as straight as a ram-rod, and was sharp enough, except that she was a little deaf. I asked about Martha Berry, her niece. "She left Lee back at Winter Quarters, and never had another thing to do with him," she insisted. Two or three times during the conversation she asked suddenly, "What you trying to do? You're not trying to make a good man out of that old reprobate, are you?"

I knew better than to argue with a woman who has lived a hundred years, especially when she is hard of hearing. She admitted that Martha's mother tried to persuade her not to leave Lee. She could remember only the three children I named, and said that the girls lived with their grandma Berry, and William Orson must have died. I didn't explain, but I had the record of where Lee baptized this young man when he was 22, in the Colorado River. Yes, Martha had remarried, she said, but she couldn't remember the name of the man, since she had not met him. "Could it have been Dennis Dority?" I asked. Her old face lighted. "That's him, and they had a daughter Roxey who married a Hall in Provo." So, anyway, I now have her full history, including 5 children by Lee and 6 by Dority. She evidently left soon after the MMM, for the last Lee child was born in 1856 and the first Dority one in late 1858.

This gal Ann Gordge[34] intrigued me. In the first place, the name is unusual; I could not find it in any of the regular places. From the 1870 census I found a wife Ann G. age 26 b. Australia, children Samuel J. age 3, and Mareb E. age 2.[35] This last name was so dim that I thought it might be <u>Mark</u> E.

Early I noted that Lee wrote on the same day letters to his two daughters Sarah Jane Dalton and Mary Adoline Darrow—and one to Mareb Philips. I tried to guess if this was a daughter I did not know, or perhaps a girl he was courting. Then he stayed at the home of Father John Philips at Beaver on one trip, and on another he called on Ann's mother at Beaver. I didn't connect the two until after he had moved to the Dell and Ann had left him, and sent the two older children, Samuel James and Mareb Emma to him to raise. Now, after two letters, I learn that Ann's father, Samuel Gordge, was drowned before they left Australia; that and her brother David came with the mother to Utah; that the mother, Merrib, was married to John Philips in California enroute.[36] Of course I still must find much in the way of dates and details, also who married her after she left John D. and what additional family she had.[37] She evidently kept her baby, John Doyle. But I will get it eventually!

As I said before, she interested me from the few mentions he made—first, she stayed snugly in bed in the wagon when they were camped out in mid-winter, while he got fingers and toes frost-bitten gathering wood and getting a fire. Later when one John Lawson[38] came to trespass on their lot and cut the willows and under-growth along the creek near her place, she and Emma[39] attacked him with boiling water, finally pounced onto him, and when the men-folks came, they had him down, Ann with one hand in his hair and the other pommeling his face. At another time she and Emma got into a fracas that Lee himself had to come to settle. Still—she did name her little girl for her mother and Emma—who, it seems, raised the child. So many, many things must be left untold!

Well, enough of this kind of gossip. I just wanted to give you some idea of how I have been entertaining myself lately.

I am sorry about your books.[40] You're fortunate if the insides are not all eaten out as well. Way back in the 1930's when I was going through the records in our court house, I found a type of termite which left the outside intact, but burrowed through and devoured the inside. Be thankful yours were not of this order.

You're right about the 1848 Lee excerpts. I hardly think Dr. Cleland would consent to their use until after they are in print. That should be right after the first of the year. He is summering at a ranch in Montana, and has asked me to meet him at the Library on October 1 for a final checkup. (I hope to have mine finished well before that time.)

I wish I could persuade Dr. Cleland to include the 1846 fragment that the Lee family secured from the Church. Did I ever let you see it? Would you like to? It begins "About 1st of Feb. 1846" to Dec. 7, 1846.[41] I think it is highly significant. I don't know whether Dr. Cleland is afraid it might anger the Church (though A. Will Lund gave a written permission for the Lee family to print any or all of the journals) or whether he is just too tired to want to be troubled by it. I think it's a shame to leave it out. The one—The Iron County Mission—has already been published, as you know, and Russ says later that he can perhaps use the Mormon Battalion mission one, too. But this is different.

Yes, the Bleak Book B. is finished, and I have my copy. I'll try to get around to mailing it to you right away.

I'm ashamed not to have read Isn't One Wife Enough?[42] Here it sits on my shelf, and I've hardly looked inside it. Seems that life is full of a number of things—only this morning I got out with the boys to encourage a campaign against the weeds, and was digging in a bit by way of demonstration, when a wasp attacked me—just struck with such lightning speed that I didn't know what hit the knuckle of my thumb. I'd forgotten how one of those things can hurt! This afternoon the back of my right hand looks like a boxing glove.

And now in about a half hour, I have a dental appointment. Which means that I must gird up my loins and march down there right away. As the Chinese(?) say, "Even this must pass."

Bye for now.

To *Virginia Sorensen*, October 15, 1954

October 15, 1954

Dear Virginia,

I have just finished The House Next Door,[43] and to say that I enjoyed it is putting it mildly. I loved your little heroine; she was so alive and human, with her own keen insight and original expressions. Luckily you slurred over the trip south, which in that day would have involved such long, long wagon trips and such a varied experience in either camping out or lodging with families. For your story, you really said enough, though.

It is a story young people will enjoy, girls especially, and it gave me an entirely new impression of what this series, "The Strength of the Union" is to be.[44] Nevada for this series poses something of a problem, first because its birth was so premature as to be almost abortive. So few people, so much empty land. The first Territorial Legislature, for example, met upstairs in a stone hotel, in a large room kept for dances and meetings. A canvas wagon-cover stretched across the room divided one house of the Legislature from the other.

The Mormons entered into the earliest settlement, the very first town of all, Genoa, being a Mormon settlement in 1855. The same year a group of missionaries built a fort at Las Vegas, but with the coming of the army and the "Mormon War" all these people were recalled to Salt Lake City. By 1861 when Nevada was declared a Territory, the center of activity was the Virginia City–Carson City area, with a population of miners chiefly. Even in 1864, when it was declared a state, it was—well, let's see: the 1860 census listed 6,857; by 1870 it was 42,491.

What I'm trying to say is that Nevada presents a problem all its own if the focus is to be on the coming in to statehood. I'm not sure that the first-person approach would be best unless the character were a prospector—or a teen-age boy who was a friend of Mark Twain; for example. That just might be an idea now.

I didn't mean to get started on this. It just sort-of oozed out of the machine.

I had a letter from Erick Berry[45] (I thought she was a man!) just as I was really burning the midnight oil on this Huntington business, so I haven't answered as yet. I shall this afternoon, maybe. She is doubtful of my ability to do this, as I am myself.

It's so good to have this stack delivered to Dr. Cleland. I feel like Atlas with the world rolled off my shoulders. He seemed much pleased with what I had done, but he also seemed not-so-well physically, and I'm concerned to push the thing to publication before anything happens to him. I hadn't thought of him as being an older man, but a heart attack has left him looking drained of energy. My Rockfeller grant expires on Jan. 1, and I'm determined to be through before that time.

Oh, yes, I'm a member of the library board here, with a meeting at 7:30 this evening. I'm taking both this House Next Door and

Many Heavens[46] with me and see that they are ordered. Also the whole STRENGTH OF THE UNION series. Our librarian is a lovely lady, but a political appointee who has never been (and is not now) a reader; so she has had a half-dozen of us appointed to help her make book selections for the library.

I'll have to take a day off and tell you of the varied reactions I've met with Many Heavens. I believe I myself enjoyed The Evening and the Morning[47] best of all your books, but this was fascinating, too. I can well understand why the Church would clamp its lips close together and shake its head over it. The Fundamentalist group must learn of it; they'd have it in every home. They should, too.

I'm so thrilled over your Guggenheim! Really, I don't think I had heard of it before. My dear, what a marvelous, wonderful thing! My heels fairly itch to get to Europe, but of course that can never be for me. My daughter Willa (do you remember her) is at the Y for her first winter away from home. The three boys, with all their different interests and problems, keep life interesting at home.

Fae Ollerton Tarlock[48] and her husband and son called the other day—the first time I have seen her in 17 years! It was good to visit again with her. I was surprised, though, to have her say that among some group somewhere I was considered a bit of a heroine because I refused to sell my Mountain Meadows Massacre to Warner Brothers. There's a long story behind that! And it wasn't loyalty to the Church that prevented the sale; it was loyalty to the integrity of the book itself. Their script was the worse possible distortion.

Yes, Mr. Musser died, and from what I hear, his wife is as foggy as ever. The patriarch of the Short Creek clan died also, but the younger men seem to be carrying on. The state of Arizona still holds the wives and children of those who live on the Arizona side of the line, while those in Utah seem to be quite secure for the time being. Their test case didn't work out too well.[49] The judge ordered 7 of Mrs. Vera Johnson Black's children taken away from her because she refused to sign the papers he had. They were to be scattered in foster homes; because the baby was not yet two years old, she could keep him. But Judge Dunford[50] reversed the decision and gave the children back. Now a family of 3 wives and 17 children has bought a big old home here in St. George, just a block east of the Post Office.

How I do run on! Bless you for being so good to me. Go right ahead and write your Masterpiece, now—another masterpiece, perhaps I should say.

Love,

To *LeGrand Richards,*[51] November 29, 1955

St. George, Utah
November 29, 1955

Elder LeGrande Richards
47 East South Temple
Salt Lake City, Utah

Dear Brother Richards:

I hope you will not censure Brother Donald P. Seegmiller[52] for showing me your letter regarding me and my book, The Mountain Meadows Massacre. After all, I have known and worked with Don for many years. He seemed much disturbed by your letter and its implications.

Your reference to "my church" prompted this reply. Anyone who knows me will tell you that I have always been active in the Church: MIA Ward President, MIA Stake Board, Stake S.S. Board, Stake Pres. of Relief Society. I financed, practically alone, a brother and a sister on missions; we have sent two sons on missions and have three more growing up to go. I went to the Temple just last Saturday. So what I said in my Preface is the literal truth.

You referred to Page 161 of the book. To deny the truth of my statement there is only to admit that you have not read the speeches of that turbulent time. Some students of the period, even among our own people, say that I bent over backwards trying to select my quotes. Certainly I could have found many more violent than any I used.

I do not want to judge, Brother Richards, but I have the feeling that you have never really read the book, very similar in other letters. If I am wrong, I apologize, but I think a careful reader might have found other things to criticize.

After I had accepted this assignment, I had a long talk with President George Albert Smith. As I left, he shook my hand and said,

"The Lord bless you, Sister Brooks, I hope you are happy—permanently happy—about what you do." I worked in the spirit—that in the long run there is no substitute for the truth. I think it is an insult to my Maker to be expedient instead of intellectually honest.

Letters I have received from members of the church, especially from the faculty of the B.Y.U. and our other universities, as well as LDS educators throughout the nation, sustain me in my belief that I have done my church a real service.

I wish there had been just ONE Elder present at my talk before the Fancher family reunion in Arkansas on Sept. 4, 1955,[53] to bear witness to the reaction of the audience. This talk will be published in the January issue of the Utah Historical Quarterly, if you are interested in seeing it.[54]

Sincere good wishes,

Source: WSU Levi Peterson Collection.

To *LeGrand Richards*, December 5, 1955

St. George, Utah
December 5, 1955

Bro. LeGrand Richards
47 East South Temple
St. George, Utah

Dear Brother Richards:

Thank you for your letter of November 30, which I shall file with the answers to the form letter sent out by Prof. Frank H. Jonas in early 1951, and other correspondence on this subject.[55]

Re: the man with the red nose. Seems that if he had a mirror, no one would need to tell him of it. He could see plainly enough for himself.

When my book, The Mountain Meadows Massacre, first came out, it was hard not to be bitter when it was condemned by people who had not even seen the outside cover. But after my interview with Brother Reeder, I was able to live above bitterness, and I had voluntarily turned down a movie contract—Before the Authorities started to protest—I decided to let time settle the question for me.

I received so many letters similar to the one enclosed. The only one that was critical came from Brother Albert R. Lyman of Blanding, Utah. He had read the book, and his right to disagree I respected. I know that he is a good, sincere man; his Friendship for my husband and for one of my sisters who lives there has lasted for many years. I answered him about like this:

"Let us not quarrel about this, Brother Lyman. You think I have injured my church; I think I have done it a great service. Let us wait ten years before we make a final decision. In the meantime, I wish you well."

Five years have passed since that. Let us wait five more, Brother Richards, and then evaluate this again. I am cheered by the fact that the BYU has had it for sale, that some classes in Church History have it listed on their reading list, that it is being read more today than it was when it first came out, and with favorable reaction.

Best wishes for the Christmas Season. May the spirit of Him whose day we commemorate be in your heart and in your home.

Sincerely your sister,

Source: WSU Levi Peterson Collection.

To *Leonard Arrington*,[56] December 28, 1955

St. George, Utah
Dec. 28, 1955

Dear Leonard Arrington,

Thank you so much for your letter Re: the Lee Diaries.[57] I'm always grateful, when anyone reads my work, and doubly grateful when I get criticism and suggestions.

First, your reaction to the "narrowness and littleness of it" interested me. I had thought that it was typical of the daily trivialities that fill many of our lives, that if I were to write faithfully at the end of every day, might record some differences and misunderstandings—more perhaps if I were weary when I set myself down to write. I grew up in a small town where there were just such bickerings, fights over the water turn, quarrels about whose washing was whitest, differences between the bishop and ward members. There were times when Lee spoke well of his associates and times when he really praised them. Of President Brigham Young he certainly always had a good word.

I like your idea that the accounts finally get beyond the Mormon and the non-Mormon. I think Lee gains more stature after he is in jail than he had before. I wish we had the account from him of his three months of freedom before his final trial, when he himself became convinced (according to his family) that he would have to pay the price.

On the same mail with your letter came one from a Michael Harrison, 4216 T Street, Sacramento 19, Calif. with his summary and reaction. Among other things, he says: "After reading the Diaries, I have an altogether different opinion of John Doyle Lee. What a rock! There are few men who would have clung to their faith as he did, in the face of excommunication and the turning against him of his friends and neighbors." So you see, we see it differently. And that is as it should be, I think. I give you this man's address because he is interested in history and has some rare books in which you might also find interest.

As to the silk industry.[58] I stand corrected. I should have qualified my note by some such phrase as "in this area" or "in Southern Utah." From all I can find in the minutes of conferences and Relief Society, President Young talked of "textiles" in general in 1872, and not until 1874 were silk worms introduced. The Relief Society took on the Project in 1875. Or I really should have learned more of the general background of the mulberry tree before I left the note. That was a plain case of slip-shod scholarship.

As to the other errors you mention, it is small comfort to me to check my carbon and find that I sent it in as <u>A.R.</u> Mortensen. (My list of acknowledgments were fused with his there at the office.) I hadn't noticed the one regarding Gustive Larson's writing in 1847, and now that I look for it, I find that I don't know where it is and the name is not in the index!

I am more disturbed by some omissions of material which I wrote or rather the way some of the "fill-in" material was compressed than by individual errors—but of this shall not write now because my household is beginning to stir and I must serve breakfast and get them on their various assignments. We'll talk about some of these things when you are here.

Which reminds me, I do hope you stop enroute to Huntington Library. Will you have the family along? We'd like to have you come and stay with us. We're not hard to find in St. George—just turn right toward the hill when you reach the only semaphore in town. We are first on top of the hill—a red stone house with large trees in front. We'll look forward to seeing you.

Sincere good wishes,

To *Anthony Bentley*,[59] February 2, 1956

St. George, Utah
Feb. 2, 1956

Mr. Anthony I. Bentley
Brigham Young University
Provo, Utah

Dear Mr. Bentley:

I am much interested in your topic for discussion before the Division of Religion faculty of the "Y".[60] I shall answer your questions as fully and frankly as I can, in spite of the fact that some friends warn me that this just might be a trap and that I could be called to answer in person before a higher group.

1—I like your statement of the topic, and am cheered that it should be brought out for open discussion. I have always insisted that we not only sell ourselves short but we insult our Maker when we do not use the highest faculties He has given us. We should bring the best we have to the consideration of every problem and accept what seems truth to us regardless of dictums from any authority. By "the best we have" I include not only mental faculties but spiritual intuition. Nor would I exclude the possibility of possible re-examination and modification of a conclusion or stand.

Unless we use that part of us which makes us distinctively men, we do not live on the plane of men. If we put on blinders or refuse to see or consider a problem, if we allow ourselves to be mental automans pulled by the intellectual strings of others, we certainly cannot realize our own full growth.

2—I think the Church should encourage creative thinking in every field, not with the idea of accepting what comes out of it, but of creating a more alert and productive society. I have said often that the ones at the top are and should be as much affected "by what seeps up from below as by what comes down from above." I think I made that observation first when the Welfare Plan was being initiated and we here in Dixie were a part of the general experimentation.

3—I'm really not in a position to answer this one very fully so far as the General Authorities as a whole is concerned. There are groups within the framework of the Church where there is a bit of yeast at work, where creative thinking is respected and encouraged.

4—I have to pass this by, too. I know what problems the Leaders must have in trying to work for the Church as a whole. There is always a sort of "lunatic fringe" attending any large group, and on the opposite extreme some ultraconservatives who want to admit no change, so that to steer a course for the body of so large an organization is a challenging task, I imagine.

5—I'm not the proper person, I'm afraid, to advise anyone else as to how to add to his freedom and security. I continue to express myself freely as a part of my American right. Perhaps if my position or income were threatened by this, I would be more careful. Within the bounds of the Church, I have protested repeatedly to the taking of the music from the Sacrament service. To me, that service has lost in beauty and meaning by the emptiness which now points up every irrelevant sound. My criticisms have been made only locally, however. The same goes for the regimentation of the deacons, or making their work more like a military drill than a passing of the emblems of the Last Supper of our Lord. As to my protesting the treatment of the Fundamentalists in our midst, I continue, because I think our attitude is far from the spirit of the Christ. (In our area they are excluded from all Church organizations and activities, while we send missionaries out to gather in other converts no more desirable.) The taking of Vera Johnson Black's children from her I consider the most wicked thing that has been done in our state since the Mountain Meadows Massacre, and I shall continue to write and speak in condemnation of it—though I learn that at least two editors say that they dare not publish my letters.

6—If most Mormons would adopt the attitude that honest, friendly criticism of each other's opinion would contribute to a sense of security of us all, I think we would have a much more vital, productive society. Certainly it would be a great incentive to creative effort. The fact of having your efforts and ideas recognized, whether they are accepted or not, would be most stimulating. I think most of us would welcome honest criticism—we don't want uncritical praise nor unqualified condemnation.

6—Your last statement is beautifully made, I think, so far as our personal problems are concerned. Within our own small area of research or study, we can well be guided by some such creed. With regard to church-wide policies or activities, those responsible could also do well to adopt the same general attitude. In my opinion, most of the revelations of the Prophet came as a result of his own efforts in applying his mind most vigorously to the problem at hand and placing himself in such a position that he could and did invite the Spirit of God to direct his final conclusion.

***

I wonder now if this is at all what you want, or if it will be helpful to you in any way. I'm glad for the opportunity to sort of crystallize my own thinking, but have had to just knock this out without much time to compose and none to rewrite.

The best of luck to you in your discussion. Would it be too much to hope that you might sometime tell me about it—the general reaction to your premises, for example?

Sincerely,

To *Mr. Hansen*, February 6, 1956

St. George, Utah
Feb. 6, 1956

Dear Mr. Hansen:

Thank you so much for your letter, and for the copy of your write-up on the polygamy question.[61] I am sure mine was published only because I happened to know the editor personally and wrote him about it. I had sent protests to other papers, but none had been used. I heard indirectly that one editor said he dare not print it.

I am glad that you found my book on the Mountain Meadows massacre interesting enough to read. I truly did spend a lot of time gathering the evidence, and I tried to consider every thing I found without leaving out any or covering up any facts.

You say that you wonder I have not been cut off the Church before this. My people here in the South treat me very well, and I don't think many of the Authorities have read the book.

You may be interested to know that I will appear on TV next Sunday, Feb. 12, channel 2 out of Los Angeles, The Columbia Broadcasting System, on the Program called "The Cavalcade of Books." I think I will have only a very short time to speak, but some man will review this last book (or set of books, for it has two quite large volumes) and then probably ask me some questions. The book is really the diaries of John D. Lee, but the main title is called A Mormon Chronicle.

Yes, I am married and have a family, but I have always just used my own name to save my good husband any embarrassment about the things I write. He is a very good church member and a wonderful husband and father, and usually approves what I do, but I thought it would be easier all around if I just used my own name to sign my work.

Thank you so much for writing

Sincerely,

To *Turnley Walker*,[62] February 16, 1956

St. George, Utah
Feb. 16, 1956

Turnley Walker
3671 Alomar Drive
Sherman Oaks, Calif.

Dear Mr. Walker:

I'm glad you are going ahead with an agreement with your agent, for I think I can clear everything. But let me give you full details, so that there shall be no misunderstanding.

Section 8 of my contract—signed August 3, 1949—reads: "That she hereby grants to the publishers serial, translation, stage production, motion picture, television rights of said work, the net proceeds from the sale of such rights to be divided as follows: fifty per cent to the author and fifty per cent to the publishers."

Section 19 says: "That when in the judgment of the publishers the public demand for said work is no longer sufficient to warrant its continued manufacture and sale, the publishers may in writing offer to transfer to the author the work and their rights in the copyright thereon, the bound copies and the sheet stock..."

The movie deal with Warners fell through in November, 1951. Mr. Foy told them, as he did me, that the material was public domain and they didn't have to ask for the rights at all, but thought to protect themselves from future trouble.

In June 1952 Stanford wrote (June 5, to be exact) "You will be interested to know that a second printing of The Mountain Meadows Massacre may be in order in a few months...." and there followed one letter from me with a few suggested changes. For example, no one so far as I know, had ever caught up with a title in the bibliography, A Summer's Journey which I had written A Sinner's Journey. Besides that, I had some few additions to make, but they seemed to be ready to go to work on the second edition at once.

Then after some delay they wrote saying that they would not put out another edition, so did I want the ms. Returned or destroyed. I had it returned. As I understand the law, copyright privileges expire at the end of seven years.

Even at that, the material is still public property. Or suppose I should have published in the meantime the Biography of Lee upon which I have been at work. Might we not base our script upon that instead. I've not been able to settle my choice of title yet, but I think that will come as I move into that last period while he is in the wilds along the Colorado and after he is in prison.

As to the attitude of the Mormon Church, I think we should go ahead with the movie. When I asked before about such a project, I was told that they could not give approval in advance, but would be glad to offer suggestions when the script was done.

Well, I don't think we should be tied by their suggestions or help. If I had told them or asked their advice, they would certainly have stopped publication of the book in the first place. Some few of the older ones still resent it, but I am cheered by its reception among influential younger ones. Among the professors at the Brigham Young University for example, and among teachers of their religious Seminarys and Institutes the book is accepted and recommended.

So I'd say, if you want to do it, and if you feel that it is material for a good moving picture, go ahead and make what arrangements you can, and get right at it. Work quietly, though, until it is about ready for final acceptance. Even then DO NOT ask permission of the Church. They will in that way be relieved of any responsibility in the matter, which will be best all around.

Re-reading your letter now, I see that I have not answered the part about Warner's. As I told you, I had already refused to OK the script Mr. Foy showed me. I enclose the letter Mr. Bean wrote about it.

It was really a privilege to meet you and work with you for a few minutes. I hope we may be mutually helpful to each other.

Very sincerely,

To *Ettie Lee*, February 28, 1956

St. George, Utah
Feb. 28, 1956

My dear Miss Lee,

The mail today brought a set of photostats from Stanley S. Ivins[63] which I know you would be interested in. They are three petitions for the release of John D. Lee after his conviction. I have made a typed copy, but I shall be glad to send you the originals if you care to see the handwriting and the signatures. I have noted that one has 181 names signed, a second identical in wording with the first, carries 262 names, and a third shorter one seems to have the names of all the people of Greenville,[64] Beaver County, Utah.[65]

I was especially interested because the reasons given for his release are almost identical with the conclusions I had arrived at from my study: that he was only one of many and not the most responsible one, that the situation was complicated by many things, that the fact that the whole territory was under military law made the act one of war, etc.etc. But more important still, I think, is the bit of the letter which shows that after his conviction he could still have had his freedom if he had chosen to talk. That he voluntarily chose death instead makes him, in my mind, a person of heroic stature.

I do not know whether Stanley is sending these for me to keep or just to look at and copy, but I am writing to ask that I may pay for them and keep them. Then I shall be glad to let you look them over if you care to.

President Bruhn[66] has gone to some convention in the East and will be back by March 14. At that time he wants an answer from me regarding next year. He wants me to teach full time or not at all. This winter I have tried the part time idea, which I like very much, except that I do not get much writing done. I had promised to do a small booklet for distribution at the National Parks on the Indians of Southern Utah.[67] While it will not net me anything, I would have the copyright and I had hoped that it might grow into something for which there would be a sale. I have it nearly one-half done—the script, that is—but have been somewhat discouraged because it should be illustrated, they tell me, and I hardly know how to go about that part of it. They want me to do all the work and take all the risk, while they will pay for the actual printing and give me a royalty of 10¢ a book as they are sold. They would put out 10,000 copies, which in time would give me $1,000. Of course, they would clear nearly 50¢ a copy. Well, of course, they would give me a chance to get it into print, for whatever that might be worth.

I have worked as I could on the story of Emma at Lonely Dell since I returned. I told you that Collier's said that they would like to see it, but of course that is no commitment.[68] I do want to finish that, though, and get it out within the next week if possible.

One of the main reasons why I did not want to make a definite promise to you about the Biography is that I felt that I should keep my word good to myself and others and actually prove that I could stay with a project to completion before I accept another. I shall pitch in for two more weeks or so and see how I can come along with these things. Then, if I can see that I am going to get them done—whether they add up to anything or not, whether they are accepted or not—Then I should like to talk to you about the Biography. Getting this new material today brings it back to me—brings back the urge to get at it and do it while it is all still so fresh.

But again I must face up to the problem of school and my obligations there and to the family. Will's retirement and my $140. Per month will take care of us, but Willa's last quarter at school will crowd us this spring. After she gets a position next year she can not only keep herself but help Karl if he needs it.

Enough of my problems. I shall send these photostats on briefly as soon as I hear from Stanley again

Best love always,

To *Asael C. Lambert,*[69] March 3, 1956

St. George, Utah
March 3, 1956

Dr. A.C. Lambert
Los Angeles State College
855 North Vermont Avenue
Los Angeles 29, California

Dear A.C.,

I'm ashamed to admit that I had not even thought of John D. Lee as a Mason.[70] I don't remember any mention of Masonry in these later Diaries, but perhaps that was because he was then far removed from it. I have a few items from his pre-Nauvoo days which I must look through again with this in mind. I find that I see in my reading what I am looking for—if I make myself clear.

My guess is that Lee became a Mason during the revival in Nauvoo, if indeed he did become one. His youth and young manhood before he joined the Church were spent far away from the centers of Masonic activity. Joseph Smith and others had joined before 1827; Lee became affiliated with the Mormons in 1838. The revival of Masonry in Nauvoo began in 1842, but Lee was on missions most of that year and in fact, was away when Joseph was killed. He returned, cast his lot with Brigham Young and was very active in carrying out the first ordinances in the Nauvoo Temple. Of all this he writes freely, but do not remember having seen any direct account of his joining Freemasonry, or any reference to it.

I notice that in my volume of the Confessions he describes the use of the Danite signal of distress, which I have seen in other places as the Masonic distress call. Lee, however, acts as if he did not know they were the same.

I am much intrigued by your question and shall keep on the lookout for the answer. If I find it, I shall certainly relay it on. And if you have any information or get any, I'd be glad to have it.

Sincere good wishes always,

To *Wallace Stegner*, May 7, 1956

St. George, Utah
May 7, 1956

Mr. Wallace Stegner
Stanford University
Stanford, California

Dear Mr. Stegner:

I am writing to you because you were instrumental, I am sure, in getting Stanford Press to accept my Mountain Meadows Massacre for publication, and because I hope that you may give me assistance again.

I have just finished a letter to the new director of Stanford Press, Mr. Leon Selzer,[71] asking that he conform to section 19 of my contract and "transfer to the author the work and their rights to the copyright thereon . . ." I hope that you will not consider this request unreasonable.[72]

I was very happy to have this book appear on the Stanford list, and my relations with them have been most cordial through all these years. But now that the edition is exhausted and six years have passed, it would seem to me fair that they should release the contract to me. Dale L. Morgan and others have criticized me for signing one so unfair—I believe "heartless" is the word Dale used.

I have no plans for a second edition at the present time, but if one should be put out, I should like to add new material and perhaps some pictures. I have said nothing in the present volume that I wish to retract, though I would modify one footnote referring to George Wood, and would make several other minor corrections. But whatever I did about it, I think should be up to me, now that Stanford Press has done nothing in six years.

Thank you for your past help and encouragement.

Sincerely,

Chapter 6

1957–1959

Writing the John D. Lee Biography

With pushing from Ettie Lee, Brooks during these years embarked on her next major project—the biography of John D. Lee. Many of her letters to friends and associates detailed her extensive research on Lee that delved into tracking down all his wives and daughters and gaining a clearer understanding of his 1847 activities at Summer Quarters, a farm established by Brigham Young to produce food supplies for later immigrant wagons. She also took several trips to locations that were part of Lee's life. In the summer of 1958 she and Will traveled to the Iowa and Nebraska sites along the Missouri River associated with Lee and then to Kaskaskia, Vandalia, and Nauvoo. Then in October of 1958 she was off with Winifred "Peg" Gregory to Skutumpah, Lonely Dell, and Jacobs Pools, all places where Lee sought seclusion in the face of possible arrest. Gregory was the editor Brooks hired to help with the biography, whom she first met when Gregory was helping Cleland with the John D. Lee diaries. They became close friends and visited and corresponded into the 1970s. In some of her letters written after this adventure, Brooks vividly described the desolate landscape surrounding areas such as at Jacob's Pools and the Vermillion Cliffs.

Throughout 1957 and into the fall of 1958 she steadily worked on the Lee biography, delivering the first eight chapters to Gregory after their journey. Another twelve chapters followed soon after. She again persistently labored on the biography in 1959 and finally sent it off to Alfred A. Knopf for their consideration. They rejected the work, as did other publishers in late 1959.

In July 1957, she eagerly wrote J. Kenner Fancher in Arkansas to encourage him and other family members of the Mountain Meadows Massacre victims to attend a centennial memorial service at the massacre site. She urged him by mentioning that Maurine Whipple had come by saying that *Newsweek* would send a photographer to the event if some of the family attended. Then on August 1 she regrettably informed Fancher that she could not get any of the interested parties in Salt Lake City to act, so it would not be worth his trouble to come out, though she could probably still pull something small together.

Brooks received the Distinguished Service Award of the Utah Academy in early May 1958. As part of their ongoing correspondence, Leonard Arrington wrote to congratulate her on the tribute saying, "We were especially pleased that we could reward one who has had such a high degree of scholarly integrity. We have, in the truest sense, honored the Academy by honoring you."[1] He then continued by requesting her expert opinion on a paragraph describing the Mountain Meadows Massacre and Isaac Haight's role for an article he had written on the early iron enterprise in Cedar City and Parowan. He suggested that many of the participants had moved away following the massacre as a partial reason for the termination of the endeavor. In answer, Brooks outlined where some of the major players had moved after the massacre and specified how he could have qualified his statement that Haight gave the order that resulted in the killing.

She expressed in a number of letters beginning in the 1940s her concern over the LDS Church's policy of excluding blacks from the priesthood, even though she had limited personal experience with African Americans, given her southern Utah and Nevada background. In May 1957 she discussed the subject with O. Boyd Mathias, who was a friend and at the time a student at Kansas City University. She maintained in this letter, "I have never felt that the color of skin pigment should be the basis of judging an individual any more than any other physical trait should be."[2] The letter continued with a story told by her mother about a temple marriage ceremony being stopped, because one of the persons to be married had a small amount of African American blood. In 1959, she again wrote Mathias on the subject in response to reading his paper on African Americans and the LDS Church. She declared, "It seems to me that it is time that we were willing to admit that we are all children of the same Father, that we are not special, chosen people, set apart by our fair skin to be superior."[3]

Among other friends with whom she maintained a long correspondence starting in the 1950s were Asael C. Lambert and Stanley S. Ivins. Asael Lambert, dean of the Los Angeles State College of Applied Arts and Sciences, supplied her with his often-controversial manuscripts concerning the inconsistencies of early Mormonism, and their discussions delved into such topics as whether John D. Lee was a Mason, the Council of Fifty, and her views about Emma Smith. Stanley Ivins, the son of Anthony W. Ivins of the First Presidency, who studied Utah and Mormon history, also provided her with photostats of documents including three petitions for the release of J. D. Lee after his conviction and the letters of George Miller, the second bishop of the LDS Church when he was dropped from the church.

~

To *O. Boyd Mathias*,[4] May 27, 1957

St. George, Utah
May 27, 1957

Mr. O. Boyd Mathias
48 D Hilltop Court
Manhattan, Kansas

Dear Mr. Mathias,

Thank you so much for your letter and the material enclosed covering your correspondence with Bro. Joseph Fielding Smith on "Blood Atonement." I was pleased that you should have enough confidence in me to trust me to read it.

I have found references in early diaries which lead me to believe that the teaching of "blood atonement" might have been more than just a teaching. Esaias Edwards[5] told how his son-in law, who had taken another wife without going through the approved procedure was fined heavily and warned, and how upon a second offence of adultery, he was forced to flee in the night or his life would have been forfeit. I'm sure I can cite page and line for several instances if you want them—mostly if I take time to dig them out.

I, too, have been deeply concerned about our official stand with regard to the negro. I have never felt that the color of skin pigment should be the basis of judging an individual any more than any other physical trait should be. One experience on this: My mother is such a sweet devout member of the church. She told how it was reported that in the midst of a temple ceremony, after the company was half-way through, they were stopped. The President had been inspired to know that someone was there who was not eligible. People were questioned, everything was held up waiting to learn who the culprit was. Finally, it was simmered down to two young couples who were going through for the first time to be married. They were taken into a private room and questioned separately as to their moral conduct. At last it was learned that one little bride had a bit of negro blood 1/32 or something like that. I'm not sure that she herself was aware of this; I do not know just how the decision was arrived at. But she was not allowed to proceed through the temple, and the marriage was held up. Now the point that Mother was trying to make was that our leaders ARE inspired to discern such things. To me, it was all ghastly. It was reported as having happened at the Mesa temple or the Hawaiian—I hope that it did not happen anywhere. The mere telling of it as inspired truth is terrible enough, I think.

I did not mean to get off onto this. It just sort of oozed out of this machine. What I had really intended to say was that I think the most dangerous thing in all the discussion is the stand of Br JFS[6] that "This is not a matter for controversy." I think everything is a matter for discussion, that nothing in our history or teachings is so sacrosanct that it cannot be re-examined.

You mentioned the fact that you had wanted to get mimeographed copies of the discussions at the USAC[7] in 1952.[8] I find that I have extras of the other three, but only this one of my own. So you may keep the others, but I'd like to have [missing]

To *J. Kenner and Florence Fancher*,[9] July 20, 1957

St. George, Utah
July 20, 1957

Dear Kenner and Florence,

Today a writer friend of mine, Maurine Whipple, came in to say that she had a long-distance telephone call from Newsweek magazine saying that they would be much interested in a story and pictures of any meeting which might be held at Mountain Meadows on September 10—I mean Sept. 11—provided representatives of the Fancher family were present.

I had talked some of the possibility of your coming earlier, before your family reunion, but after your word that they had decided not to make a family trek of it, I told the local people who had been interested, and had thought no more of it.

Now Miss Whipple insists that if a couple of car-loads decided to come, there would be money to help defray travel expenses. I don't know how much difference that would make, but if any number cared to come, I think there could be some provision to do this. I am sure that accommodations would be furnished also, and that every effort would be made to have a memorial service which would please you.

Perhaps the attention of this national magazine would result in full picture stories by Life, or other magazines. Miss Whipple thinks so. It is not that I want publicity, and I am sure you do not, but if such a gathering could be held, in the right spirit, it might help point the way to the settlement of similar differences in other areas.

Use your own judgment. Don't let us pressure you into anything against your will. But if you do decide to come, we should be most happy to have you. I told Miss Whipple that I had extended an invitation earlier which I would be glad to repeat and to hold open indefinitely, but she thought I should tell you of this telephone conversation with Newsweek.

Sincere good wishes. I hope you are having a pleasant summer.

Always,

To *J. Kenner Fancher*, August 1, 1957

St. George, Utah
August 1, 1957

Dear Kenner,

It is with genuine regret that I write this letter. When I went in to Salt Lake City last week, I talked with Dr. Mortensen and learned that nothing has really been done about a meeting at the Mountain Meadows this fall,—at least nothing definite enough to count on for certain now.

Mr. Nicolas G. Morgan[10] who says he is going to have a permanent bronze plaque set out near the road had been called east on some other urgent business and had done nothing about it. Seems that he probably could not get it done now in time for Sept. 11. That would have been the occasion for the meeting of the Sons of Utah Pioneers at the spot.

I called several others, but could find no one who was heading any group to meet at the Meadows, though every one I spoke to said that he personally would like to attend a memorial service there if one were held.

The John D. Lee family held their annual reunion in Arizona near the end of June. Several members from this area have expressed interest in a gathering there, but the family as a group feel that the incident is one of which they cannot be proud, though their ancestor did pay the supreme price for his part in it.

SO—what I am trying to say is that I'd hate to have you make the trip out here unless something really worthy was to be done. I think that if you and Kit Wilson[11] and a few others come anyway, and we know for sure a couple of weeks in advance, we could publicize the fact locally and still have two or three hundred people in attendance. We would expect both of you to speak, I am sure that Dr. Mortensen would come and speak as a representative of his father—and also Mrs. Ettie Lee. We could have appropriate musical numbers from the college here and also some from Cedar City. We could also arrange for the seating and loud speaker, and have that access road improved.

The massacre is the one really black spot on the name of Utah. We all look upon it with the humility and contrition of people sincerely sorry. But we hesitate to call public attention to it unless we could unite with some of you, the descendants of those who were killed, in a memorial service dedicated to the hope that we shall never allow our passions to be so aroused again in any condition where similar acts of violence are committed . . .

But let's think it over and talk about it via the mail, and when you decide IF you will come and how many will come, we'll swing into action here. Thanks for just being your own very fine CHRISTIAN self.

To *A. William Lund*, August 9, 1957

St. George, Utah
August 9, 1957

Mr. A. William Lund
Assistant Church Historian
47 E South Temple
Salt Lake City, Utah

Dear Brother Lund:

Thank you for your prompt answer to my letter regarding the people who died at Summer Quarters.[12]

John D. Lee's Diary No. 6 as published by Charles Kelly in 1938,[13] gives an account of the meeting held Tuesday March 23, 1847 in which "the following members of Pres. B. Young family assembled at Bro. Robert Pearce's, namely: Edmund Ellsworth, A.P. Rockwood, J.D. Lee, G.D. Grant, Isaac Morly, John Lyttle, Robert Pierce, Addison Everett, T.O. Angel, Major Wm. Weeks, Chas. Shumway, S.A. Dun, Thos. Grover, Fredrick Kesler, Phineas W. Cook, David Davis, Jas Busbee, Solomon Angel, Willen Atwood, Samuel L. Sprague, Jacob F. Hutchinson, Sylvester H. Earl, Wm Empey, Daniel Carns, Jos. S. Scofieıd, Moses M. Sanders, Hyrum Dayton, Jacob Wilder, A.P. Free, Edward D. Woolev, E.P. Dusette, Samuel Gully, George D. Grant, Benj. Brown, Isaac Chace and Sidney A. Hanks (37) and Chas Decker (38)[14]. . . . . Come brethren, who will be set apart to stay and farm? Here is Bro. J.D. Lee, G.D. Grant and David Davis that I will select to farm (Bro. J. Busbie also). . . . As for a location for a farm I know of no place to equal a piece of land lying a short distance above the old fort and about 16 ms. From this point. There is about 600 acres that has been cultivated which is just as mellow as an ash heap. We can enclose with a very little labour some 2000 acres including the broke land, where you can by industry raise any amount of grains . . ." (p. 133–134)

I must not go into further detail here, but of the thirty-eight named above, twelve others were added to the first four selected to stay and still others later until he said some 80 names were entered. Isaac Morley was put in charge of whole enterprise, with John Vance[15] and John D. Lee also captains.

They arrived on the ground on March 31 and began laying off the land and selecting sites for their homes on April 1, 1847.

As I said before, this journal ends on July 23, with many of the colony ill. David Isom Young[16] had been buried on July 20, in a cemetery which they decided to call "Fairview" because it was on top of a hill. A footnote by Kelly says that seventeen others were buried here.[17]

I have also had correspondence with Edith L. Neale[18] who is in charge of the old Fort Calhoun there in Nebraska and is going to write an article on the farming activities of the Mormons in that neighborhood. She also has mentioned the cemetery, but does not have a list of the names.

Lee's next journal that has been found begins on February 29th, 1848, and continues with the preparations for migration west and the trip across as far as Weber River.[19]

Between these two records is a lapse of some seven months. I wonder if his book covering that period is not in your archives with those which Brother William R. Palmer has repeatedly told me and also members of the Lee family are there. In April of this year he told Br. Omer Smith[20] and his wife that there are many Lee records there. Seems that Lee kept small day books which he later transferred into larger ledgers—at least that has seemed true of the originals which I have handled.

Because of this, the story of this farming venture at Summer Quarters, called by Hosea Stout[21] and others "Brother Brigham's Farm," has not come into the official church record. It seems that it should, though, because the grain raised here was very important in the 1848 migration.

I hope to leave by plane on October 20 to visit this area. If I find any pertinent information I will let you know. In the meantime, if you should locate the official record, it would be a valuable addition to the story of our people.

Very sincerely yours,

To *Asael C. Lambert*, September 2 [1957]

St. George
Sept 2

Dear Alfred:

Congratulations! I'm so happy to know that the YTFIF[22] paper is finished and may see publication. Be sure that I shall use what influence I have—if any—to the end. I think it will be something of a milestone in modern Mormon history when it appears. As for anyone's membership, well, just don't worry about it. Long ago I decided never to be afraid again, for I went into the office of a high dignitary to defend my action in writing the MMM, and came out with the same sensation that Christian must have had as he journeyed on his Pilgrim's Progress[23] and found the way guarded by the fierce lions. When instead of turning back, he approached them resolutely, and found they were chained! I saw this good brother so embarrassed and humiliated before me that I decided that never again would I be afraid or act afraid. A part of the Christian life is to love the Truth, before which the lions are literally chained and helpless.

Forgive me. This machine got out of control again.

Strange with what new vision one reads when a new problem is opened up. For example, I was looking for something else a while ago on the Emmett company (Utah Historical Quarterly January, 1955 p. 7)[24] in which Dale L. Morgan quotes from the Kartchher[25] diary:

> "An expedition was ordered by Joseph the Prophet prior to his martyrdom for a few families to migrate to the Missouri River and put in crops preparatory to the Church moving from Nauvoo westward under the charge of Bro James Emmett and John L Butler his counselor, I was called upon to go, being just married, as they wanted young men mostly. I was instructed to keep it a secret as all would want to go if word went forth that we were going west. This instruction was given us by Zachariah D. Wilson, the Presiding High Priest of Liberty Branch, situated on the head of Cedar Creek, twenty miles below Nauvoo. We were told by Bro Wilson that he was in the highest court on earth. . . ."

As part of their secrecy was an attempt to by-pass Brother Brigham, and the inference is that the YTFIF considered itself independent of him. The whole article is an interesting commentary on the decisions of the council.

Then in the Journal of Discourses Vol. 2[26] p. 168 I found a report of the speech made by Joseph Smith upon his return to Nauvoo after having been taken a prisoner at Dixon.[27] Although the prophet is quoting an old man, the fact that he said this and that there were no doubt some men in the audience who got the full import of what he said seems to indicate that the council might have been organized at least in part on that day—June 30, 1843:

". . . and if you never learned manners in Missouri, we'll teach you that gentlemen are not to be imposed upon by a nigger, driver; you can not kidnap men here if you do in Missouri; and, if you attempt it here, there's a committee in this Grove that will sit on your case; and, sir, it is the highest tribunal in the United States, and from its decision there is no appeal."

This is not to affect in any way what you have written, it is only to show that now whenever I read it is with an extra dimension.

Seems that there will be nothing done on Sept. 11 in the way of a gathers at the Meadows. The Fancher family voted against the trip at their reunion earlier, and the SUP[28] evidently got cold feet or were strongly persuaded from above to do nothing. So the Centennial will pass quietly.

As you see from the numerous errors, I am typing under a tension. My second Brooks boy, Kay, just bounced in with a friend and both declared that they were going to tell the Bishop they want to go on a mission. We have suggested it to Kay a number of times but he was determined to go on to school. Now in just an instant many plans must be changed. We're wondering if they really mean it, or if they are just kidding.

The chief immediate result is that I have written most of this with only half my mind.

Congratulations, again. It's cheering to know with what enthusiasm you have attacked this problem—and what immediate results you have achieved.

Good luck always

To *A. Russell Mortensen*, October 3, 1957

St. George, Utah
October 3, 1957

Dear Brother Mortensen,

I'm trying to talk myself clear on the matter of Nancy Bean[29] and her association with John D. Lee, and also on the matter of the birthdate of her daughter Cornelia.[30] I know that you have it from the record as 15 January 1846, but I just sort of wondered if it might not have been a year earlier. As I said, I'm just thinking this out on paper.

In Lee's handwritten Diary Book 14A I found this notation which I copied:

"Feb. 5th, 1844, Nancy Bean adopted into my family.... April 19th, Louisa Free, Caroline Williams, Abigal Woolsey, Rachel Woolsey."[31]

This would seem reasonable enough, for The Prophet married his first admitted plural wife, Louisa Beaman,[32] on April 5, 1841. A few close friends knew of this, and it was talked among the Authorities. A little more than a year later, on June 15, 1842, Brigham Young took his first plural wife, Lucy Decker.[33] He took two more the next year, and five in 1844—at least when he left Nauvoo in February 1846, he had 16 wives.

I mention this only to show that since the two men, Brigham Young and John D. Lee, were working closely together, it does not seem unlikely that Lee should have been allowed to practice polygamy at this early date.

NOW—Lee left for a mission to help with the campaign for Joseph Smith on March 28, 1844, and did not return until August 19, 1844. Having married Nancy on Feb. 5, 1844, he could well have fathered a child by her that was born on January 15, 1845. Or would he have been at home 8 months more before she conceived.

Either way could be right, of course. George Laub, one of Lee's adopted sons, tells of the move across the river on the 12 of February 1846: "Myself & John D. Lee Nancy Lee & Polly Lee took up our Line of march for the west for pertection from our Enemys who ware seeking the lives of the Twelve.... Now I took across from the State of Illinois one waggon Two Horses one cow and Provision suficiant to sustain them for about Two months or more. . . ."

Now little Cornelia might have been either less than one month old when this move was made, or just under a year of age. In either case, she was not mentioned, but certainly she was along. It makes some difference how I write the story, the age of this child. Nowhere is she mentioned until at Winter Quarters, May 12, 1848, when Lee notes that ". . . returned to the Ferry about 4 P.M. Found Nancy 1st an her litle Daughter Eliza waiting to cross . . ."

Here again a year's difference in age does make a difference, for while a 2-year-old would have to be carried part way on any long walk, a three-year-old in good health is quite able to go on its own.

As I said at first, I'm trying to clarify this in my own mind so that I can write of it more consistently. I've seen so many family records where there is a year—sometimes more—difference in the age of a woman by having it put down from memory years later. Nancy couldn't have had her endowments until after December 10, 1845—between that date and Feb. 8, 1846, when the ceremony was closed in the Nauvoo temple. If the baby had been born on Jan. 15, it is not likely that she would have gone before the birth (since this was still not made public, this matter of plural wives) and she would likely not have gone after because of their idea that after childbirth a woman remained quiet for a month . . .

The census taken at Parowan in 1850 lists Zechariah B. Decker 33 N.Y., Nancy, aged 23, Mo, Eliza aged 5, Ill., and Zechariah aged 1, Deseret.—Now that I think of it, this may confirm the later birth date, for they did not arrive in Parowan until late 1850, and the census was not reported until after the turn of the year 1851.

Forgive me for troubling you with this. I'm just trying to clarify it exactly in my mind so that I can write of the trip across the river on February 12.

This Biography is a fascinating thing. I become involved in some detail such as this, and my eagerness to have it right, I sometimes delay my own progress.

I hope that all is well with you. I'd be glad to hear from you on this.

Sincere good wishes,

To *Leonard Arrington*, May 12, 1958

St. George, Utah
May 12, 1958

Dr. Leonard L. Arrington
Utah State University
Logan, Utah

Dear Leonard:

After another week-end in Salt Lake City, I am back and at work again and shall try to answer your letter of May 5.[34]

I am probably responsible, in part at least, for the idea that participants at the MMM left Cedar City within a very short time, though actually the documentary evidence consists chiefly in the census figures of 1860 and in a few casual comments which I shall take time to locate definitely later, if I have time.

But you must remember that they were in war, that all were under martial law, that no one was allowed to move from one place to another without consent of the leaders. Particularly was it most dangerous for any Mormon to attempt to leave the territory. This is shown definitely in Lee's Diary for August 3 to 6, 1858. (See also the MMM p. 122)[35]

At this time "the people were told that they were at liberty to move to any settlement where they thought they could better their condition." Nephi Johnson, who had helped to manage the Indians at the MMM affair, moved far up into Zion canyon early in 1858; Philip Klingensmith moved to Pocketville, just below the present site of Springdale, and across the stream. Haight moved one of his wives to Toquerville in 1858, and himself spent much time there after his release from the Stake Presidency on July 11, 1859, soon after the return of Judge Cradlebugh from his fruitless mission south in an attempt to arrest the leaders.

By early 1860 Dame had been called on a mission to England, James H. Martineau had moved to the Logan area and spent the next several years surveying in the northern Utah and southern Idaho. (He was Dame's adjutant.) Laban Morrill and Wm Bateman both moved to Cache Valley; the Slades to Pine Valley; the Wildens to Cove

Fort; the Pearces to the Ferry at the confluence of the Virgin and the Colorado.[36] Before Lee's capture in 1875, most of the participants were moved away or dead. Haight, Higbee, and George Wood and Bill Stewart[37] were in hiding much of the time after peace was declared certainly after early 1859.

I believe in their quarrel as to the responsibility for the massacre, Haight pretty well established that Dame had issued the orders, though probably had counseled together earlier.

I too think you could well have qualified the sentence that he was the one who ordered the attack. Is this paragraph all that you say about the massacre?[38]

The people who were trying to manufacture the iron were, most of them, new converts from England and Wales, I thought. From what I have read of their efforts to make a good grade of iron, I gathered that their difficulties lay in the smelting process and in whatever they did not know of the proper chemistry to use. Add to these their poverty and the struggle for existence here and there is ample cause for discouragement.

I wish I might have visited further with you at Provo. I was so happy to hear of your opportunity to go abroad.

My best wishes to all the family.

Sincerely,

P.S. You really might do well to black out the last two sentences, since the last is dependent for meaning upon the one immediately preceding.

To *Stanley Ivins*, October 18, 1958

St. George, Utah
October 18, 1958

Dear Stanley:

Thank you so much for the photostats of the Miller[39] papers. I'm very glad to have this item in my files, and just looking through it again makes me feel that it may clarify a number of points upon which I have been hazy. It almost leads me off to considering that YTFIF thing again, for Miller's note for May 5 & 6 on Page 121 is so much like the account of the Prophet in the Historical Record pp. 493–94.[40]

As I have told you, I'm inclined to take the date of the revelation—as given in the minutes of the re-organization meeting held Saturday, Aprii 10, 1880, literally.[41] And they say it was organized by the Lord, April 7, 1842, and the name was "The Kingdom of God and His Laws with the keys and powers thereof and Judgment in the hands of his servants."

But why bother you with this? Or myself, either, for that matter, when I have more interesting things to talk about.

Mrs. "Peg" Gregory[42] who did all of Dr. Cleland's editing on the Diaries has been here for the past two weeks, going over Lee's trials. I went with her to the Meadows, to Harmony, and Washington. She went by herself to Beaver and Panguitch. Then last Friday afternoon we set out together in her little new French car for a week-end of exploration. We went to Kanab via the Hurricane Ridge, Short Creek, Cane Beds, and Pipe Springs, arriving just at dusk.[43] Early the next morning we went out past Johnson's Ranch over the Brigham Young exploring route of Sept. 1870,[44] and over a ridge to the east to Skutumpah Valley.[45] The place is now owned by the Robinson family, and two of the boys happened to be there getting ready for the deer hunt. They showed us the ruins of two of Lee's houses, and insisted that the one which stands was built by him. Certainly it is a polygamous house, built with two identical sides—fireplaces, stoves, or I should say instead with living room, kitchen (each with another outside door) and bedroom exactly alike, and the same dimensions that he gave for the double home he built. The place is still called "Skutumpah", and Mill Creek marks the site of the portable saw mill that he and Levi Stewart[46] ran.

On Saturday we went on to the Lonely Dell and back to Green's,[47] where we spent the night. Sunday Morning a Texan who is out there prospecting, took us to the Pools in a four-wheel-drive truck. This was Jacob's Pools[48] from the time he and Thales Haskell dug them out and walled them up in 1859, and was called by Lee his "Retreat" or his "Ranch."

Oh, Stanley, it was horrible! Simply horrible! I don't know how to tell you what it was like. Have you seen the picture of Lee and his family and the willow house that he built here? He tells of the taking of the picture in Vol. 2 p. 200,[49] and of building the shelter a few days earlier. In the picture he stands, heavily bearded, near the center, with three or four small children about and his daughter Amorah or else her mother Rachel at one side, one stranger sitting on a chair, another opposite holding a pick. The foreground is bare with a white talus slope behind, and behind this the bluffs.

Well—as we rode the 12 miles from Greens back toward Kanab via Jacob's lake, we watched those vermilion bluffs, and it looked as if the land from the road sloped right up to their base. Then we were shown a block fault, where a piece had slipped down, leaving a seam on each side near the bottom of which there was just a hint of green. We went through a gate, up an incline toward this place. The rock house Lee built on the plain still stands and is visible from the road if you know where to look for it. But beyond this house the ground fell away into a wash that paralleled the ledges.

I picked up a dim trail and walked to this and skirted it, and there below me was the place. And such a place! Totally barren, not even in mid-October, the talus a blue formation, dark blue nearer the bottom and shading to gray near the top, a poisonous accumulation that reminded me of blue vitriol and that our Texan said was an arsenic combination. Anyway, not one blade of anything could grow on it. There on the slick rock at one side were the piles of rock which marked the pig pen, the rock wall which conned the cattle, the trail running west over which the pack trains had approached the place, and along the eastern seat on the vermilion ledges behind, a faint almost perpendicular trail. If I have never looked upon desolation before, I saw it there. On the slope approaching it nothing grew tall enough to shelter a jack-rabbit. Here, nothing grew. Period.

I must go back again when I can stay a few hours at least and don't have dead-lines to meet. I must go this very fall back to Kanab and from there out to the Pareah settlement, some houses of which still stand, they tell me, and to the old Peter Shirtz[50] fort.

I didn't mean to go on such lengths. Do you ever go into such by and forbidding areas? Perhaps you should, if only to give yourself a chance to be grateful for what you have.

So-long for now, and thanks again for all your help.

To *Dale Morgan*, January 22, 1959

St. George, Utah, Jan 22/59

Dear Dale,

The welkin stopped ringing some time ago, but one bell or another keeps clanging at me all of the time. I was glad, though, for your reference to the Thurber[51] diary because it makes me conscious of one more of Lee's brothers-in-law.

I knew of his marriage to Martha Berry and of their difficulties at Summer Quarters. I knew that John Vance had holdings near Lee on Mill Creek, but didn't know that the Berry family was near also. I think I told you how I discovered when Martha left the Lee household in early 1858—whether as a result of Lee's bringing Emma Bachellor to share her apartment or whether the MMM figured in it at all. But she married one Dennis Dorrity—technically, Dennis Smiling Dorrity—as his third wife, and bore him six children. She had five by Lee, but two little girls died very young.

I'm sure that I told you also of my adventures in locating the last wife, the Australian girl, Ann Gordge, and of getting pictures and a full history of her. One of the greatest tragedies in all the Lee stories is that of her two children—2-year-old Jim given to Emma at Lonely Dell and 4-year-old Merab (called Belle by the family) given to Rachel at the pools.

Now just lately I feel sure that I have located the missing wife. He always said that he had <u>nineteen</u>, and the list in the <u>Confessions</u> was garbled—as garbled as it might well be if Lee were talking and someone unacquainted with the family had taken the notes. Nancy Bean is called Nancy Berry, Rachel Andora is made two wives, and Emoline Vaughn Woolsey is the sister to Aggatha and Rachel. What I am trying to say is that one wife was not listed.

I argued that this one wife was one that he had taken during the Nauvoo period, one who had probably left him during the wretched time between 1846 and 1848. Following an inspired hunch from the fact that Lee spoke of "Father" John Vance a couple of times in Vol 2 of the <u>Chronicle</u>, I looked up the Vance family records and found one Nancy Ann[52] who would fit all the requirements, especially since in the Kelly volume she is named twice among the wives as husking corn or planting garden.

Consider these facts and see if I have jumped to too many conclusions:

John Vance was ordained a High Priest in Nauvoo on 12 Fe. 1845, which means that he was likely in on this business of plurality and would consent to his daughter's entering into it. At this time Nancy Ann 21—she had been baptized 9 Oct. 1839. Her marriage to William Shin Wordsworth evidently did not take place until she reached the Valley—their first child, Eliza Jane, was born 1 May 1850 at S.L.C., the second in l852 at Alpine, the third in 1854 at Lehi, Utah.

I thought I had rather established my hunch when in Pioneers and Prominent Men of Utah[53] I found the notation under his picture:

> Wordsworth, William
> (son of Catherine Morgan)—
> Came to Utah July 24, 1847, Brigham Young Company.
> Married Nancy Ann Vance (daughter of John Vance, Salt Lake City pioneer 1847—mother of Hannah,[54] born at Winter Quarters by a previous marriage.) . . .

From the index of the genealogical library I found her listed as Hannah L. Wordsworth or Wadsworth. Nothing except her death date as 6 June 1917 and the fact that some one did her work in the temple—baptism in 1935 and endowment in 1936, and a note m. Mr Harris.

From the Journal History I find that William Wadsworth was with the Parley P. Pratt exploring expedition in December 1849, that Bishop David Evans wrote from Dry Creek (Lehi) on Feb. 5, 1852, to the effect that William Wardsworth was settling on the head of Dry Creek and would take too much of the water, and in the summer of 1853 William Wadsworth is named as one of the members of the battalion to go south to Fillmore. Add the date of the birth of their third child and you have the last account to date—9 Feb. 1854.

Because none of these children were baptized until they were in their middle life, I assumed that perhaps the family left the state. I saw that there was a town in the Reno area called Wadsworth and have wondered if he might have moved there. Also there are so many Wadsworths in the Panaca-Pioche area that I shall start looking there. Because even on the genealogical cards the "Shin" has been dropped and both spellings been given, I'm sure that the name has now become "Wadsworth."

Knowing all this, you may be conscious of this man if you ever happen across him. No record in the Vital Statistics of the death of Hannah L Wadsworth Harris. She must have died in another state.

Just plain curiosity, all of this. But I'd like to see what Lee posterity there is carrying the Harris name—who and were they are, and in so far as I can, what they are like.

***

Feb. 26

So here it is, days away, and I've had my run up to Salt Lake City & back with little accomplished except going through the motion of being a member of the HQ Board[55] (bored). Was glad to see that you are to do an article.[56]***** We'll be sure of one really good thing.

And here I've been interrupted again with a telephone call from Willa to the effect that she is to be married before February is out! Horror Why couldn't she have taught the year out??? He's a jet pilot who has been on temporary duty at Nellis Air Force Base,[57] and will leave for his home base at Phoenix about the end of February. So forgive me if I seem totally incoherent.

So many things else I had wanted to talk of, but mostly to ask of you and your doings—and to add that above and beyond almost everything else I prize your friendship—I mean that in spite of all the lapses and silence and diversity of interests, I'm glad that you are alive somewhere.

To *O. Boyd Mathias*, February 8, 1959

St. George, Utah
February 8, 1959

Dear Mr. Mathias:

Thank you so much for the copy of your paper, "The Mormon Church and its Negro Doctrine."[58] I am glad to have it in my files for reference and happy for the chance to read it through.

It is a subject upon which I have done little research, but one to which I have given some thought. I have been much embarrassed at some of the things that have gone on in Utah: at the fact that boy scouts in uniform gathering at Salt Lake City to take train for a national Jamboree found that those little fellows with dark faces could not be put up in hotels. Mr. Rulon Doman[59] who was in charge told me of his own personal humiliation at the fact that he had to find lodging for these boys in private homes.

It seems to me that it is time that we were willing to admit that we are all children of the same Father, that we are not special, chosen people, set apart by our fair skin to be superior, but given an opportunity to become worthy only by the same achievement that is open to every individual without regard for skin pigment.

I am glad you have written this. It may seem not to make any difference; it may actually not make any immediate difference in Church policy. But the very fact that you have set it down, that it is on paper and available means that it will set some ripples into motion and strike some sympathetic hearers. I think also that it is wholesome for some of us to be willing to take a stand openly and defend it. On this I am with you.

In a world full of tensions and misunderstandings, at a time when Christianity itself is questioned, we must each make some contributions as we can toward brotherhood and fellowship, toward the evaluation of each man upon his worth as a person, toward the sluffing off of some erroneous myths.

I'm being rather awkward at this. But I do thank you heartily for your work on this subject and for sending me this copy.

Sincerely,

O. Boyd Mathias
University of Kansas City
Kansas City 10, Missouri

To *Hamilton Gardner*,[60] May 10, 1959

St. George, Utah
May 10, 1959

Mr. Hamilton Gardner
4 Cogswell Avenue Apt 25
Cambridge 40, Mass.

Dear Mr. Gardner:

I'm sure that you will guess at once that I need help, and I'm equally sure that you are busy with your own projects. Let me state my problem, and if you don't know about it or are too busy, I'll not blame you if you don't ever answer.

I am in the midst of a biography of John D. Lee, and for a long time have kept a search for his 19th wife, of whom no record has yet been found by the family. I wondered how much of a posterity, if any, he had by her.

Now I have decided that the wife was Nancy Ann Vance, daughter of John Vance, and that she bore Lee but one child, a daughter named Hannah. The mother married William Shin Wordsworth, so the child grew up as Hannah L. Wordsworth. Family legend says that she matured early, that she was high-spirited and hard to discipline, and that she fell in love with an officer who was stationed at the point of the mountain, and went back with him when the army left in 1860 or 1861.

The elderly lady who told me the story insists that the officer was William Sherman. Now I feel quite sure it could not have been General William T. Sherman of Civil War fame, but the lady insisted that name was right. Seems that Hannah returned to the East, where she was deserted, either because her husband was away to the war or because he had another family. Hannah bore but one child so far as the family knows, and they have pictures of both the mother and the child. There were letters, too, they claim, though they cannot now find any of them.

Knowing your interest in the "Utah War" and your knowledge of the personnel of both armies, I thought you would perhaps run across something about any Mormon girls who might have followed the army when they returned to the East. I'm sure there were some who did marry soldiers or serve as mistresses to them.

So much for this—

I hope that you are employed at something interesting and stimulating, and that we shall see other articles from you as scholarly and rewarding as the one on the Mormon Battalion which appeared in the Utah Quarterly.[61]

Sincere good wishes,

To *Robert Ashby*,[62] 20 July 1959

St. George Utah
July 20, 1959

Mr. Robert L. Ashby
American Fork, Utah

Dear Brother Ashby:

I have just finished reading your book The History of Holden[63] and wish to congratulate you on a very fine piece of work. You have collected a great deal of material and presented it in a very clear, fine way.

I borrowed this book from our friend, Maiben Ashby.[64] Now I wish to own a copy. Are there others for sale? What is the price? I shall be glad to send a check, if you will tell me, or you may send the book C.O.D.

I am much interested in your entry on page 21, in which you say of Father William Stevens[65] that "He was a great financier and helped the poor in many ways. Before his death he donated $5,000. to the Church—a large sum in those days. He operated Holden's first store."

Did you have documentary proof of this in a Church record book, in letters or diaries or a private account book? I ask because I talked to one Sister Stevens in Holden who says that she is writing a history for the family, but is not going to include this item because she thinks that it simply cannot be true. How could any man collect that much money, she says, when people were trading mostly by barter? On the other hand, another Sister Stevens in the same town told me the story before I saw it in your book. According to her, Brother Stevens wrote to President Young telling him that he wished to make this contribution, and that while President Young did not come for the cash himself, he did send a man to get it. I'm not sure that she said in a buggy from Salt Lake City—I assume that he would come by train to the nearest terminal. But she does tell the same story that you do, of his taking back $5,000.00.

Those who don't accept the story are so positive that he could not and did not have that much money that they discount anyone who would repeat it. I'd be glad for any information on this.

On page 3 you speak of "At the west edge of the settlement near a "Cold Spring" (or a Gold Spring) Father Stevens made his dwelling large enough to become a social center. School was conducted here in the winter of 1851–52." I'm sure you meant the first, but it looks in this book like the second had been written.

Please do not think I am critical, I am not. I think you have made a fine contribution to local and state history.

Sincerely,

To *A. Russell Mortensen*, August 6, 1959

St. George, Utah
August 6, 1959

Dr. A.R. Mortensen
Utah State Historical Society
603 East South Temple
Salt Lake City, Utah

Dear Dr. Mortensen:

Thank you for your letter of August 3. I had not seen the reprint in the Deseret News, since I do not take the paper, but my sister called my attention to it.[66] I was about to write to you. It may be none of my business, since I am only the author, but something about the deal stinks.

For example: What is this magazine "Holliday"? Was that word only a deliberate attempt to mislead their gullible readers? Or is there such a magazine? If the article had been reprinted from Holiday, I'd naturally assume that I might have been notified. Was the change of title just another bit of deceit, or were they ashamed to print it twice under the same caption? Brother, they must be hard up for newsprint and fillers!

As an example of their integrity, editorial and otherwise, I think this is a classic. A publication that has received my real work with such stony silence, now to take this and use it twice! Next time they'll print it under a fictitious name or will claim it as their own—whoever it is that is in charge of this page and too lazy to do his own writing.

Maybe it's as well they use what they want now, for after this Lee Biography appears, I'll be cut again. By the way, it's really coming along. I shouldn't leave it long enough to even write letters.

Would I be allowed to use this article, along with some new pictures of Art Bruhn's myself, do you think?

Sincere good wishes,

Chapter 7

1960–1961

Move to Salt Lake City and the Reinstatement of John D. Lee

In June 1960, the Brookses moved from St. George to Salt Lake City so that she could take a position as research associate at the Utah State Historical Society for a term starting July 1, 1960, and ending January 1, 1962. Her appointment was eventually extended so that she could finish the editing of the Hosea Stout journals, her major assignment during this employment. They first resided at 1218 Third Avenue and then relocating to a house they bought at 1295 Crystal Avenue in March 1961. Their final location in Salt Lake City was 98 U Street.

She continued her efforts with the John D. Lee biography, accepting during the summer of 1960 Arthur H. Clark's offer to publish it. She received and reviewed the galleys of the biography in May 1961 and the book finally appeared in November of that year.

Perhaps the most trying and stressful confrontation of Juanita's career was the one over her unyielding insistence in 1961 that a notice of the LDS Church reinstatement of John D. Lee be included in her biography of him against the demands of Apostle Delbert Stapley and many members of the Lee family, including Ettie Lee. Her letters summarize how she came to write the biography, her reasons for not complying with Elder Stapley's mandate, and the events surrounding the controversy. True to form, Brooks argued that she could not suppress known information, that doing so would amount to her writing dishonest history, a prospect she had spent her career fighting. In a concerted attack, Stapley first met with her and attempted to convince her of her folly. She later described the meeting to Ida Hamblin, a John D. Lee descendant: "When I talked to Apostle Stapley and told him of our meeting at Panguitch, and that I had felt that the book had been delayed because there was new material which should be added, and this came as an answer to all our prayers, he just slapped the table and said, 'IT IS FROM THE DEVIL.'"[1]

Under threats from Apostle Stapley that President David O. McKay would rescind the reinstatement if mention of it appeared in the biography, the Lee family under the direction of Judge Jesse Udall of the Arizona Supreme Court summoned Brooks to Phoenix in July 1961 so that they could force her to reconsider. At the meeting, she faced twenty-three opponents all trying to convince her to change her mind with her saying no after each speech. She had support from only one uninvited participant, J. Wesley Williamson, a John D. Lee great-grandson and Brooks's friend, whom she requested attend and tape the proceedings. In the end, she agreed to leave the notice out of the first edition of the book but include it in later editions. At her request, the Arthur H. Clark Company, the publisher, printed just 209 copies of the first edition and then immediately went into producing the second edition with the announcement.

Even her friend and a major supporter, Ettie Lee, attempted to convince Brooks not to include the notice of the reinstatement in the book. Brooks later reminisced about the ordeal in a letter to Ettie Lee in 1967, observing that members of the family would now thank her for standing firm and including the statement in her book, given the passage of time. She also summarized the incident at the request of Everett L. Cooley of the Utah Historical Society in 1969 and recalled the event in a letter in 1971 to Sana Williamson, wife of J. Wesley Williamson. In the end, David O. McKay not only did not reverse John D. Lee's reinstatement, he eventually instructed Stapley to leave Brooks alone. According to a conversation as recalled by William Delves, a stake president, between him and Stapley, the latter related, "President McKay is a more compassionate man than I am."[2] Upon meeting Brooks at a gathering in 1965, Delves related to her his discussion with Stapley, reportedly causing her to tear up. However, she never mentioned this exchange in any of her correspondence discussing the subject.

Brooks continued her correspondence with Asael Lambert during these years, exploring such subjects as her feelings about Emma Smith and the Council of Fifty. She also commenced a long-term letter-writing relationship with Alfred L. Bush, curator of Western Americana at

Princeton University who had known Brooks since his student days in Utah. They often discussed American history and traded gifts such as books and documents and later, in the 1960s, aided her in her search for employment and travel grants. As her original engagement period with the Utah State Historical Society was winding down, she reinitiated contact with Wallace Stegner, then serving as assistant to Secretary of Interior Stewart Udall, seeking new opportunities in the Department of Interior. She later in the year informed Stegner that her arrangement with the Utah State Historical Society had been extended but agreed to supply him with an annotated bibliography for his upcoming writing project on the Mormon Trail that became one of the landmark books on the subject.

She also wrote Secretary of Interior Stewart Udall, a great-grandson of John D. Lee, in September 1961, summarizing her trip to Phoenix at Judge Udall's expense and why she was including the reinstatement in her book, ending her letter by stressing, "And I think that facts suppressed or ignored constitute a lie as real as facts distorted."[3] In a later letter from October 1961, she started her crusade to secure the Mountain Meadows Massacre site under federal management and ownership.

Throughout 1961 she continued to edit the Hosea Stout journals, commenting on different aspects of the journals in letters to friends. In one letter she offered Reed Stout, who edited his great-grandfather's autobiography, editorial guidance and her editorial procedures. She also contributed to the St. George centennial by preparing and authoring much of the July 1961 issue of the *Utah Historical Quarterly* dedicated to St. George and the Cotton Mission and answering questions from George Romney, president of American Motors and 1968 U.S. presidential candidate, about his ancestors Miles Romney and Miles P. Romney, for his St. George centennial speech.

~

To *Dean R. Brimhall,*[4] October 26, 1960

October 26, 1960

Dear Dean:

Thank you so much for letting me see the enclosed review. Fawn always does a wonderful piece of work, doesn't she?[5] Somehow she gets the right perspective and evaluated the work as a whole instead of picking at little things.

I don't know when I have enjoyed an evening more than I did the one we spent with you. It's not often that I meet people for whom I feel such an instant fellowship. We shall always be indebted to Ernie and his lovely wife for implementing the meeting and to you and Lila for such perfect entertainment. The only thing I can think of that would be as good, would be a visit with you in the great outdoors which is your back yard there. Maybe—sometime.

I'm sure that you will want to keep this in your files. Thanks again for sending it.

Good wishes,

Dean R. Brimhall
Fruita-via Torrey
Utah

Source: MS 114, Marriott Library Special Collections.

To *Asael C. Lambert*, November 17, 1960

November 17, 1960

Dear A.C.:

Thank you so much for your work on the "EPISTOLE",[6] which I received last night. I have spent a pleasant several hours with it, but must still go back to it.

The closing section on Emma Smith impressed me for two reasons: I have long resented the attitude our people have toward her, and I have copies of two pieces of her writing. I am enclosing copies of these for your files. I think the "blessing" which she wrote for herself is eloquent of the strain under which she lived and of her sincere attempt to accept Joseph's marital irregularities.

Maybe I should bring you up to date on my activities. I'm here at the Historical Society, at least I am until next July, to fill in a vacancy occasioned by the moving of Dr. Cooley[7] to the USU.[8] I am not doing his work, but am editing the diaries of Hosea Stout for publication. This is largely an act of faith for us all: we believe that they are worthy of publication and that they will be a most significant addition to Mormon history, but they will run into two very large volumes at the least and in our economy conscious government there is no money to finance their publication. My own feeling is that I should get them ready, and then trust in the dear Lord or in some Foundation or some grant from somewhere to come forward with the means.,—with the proper pressures, of course.

We have two sons attending the University, so that the arrangement is a happy one for us at home.

I'm deep in Hosea's activities at Nauvoo. He is Captain of the City Police, and writes frankly of their doings in this time of great stress. He speaks of "abating a nuisance", of various encounters and of the "fur company" and its activities. He even includes speeches wherein Brother Brigham rebukes the guard for drinking too much whiskey, etc. This Alexander McRae[9] of the poor spelling is one of the leaders in this raiding group, the fur company.

Many things I'd like to talk to you about.

My Lee biography is being published by the Arthur H. Clark company, and should appear in February.[10] If I get to come that way in the meantime, I'll contact you by telephone.

Thank you so much for this study. It helps to clarify my thinking in some areas.

Sincerely,

To *Alfred L. Bush,*[11] January 26, 1961

January 26, 1961

Mr. Alfred L. Bush
Princeton University Library
Princeton, New Jersey

Dear Alfred:

Somewhere between this office and home I have a one-page letter to you in which I told you something of my acquaintance with Dale L. Morgan. I started thus at the wrong end of our correspondence because my copy of <u>Let Every Sluice of Knowledge be Open'd and Set</u>

a Flowing[12] was out of my hands at the time, and I didn't want to say my thanks before I had read it through. Mr. Dan Walker of the English faculty at the University saw it—his wife is our receptionist—and he was really excited about it, so excited that he kept it for several days. He conducts an "Institute of American Studies" for which this seamed a priceless item.

Then a boy who lives with us—R.J. Snow, son of Glenn E. Snow of the NEA,[13] now in Washington—is majoring in history, and he too borrowed it to show to his teacher, Dr. J.D. Williams.

Now that I have gone through it more thoroughly; I am more impressed with the truth and the beauty of it, with the continuity of history, with the contemporary values so forcefully and so aptly put. As I listened last night to our youthful President at his first press conference, I caught something of the same feel of urgency, the same attempt to put first things first.

I am glad that you put the printed text alongside the handwritten one. For many readers deciphering the original becomes so laborious that they lose the impact of the idea, while for those of us who have handled many such documents the very handwriting is often as eloquent as the words. I think, for example, of John D. Lee's entry, "Today is my chill day," written in such a trembling script that one can almost feel the chill himself.

Thank you so much for this, a thing of beauty and a joy forever for its intrinsic value and its appropriate and exquisite format. Only one word distresses me, and at the risk of being labeled a "hen-minded" reader scratching for flaws, I think I shall call it to your attention. Perhaps I am not the first to do so. It is the word Pictures in the sentence ". . . like apples of gold in pitchers of silver." Oh, Alfred, what that does to the quotation! Can't you just see one of those long, low silver pitchers with its scroll handle, its flowing lines melting into the small lip opposite, its slightly enlarged center piled high with golden apples? Not hard, metallic gold, but ripened golden apples with perhaps just a flush of pink—the dish, the fruit, the arrangement combined to create a sense of wholeness and perfection?

I'm a bit ashamed to have pointed up this one trifle. I apologize sincerely. But let us not take liberties with the King James Version. Yet I think I am not like Carlyle's "critic fly,"[14] for I do sense the enduring nature of this publication, the music of its lucid prose, the combination which makes it the finest tribute possible to a great man—better than a plaque or a statue or a medal to display. Appropriate and not over-done.

More and more each day I sense the importance of what I am trying to do here. In reading the typewritten copy against the original, how important one letter often is! I think I showed you the difference in John E. Page as compared to John E. Hoge of the first reader's version. At any rate, here is a man who was in an important position during those crucial years in Mormon history, who writes clearly and frankly of the things that happen.

I think perhaps I should mail this now and send along another installment later. I suggested that we make our summer issue of the Magazine center in the centennial of The Cotton Mission, and now find myself in the midst of a whole group of short articles which I must write for it.[15] Happy as I am to see this done and to help with it, I still regret anything that takes me away from Hosea.

I catch the mid-night bus tonight for St. George to gather up some material from my files there that I did not bring with me and to talk over our plans with the local committee. By arriving back here at midnight on Sunday night I can meet my friend-husband as he returns from his trek with the Mormon Battalion caravan to Washington, D.C., for the inauguration.[16]

So until sometime next week—maybe—

Sincerely,

To *Arthur H. Clark*, May 15, 1961

Salt Lake City, Utah
May 15, 1961

Dear Mr. Clark:

Here is the Bibliographical Essay of sorts. I've wondered if I should state that with the listing which I made at the end of the MOUNTAIN MEADOWS MASSACRE as a basis of research, these represent additional or specific materials used here.

Several days ago I received a letter to the effect that the leadership of the Mormon Church have issued a formal statement to the effect that John D. Lee might be re-instated into the church through their temple ceremonies. They wished no public announcement to go out to that effect, though they were willing that the family should know.

I had felt that this would be a fitting and dramatic climax to this book—certainly it is a thing that I have not expected to live to see. I have written a short paragraph which I should like to have appended to the last chapter, but do not dare to use it without official consent. There is so much of diplomacy and time and tact required that I may have to discard the idea, but if I get permission, this is what I should like to say:

(APPEND TO LAST CHAPTER)

Through all the eighty-four years which have elapsed since the execution of John D. Lee, the dearest hope of his descendants has been that his name should some day be cleared. An action taken on Thursday, April 2, 1961, has made that hope a reality for them.

On that day the First Presidency and Quorum of the Twelve of the Mormon Church met in a joint session and "It was the action of the Council after considering all the facts available that authorization be given for the re-instatement to membership and former blessings of John D. Lee."

On May 8 and 9 following the necessary ordinances were performed in the Salt Lake Temple.

***

If I can clear this, I'll telephone. Otherwise leave it out.[17]

Sincerely,

To *Merrit L. Norton*,[18] [May 15, 1961]

APPEND TO LAST CHAPTER

Through all the eighty-four years which have elapsed since the execution of John D. Lee, the dearest hope of his descendants has been that his name should some day be cleared. An action taken on Thursday, April 2, 1961, has made that hope a reality for them.

On that day the First Presidency and Quorum of the Twelve of the Mormon Church met in a joint session and "It was the action of the Council after considering all the facts available that authorization be given for the re-instatement to membership and former blessings of John D. Lee."

On May 8 and 9 following, the necessary ordinances were performed in the Salt Lake Temple.

***

Dear Brother Norton:

My Biography of John D. Lee is finished, I have corrected the galleys, and the page-proofs should be here soon. It is scheduled to appear in July. As it now stands, it closes with a question, or with the idea that many questions remain unanswered and may never be answered.

The fact of his re-instatement into the Church would seem a fitting climax to this long study. It could be added to the last chapter as suggested above, or could be attached as a foot-note on the date of his excommunication. I have no desire in this except for the happiness I know it will bring his descendants. Since the edition is small, and the purchasers will be chiefly members of the family, I see no harm in putting it in, though I would not do so without permission.

Thank you for all you have done to bring this about. I'm sure that no one else among all his respected posterity was in a position to do it; I'm sure it will be the occasion for deep prayers and thanksgiving from them all. Though not of the family blood, I too am humbly grateful.

Sincerely,

To *Jesse Udall*,[19] June 23, 1961

603 East South Temple[20]
Salt Lake City, Utah
June 23, 1961

Dear Brother Jesse Udall:

Please do not thank me for complying with your request to call Mr. Clark again asking him to put no word on the jacket of the John D.

Lee biography regarding his reinstatement into the Church. Since I had already called once and written twice, it made me appear a little ridiculous. And I certainly would not accept any money for such an act.

I know that this letter will not change your attitude in the least, but I must write it for my own conscience, and for my record as well as your own. I should like you to hold it until the Church begins to receive high praise for this far-too-long-delayed action and then perhaps you will dare to admit what was done.

Let me begin at the beginning: In 1945 I received a grant from the Rockefeller Foundation, through the Henry E. Huntington Library, to do a piece of research on the Mountain Meadows Massacre. I accepted it and set to work. I did tell my stake president, Brother Harold S. Snow, but I did not mention it to anyone else. I knew that I would be commanded in the name of the Lord to leave it alone.

After the death of President Grant, and after I felt that President George Albert Smith was oriented into his position, I wrote him telling him what I was doing and asking for an audience. He granted it and was most gracious, though at first he made me feel that he could not see what good such a study would be. At the end of our interview, he walked out the hall to the front door with me, shook hands with me again, and said, "The Lord bless you, Sister Brooks. I hope that you are happy, permanently happy, with that you do."

"Thank you, President Smith," I said. "I do not want to do anything for which I will have to apologize ten or twenty years from now."

I believed then, as I believe now that nothing but the truth is good enough for the Church to which I belong, and that God does not expect us to lie in His name.

Not until the book was almost ready for publication did any of the Lee family know of it. No one of them ever saw the manuscript before it appeared in print. I tell you this in order to dispel any idea that I have been working for the Lee family. I have only been trying to write history.

Before the book appeared some of my friends here in Salt Lake City warned me that I would likely be excommunicated; at the last minute the Stanford Press people wrote suggesting that I reconsider and count again the possible cost. I insisted that the publication proceed.

Nearly two years after the book appeared (Nov. 1950) Dr. Frank H Jonas of the University of Utah Political Science department wrote a form letter to five of the people interested in history and employed at 47 East South Temple.[21] Briefly, Jonas asked: "Have you read the book, The Mountain Meadows Massacre, by Brooks? Do you think she has found any new material? Would you class her with such writers as Fawn Brodie, Vardis Fisher,[22] and Maurine Whipple?

Without exception the five Authorities answered that they had NOT read the book, but on the basis of a report made by Brother Reeder, they assumed that it was bad, that it contained no new material, and that the author could well be classed with the others mentioned. Dr. Jonas gave me all the answers, their letters, I mean. I can present them in court, if necessary.

When I had a chance to sell the book to Warner Brothers for a moving picture, I went to Brother Reeder, took a copy of the book along, and asked to discuss his objections to the material in it. He was much embarrassed to have to admit that he had never even seen the book: he thought it was a pamphlet put out by Caxton Printers in Idaho! And yet upon his report, others had decided that it was bad!

I have often said that no one will speak as eloquently for John D. Lee as he himself, so when his Diaries appeared in 1955, I felt that he defended well his own case. These printed books constitute less than half the handwritten material to which I have had access. Because of this, I decided to do a Biography—not for the Lee family, but for a great man who has been judged and mis-represented for more than a hundred years. With this in mind I visited his birthplace at Kaskaskia,[23] I followed his boyhood travels, came across the Plains, to Southern Utah, and have stood in his tracks in the most desolate areas of the Colorado River basin.

By 1958 I had the book written and ready, I thought, to sell. I am not a good salesman; I knew not how to market my own tares. Finally, in June 1960, I signed a contract with the Arthur H. Clark Company, with the understanding that the book should appear in the spring of 1961. At the family reunion in Panguitch in August, 1960, I told the group that, because I had tried so diligently to get this out and it had been held up by forces over which I had no control, I believed that it was delayed for a purpose, that there was new material which I had not yet found which should be included in it. When this appeared, I felt, as many others did, that it was the answer to our prayers. (My talk at Panguitch was put on tape; you can hear it if you care to)

I find it very hard to understand all this hysteria, these frantic calls. Brother Stapley said over and over like a broken phonograph record that "If this appears in print, President McKay will rescind the action." Of course he knows, as I do, that that is only a bluff. If such an ordinance, so impressively performed, can be annulled the next day, it makes all temple work, past and present, null and void.

I myself could not help observing that neither Brother Stapley nor Brother Norton had ever read The Mountain Meadows Massacre, and neither had seen or heard of A Mormon Chronicle: The Diaries of John D. Lee. Brother Norton's family is not even included in Manetta's[24] book—and yet they talk of "all the available information."

Now it all boils down to this: You boys evidently promised not to give this action undue publicity, but to try to keep it within the family. Like a fire in grass, it got out of control. Whom can you blame? I got it from five different sources, two by long-distance telephone, one by local telephone direct through one person from Brother Norton himself, with more of detail than I had elsewhere, and two by letter. Oh, yes, a sixth couple made a special trip up from Orem to tell me all about it—and they too knew the details.

Now I myself have no desire to give this undue publicity, either. I do not want it on radio or TV or headlined in magazine or newspaper articles. But I do think that as an honest historian—as I have tried to be, I owe it to myself and to my readers to tell all the truth, for truth suppressed is its own kind of a lie. So to protect your integrity and to help you keep your word, I must act the part of a prevaricator myself in that I fail to use important and pertinent information or deliberately pretend that I do not have it. This is a role which I do not enjoy playing. This is the reason that I feel I cannot fraternize with the Lee group at their reunion.

I am not sure that you understood my promise to Brother Norton and to Apostle Stapley to be only that I would keep the information out of the first edition. After that is out, after the reunion, I shall use it in such a way that I may retain my reputation as a reliable historian, but still not give it "undue publicity."

Please file this letter where in a year or two, when the Church leaders are being praised for their attempt to correct this hundred-year-old injustice, you may read this again and not be ashamed of the part which you played in bringing it about. For this action will redound to the good of the church; it will give increased faith in the vision and inspiration of its leaders. Everywhere it has been greeted with, "it's about time!" by everyone who knows, both in the family and out.

Very sincerely yours,

To *Reed A. Stout*,[25] July 30, 1961

603 East South Temple
Salt Lake City, Utah
July 30, 1961

Dear Mr. Stout:

Here at last are your notes. I'm sorry about the delay, but I had taken last week off to work at home on my own book.

It was good to visit with you over the telephone. Mail man's here!

He left without this, so I'll take time to summarize our discussion, and then carry this out myself.

Dr. Mortensen is in Dixie today and tomorrow; when he returns, he may wish to modify this. Roughly, this is about what I have done.[26]

1—I divide the material into paragraphs to facilitate the reading. To me, the editor is a go-between from the writer to his audience, and a part of the business of the editor is to be interpreter and guide.

2—I insert little punctuation, often just making a double spacing indicate a place where a period should be. There are times, however, when for clarity or to prevent mis-understanding, I do punctuate. There are arguments both for and against this; the fact that I myself may misinterpret on the one, and the fact that I should not expect every reader to take as much time to decide that this man is trying to say as I have had to do.

3—When a name is variously spelled, I footnote it as it appears first, explaining that there will be changes in the text and giving the final or correct spelling. Then I leave the variations in. For example, Lee is consistent in spelling "Kimble" and after the first note to that effect I leave it misspelled. In the index it is correctly spelled, and he finally does get around to writing it correctly.

4—In long quotations which are single spaced and indented, I spell exactly as in the original without comment, and in short sentences also unless the error is such that it might be assumed to be a typographical one, when I use the [sic] note.

Actually, I think an explanatory note at the beginning stating exactly what you plan to do in this regard is sufficient.

It's a great business, this making a public figure of a man who was before only a name, a challenge and a rewarding occupation. Good luck to us both!

Sincerely,

To *George Romney*,[27] [July 1961]

UTAH STATE HISTORICAL SOCIETY
603 East South Temple
Salt Lake City, Utah

Mr. George Romney, President
American Motors Corporation
Detroit, Michigan

Dear President Romney:

I had delayed in answering your letter, thinking I could send the summer issue of our Quarterly[28] along at the same time, but now that it is to be delayed for another few days, I think I should not wait longer. As I told you before, it is to be dedicated to St. George and the Cotton Mission.

I understand that a book has been published on your own life, which gives in addition a sketch of your ancestors, but I have not had access to this book.[29] I hope you will forgive me for including items that I have gleaned from the sources available here regarding the two men, Miles Romney and his son Miles P.

MILES ROMNEY[30] joined the Church in 1837 in England, and for a time served as local preacher in the town of Preston. When he decided to come to America, he sailed on the ship Sheffield, embarking on 25 February 1841 and landing at New Orleans. From here he came up the Mississippi river to Nauvoo, Where, according to one account, his wife traded a paisley shawl for permission to live in a small house.

In Nauvoo Miles Romney worked on the temple as foreman. When the Saints were driven out, he took his family to Burlington, Iowa, where he spent the winter. He did not come to Utah until October 18, 1850. He camped on the Temple Block that winter, his family living in their wagons. He was made superintendent of public works in Salt Lake City.

In 1856 he was called on a mission to England, where he served for three years. In 1861 he was called to Dixie on the cotton mission, his name being listed with the first company.

He is listed as "Architect and Builder" of the St. George Tabernacle, and as "Assistant Architect and Chief Carpenter" of the Temple. He died on May 3, 1877, not long after the building was dedicated.

MILES P ROMNEY[31] was born August 18, 1843, in Nauvoo, Illinois, so he was only a boy when the family moved to Dixie. James G. Bleak's record says that while he had been made a Seventy "Sept. 1862 Brother Miles P. was in Salt Lake city and not set apart at this time." He filled a mission from 1862 to 1865—in England.

From James G. Bleak's Book B (1869–1877) we learn much of the activity of this young man. On Nov. 8, 1869 he was made a High Priest and set apart as a member of the High Council. March 29, 1870, he is listed as Major Miles P. Romney under Col. Richard Bentley. July 4, 1871, Miles P. Romney was orator of the day. August 2, 1872, he was made Stake Superintendent of Sunday School.

In 1874, in an effort to standardize their products, he was in charge of "erecting a canning and wine house." This was later enlarged to be the Opera House, and was built under his direction as head of the Builders Union.

In the setting up of the United Order in 1874 he was appointed Superintendent of the Carpenter Department. Later he was chairman of the convention of Mechanical Labor and it products.

From the Diaries of John Laub, Charles L. Walker, Lorenzo Brown,[32] and others, we find that he was in charge of the building of the Court House, the Brigham Young Home, and other homes; he was a member of the Dramatic Club and the Library Association; in 1876 he was awarded a contract to build a bridge across the Rio Virgin River. In January 2, 1877, he was a Director of the Winsor Castle Stockgrowing Company.[33]

From all this it is clear that he was a dynamic person, much loved and trusted among his peers. I should add perhaps—though you need not feel any obligation to use it—that on August 25, 1878, he made a public confession getting too much wine on election day. That is, he wrote a letter which was read to the congregation which "showed a very contrite spirit being full of grief and sorrow for what he had done. . . ." He was in good company, however. David H. Cannon,[34] later for so many years president of the temple, made a similar confession just two weeks earlier, and Henry W. Miller[35] made one the same day. (This is told in the diary of A.R. Whitehead.)[36]

I realize that these are sketchy and disjointed, and that you may not care to use any of them, but am so happy that you have consented to come and to stand in the pulpit of the building designed and erected by your ancestor that I think it a privilege to assemble this material. To me, as to most Dixieites, the Tabernacle is the most beautiful building in the state, a credit to any community. My husband takes great pride in the fact that his father, then a teen-age boy, cut the caps for the doors and windows as his contribution.

Sincere good wishes,

To *Ida Hamblin*,[37] August 7, 1961

1295 Crystal Avenue
Salt Lake City, Utah
August 7, 1961

My dear Ida,

The longer the time goes on, the worse I feel about the meeting I attended at the home of Judge Udall. I am sick with the thought that such men as Al Lee and Ewart and the others should feel toward me as they do. After the wonderful reunion at Panguitch, I feel deeply that the family will be split on this basic issue, or that I have caused such a division.

It is so hard for me to understand this hysteria, this fear of apostates, this threat that the action will be rescinded. This last I do <u>not</u> believe. I do not think President McKay would punish all the Lee family (and that would be a real punishment to them) because of something I do. I know he COULD, but I don't think he would. I think they should discipline ME if they think I need it.

They forgot the fact that after a hundred years the Lee family is very large, or perhaps they would not have said to tell the family. They would have said, "Tell only the bishops in the family, or those who are regular ordinance workers at the temple, or those who keep the Word of Wisdom." But they didn't: They said "You may tell the family." Now in this area they have been taken at their word, and the family has been told, down to the last and the least—Evan Lee in this area, Russ Mortensen here, Ken & Peg Whitwood and others have been so very happy to tell the family. Once they have all been told, it would give the church the kind of publicity they do not want to have to pass out the word that the action has been rescinded. The Jack-Mormons and apostates would really have a holiday then.

I hope you will not think I was too bitter that day. Several things had troubled me: First that Bro. Norton himself told it in great detail, and then was all upset that others had; Second, that neither he nor Apostle Stapley had ever seen even the outside cover of The Mormon Chronicle or diaries. If they had read them, they would feel different. Third, that when I talked to Apostle Stapley and told him of our meeting at Panguitch, and that I had felt that the book had been delayed because there was new material which should be added, and this came as an answer to all our prayers, he just slapped the table and said, "IT IS FROM THE DEVIL." As if maybe the Dear Lord wouldn't hear humble people who have worked on this problem for more than twenty years as you and Edna and others have done, or for more than fifteen years as I have done.

I want to copy a little from my letter to Judge Udall, so that you will see my thinking more clearly:

> "Now it all boils down to this: You boys evidently promised not to give this action undue publicity, but to try to keep it within the family. Like a fire in grass, it got out of control. Whom can you blame? I got it from five different sources, two by long-distance telephone, one by local telephone direct through one person from Brother Norton himself, with more of detail than I had elsewhere, and two by letter. Oh, yes, a sixth couple made a special trip up from Orem to tell me all about it—and they too knew the details.

"Now I myself have no desire to give this undue publicity, either. I do not want it on radio or TV or headlined in magazine or newspaper articles. But I do think that as an honest historian—as I have tried to be, I owe it to myself and to my readers to tell all the truth, for truth suppressed is its own kind of a lie. So to protect your integrity and to help you keep your word, I must act the part of a prevaricator myself in that I fail to use important and pertinent information or deliberately pretend that I do not have it. This is a role which I do not enjoy playing. This is the reason that I feel I cannot fraternize with the Lee group at their reunion."

Well, it was a long letter, and I'll not copy more from it. But please do not misjudge me or be angry with me. I simply COULD NOT promise what they asked, or it would never have come out in this biography where it belongs. It would have been picked up by someone else who does want to make a smash hit with it, and I would be blamed by all true historians for not having included it.

I'm so glad for it; so happy and grateful. It answers everything. It settles everything. That of all those responsible, only Lee and Haight were cut off the Church and that Haight was re-baptized in less than two years, still left full responsibility on the shoulders of Lee. Now it is lifted—many, many years late—but still lifted. And if Brother Stapley and Brother Norton have not had time to become informed as to the true character of John D. Lee by reading his own words, thousands of other people have. And all who know will rejoice.

My best love to you, Ida. I appreciated your silence during that horrible, horrible afternoon.

To *Ettie Lee*, September 3, 1961

1295 Crystal Avenue, S.L.C.
Sept. 3, 1961

My dear Ettie:

Your letter came some time ago, and I did not plan to answer it, but yesterday the check was returned and I thought you should know.[38] Will is still in Dixie, having the time of his young life, and won't be back until Monday at least. It warms my heart to see how genuinely glad people are to see him. I don't think he has an enemy in all the world, or a person that would doubt his word.

I was deeply troubled that you should write again in that vein. What does the Judge mean by AT THIS TIME. He knows well that when a book is published, it is published, and at this time after it is out means that there would be the same forces a-foot to prevent a second edition.

He said several times that "the brethren felt good about it." I'm sure that they still feel good about it, as does everyone else here. In view of the conditions in this state regarding it, the attitude there is positively ridiculous. Take Marian Lee Pulsipher's father: He took his letter straight to the temple to President Harold Snow. Since four or five of John D.'s descendants are ordinance workers there, every person in the house knew it before the session was ended, and there was general rejoicing. Or Wes Williamson[39] who left the main highway to visit Harmony and told every person there; or Evan Lee who has passed it on freely in southern Utah. In my own case even people I have never seen have taken occasion to come into the office—on Friday last a Mrs. Ashworth from Beaver, and I told you of the Mrs. Banks whose husband is a retired school teacher at Pleasant Grove and who herself is a Lee from Panaca. What I'm saying is that it is no secret and that not a single person has said a word except praise of the General Authorities for the action. Truly they should feel good about it. Every person who has read either the Mountain Meadows Massacre or the Diaries will feel good about it, as I have come to learn from having my own words quoted back to me. Righting a hundred-year-old wrong can bring only commendation.

As to the meeting there—I was not there five minutes before I could see that it was packed, with every speaker instructed and words put into his mouth. Of course I know that President McKay has the power and authority and CAN rescind the action about which they all feel so good, but does it follow that he must do it just to prove that he can. I cannot believe that a rational being would punish John D. Lee and through him the whole Lee family because of what I do. He was pronounced worthy of being readmitted to the church; the decision was unanimous; the ordinances were performed and recorded on earth and we believe in heaven.

Oh, Ettie, if you could have seen our dear President last Tuesday morning when they brought him out to have his picture taken with the leaders of the "Covered Wagon Trek" that was advertising the Dixie Centennial! Supported by two strong men, he could only shuffle along, and was lifted down and back up about five steps. When they got him arranged, he took a good picture, but it was a shock to all the crowd to see how he has failed in the last weeks.

Please, Ettie, do not make yourself miserable about this. Thank God that it is done, smile and be happy and know that all is well. I'm so grateful for the tape recording that was made there.

I have not heard again from Wesley about the monument,[40] but assume that it is moving along. I have spent the better part of the last three weeks indexing the Lee Biography, and hope that it will appear on October 1 according to contract. We love you dearly as we have done from the day we met. The extent of your good works can never be measured, and the Dear Lord knows that your heart is right.

Be of good cheer; lift up your head and be happy; enjoy your sunset years in the assurance that the cause to which you have dedicated your life is accomplished.

To *Stewart Udall,*[41] September 7, 1961

Salt Lake City, Utah
September 7, 1961

Dear Secretary Udall:

I've held this silly card because it really doesn't tell anything except that I am thrilled to have the picture.

The poetry bits were both by Lydia Hall,[42] a recluse so shy that she could never lift her eyes to talk to people, hardly even to me. I discovered a bit quite by accident and went to see her, for I sensed a true poetic touch. I took two short items (they are all very short), typed them up for her and sent them in to the Relief Society Magazine, where they were published. Several of the others, these two among them, are in Under the Dixie Sun,[43] a large book put out by the County and the Daughters of the Utah Pioneers, St. George chapter. Lydia died unmarried a few years ago, her gift quite undiscovered I think by her two brothers. I think that six to ten pages would hold all she ever did, and I have considered getting them together as a sort of memorial to her.

My reference to Judge Udall stems from a trip to Phoenix which he financed in an effort to make me believe that "if any word of this [John D. Lee's re-instatement into the Church] appears in print, President McKay will rescind the action." He had stirred up such hysteria on the subject that most of the family there thought that if I include a short statement of the facts at the end of my Biography, poor John D. will be put back into Hell and not redeemed until the Millennium.

I had promised to keep it out of the first edition to please them, but would make no further promise. They (Judge Udall) wanted a pledge that no word would appear in the book, on the jacket, or in any review of the book.

The family in Utah are pleased, ready to tell it to the world. I myself insist that it is public information; a card giving full detail of name of participants in the ordinances, date, date of Letter of Approval from the Presiding Authorities is on file at the Genealogical Library for anyone interested to see. And I think that facts suppressed or ignored constitute a lie as real as fact distorted.

To *Stewart Udall*, October 16, 1961

October 16, 1961

Dear Secretary Udall:

I know that you are to be in the area today, but I doubt that I shall get to see you. Anyway, this matter is best put on paper.

Last week Howard Foulger of the Forest Service at Cedar City called on me to say the Church had sent Apostle Marion G. Romney[44] to try to purchase the land upon which the Monument stands. It is now owned by Ezra Lytle.[45] He declined to donate it to them; in fact, he asked a price which they considered exorbitant. I am not certain enough of the figure to quote it.

Mr. Foulger had hoped that there might be some exchange of land that would bring this two-and-a-half acres under the Forest Service, so that he could improve the road to it, erect a foot-bridge across the gully, plant some trees and grass around it, and take measures to prevent further erosion. He talked to Apostle Romney, he said, and was informed that the Church does not want any of those things done, nor do they want any publicity which would encourage people not already interested in finding the place to go to it.

I have tried without success to get local people to make a few improvements, the County Commissioners or the Sons of Utah Pioneers.

I have long felt that, this should be under Federal supervision: the people buried there were from other states; the whole matter is of national, not local concern. And our State Parks and legislature are both Church-dominated.

I know that the Forest Service is not under your supervision, but felt that you would know how it might be perhaps designated as a National Historic Site, or National Cemetery, or in some other way be placed where it will be accessible and well cared for.

I returned yesterday from the Lee reunion at the Marble Canyon Bridge. The crowd was smaller than usual, but seemed congenial and enthusiastic. At no time was our point of difference mentioned, except when I told them that volumes of the FIRST EDITION would be mailed soon to all who had placed pre-publication orders.

Your sweet mother was there. She makes a most efficient secretary.

Good wishes always,

To *Arthur H. Clark*, November 2, 1961

1295 Crystal Avenue
Salt Lake City, Utah
Nov. 2, 1961

THE ARTHUR H. CLARK COMPANY
1264 South Central Avenue
Glendale 4, California

Dear Mr. Clark:

Thank you for the "Prospectus" just received.

I have no criticism of it except that I do feel rather deeply that the phrase "even to official Church action as recent as 1961" should be omitted. It will make no difference in the general sale of the book on the one hand, and on the other it will be like defiantly waving a red flag in the face of many who are concerned about it. The facts are all there, in normal print, where they belong, and whoever reads the book will find them.

I made the family a promise on the one hand; I stood alone in defiance of all the most influential of them in insisting that this matter be printed in the second edition. Now that it is there, I think I have filled my duty as an historian, but I think it would be poor taste to flaunt it in their faces. As I said earlier, I do not think it will make any difference at all in the sale of the book.

I have already written Wes asking him if he will get busy on his list of people from that area, and I'll call or contact Mrs. Henrie at Provo. She may have such a list from her work in distributing her book on the Lee genealogy. You might write Evan Lee at Virgin, Utah, and ask if he would address a number of circulars to the members of his immediate family, the descendants of Mary Leah Groves. I shall write to Mrs. Louise Udall in Phoenix and also Ida Lee Hamblin at Mesa and ask them to contact you direct.

I shall be very happy indeed to see this book in print.

Sincerely,

To *Wallace Stegner*, November 4, 1961

November 4, 1961

Dr. Wallace Stegner
Department of the Interior
Washington 25, D.C.

Dear Wally:

Thank you so much for your prompt answer to my letter.[46]

I hope you'll not think I was crying "wolf!" too soon. Director Cooley[47] had told me that things looked pretty hopeless and that I should cast about for other opportunities. Now he thinks that he can guarantee me employment until July 1, provided I can guarantee to finish the second volume of Hosea Stout by that date. I can and will, though I dislike this business of having to solicit contributions to get the pay.

On the other hand, I think this record is significant enough that it should be finished and I cannot stand leaving a job half done to either dangle unfinished indefinitely or to fall into the hands of someone else to do.

As I see the situation now, I can spend some time for you.[48] Is the thing you want chiefly the bibliography of the first-person accounts of the trek across the plains. Since you are on one side of the Platte and I on the other, I assume you mean that it is east of that stream that "doesn't offer much in the way of interest." Right?

Without moving from my chair I can list a least twelve day-by-day diaries besides Hafen's Handcarts to Zion.[49] It's Saturday and the library upstairs is locked, but I can send a preliminary list right away. Or would you prefer that I copy, or have copied for you some excerpts. I'll try to get a full reproduction for you of the most significant, most revealing account I have seen of a member of the ill-fated handcart group. I found it only recently in Idaho, and we have only a microfilm. It's one you MUST see. Then Burton W. Musser has been teasing me for a long time with some letters written by Mary Barr Neff to her sister Anna Barr Musser[50] in Winter Quarters giving a woman's interpretation of the 1847 journey of those who followed close on the heels of the Pioneers. I'll be [not clear] I trouble him enough without this. And expect a preliminary list and some notes with in the week.

Thanks again

To *Klaus J. Hansen*,[51] November 7, 1961

November 7, 1961

Dear Klaus:

I'm embarrassed to be so long acknowledging your letter and thanking you for the "Kingdom of God" paper. Duties press in on every side and as the old-timers used to say, "The squeaking wheel gets the grease." At any rate, the more persistent demands do get first attention.

I like your paper very much. A few ideas suggest themselves to me in the attempt to understand the early Mormon Church in its setting, one of the most important of which was the general belief in the immediacy of the Second Advent. This was shared by many, indeed, by most of the Churches. Everywhere was the feeling that the END was near; Jesus Christ would soon return to gather his children, while the wicked would burn as stubble.

This, I think deserves some mention, not because it was peculiar to the Mormons, but because it was in the air. They were different in that they meant to do something about it—something more than clothe in white robes. They were to establish His Kingdom upon the earth, with His holy Temple ready to receive him. They talked of powers, thrones, and dominions in the eternal worlds, but they talked also of getting ready to receive Him on this earth. Irene Haskell Pomeroy's letters and those of her mother—in fact of so many converts—show their great eagerness to get to Zion to be one part fear lest they shall not get the Kingdom established in time.

Joseph Smith had fired these chosen ones, the YTFIF with such a zeal that they never lost the sense of their responsibility in this tremendous undertaking. Because of it, they could pull up roots to establish new settlements wherever the needs of The Kingdom demanded it.

I am sure that the YTFIF controlled the political life of the Territory, and also for the young state; I think it also had great influence upon the economic development. You probably noted this item, also from the Mormon Chronicle:

"... Pres. Young said that he would let Bro. A. Lyman nominate that commity: James M. Flake, William Crowsby & John D. Lee. Pres B. Young Said that he had no objection to the men, provided J.D. Lee is the chairman of that commity, and further Said that when a man was taken out of this council to do buisiness, let that man be the chairman of whatever commity he may belong; thus the chairman can report to the council."

Dr. Cooley tells me that in the 1857–1858 election in Box Elder County, they had a regular election and the man receiving the most votes was not one of the Council, so they had him disqualified and seated Jonathan C. Wright,[52] who was a member, instead. His article in the Quarterly [Vol XXIV No. 2,3,4][53] does not show this, but he says he has the correspondence which does. His secretary, Mrs. Ward, has papers to show that they always made two reports of [incomplete]

To *Arthur H. Clark*, December 1, 1961

December 1, 1961

The Arthur H. Clark Company
1264 South Central Avenue
Glendale 4, California

Dear Mr. Clark:

I'm much disturbed about the wrapping-paper covers of the First Edition of this Lee book.[54] People who get them seem so disappointed, so let down. Today I have taken the jackets off the two that you sent to replace these ugly, empty ones for people who wanted the books as gifts and thought they should look like gifts.

Can you send extra jackets for the ones you sent? I thought I ordered and paid for ten copies of the second edition, but I got the first. I could sell them here at a meeting tonight if they had the other covers on. I'll pay extra if necessary to get the jackets for all that I buy hereafter.

Don't you think that the difference in the bound cover, the paper and the title print is enough?[55] One lady who ordered hers by mail, or sent in a pre-publication order, came in to complain that she didn't get the book that was advertised in the brochure and was most disappointed.

We should have our best sales here in the next two or three weeks, but we can double them with the new jackets.

I don't know what Sam Weller of Zion's Book Store got, but his hands will be tied for any publicity with those covers. How could he make a window display?

Please forgive me. I've had four callers today—one to complain at the looks of what she had, two to buy First Editions with the jackets of the two Second Edition books, the third to take hers with the promise that I would somehow get a dust jacket for it before Christmas.

Sincerely,

To *Arthur H. Clark*, December 5, 1961

December 5, 1961

The Arthur H. Clark Company
1264 South Central Avenue
Glendale 4, California

Dear Mr. Clark:

Thank you for the letter of November 28 explaining why an author must not expect to be classed with a dealer, even though she pays cash in advance and sells twice as many books.[56] I feel that authors should be kept in their places also and have no hard feelings in this matter. Huntington Library had spoiled me; that's why I asked.

Enclosed is my check for one hundred forty-four dollars and fifty cents ($144.50) for which please send me twenty copies of the regular advertised edition. If possible I should have them before December 10; I can sell them all on that night—rather, I have orders for them all. If the five copies I am allowed arrive rather soon, it will take off the pressure of people who want them for mailing before Christmas.

The advertising through the Historical Society is really paying off.

Sincere good wishes,

To *Asael C. Lambert*, December 11, 1961

December 11, 1961

Dear A.C.,

Thank you so much for your letter of December 6.

Yes, there is a story behind the last paragraphs of page 376, but I am not sure that I can tell it all. I do not care to tell any of it in public, but to you I will give my version.

The Lee Family Reunion was held at Panguitch a year-and-a-half ago in August. A wonderful crowd was there and a fine spirit. The Panguitch stake house was full to overflowing; Manetta Henrie had just got out her 1200-page book on the John D. Lee descendants, and was the guest of honor.

I was asked to speak. I told them that the Biography was finished, that Arthur H. Clark had accepted it, and that it was scheduled for a spring appearance—last spring. Pre-publication orders would be accepted for $7.50, etc. etc. Then I explained how restless I had been at the long delays on the MMM book, and then finally this item, the most important thing in it, came after it was being set up in the galleys. Dale Morgan found the hand-written letter of the father of two of the victims—It had arrived in D.C. too late to be included in Senate Document No. 42, and was filed, unlisted, among the Indian materials.[57] So, I explained, since so many questions remained unanswered, it might be that there was new material forthcoming for this book also.

Immediately after I spoke, a tall, good-looking man stood up in the midst of the audience and made a motion that this body go on record as requesting the re-instatement of John D. Lee into the church. Everyone was saying, "Who is he?" He had voiced the hope of them all, but all supposed that such an request would be futile.

He was Merritt L. Norton, a grandson through Caroline Williams,[58] who is a regular ordinance worker at the Salt Lake Temple. He evidently worked with Apostle Stapley and the president of the Temple. At April conference last spring they called in Judge Jesse Udall of the Supreme Court in Arizona and Bishop Ewart Lee,[59] also of Arizona, and talked the matter over with them. Later the council met, the action was taken, and the ordinances performed.

A copy of the letter of authorization signed by James Anderson, also word that the ordinances were performed, was sent immediately to Miss Ettie Lee, who sent them immediately to me. There was no word of secrecy in Brother Anderson's letter; in the one from Norton to Miss Lee was the statement that, "You may notify the family," but the suggestion that this be not given "undue publicity." Well, the Lee family is pretty large, and the word went like wildfire. Such rejoicing, such tears and prayers of thanksgiving you could hardly imagine. Miss Lee sent all the material with the word that this is just what we have all been waiting for, a fitting climax to the book.

Immediately there was a panic. Norton stated that if this were to appear in print "President McKay would rescind the action." My answer to him was, "How crazy can you get? He cannot rescind the action!" I felt, like Lady Macbeth that "What's done is done." Well, there were long telephone calls from Zion to California to Phoenix, around and around, until at last Miss Lee in tears implored me not to put it in the book. Reluctantly I promised not to use it in the First Edition. I was called in to an interview with Apostle Stapley. He seemed not to hear what I said, but repeated over and over like a broken victrola record the words, "If this appears in print anywhere—in the book, on the jacket, in a review—President McKay will rescind the action." I could only insist that I had made a promise to keep it out of the First Edition; more than that I would not promise.

Now they put on pressure from another source. I was invited to a meeting of the Lee family in Phoenix; they paid my fare down and back on a jet plane. The meeting was held at the home of Judge Jesse Udall, whose wife is a Lee. Present were the official officers in the Lee organization along with six young Bishops. They each spoke, bore testimony that Pres. McKay was the only man on the earth authorized to speak in the name of God; that he could rescind the action; that if he did, Poor John D. Lee would have to wait out another hundred years....

Well, we decided to make the First Edition 250 copies, identical with the regular one except for this last short item and with the front WESTERN FRONTIERSMEN SERIES IX omitted. These are now all sold out. So far as I know, no mention has been made of this reinstatement. I hope that for the time being, it will be overlooked, though a printed card in the files of the genealogical society has long ago made it public. I enclose a copy. Most of the Lee family have it in their books.

I wish that Jesse (Judge) Udall could know that people like you regard this action as a credit to the church, as a reason for renewed faith in the inspiration and humanity of the Leaders—without connecting the word with me directly. He insisted that it would injure our missionary system, cause apostasy among the converts, and be a terrible thing. I felt that it would bring into good fellowship many who are now estranged, including many of the Lee family.

Thank you for book on BLOOD which may be delivered later today. It did not arrive this morning. I saw the work on THE SERPENT, but do not have a copy.[60] I had hoped to get you a copy of this book, but they gave me only five free ones and they went quickly nearer home. I have ordered and sold one lot of twenty—I mean, I have sold some of them and sent out the others. After the holidays I still expect to send one to you.

Gratefully,

To *Asael C. Lambert*, December 20, 1961

December 20, 1961

Dear A.C.,

What a tremendous amount of research you have done! And what significant research!

I have been looking through again this on the Kingdom of God. Since I first got a glimpse of the YTFIF or Council of Fifty, I have been conscious of the great part which their belief in the immediacy at the Second Advent played in their lives. IF the Savior were to come within this generation, or within eighty years, IF at his coming the wicked would burn as stubble, the moon be turned into blood, the waters into gall, it naturally behooved them to get the Kingdom established and the Temple built.

This physical, political Kingdom grows as we read; this Council of Fifty takes on stature and importance. No, I have never heard of ELU of Fifty of which you speak. I have been tracing down the secret "Living Constitution" of the Kingdom, perhaps wrongly assuming that this inner circle consisted of twelve men. Now I think perhaps it was SEVEN instead.[61] Stout names five of the members of the "Living Constitution;"[62] Lee mentions the group but does not say how many.[63] Jones says that Alphaeus Cutler[64] was a "member of a certain quorum or committee of seven, who had been set apart by Joseph the Seer in Nauvoo. Present-day Fundamentalists base much of their claims to a group of Seven set apart by John Taylor (perhaps the group re-activated or new members supplied) at the time he was wrestling with the problem of keeping or rejecting polygamy. These Seven were commissioned to see that there were those who would live the Celestial Law until the coming of the Son of Man.[65]

As nearly as I can check, members of the YTFIF were men of practical skills and training. Those named as the "Living Constitution" were men who could well have been the law-enforcement group. Stout named the five as: Samuel Bent, Charles C. Rich, Edward Hunter, John Taylor, and Theodore Turley.[66]

How closely this all ties into the Blood-Atonement or blood-vengeance deal I cannot yet tell. There were killings in Nauvoo, but chiefly of spies or traitors, I think. Between the Mississippi and Winter Quarters young men were whipped severely for moral lapses and there were threats that "The Law of the Lord" would be put into effect, if not now, certainly when they reached Zion. I am appalled by the number of murders in Salt Lake City—in the Territory, to be more exact. Some of these were characters who had been suspect for months or years; some were apostates or outsiders who were trying to edge in on the land or water rights. Added up, they will give positive evidence of the theories which you advance.

To change the subject a little:

I have seen no criticism of this John Doyle Lee thing in print, but I understand that some important people who have looked into it say that while it may be true "She didn't need to bring this thing up," meaning the suggestions of blood atonement or other of the current beliefs, including polygamy. I could as well have left out the things upon which the leaders are sensitive, they argue and it would have been a better book.

Daily Dr. Cooley wonders how long before I may get called in before Brother Stapley. I have no fear, since at the meeting in Phoenix I insisted upon having a tape recorder. I rather surprised Judge Udall by that—He didn't want his voice on it at all. When Miss Lee insisted that I fly down at their expense, I told her that I would appear only on that condition. I knew that Wes Williamson would support me and be there with his machine. Now if there is to be a questioning, I can produce the tape.

I don't want to burden or annoy you with this, but I think I'll let you see the correspondence which led to the meeting. Slip it into the enclosed envelope and get it out of your way.

I have a First Edition copy saved for you which I'll get out after this Christmas rush.

Since it will be over before this arrives, I hope you had a happy day, and a year ahead of continued achievement and success.

Sincerely,

Chapter 8

1962

Completing the Hosea Stout Journals

By the 1960s, Brooks's letters reveal a senior historian at the pinnacle of her career responding to numerous requests to review manuscripts, for information and her ideas on historical subjects, and for copies of her books. She kept busy replying to these appeals for help and the number of letters she produced increased over previous years, peaking at sixty-two extant letters during 1962. These include the steady stream of correspondence she maintained with a number of good friends, who furnished her with stimulating conversation and support.

As 1962 dawned, she composed a newsy letter to Dale Morgan summarizing the events in her life and, as always, asked his opinion on questions arising from her editing efforts. These incidences included moving to the 98 U Street location in Salt Lake City; receiving two offers to republish her Mountain Meadows Massacre book, one from the Oklahoma University Press and another from Arthur H. Clark; obtaining an extension of her employment with the Utah State Historical Society to complete the Hosea Stout journals; and A. R. Mortensen's promotion from director of the Utah State Historical Society to the University of Utah Press. During her editing of the Stout diaries, she encountered the phrase "arrested & nepoed today." She took "nepo to be the root of nepotism and assumed that the boy was put into custody of white parents."[1] Morgan quickly replied that nepo is the word *open* spelled backwards and "symbolically if not in actual fact, it means opening up a man's belly, filling it with rocks, and sinking it in a river."[2]

Among the friends with whom she conversed was Peg Gregory, the editor who helped her with the John D. Lee biography. Brooks reported that several local newspapers had favorably reviewed the biography and the *Los Angeles Times* actually started their review with a quote from the controversial notice of Lee's reinstatement that appeared at the end of the book. She crowed about Apostle Stapley's threat that "'if this appears in print, in the book, on the cover, or in any review, President McKay will rescind this action,' must either put up or shut up, as the locals say. Well, I think he has shut up."[3] Other friends she wrote included Obert C. Tanner, encouraging him to run for governor of the State of Utah, and Gustive O. Larson, discussing the use of "B'hoys" in the Stout diaries.

She continued to correspond with Wallace Stegner, addressing him as Wally and listing the various trail diaries and the location of copies for his Mormon Trail book. She also fed him historic nuggets that she encountered during editing of the Stout journals. One such tidbit was her suggestion that William Clayton was the unnamed person that Stout caught being delinquent in performing his guard duties and threatened with cutting behind the ears. In her next letter, she quickly cautioned Stegner that her thoughts on Clayton were only speculations without historic documentation. She then corrected him on the best way to approach the LDS Church history department to gain access to some of the diaries held there.

To Stegner's question about the non-Mormons present in the 1847 pioneer company, she discussed for probably the first time in her letters the "notorious" Tom Brown, a topic she would turn to throughout the decade and into the 1970s. Nathaniel Thomas Brown was a member of the 1847 pioneer company to Utah who was listed on the "This Is the Place" monument as "and one other man, whose name is not of the record." Juanita identified him as the man who was involved with Stephen and William Hodges in the murder-robbery of members of the Miller family in Iowa on May 10, 1845. The two Hodges brothers were apprehended, tried, and hanged for the crime shortly thereafter, but Brown, the real instigator, took refuge in Nauvoo, traveled with the first pioneer company to the Salt Lake Valley, and was eventually killed in Iowa.

Brooks accepted temporary employment in October 1962 with Assistant U.S. Attorney Parker M. Neilson to research the history of the upper Green River. Her research would be used to counter a suit by the State of

Utah to gain possession of the riverbed. This task presented an opportunity for her to study the fur trade, writing Morgan that his *Jedediah Smith* was her Bible. She then went on in the letter listing all the diaries she had reviewed.[4]

An adventure for Brooks near the end of the year was a trip to Los Angeles to speak at the invitation of George T. Boyd, instructor at the LDS Institute of Religion at the University of Southern California. Upon returning, she apologized to Boyd if she had offended some members "with my comments on the use of wine in the sacrament or by intimating that 'the testimonies went on until sundown,' after the proper spiking of the noon meal."[5] She explained that the people of Dixie do not take such matters so seriously and then concluded the letter with a couple more stories that she luckily did not repeat during her talk.

~

To *Dale Morgan*, January 15, 1962

January 15, 1962

Dear Dale:

How many weeks—yes months—I have thought I'd take time to write to you, but always nearer pressures had their way. Two things make it imperative that I act immediately.

First, I had a note from Howard Cox of Manti to ask why he had never received his copy of John Doyle Lee ordered and paid for in advance. At once I looked up my record and found that his was mailed in the lot of ten which I myself accompanied to the Post Office. My son Kay was with me, carried the books in and attended to the business. We did not insure them, perhaps because of our long experience in the Post Office which had developed a great confidence in the efficiency of the postal service. In the same shipment were books to you, to Alfred L. Bush at Princeton, and to Otis Marsden at San Francisco, neither of whom has acknowledged receipt of it. I was so sure all would arrive well before Christmas. Will you please let me know if you got yours???

Second, Things have cleared somewhat for me and Hosea. Dr. Cooley has scraped together enough so that I can finish the editing, if my eyes will hold out at the microfilm. For a while I thought I could never endure it, not because of the immediate effect, but because of a delayed aching in the night hours far at the back of my eyes. Lately I limit myself to two hours a day at the microfilm and seem to get by OK.

Then too, we have moved.[6] We liked the house on Crystal Avenue very well, but it was set up on a long-time payment plan which we knew we could never complete. So when Dr. Hal Bentley was to go to Ethiopia he sold us his little, OLD house on 98 U Street. He took a lot of ours in St. George and a part cash payment for his equity in the place and it will pay out at $85. a month in six years. It is such a house as we can leave one of the boys in if and when he marries; it is only ten minutes walk from the University Library and nearer my work here.

Moving is a distracting business, though, attended with a certain amount of confusion, in spite of everything.

You were right about Hosea's journals being about ready to publish.[7] In fact, if we had a clearer ribbon copy, I'd protest even copying them again. I have listed changes I noted in the first two volumes, if you would care to check them. They're really not too vital. In this volume four where I am working now, I've met this P. 88 and several times later "Traver and Conversion" and discovered that it is a legal trespass by people who do not return property or animals they have found to the owner. On p 90 where the young Indian was "arrested & tried & <u>nepoed</u> today" I have taken <u>nepo</u> as the root of <u>nepotism</u> and assumed that the boy was put into the custody of white parents who would be responsible for him. Any suggestions??[8]

Another interesting development: for several years I have hoped that I might get a reprint or a second edition of the <u>MMM</u> out, but no one seemed interested. Now suddenly I get two offers in one day: Lottenville[9] of Oklahoma University Press called to say that they are all ready to proceed, had the typescript on the desk before him and a contract in the mail. More than two years ago I had let Dr. Mortensen have a copy to send to him and had never had a word of it since.

The very next day Mr. Clark of Arthur H. Clark company called to say that they would also be interested to do a reprint if they could get a copy to work from. Their proposition would be about the same as Oklahoma.

Now I don't kid myself that there'll be any money in it from either source, and certainly none for me. Most of the people here think I would do better to have Oklahoma do it, since they are already into it, they put out nice books, and they have perhaps a wider circulation. On the other hand Clark did take the Biography. By the way, it is getting better notice than I had dreamed it would. About this reprint—second edition deal, what is your opinion?[10]

You know, of course, of Dr. Mortensen's promotion to the University of Utah Press. His wife has been desperately ill for several weeks now and is still not off the critical list, though she is some improved.

I must know if you did not receive your copy of John Doyle Lee. It will be a hard lesson for me if you did not, but another will be on its way immediately.

Always,

To *Winifred (Peg) Gregory*, February 2, 1962

February 2, 1962

My dear lady:

I've been positively hungry for a visit with you. Would have used the telephone except that I wanted you to see at least two of the reviews I have had, so that we could visit with more definiteness. I think you know the first—perhaps I sent it to you earlier—the one from the San Francisco Chronicle. I promise myself that I will do these things so faithfully that I sometimes come to believe that I have actually done them.

Anyway The Salt Lake Tribune, my own home town paper, the Washington County News, the weekly L.D.S. Intermountain News, and other have been more than generous with me.[11]

Then The University of Oklahoma wants to do a reprint of MMM, and the next day after their call Clark Company asked to do it. For a time, I was in a quandary, but nearly everyone with whom I have talked has advised me to let Oklahoma do it. I'd feel more indebted to Clark if they had not been so penurious with me about this Lee book. I cannot do much about it now; my eyes will not take more than I am giving them.

To add to this, Miss Lee writes that she had found a few copies of the MMM which she will send to me to "place where they will do the most good." My guess is that there are five, or maybe, ten, and I'm sure that she may want me to present some and sell others. But that is a bridge I will cross IF and WHEN the books arrive.

Of the Los Angeles Times[12] article I was almost shocked—that they should actually begin with a quote of the disputed closing of my book. Poor Jesse Udall, that would really have him on the spit and turning before a hot fire, while dear Apostle Stapley with his threat that "If this appears in print, in the book, on the cover, or in any review, PRESIDENT MCKAY WILL RESCIND THIS ACTION," must either put up or shut up, as the locals say. Well, I think he has shut up.

I am invited to speak before the Hamblin reunion in Mesa on Feb. 10—and accepted in part because it will give me an excuse to get into the area again. I shall fly down a week from today. I feel sure that Louise Udall will be there and perhaps Jess and his wife, for they are Hamblins too, you know.

Enough of this:

My son Kay is graduating this spring in Spanish and hopes to continue with a view of getting into the communications program somewhere in the government or with business. He considers a summer at the University of New Mexico, then would like to do graduate work there at the University of New Mexico if perhaps he could get some kind of a teaching assistantship in Spanish I by which he could pay his way. He has a good part in a Spanish play which is being put on in the department upon which he has had many compliments as to his phonetics or enunciation—his speaking as it should be spoke. His professor is from Chile.

He must write to the department himself I know, but I thought also that you will know about the general rating of the school, size of the department, and general opportunities.

Tony's grant in this radiation fall-out study takes him out in a camper every week-end to the remote corners of the state. In the spring and summer it should be fun, but with this unusual amount of snow and fog, it is something of a hazard. He is really thrilled with it, though.

We all keep well. Father William, bless him, is the very busiest one. He keeps the accounts and handles the money; he writes in his diary every day. He sends greeting cards and sympathy cards and get well cards; he has such good times attending funerals. Yesterday it was Matt Chidister, 88, who lived his early life out in Dixie, in Pine Valley and Damcron Valley during the summer and in St. George during the winter. Will met so many old friends at the mortuary and at the church, people he hadn't seen for years, and brought one home with him to finish out the afternoon and have dinner.

I've done this at the office while I rest my eyes from a couple of hours at the microfilm. If I don't hear from you by the time I get back from Mesa, I'll have to call you.

Take care of your precious self and keep me posted as to the family—Reggie & Chilt. Give them both our love.

And to you also
Love,

To *Obert C. Tanner,*[13] February 6, 1962

February 6, 1962

Dr. Obert C. Tanner
Department of Philosophy
University of Utah
Salt Lake City, Utah

Dear Obert:

I cannot tell you how happy I was to get your letter. Like Socrates, I value the opinion of those whom I know to be wiser and better than I far more than I do general public acclaim, and the fact that you would see in my attempt something praiseworthy means much to me.

I too have found it impossible to yield "unquestioning obedience," even to the leaders of the Church. As I study more and more of the lives of the more loyal and more skilled of our early people, I marvel at the willingness to move into the most forbidding areas—often against their better judgment—because they are Building the Kingdom. These Fifty, especially, who had been fired by Joseph Smith, carried a responsibility beyond the strength of man to establish towns where neither God nor Nature had intended towns to be, and who again and again fought a losing fight against the elements. Of such was John Lee, but he was only one of an army.

At a tremendous price in human life and energy some spots of the desert were conquered—temporarily, to be sure, as witness the present state of many of our smaller villages in different parts of the state.

***

An interruption here.

Another reason why I was glad for your letter is that it gives me an opportunity to write one to you that I have thought of many, many times during the past year, This is it: Why don't you begin now to plan to run for Governor of this state at the next election? Certainly we need a governor with your qualities: education, vision, a solid philosophical foundation, practical business experience, ability to work with people.

As a public service, not for financial gain or public honor, you should do this. You have a responsibility to leave the state a better place than you found it, to bring into state government for the sake of youth now growing up more interest in education, in the creative arts, in the whole field of general welfare. I know you are not a politician, but we don't need a politician. We need a man of your stature.

To *Gustive O. Larson*, April 3, 1962

April 3, 1962

Mr. Gustive O. Larson
324 Jesse Knight Building
B.Y.U., Provo

Dear Gus:

It's always good to hear from you.

The quotation you want is in A Mormon Chronicle, v.1 p. 108, a little below the center of the page and beginning in the middle of a line.[14] You will likely want to use the entire statement on this subject.

I'm in the midst of the Mormon War period in Hosea Stout, which means that I am in volume seven of the typescript. As the book is now projected, I am in part 4 of volume 2. Hosea writes little after the beginning of 1861, but he lived until 1889, which means that I must fill in the gap or at least summarize this period.

Right now I'm intrigued by the term "B'hoys" as applied to a select group of cavalrymen.[15] On March 8, 1858, Stout writes that "Col Kane accompanied by Egan, Rockwell, Hanks and several others of the "Be'hoys" left for the United States' troops' Camp to go by the up Weber route"[16] On August 27, 1853, William H. Kimball,[17] on his way out to take over Fort Bridger writes from the West Foot of Little Mountain telling his plans and listing his 42 men. He closes with the statement: "No More at Present Give my Respects to all the B'hays"[18]

I have seen this term in other places, but have not tried to pin-point it before. An intriguing game!

Thank you for your invitation to join you on April 19. I'd like it, but I doubt that we can come. We hope to go south to Dixie about that time, since it's Will birthday on the 23 and we may step it up a day or two and arrange some way in which he may greet his neighbors and friends.

Sincere good wishes,

To *Marba C. Josephson*, April 17, 1962

April 17, 1962

Marba C. Josephson
THE IMPROVEMENT ERA
135 South State
Salt Lake City, Utah

Dear Marba:

I should have sent this on several days ago but just became involved in other things.[19] I hope you like.

I agree with Wes that it would make a wonderful cover picture, and that use should not interfere too seriously with its use in other places. So if you think you want it, will you please let us both know? I've written his return address on his letter-head. When you are through with this, return this to me and I will hold it until he comes next month.

We were talking of doing an illustrated article on the "Marriage Trail," as it was called during the late 1870's, with pictures of at least some of the watering-places en route: Gould's Place, Canaan Springs, Short Creek, Pipe Springs, Kanab Creek, Hogan's Wells, House Rock Spring, Jacob's Pools (or The Blue Pools, as it was later called), Soap Creek, and the Paria. Each has its own fascinating story.[20]

The ferry crossing of the Colorado River[21] was always the climax, the most dreaded experience of the trip, and here too were many stories both of comedy and tragedy.

I am too deeply involved here right now to do the actual writing, but I have complete notes and references, and have visited every spot along the way. I have hoped that perhaps ARIZONA HIGHWAYS might like it, but did not want to approach them until I am ready to produce a finished product. This should be within a couple of months.

Or could you consider such an article—done by me? I don't really expect an affirmative answer; I just asked. Call me some day when you have time at DA 2- 0467.

Cordially,

To *Wallace Stegner*, August 14, 1962

August 14, 1962

Dear Wally:

I called Olsen[22] at the L.D.S. Historian's office only to be told what I had already guessed: that they do have the originals of Heber C. Kimball, Wilford Woodruff, Thomas Bullock, and George A. Smith in their files,[23] but that they are available only to people who come there and work with the permission of Brother Joseph Fielding Smith. If it were at all possible to do so, I suggest that you do just that. I feel sure that you would be given permission to read the volumes, your name and reputation being what it is, and though they might examine direct quotes, they could not take away your own mental image of the various characters or prevent paraphrasing.

I imagine that the Cowley edition of Wilford Woodruff's life[24] is quite a faithful reproduction of the journals, but nothing can be as good as the original.

I talked to T. Edgar Lyon[25] last night about the Orson Pratt writings. He says that the Millennial Star pieces have never been put together.[26] His Master's Thesis from Chicago [1925, I believe] was on Orson Pratt. The family had consulted him about doing a biography and had made preliminary moves to collect the many diaries, but the man who was to have financed it died very suddenly. A home fire destroyed some of the diaries, he thinks.

John says that the photostats of the Huntington and other items have not been returned as yet, but he will check to see if there is any way they can be speeded up. Seems that they sent them to San Francisco to be done.

This William Clayton[27] statement on Sunday April 11 "I told Winslow Farr concerning Hosea Stouts threats to take my life after the Twelve are gone" and again on Tuesday 13 when he told Brigham and Heber[28] interest me very much because Clayton's name does not appear in the Stout record at all during any of this time—From February 1 through April.

Was William Clayton a member of the guard? On March 5, 1847, Stout reported that "In the evening I went on guard and found one of the guard absent and in fact he had been reported absent more or less all winter I could never find him at his post, but he was sure to be at a party or dancing school every time. Now I thought it was time to report him . . ."[29]

Stout found the man at a party in the home of Phineas H. Young;[30] Stout watched and found that the man came on guard only long enough to call out his relief. He reported to Brother Brigham, who authorized him to deal with the delinquent, who was brought in "Whipped and Cleared" and "if he will profit by what has passed he will do well if not he had best leave the police before he is disgraced." Through all this, no name was given.

On March 13 a man who was named was up before the police for stealing some guns. Stout defended his right to stay on with the guard and then continued "I spoke quite lengthy on the subject and was for keeping him in fellowship as I could fellowship any man that could be suffered to live amongst us and when we could not stand it any longer to cut him off—behind the ears—according to the law of God in such cases."

Might Clayton, hearing this, think it applied to him? There is no direct evidence as yet that Clayton was one of the police or that he was the delinquent one, or that he was present here.

On March 15 at a meeting it was "decided as the best policy for this people to pursue after the Twelve & pioneers are gone . . . to keep up the police under its present organization. . . ."

Nowhere is William Clayton mentioned at all. So your guess is as good as mine. I shall look into contemporary records, though, just out of curiosity.

At present we can't let either copy of Stout out of our hands. A strange behind-the-scenes struggle goes on as to its publication about which I must not write.

An interesting person was in during this last week—William L. Knecht[31]

2855 Telegraph Ave
Berkeley 5, California

who is doing intensive research on the Martin Handcart Company, and who seems to have more in the way of original material than we have.

I suppose you notice how out of form even my typing is. I'm due to be on the way with my husband and two of my sons to Grand Junction to visit a third son—this one married and for five years in a new home which I have never seen. He has also five children, and since they make a semiannual visit to my home, I had not troubled to get out to theirs—to see the house, I mean. My baby boy was married on July 24 in the Los Angeles temple. These two unmarried brothers—Karl, who teaches in the Virgin Valley, Nevada, and Kay just returned from summer school at Mexico City, who will do graduate work in Spanish this winter—have decided that today is a good time to go. So be it. Hosea can wait.

I'm glad, for I'm at this difficult and violent year of 1859 when there were too many murders in Zion.

Good wishes and more help
later—I hope

To *Wallace Stegner*, August 31, 1962

August 31, 1962

Dear Wally:

Remember that I'm not sure that the "delinquent policemen" was William Clayton.[32] I'm only saying that it could well have been him

IF he were a policeman, present at the meeting where Hosea said that when they could no longer fellowship a member they should "cut him off behind the ears" and IF Stout turned his piercing black eyes on Clayton, that worthy might feel that his life had been threatened. Evidently, "the shoe fit," in this case.

You should address the Apostle as "President Joseph Fielding Smith."[33] He is president of the Quorum, and as such next in line to the throne. He has waited for and doted on this position for years, I am told. But he may be disappointed, since he, too, is getting older. He is the official Church Historian, and as such has the final say. Why don't you address the office attn Earl Olsen first? For all intents and purposes, Earl manages, and if he understands your project and what specifically you want, he can at least clear the way for you. (The Joe Smith you know is younger, a nephew, I think.)

Now, about the non-members in the 1847 company: I doubt that there were actually six—the term "half-dozen" is used so much to mean an indefinite number from four to eight, say.[34] The negroes, at least two of them, were members, I understand.[35] The ONE non-member in whom I have been interested in is Tom Brown.[36] I met him first in Nauvoo when the two Hodge brothers were convicted of murder and hanged on July 15, 1845. These men were involved, the third being this Tom Brown, then a well-known desperado, who was supposed to have engineered the intended robbery. He with the eldest Hodge entered the house with intent to steal a chest; they became involved in a struggle with Old Man Miller and his son-in-law, in which Miller was stabbed and died instantly and the other died later of wounds. It was said that the knife embedded in Miller's chest belonged to Tom Brown, and the description of the wounded man was of Brown. The two Hodges were caught and both hanged, though the younger had remained out by the boats as a watch.

I think you would not want this long list of references on the subject, but I'll enclose it and you can send it back. The Edward Bonney book has much to say about the exploits of Tom Brown.[37]

Practically every diarist of the 1847 company mentions the arrival of a group of horsemen on April 19; no one seems to name them all, but give a few and then say "and others," or "and one other."[38] Norton Jacobs[39] lists "Porter Rockwell, Redden, J.C. Little, Thomas Brown and another young man overtook us . . ." As I remember it, Brown later returns with Norton. Egan[40] mentions Rockwell, Brown and Joseph Matthews, who might be the one other omitted by Jacobs. Erastus Snow calls the new-comer "the notorious Tom Brown", so we may be sure of his identity. Now while Port Rockwell and Jack Redden and perhaps others were baptized Mormons, they were not the preaching-praying kind, and in general could hardly be classed as saints.[41]

It is this group, and some of the kindred spirits among the assigned teamsters to whom Brother Brigham spoke, I think. Or was he only using them as whipping boys? I would not take the number six too seriously myself.

I must add that Hosea Stout is dead and for present purposes buried, though I mean to stand by until the notes are copied, in case Mrs. Walker needs a urim and Thummin.

My only prospect for employment comes from Assistant U.S. Attorney, who wants a bit of research done on the Upper Green River from where it enters Utah to a point some twenty-two miles below the town of Green River, Utah.[42] This should take about two months, he estimates. I should tell him how much I expect to be paid for this service, a question I find difficult to answer. I'm sending some items about myself to him.

Too many interruptions. Hope this bit helps.

To *Elizabeth Lawrence*,[43] September 17, 1962

September 17, 1962

Dear Mrs. Lawrence:

When I actually got into this business, I found that I had two stories of water rather than one. The first is informal and largely autobiographical, the old man being John Whipple[44] who is now well in his nineties. He has told me histories and has them typed up very briefly.

This one is enclosed.[45]

The second I shall call THE INVINCIBLE DESERT AND THE MORMON WAR. Now that I have it blocked out, I am quite excited about doing it. I shall send it to you or to Mr. Monjo[46] first. It deals with the problem of the geography as related to the Mormon defense and strategy in 1857, when they thought they were at war with the United States.

Briefly outlined it includes:

1—The attempt to mine lead at Las Vegas, Nevada, in preparation. This is graphically told in the diaries of participants.

2—Calling the people home from the far-flung settlements in the Carson Valley. Two members of the 16-man party kept excellent diaries of this so-nearly tragic trip.

3—Searching for a place of refuge for the Saints. This is a little-known episode of which I have the original journals. A company of twenty wagons sixty men and sixty horses was sent out from the Parowan–Cedar City area of southwestern Utah into an uncharted desert with the hope that somewhere beyond it they would find a haven to which the people might move.[47] Here again was near disaster.

I believe that this article will throw significant light upon the much written about "Mormon War." It is an angle which no one else to this time has considered.

This is something that I must do, but having all the material now at hand, I should not find it too difficult.

The QUICKSAND AND CACTUS is also a pleasant prospect. I may send excerpts from it with little change.

It's really a good experience NOT to have a regular, demanding position, but to be left to my own devises for a time, at least.

To *Conway B. Sonne*,[48] September 20, 1962

September 20, 1962

Mr. Conway B. Sonne
3348 St Michael Drive
Palo Alto, California

Dear Mr. Sonne:

Thank you so much for your letter of September 16. I appreciate it sincerely.

More and more I am impressed with how small the world is and how intricate the webs of interest that tie us together. As I walked into our group dining room with the mail in my hand, your letter among others, one of the boys at the table held up a book and asked, "Have you read this?" It was your book on Chief Walker.[49]

I have not read it yet, but I shall soon. He let me take the copy long enough to leaf through it, and I am much impressed.

I saw in it the announcement of Knight of the Kingdom,[50] which I now have on my desk. Isn't it interesting that my own son, Karl F. Brooks, wrote his Master's Thesis on Amos Milton Musser?[51] And that my last project has been editing the diaries of Hosea Stout, who was called at the same time to fill a mission to China and traveled all the way to San Francisco in the same company.

Which reminds me—I hope that the diaries of Richard Ballantyne[52] have been photostated and microfilmed, so that the original, hand-written words remain. The journals themselves cannot—must not—be handled, even by the most dedicated and careful, but the reproductions should be available to scholars who wish to cross check parallel records.

Thank you again. Let's hope that we both have other books ahead of us, books that may help to interpret our people and their times.

Sincerely,

To *Bent and Geneva Larsen*, September 27, 1962

September 27, 1962

Dear Bent and Geneva:

I have just finished reading While the Desert Blossomed,[53] and shall take it home for Will to read.

It is a beautiful book, beautifully-written and made up. I must contact this J. Grant Stevenson when I get the life of Grandpa Brooks ready and see if I cannot get something as nice as this out of it.

Yes, I enjoyed the book very much, but I do think it is one of the saddest stories I have ever read. Irene seems all her life so starved for love, and too afraid to take it or return it when she had the chance. The first suggestion right at the beginning that this little girl felt rejected by her own mother—that the mother always kissed Ezra, but never

Irene, that she always turned her back to Irene, even in bed—yes most pathetic and frightening, at least to a mother of many.

Then when she dare not accept Julian's love, and marry him at once when she know how he wanted her. She wanted him, too, so desperately, but didn't dare let herself go. She could so easily had him back and been first if only she had written a different kind of answer to his letter; she had only to say the word, and he would have come to her immediately. Why didn't she? And then—of course, after he had married, the first wife was important. But that important?

Then to marry without love and never secure it in all her life! To be only <u>respected</u>! And to give in return only respect. Even in her later years to be afraid to read a message from her early lover because she could not face the emotions it would stir up.

She was a wonderful person, and a superb mother, and a model of true Christian living with regards to everyone but herself. She was a sacrifice to her own suppressed desires.

I write free about this because it is so truly the story of my own grandmother Hafen.[54] She married the man she loved, but he was killed within ten days. Before she had time to get over the shock and to adjust her life and emotions, she was married to my Grandfather. He knew that she did not love him—she made no effort to, or to have him love her. But she dutifully bore him seven children, and in her old age did not want him in her house.

It is cases like this that make me doubt that the law of plurality was ever Divinely given. I wonder if, from the first, it was not a mistake.

Or does it prove that some of the most superior off-spring are produced from unions that are devoid of emotional ties? I wonder how the fifth and sixth generation will interpret this "Celestial Kingdom" deal that was so important to their ancestors.

Forgive me. I forget that I am writing rather than talking, and perhaps this machine gets out of hand. As I said at first, Floy is to be congratulated on the sensitive, delicate manner in which she had handled it. I feel that it is told much as Irene would have told it herself, with all the rich background of life and custom, with all the restraint and delicacy of one who completely understands. And for all its tragedy, it is a beautiful life, fittingly presented.

For the first time in all our married life, Will and I are alone. Makes quite a difference, I find.

To *Dale Morgan*, October 24, 1962

98 U Street, Salt Lake City
October 24, 1962

Dear Dale:

Life is full of quirks and surprises, but it is certainly never dull. As you know, I'm officially through with Hosea Stout, though I'll never actually be through with him. We didn't even get the notes to the projected volume two read through yet—Margie Walker had to go to the convention of Western Writers in Denver, and then out on the deer hunt. Now the time may have to wait another week or more.

Meantime, I'm on a brief assignment with Asst. U. S. Attorney, Parker Neilson, to do research on the history of the Upper Green River. The State has opened litigation to secure if it can possession of the stream-bed. I'm getting into the early fur-trade history and finding it exciting and interesting reading.

Your Jedediah Smith[55] is my Bible, of course. I note where you say that "I hereafter expect to publish it in full in a documentary collection of Ashley Papers," but since John has heard nothing of its appearance, I assume that you have had too many more important things to do.[56]

Judging by the interpretations made in other decisions, the river is considered "navigable" if at the time of statehood, 1896, the stream, in its natural state were navigable. So much hinges on the interpretation of that one word. At any rate, I must know the details of the Ashley trip down and of succeeding ones to 1896, especially, and then the later history also, though with perhaps not such great detail.

To date I have been in diaries—Smith, Broken Hand, Beckwourth, Sublette, Ferris, to name a few, along with Chittenden, Billington, and some other general books.[57] Right now I'm getting into the Powell records. I noticed that he spoke as though the Ashley trip were "disastrous," but from the Ashley papers it would seem that he lost no men.

My work here will last until mid-December or January first, and I may go wherever it will be necessary or beneficial to examine original documents. While going either east or west would be pleasant, I do not want to go just for the fun of it, unless there is reason to believe that such examination of either Powell or Ashley originals would add significant items. I think I should exhaust the sources here first, which I have not yet done.

Add to this the fact that my page-proofs for the second edition of the MMM indexing will be here early next week, and you can see that I will be fully occupied.[58] I would not have become involved in this right now had not the Oklahoma University Press made such an unexpected and headlong drive. Here for three years I had waited for some word from them. Well, that is life, and we must take it as it comes.

Will's brother Sam,[59] who lived in McClelland and served so many years as a postal clerk died of a heart attack yesterday, which for a few days will compound my problems. And my nephew, Carrick Leavitt,[60] whose mother died when he was young and who has lived in my home for three years, is going on a mission to England and wants me to speak at his testimonial on Sunday. This is in Cedar City.

Fortunately my health is good; I'm at peace with the world in general; even the fall is perfect. So I guess I'll continue to bite off more than I can chew and then proceed to chew at it—with the net result that nothing will be really well done.

I think of you often, and grow in respect of the monumental things you have already done, all the more profound knowing what lies ahead in production for you.

Good wishes always,

To *Mrs. McKnight*, November 9, 1962

505 Federal Building
Salt Lake City, Utah
Nov. 9, 1962

Dear Mrs. McKnight:

On this business of pioneer games, I think I'll just talk about indoor ones, since that is what you need now. I hope the party is to be held in a scout den or rumpus room rather than on an expensive rug, for boys need room and action.

Forfeits These are used for many games, when a boy is "caught" or fails to do as he should. He hands to the manager some personal item—a knife or marble or top or yo-yo—and at the end of the game all forfeits are redeemed.

The judge sits in a chair with the auctioneer standing behind him. Holding the item over the judge's head and in full view of the guests, the auctioneer says:

"Heavy, heavy hangs over your poor head."

"Fine or super-fine?" asks the judge. (boy or girl?)

"Fine." in this case where all are boys. "What shall the owner do to redeem it?"

For a mixed crowd, especially an older one, there are many fines such as "Haul a load of wood," which means rubbing the forehead down a door making it bump along as though the road were rough; "paint the plow with"—the boy kneels on one knee with the other bent, the girl sits on his knee and he kisses her cheek. If he must paint it on both sides, she stands up and reverses her position so that the other cheek is toward him. "Bow to the wittiest, kneel to the prettiest, and kiss the one that you love the best." As you see, these are for mixed, older teen-agers.

For these boys, the judge should let the fine be a song, a poem, a trick, an acrobatic stunt such as turning a summersault, walking on his hands, holding his toe with one hand and jumping through it. Usually jokes or poems are easier to get done, but the boy must pay his forfeit or fine before he gets the item back.

One good game for forfeits is "Going a Journey." In pioneer days they named each child a part of the outfit: the father, mother, a little boy with a name, a little girl, the dog, the harness, whip, singletree, tire, endgate, etc.etc, and then the story-teller proceeds to tell of the preparation and the trip, and at any mention of his name, the child must jump up quickly and turn around. If he forgets or has to be reminded, he pays a forfeit, and the story proceeds.

In this case you should use an old car and name the horn, the tires, the windshield wiper, etc. etc. and then make up a story interesting enough to hold the children in addition to having each one jump and turn around. The narrator needs to be sure that every child is mentioned several times.

"Musical chairs" was another favorite, where there is always one chair less than there are players.

“Fruit Basket Tipped Over”. Every child is named a different fruit. The one in the center calls out two fruits like, “apple and pomegranate” which means that these two must exchange places. [unclear] Occasionally he may say “The fruit basket has tipped over,” at which every one in the room must take another seat, the one who does not get one being “it.”

“Pass the Button” was another favorite. The leader, with the button held tightly between his two flat hands, pretends to put it into the hand of every one in the room, and when he has reached the end of the circle he says, “Button, button, who’s got the button?” and calls on one to guess. If he guesses wrong, he is “it,” if he guesses right, the one who has the button is “it.”

“Hunt the Slipper” is another. The group sits in a close circle on the floor, passing a shoe behind them, all pretending that is just in their hand or just going by; if the boy in the center finds the slipper, the one who had it must take his place in the center. Occasionally one who has the slipper may strike the searcher from behind to give him a new lead.

“Barnyard Chorus” has each boy represent an animal, and when called upon or pointed at, he must stand and make the call of his animal. The game ends when all stand together and do their “song.”

In trick games where the one who is to be the fall-guy or “it” must be picked from the crowd, the selection was made by saying a jingle. You probably know others but this is the one we used, pointing to a different boy in the circle every time: “onery, orrey, ickory, Ann, phillasy, follisy, Nichole, John, Queever, quaver, English, naivor, stinklum, stanklum, you-may-be-buck, OUT.” This takes care of a circle of 17, but the counter has the one called OUT sit each time around until only one is left to be IT. This does away with the feeling that any special one is being made a fool of, or with the more aggressive being “it” all the time. Two of many games where this has been used are “Wipe the Water up,” and “Going to Heaven.”

In the first there must be a small puddle of water on the floor /See why it must be linoleum?/The boy who is IT is seated on the floor with the water between his legs, and given a fork in each hand with which he is to jab the hands of any who try to wipe the water up. Two boys with rags pretend for a minute to wipe it up, then suddenly grab the seated one by his feet and drag him through it.

In "Going to Heaven" the boy who is it is blindfolded and stood upon a plank on the floor, his hands on the shoulders of a taller boy in front of him. Two other boys lift the plank only a few inches from the floor, while the boy in front slowly sinks down and the crowd keep up a line of, "not too high, now" "Don't let him hit the ceiling," etc. The blindfolded boy is urged to keep his balance and try to stand after his support in front has completely faded away. Then he must jump back to the floor. Usually he thinks he is very high up indeed.

If the crowd is large enough to choose up sides, or better still, to be divided into three groups, they will enjoy competitive activities. One is a kitchen band, in which they see which can produce the best music on improvised instruments.

Then there are stunt games like: "Eagle Writing on the Floor" or "Hypnotism" in which only two people are in on the secret.

Still another is aimed to keep the crowd laughing, or to get each individual to laugh. The one who is IT often puts on a shawl and spectacles or a false nose and stoops over a broom-handle cane and goes tapping along to one or another in the crowd saying "Here comes Old Grandmother Graff, with her stick and her staff, and you must neither smile nor laugh, but say right down I WILL." Then he proceeds to ask foolish questions to which the person must always answer soberly, "I will." If he laughs he either pays a forfeit or takes the place of Grandmother Graff.

Well, I think this really is enough to wreck your place or at least to help with having fun. I hope that, with whatever you already have, you can make a pleasant evening for these youngsters.

Good wishes

To *George T. Boyd*,[61] December 11, 1962

98 U Street, Salt Lake City
December 11, 1962

Dear George:

The check arrived OK, and is more than adequate. In fact, I feel a bit guilty at accepting it when I did so little in preparation.[62]

Since I have been home and see things in perspective, I'm a bit afraid that I offended some members in the last meeting with my comments on the use of wine in the sacrament or by intimating that "the testimonies went on until sundown," after the proper spiking of the noon meal. We in Dixie have not taken this matter so seriously as some members of the church who have not been so close to it. I did not want to offend or to appear flippant.

It's a good thing I didn't tell Grace Woodbury's[63] story of Uncle Hughie Cousins whose wife was home-bound, so he would take a bit of the bread and a small cup of the wine to her "and would run all the way home in order to get there before the blessing should dissolve."

You would not remember how they uncovered the butter and other dishes, and lifted up the lids of the pitchers in church—so carefully and solemnly—that the blessing should lose none of its potency.

Forgive me, I started to say only thanks and to wish you and your lovely wife the happiest Christmas ever, and a busy, healthful New Year ahead.

Sincerely,

Chapter 9

1963–1964

Back in St. George and Receiving an Honorary Degree

In early January 1963, Brooks had the pleasure to write Savoie Lottinville of the University of Oklahoma Press thanking him for a job well done on the second edition of her Mountain Meadows Massacre book after receiving five copies. She also started casting her net for a worthwhile project as her employment was winding down. She mentioned to Alfred Bush that she had plenty to do but felt, "Yet all this seems just busy work for children, or finger exercise. I want something that will present more of a challenge and offer more of a reward."[1] Among her projects was a biography of Will's father, George Brooks.

Brooks also spearheaded several writing campaigns to protect other historic sites and buildings. In 1963, she made a major push to save the Washington County Courthouse, writing the county commissioners among others arguing that they were smart enough to figure out how to build the new courthouse on a block owned by the county, next to the old one. She emphasized, "Surely our people as a whole will not sanction the destruction of the Court House, which in its own way is as historic and important as the Tabernacle or Temple."[2] Regard for the latter two was perhaps greater beyond St. George, but in the end the courthouse was saved and repurposed as a civic center.

The deplorable condition of the Mountain Meadows Massacre site, though, particularly compelled her to write letters. She wrote the U.S. Forest Service in 1964 suggesting that the federal government obtain control and manage the site because "the people whose bodies lie there were not from Utah, but from Arkansas and Missouri and other points east, so the spot has national significance."[3] She also encouraged her friend Wesley Williamson to write Secretary of Interior Udall concerning the massacre site and kept him posted on the status of the cause.

Another issue that she repeated several times in her letters was the depiction, particularly in the writings of Preston Nibley and lesson manuals, of the early Mormon leaders as having only one wife—only two women were cited in the life of Brigham Young, and Parley P. Pratt was portrayed as marrying just the bride of his youth.[4] In other letters she questioned the official story of the killing of A. W. Babbitt in September 1856 on the overland trail near Ash Hollow as he was returning from Washington D.C. and speculated on Porter Rockwell's role.

In 1963 and 1964, she continued to receive more acceptance, recognition, and honors in Utah. One such indication of her acceptance was that a student at Brigham Young University, Pansy Hardy, wrote a master's thesis discussing the influence of southern Nevada and southern Utah on the writings of herself and LeRoy Hafen. Deseret Book started carrying her Mountain Meadows Massacre book, which they had refused to sell previously. The editor of the *Journal of American Folklore*, John Greenway, requested and published three of her stories written originally in the 1940s for her unpublished *Quicksand and Cactus* book.[5]

One of the greatest honors in her life, which she described as "one of the rare 'sun-bursts' of my life, the highest point to date, certainly" came on June 6, 1964, with the award of an honorary doctorate degree from Utah State University.[6] Also on the stand receiving the degree was LeGrand Richards of the Quorum of Twelve, the apostle she traded letters with in 1955 concerning her Mountain Meadows Massacre book. During that debate she predicted that, given time, her work would become more and more accepted throughout the Mormon community, so as Brooks wrote J. Wesley Williamson prior to the event, "Life is full of paradoxes, certainly."[7] She also thanked Leonard Arrington for his congratulations saying she was gratified that people in his position thought she deserved the honor. In thanking Ellvert Himes, chairman of commencement activities at Utah State University, following the award she disclosed the amusing scene of her modeling her doctorate hood over her kitchen apron while she was serving lunch to members of the Lee family when they arrived, a noteworthy contrast between her scholarly and domestic activities. She went on to receive many more major honors, including honorary doctorate degrees from Southern Utah State College in 1969 and the University of Utah in 1973.

~

To *Savoie Lottinville*, January 10, 1963

98 U Street, Salt Lake City
January 10, 1963

Dear Mr Lottinville:

My five copies of The Mountain Meadows Massacre were here when I returned from a short trip to Southern Utah.[8] Thank you.

I am highly pleased with the whole production—the format, titles, and general make-up. The pictures reproduced rather well, I thought, and add materially to the value of the book. I wish there could have been others also—I might have sent one of his "mansion" at Washington by way of contrast to the willow shanty, for example—but I liked the selection of the ones used.

Please send me ten additional copies as soon as they are available, and bill them to me.

I should like also a copy of Miguel Leon-Portilla, Aztec Thought and Culture,[9] as soon as it is ready.

My sincere thanks to all the Oklahoma Press staff, and most especially to you and to Miss Martha Tait for the excellent way in which this book of mine has been prepared.

Sincerely,

Mr. Savoie Lottinville
University of Oklahoma Press
Norman, Oklahoma

To *Alfred Bush*, January 17, 1963

98 U Street, Salt Lake City, Utah
January 17, 1963

Dear Alfred:

Your enthusiasm almost convinces me. At least it gives me courage to ask if perhaps I may <u>help</u> to do the Utah papers.[10] I looked up the Carter publication,[11] and am sure that you are right in your statement that others remain un-done ahead of Utah. Few, I suspect, have a greater mass of material of a more controversial nature.

I think I should probably write to Mr. Grover[12] himself first. Or should I contact Senator Moss[13] or Secretary Stewart Udall? I know Stewart quite well; have had a rather good relationship there due in part to my biography of John D. Lee, his great-grand-father.

If I understand the workings of the Government, their wheels, like those of the Gods, grind slowly. If I set them in motion now, I might get action by the beginning of the fiscal year—if I am to get it at all. That would be soon enough. What I need most right now is the assurance of something ahead.

I have plenty to do. A biography of Will's grandfather is waiting to be finished, and it's a tremendous story.[14] It's one that I should not postpone longer. Our local ward has launched a project by which they expect every adult member, that is, every head of a household, both husband and wife, to write a biography not to exceed 1200 words.[15] They count on having four hundred of these and want me to help edit them. I could give this much more time than I am willing to; I did promise to help and to scatter the writing among some seven or eight other readers.

Yet all this seems just busy work for children, or finger exercise. I want something that will present more of a challenge and offer more of a reward. I don't mean just a financial reward—I mean a satisfaction of having done something that is worth doing.

So thank you again for your encouragement. I'll sleep on it another night or two, perhaps, but I'll get something out somewhere.

Hosea is still in the hands of Oklahoma Press. One of their representatives, seeing the bulk of the copy in Dr. Cooley's office yesterday, said that he felt sure they would NOT take it. Just too big! If they refuse it outright, Everett may find himself more at the mercy of Mortensen than he may like.[16] But who am I to prognosticate?

To *Evan Woodbury*,[17] January 24, 1963

98 U Street
Salt Lake City, Utah
January 24, 1963

To the County Commissioners of Washington County,
Evan Woodbury, Chairman:

Dear Evan:

I address this to you because yesterday I received a letter from a citizen of St. George urging me to write to Mrs. Annie C. Johnson to try to persuade her to sell her home to the county in order to save the Court House.[18] The Cottam corner one block east would not do, "because, as everyone knows, it would utterly ruin the businesses on the lower street." If the Court House cannot be built on the Johnson corner, it must be erected on the site of the present Court House.

I feel sure that this is not true, and that you as a county commission have never made such an ultimatum. I am sure that you are all level-headed and honest. You have no private ax to grind, and if you did have, you'd be too honest to grind it at public expense.

Who is it that is so disturbed about his financial gain that one block difference in the placing of the Court House should be so crucial? In these days of cars, who cannot expect to ride a few blocks? Safeway Store moved away from the center; here the whole tendency is to move out where parking space can be had at less cost.

Since the County already has property, Why not use it? Please forgive me. You know your business better than I do. But in the solving of problems, surely our people as a whole will not sanction the destruction of the Court House, which in its own way is as historic and important as the Tabernacle or Temple. The people who own motor courts and who cater to the tourist should realize the potential of this building.

Everywhere else in this nation, folks are preserving their heritage; our Church is expending a large amount to restore old homes in Nauvoo. Salt Lake residents still lament the destruction of the Old Social Hall here.

Decide to put the new court house where you will, but please be slow to destroy the old one. You would not want that blot on your name, I am sure, and SOMEWHERE funds can be found to restore it as typical of the civic pride of our pioneers, and the fact that they were Americans, all of them, jack-Mormon,[19] emigrant, outsider, as well as the pulpit-pounding ones.

Sincere good wishes to you all.

To *Alfred Bush*, February 5, 1963

98 U Street, Salt Lake City
Feb. 5, 1963

Dear Alfred:

I'm overwhelmed that my unpretentious little Dudley Leavitt should suddenly become an antidote for flu, and I'm sort-a glad that something provided time in which you could read it. As you noted, it was done long before I had really got started in research, though for that matter, his name didn't get into the official records very often.

Such a good story about the Indian wife I didn't learn until after the book was out. It was told me by Dudley's eldest child, Hannah Terry.[20] I have written it in some detail and re-told it many times, but it is not yet in print.[21]

According to Hannah, the three wives were all waiting for Dudley's return from the big city. When the other wagons passed in late afternoon, they found it hard to understand why Dudley was so late. At last the wagon drove into the yard and they all hurried out to greet him. The sight of a female figure on the spring seat beside him troubled them all, but when he lifted her down and introduced her as "my wife, Janet," it was a shock. Mary, the first wife, had better control than the others. She extended a perhaps not-too-hearty invitation to "come on in." Maria, more quick tempered, began to sputter, but Thirza, my own grandmother turned on her heel without speaking to her husband, went around to the back door and into her bedroom, bundled up her clothes hastily and cut cross-lots to her parents' home.[22]

Her mother scolded her and told her to go on back, but Thirza insisted that she would not be a wife to a "squaw man." "His other wives welcomed you and treated you well," her mother reminded her. "Do you think they were happy when Dudley brought you home? Now you act your age, and go on back. And you treat that little girl as well as you were treated."

As I remember now, without referring to a book, Thirza was not yet nineteen and a bride of only six months.

Well, things went on at the Leavitt household, but not well. In the first place, Dudley would not unload the wagon and divide the things until all the wives could be present. Nor would he go to try to coax Thirza back. She had left of her own accord; she could return when she was ready.

More pressing and more important, they had lost the mush kettle. Now they could hardly keep house with that kettle. They had a very large one to use over the fire outside to wash with; they had a brass bucket and a dutch oven with lid, but only one kettle for mush and soup.

Then on the second night, after they had borrowed a kettle from a neighbor, the door opened softly and Thirza put her head in. "I just remembered about the mush kettle," she blurted out, almost before she was inside. "I was out back scraping it into the swill-barrel when Dudley drove up, and when I saw Janet on the seat there with him, I just opened my mouth and dropped the kettle and forgot about it until just a while ago. How did you ever manage without it?"

She held out the kettle. The action of the sour milk in the swill barrel had made it bright and shining inside, and taken off much of the black on the outside.

"Thirza ran and kissed Pa, and held her hand out to Janet, and said 'Hello, Janet, I'm sorry.' And everybody was glad because now Pa would unload the wagon. At first we worried a little for fear maybe the brass kettle had poisoned the swill, but we remembered that we had fed the pigs out of it and they acted the same." So Hannah concluded her story. I thought it was rather precious.

I had already written to thank Mr. Grover. Told him that I am happily employed until July 1, with a possible extension for a month after, that I am sure I shall have other opportunities but had made inquiry of him because I am genuinely interested in and intrigued by the Utah territorial Papers. Privately, I'm afraid they would be an extremely long—I mean perhaps more than two years long—job, even for a team of workers.

Your own project on the Utah Imprints sounds important, too.

No more now—Time's up

Good wishes always

To *Hoyt Palmer*, May 29, 1963

98 U Street, Salt Lake City
May 29, 1963

Mr. Hoyt Palmer
LDS Genealogical Library
Salt Lake City, Utah

Dear Hoyt:

I have spent the better part of two days on your ms. "The Rocky Road to Glory," and feel that I should write my reaction and get it back into your hands at once.[23]

In the first place, no one knows better than I what 400 pages of finished writing cost in time and energy—in re-writing and reorganizing and typing—than I do. Folks who think that books just happen, or that they can be dashed off quickly and easily, just DON'T KNOW. So I certainly salute you for your industry and skill.

You write well. There is no reason why your work should not sell, judging from that standpoint. My doubts grow out of the subject itself and your treatment of it.

As I suggested when I talked to you, I have listened to these talks of the imminent return of Christ to the Earth with all the horrors preceding it, for many years and from many sources. It is a favorite theme of "Jehovah's Witnesses," too. My reading of early diaries shows that our people at Nauvoo expected it to be soon—they sent the architect, William Weeks,[24] with the 1847 emigration that he might be on hand to get a temple started. From letters and diaries, folks expected it "within this generation," as promised at Nauvoo earlier.

The earlier settlers in Dixie, many of them, had to be told that it would not be right away, and that they should settle down to making permanent homes. Easton Kelsey[25] kept his wagon painted and ready to return to Jackson County. Most of the patriarchal blessings of that time gave this promise definitely. There have been recurring periods when the second coming has been emphasized, and a few speakers for whom it is a perennial theme, but, frankly, they all leave me cold. I just do not believe them.

From this point of view, I am a poor judge of your book.

It seems to me to be a piece of propaganda, with the characters and the situations only pegs upon which you hang your arguments and sermons. It is clearly written for an LDS audience; I think it will have little appeal beyond the Church. Within the Church you will get varied reactions, but many will agree with you whole-heartedly and will bless you for making it all so plain.

Your description of the atomic bomb, the suffering which followed, the anarchy and violence, the complete overthrow of the government, are all clearly and convincingly done. Your thesis that the Welfare Plan or the United Order is the salvation for mankind has too small a group. I had been led to believe that God is over all the world, and not just a few acres around Independence, Missouri, that all men, everywhere, are His children, and that He is mindful of them all. Just as I love my one brown-eyed, dark complexioned boy just as dearly as I do my blonde, blue-eyed ones, so I believe He loves all of his regardless of skin pigment or other differing qualities. Your novel seems to imply that these few at Independence have some special value over others.

You are very good on the kissing deal also. I felt that your description of the techniques of Roger (pp. 110–112) might be cut by an editor as being too pornographic. At least they cut some of Maurine Whipple's scenes that were not nearly so suggestive. The same is true in the business of the Devil's Secret Society. Your account of their orgies there sounds as though you had been reading some of the early anti-Mormons on our own temple ceremonies. This is exactly what they said went on, so that John Hyde's[26] expose was tame.

Re: kissing again—how could you have those women at the hospital kiss their plague-ridden, dying husbands on the mouth? UGH! The thought nauseated me. Surely there are other demonstrations of endearment less deadly. But that is nothing, really—I mean, it is a very minor point. Yet in time of mass extinction by a highly contagious disease, they should have been more realistic.

Your black is so very black. These men openly and admitted sworn to Satan and dedicated to destruction smacks of John Milton's hosts in Hell. My own observation is that much of the wrong and suffering in the world is due to people who think they are doing right, and who pursue their evil ends with a zeal and earnestness that could only come if they thought they had Divine Approval. It was so with Hitler and the Jews; it has been so since the beginning with self-appointed "servants of God" killing masses and destroying in his name.

As I said earlier, your presentation of Mormon doctrine in the funeral sermon, in the welfare plan, in the court scene, in the miraculous healing of Collin Lee are easily recognized. I haven't taken time to go back to some of the texts, but I think I could find them all.

The Second Coming itself makes me glad that I may not be among those "caught up." I have no desire to dangle in the air. If I am to go to Kolob,[27] I'd like to know about the where and how. I had assumed that we would remain here, busy and happy—and still human. The burning as stubble—well, its pretty hard to separate the wicked from the righteous. "There is so much good in the worst of us, and so much bad in the best of us . . ." Calamities do not seem limited to the wicked as I see life about me.

If I seem too critical, Hoyt, forgive me. You have done a remarkable piece of work here, a moving piece, and one which I know many will enjoy. If you can write fantasy like this, why not try a biography, for example, and deal with a living man and some actual situations. Sometimes the Truth is stranger than fiction.

Good wishes,

I wondered about the return of the Ten Tribes   you didn't even mention them!

To *Wallace Stegner*, June 13, 1963

Salt Lake City, Utah
98 U Street
June 13, 1963

Dear Wally:

You are at your superlative best here.[28] Your story is vivid, readable, fair. I find only a few points of difference, some of which you may not accept. For better or for worse, here they are:

1—p. 13

I called Earl Olsen at the Church Office for official figures, and when he said that he could do nothing about hunting them out for a week, I took those complied by Kate Carter in <u>Heart Throbs of the West</u> v. 12 p 463–465.[29] According to these, the total European immigration between 1848 and 1868 added up to 46,972, with the year 1855 as the peak—4,544 people having come over.[30] I'll fire Olsen's figures on if and when he calls me.

2—p. 23

You should cut the sentence "Brigham Young, for the first time given a task, etc . . ."[31] It is not true. It represents the story as it was told later when A.M. Musser[32] and others were busy "re-writing" our history. Contemporary records simply do not bear it out.

Brigham Young did come into the area on March 14, 1838, but he took up a farm out on the prairie away from Far West, so did not become involved in any of the trouble. He came into the town along with John D. Lee, Levi Stewart, and other later comers and was there when the Prophet surrendered. His name is not mentioned anywhere in any list on either side until December 10, when he was present at a meeting in Far West and was fifth in a committee of nine to draw up some resolutions. John Taylor was always more active than he.

Brigham Young presided at a meeting on December 19; on December 26 John Smith[33] presided and Elias Smith[34] acted as clerk as they did again on February 1. "Elders Taylor and Young in the most forcible manner addressed the assembly on the propriety of union in order to carry out the resolutione," the clerk wrote. Brigham Young's name was number 12 on the list of 87 who signed, but in two weeks, February 14, he fled the place, crossed the river, and set himself up near Quincy, leaving others to manage the evacuation.

I'm sure that your account—now the accepted Church version—will be accepted by all but a few like Dale L. Morgan and Stanley Ivins, and others who have examined the contemporary sources.

3—p. 25

You do well by Thomas L. Kane.[35] I'll try again to see if any Patriarchal blessing is on record. I have heard of one pronounced by Brigham Young—who was not a patriarch—in which Kane was promised life, health, and posterity. According to folklore Kane appreciated this last, since his health had been so poor that he thought he should never marry. They did shave his head and give him repeated baths to reduce the fever, and did ask that "Dr Sanderson or some other experienced physician /come/Post Haste not to wait for tired horses or broken carriages to bring him such things as would nourish & strengthen him. . . ."

4—p.31

I cannot resist a sidelight on Lucien Woodworth.[36] I had come across several references to "The Pagan Prophet" several times without being able to identify him. Then Lorenzo Brown,[37] writing on March 14, 1851, as he was in the neighborhood of American Fork, wrote: ". . . Stopped both nights with Mr Luceen Woodworth known as the 'Pagan Prophet.' He would be a pretty good Mormon if he could be made something of & put in a situation that he could get plenty of money without work. . . ."

Woodworth later accused his friend Braffitt of seducing his young wife, Margaret. In the law-suit which followed, Braffitt confessed "that he had done what he had done," and offered to be decapitated to atone. A most interesting side-light on early Mormon justice. They did NOT kill him. Just took all his property.[38]

5—p. 37

Re: Rockwell who "in a long life that his enemies said included upwards of a hundred holy murders," you might be interested to know that Harold Schindler is deep in a biography of Porter and has collected an amazing amount of material.[39] Schindler insists that he cannot find as many as twenty murders that can be laid to Rockwell, not even counting such doubtful ones as the shooting of Brewer, the counterfeiter, and Johnson, the horse thief. His estimate cannot be farther off than Kelly's.[40]

Schindler has an almost daily chronology of Rockwell's whereabouts, his trips with the mail and with the Authorities, his various expeditions. His research includes a list of all the murders committed, with source material as to who did the killing.

Kelly is so far out. Truly there were many killings, far too many, and most of them unjustified. But there were many other gun-men, also, and some murders were between the rival gangs of 1858–1861.

6—p. 38

The Mormon-Handcock County negotiations always stipulated that the Mormons should leave "as soon as the grass grows and the water runs." They could hardly promise to leave earlier than that, but tensions mounted until the vanguard did get out before the set time. Those who remained had little trouble, except those who tried to stay long enough to harvest their crops. They were brutally treated for not living up to their agreement.

7—p. 42

John D. Lee wrote: "Nov 28th 1845 I was called to assist in fitting up the rooms for the endowment in the House of the Lord—10 days & I might as well say nights I was engaged in preparing the rooms refered to & on Thursday at 5 p.m. Dec 10 1845 myself and wife received our washings & anointing . . ."

Another party had gone through the ceremony earlier that day.

4—p. 38, 59, 60—

I have included a page of gleanings re: Henry B. Jacobs and Zina D. Huntington. Zina's son Zebulon was born January 2, 1842, lived to come to Zion, at the age of 24 married Frances W. Carrington, daughter of Albert and Rhoda M Carrington. He filled the regular missions, was a conductor on the Oregon Short Line railroad and later a guard at the state penitentiary, and donated the log house in which his wife was born to the state for preservation on Temple Square.[41]

His younger brother Chariton, whose birth you note here always went under the name of Jacobs. Zina bore Brigham Young one child, a daughter named Zina

[missing]

10—p 108

As I suggested before, Rockwell is not yet the murderer of many men. He is a man of 33, whose first wife, married when they were both very young, has left him with three children. They are in the migration, with the John Neff group. Rockwell will later marry Neff's daughter.[42]

Up to this time Rockwell can be held for the attempted assassination of Governor Boggs and for the killing of Frank Worrell.[43] For this last, he was held in honor by his people, for Worrell had led the Carthage Grays in the assault on the jail where the Prophet was killed. Rockwell is now, and will be for some twelve years, a messenger and a bodyguard. His real career as a killer begins after the outbreak of the "Mormon War."

11—p. 117

I do not want to be skeptical, but I wonder if the miracle of the quail, properly investigated, would not show that the Mormon refugees had camped at one of the annual roosting places of the passenger pigeons on their migration south.[44] I have read accounts of how settlers in various places located these roosting spots and waited for the birds to circle and settle and then went in and killed them by the thousands in one night.

But don't let me spoil one of our best stories!

***

Earl Olsen has just called, and his figures have knocked me for a loup! Brother Jensen's figures for the total immigration from 1847 to 1868, with just 2,000 coming the first year, is 68,028. According to his figures, the peak year was 1851, with 5,000 coming that year and 4,684, in 1852.

I have wondered if this is not the total emigration, including that from the U.S. also. Maybe you can find something more reliable than either.

12—p. 168

I have wanted to write in some detail about Clayton's statement that Stout said he would kill him. I studied a long time to learn if I could what the basic trouble was, and I think that Clayton was the un-named "delinquent policeman" who had to be brought in at least twice. The last time he was at a dance instead of at his post.

Soon after, at a policeman's meeting, another was up for discussion and Hosea said something to the effect that he was in favor of holding a man in fellowship as long as they could, and when they could no longer trust him, to cut him off behind the ears. If he bored into Clayton with those fierce eyes of his, the man would take it as a threat.

To *Pansy Hardy*,[45] August 14, 1963

98 U Street, Salt Lake City
August 14, 1963

Dear Pansy:

We got back from our trip with a month's correspondence on the desk and with things in such a general state of confusion otherwise that I may have to answer your letter in installments.[46] I wish I knew more about your thesis topic—if you use only Dr. Hafen and me, or if you include such people as Israel Abbott, for instance, or Marion Earl, or others who have gone on in professional fields.[47]

If you use but the two, it seems that any linking or likeness would more aptly be genetic rather than Mormon-desert-ethnic. This last was Tony's conclusion when I mentioned the problem to him. It might bear some consideration.

Have you seen Mother's family history? It is something of a jumble in some ways, but it does give authentic dates of our progress through school and the names of many of the teachers as well as any little distinction which we received.

Mr. Nisson of Washington told me once that he had some themes which I wrote when I was in his class somewhere in the grades. This was a surprise to me—I hardly believe it, in fact, for I have no memory of it. Still, you might ask.

My early life was conditioned by a number of things:

1—as the eldest of a large family, I was given an extra responsibility with regard to the younger children. I was also given the care of the animals, since Daddy was absent so often on the mail run.

2—I was a puny, homely child. An early memory of soon after Pa returned from his mission is of sharing a No.3 tub with Charity. Mother usually bathed the two of us together, letting one soak while she scrubbed the other. I saw that she was crying about something, the tears running down and falling from the end of her nose. Father said, "The child is all right. Don't snivel over her." Charity was so healthy and plump and pink. I didn't realize how skinny I was, and hollow-chested, my shoulder-blades like sprouting wings, but I did know that I was smaller. Lillian Correy (?) who gave me all eight of my music lessons, told me that I had a "swill-pail complexion." Because of chronic catarrah[48] I breathed through my mouth, so that Annie Cox often hit me between the shoulders and told me to straighten up and shut my mouth—I looked stupid when I played the organ in Sunday School with my mouth hanging open. Con Adams said once that "she could eat corn off the cob through a picket fence" referring to my protruding teeth. I could enlarge upon this and may do so later. I should tell of the braces or harness which mother subjected me to in an effort to hold my shoulders back.

3—This delayed development—Charity was a young lady more than a year before I was—and the fact that I was one grade ahead of my years because school had been held in the large room of our 2-roomed brick home so that the $7.00 a month rent could help finance Pa's mission—brought me into the sixth grade early. The schools were divided into beginners, first and second; 3,4, and 5; 6, 7, and 8. John Gubler was the teacher. Here was I, undersized and puny, in a room of young men and women, as some of the eighth graders had come back into school after some time out.

He recommended that the folks take me out of school entirely, put me out of doors to sleep at night and on a horse in the day so that I might perhaps have better health. I did not attend at all until late spring when I went back to Aunt Martha Cox's room. I was heart-broken when she issued certificates of graduation to all the class but me until she explained that I had already graduated the year before and needed none.

I must stop now, but will either write or talk to you further later on. I think my personality was affected as much by the fact that my father had the contract to run the mail during the years when I was 8 to 16, and for much of the time I was responsible for his string of ponies. This put me out-of-doors a great deal and made me something of a nature mystic, conscious of the seasons, the phases of the moon, the position of the stars, etc . . . the signs of each coming season.

I learned to substitute a pair of nimble heels and a cheerful "line" for a pretty face, and found that I had my share of dances and some dates. I married and intended to settle down on the lower Mesquite flat and raise a family of children. When fate decreed otherwise, I was for a time bitter. After I outgrew this, I decided upon a teaching career.

I did not then, nor do I now, consider myself a writer. Prof. Harrison R. Merrill,[49] short of material for his Utah Academy Section about 1927, asked me to join the Academy and to submit a paper. I did, but I don't remember what the paper was about.

Goodbye again. I may be seeing you

Love,

To *Grace Woodbury*, October 22, 1963

346 North Main
St. George, Utah
October 22, 1963

My dear Grace:

I'm sorry that we couldn't arrange a meeting while I was in town this time. There simple are too many demands and too many directions in which I am expected to go. What I am saying, actually, is that I let myself sometimes get so involved in trivia that I miss some of the really important things I would like to do.

I wanted especially to talk to you about Virginia's last book, Where nothing is Long Ago.[50] I was delighted with it. I'm sure it is true that one gets from a book in proportion to what one brings to it, and in this case I felt a perfect rapport from beginning to end. My own rural background was so similar, except for our River.

Virginia's craftsmanship impressed me, too—her deft, delicate way of saying exactly enough but never too much, of being able to suggest and to leave much to the imagination. Would it be heresy to admit that I enjoyed this book better than any others of hers that I have read?

I must apologize, too, for being so crude over the telephone. I don't remember myself what I said, but it was inappropriate and—well, just crude. Forgive me. I must have just had a cup of coffee. It sometimes turns the Devil loose in me.

Now that I am set up at home again where I belong, I do hope you will call on us if and when you are in our town. I'll probably serve scrambled eggs or bread-and-milk-and-onions or something equally inappropriate.

My best to you and to your wonderful husband. I've had a sort of hero worship of him for a long time—I like his broad, humanitarian approach to problems local and national, and the background from which he speaks.

Good wishes,

To *Virginia Sorensen*, October 22, 1963

346 North Main
St. George, Utah
October 22, 1963

My dear Virginia:

Your book, Where Nothing is Long Ago, came to me here on a Saturday afternoon and never in my life did I miss a Stake Conference with so much pleasure. I had it finished by the time the afternoon meeting closed—only thing, I forgot and let my baked potatoes get—well, not quite charcoal. I smelled them in time.

How alike our childhoods were, I kept saying to myself. Where you went after milk, I went for yeast and had most of it sipped away before I got home. As soon as I turned eight, I started milking, and from that time into my teens I carried the buckets I had milked.

Your pet was a cat; mine was a dog, Old Griz. And I had my very own pony, Selah, who was stolen and never recovered. The name comes from the Old Testament, as you will know—the closing word to many of the Psalms.

My only difference was in the manner of eating pomegranates. Some day I'd like to sit down with you and a couple of nice ripe ones and proceed. Our favorite indoor sport was watching a new school teacher or any other stranger tackle one for the first time.

But the book! How I did enjoy it. I must thank you for your chapter on "Ghosts." You have said for many of us what we want to say, and said it better and more effectively—without rancor, but still with force. "The Other Lady" was beautifully done, too, with just enough told and just enough left to the imagination.

Congratulations for it, for every story in it. My prediction is that it will make a best-seller list. If it does not, I'll still think that it should.

I hope to see you when you come to Zion again.

Love,

To *Savoie Lottinville*, October 25, 1963

346 North Main
St. George, Utah
October 25, 1963

Mr. Savoie Lottinville
University of Oklahoma Press
Norman, Oklahoma

Dear Mr. Lottenville:

Now that I am moved back to my little village,[51] I have so many requests for my Mountain Meadows Massacre that I think I should keep a few on hand. The local bookstore has had none in the last month.

Please send me ten copies and bill me.

I was happily surprised to see it on display with the Deseret Book Store collection. I never thought I'd live to see the day.[52]

I really enjoyed the convention, and hope to attend next year in your state.

Sincere good wishes,

To *Editor,* Salt Lake Tribune, November 30, 1963

346 North Main
St. George, Utah
Nov. 30, 1963

CONTRIBUTOR'S COLUMN:
or
PUBLIC FORUM

Editor, Tribune:

My sincere thanks to Susan M. McDonald for her criticism of St. George in this morning's paper.[53] She spoke well for many of the citizens of our town, who felt as keenly as she did the lack of respect that was shown to our martyred President.

I myself sat glued to the TV unashamedly weeping so much of the time that I was perhaps not conscious enough of what went on elsewhere until Sunday. By that time I began to ask what was to be done on a community basis to show our respect to our great leader, only to be told that each of the schools was having its own memorial activities. On Sunday the LDS Wards of the town evidently followed each its own pattern, with little said of the national tragedy.

When I expressed my criticism in the home of Karl and Kathryn Larson,[54] she gave us all a deserved rebuke: "That is in part your fault and mine," she said. "We knew that the minute the news broke our Tabernacle bell should have begun to toll, and should have continued for at least an hour. That is the traditional signal to our people of great mourning—not to ring the bell, but to toll it. You knew that, and so did I, but neither of us did anything. It would have made a difference I am sure, if we had."

So for myself and my town I apologize, and thank Mrs. McDonald for speaking out in behalf of so many of us who share her feeling.

To *Stewart Udall*, December 1, 1963

346 North Main
St. George, Utah
Dec. 1, 1963

Dear Stewart:

I had read the preview of your The Quiet Crisis[55] in the Saturday Review of Nov. 23,[56] and intended to write my congratulations then, but the tragedy of our President's death left me incapable of doing anything much for a week.

Yesterday's Salt Lake Tribune carried this review by Ernie Linford, in case perhaps your clipping service missed it.[57]

I am proud and happy that you have thus put your ideas into permanent form. While a comparative few may read it, those who do will be among the people who count, and you will have set the record straight for all. I hope that you can carry out your plans inspite of political forces who oppose merely for the business of opposition. We had as well face up to the fact that for the next two or three hundred years the cosmic forces promise, not more water for the southwest, but less, and only by wise and decisive action can we preserve—or conserve—enough for our needs.

As you see from the address, we are back at our home in St. George. Now that I have no permanent employment, I expect to devote the winter to a biography of Will's father, George Brooks. It will not be a large book, but it needs to be done, and I must do it. In the spring I hope to spend some time in Washington, D.C., in the Library of Congress to work on a more important piece of work.

Miss Ettie Lee and two of her "home parents"[58] are with me today. Though we differ sharply on politics, we have many things in common and a genuine affection for each other. I'm afraid my picture of President Kennedy hanging over the piano troubles her a little, but I'm proud to have it there.

Sincere good wishes to you in your very important role, and all my confidence in your success.

Hon. Stewart L Udall
Sec. of the Interior
Washington, D.C.

To *Fawn Brodie*, December 30, 1963

346 North Main, St. George, Utah
December 30, 1963

Dear Fawn;

I have two reasons for writing you—yes, three—besides the wish to send greeting at this time of year.

First, Alfred Bush sent me the section from the New York Times Book Review containing your article, "Who Won the Civil War, Anyway?"[59] I had not seen it before. I am proud that you should so expertly de-bunk so much of the writing about the south. This denial by omission, this creation of a whole new atmosphere by a change of emphasis is so common in the history or our people—I have been so conscious of it, I mean—that I had missed it in the area of the south and civil rights.

When Amos Milton Musser noted that day after day he was helping to "rewrite" Mormon history, he meant just that. Somewhere in the 1870's and 1880's the whole story of the Three Witnesses was re-aligned, and more recently Preston Nibley has done profiles of leading Mormons in which all mention of any wife except the first is carefully left out. Young seminary teachers carefully impress upon their students that the pioneers did not use wine for the sacrament, but "the pure, unfermented juice of the vine." It would have done your heart good to hear my husband and several of the other older members of the congregation set him straight. These are trivial, but they are straws in the wind.

Second, I received my copies of Overland in 1846[60] yesterday and noted that Dale had dedicated it to you, Wonderful! I'm not yet through his introduction. I am more deeply impressed with the quality of his scholarship with each new publication. To have this monumental work dedicated to you is an honor which I think you deserve.

Third, if and when you have time drop me a line and bring me up to date. I expect to go in to the "City" this week-end and pick up my Christmas gifts to myself—your edition of The City of the Saints[61] and Frank Robertson's Fort Hall[62] among them. I have Virginia Sorensen's last.

All good wishes for another successful year ahead.

Sincerely,

To *John Greenway*,[63] January 31, 1964

346 North Main
St. George, Utah
January 31, 1964

Mr. John Greenway, Editor
JOURNAL OF AMERICAN FOLKLORE
University of Colorado
Boulder, Colorado

Dear Mr. Greenway:

Here is the story of the Outsider.

I had to cut this somewhat in order to avoid long explanations. For example: The Outsider actually came to try to persuade the children of my grandfather's Indian wife to accept a free education at Carlisle—I think it was. Anyway, none of them would consider it, because they would not be counted as Indians. Their mother might be a squaw, but their father was Dudley Leavitt, and they were NOT Indians. I have a chapter in which I told the story of Grandma Janet—"Five Grandmas," I call it—Grandpa was a polygamist; my father was the youngest son of his third wife, a girl from England. So as I said, all this was so complicated that it seemed easier not to tell what the Outsider's business was.

Do I understand that you want all three items—"Tubucks," "The Outsider," and "Selah" all in one issue?[64] If this is the case, let me know so that I can get it in by the middle of the month. I'm being pushed a little by other things.

I will appreciate suggestions.

Sincerely,

To *Stanley Ivins*, February 7, 1964

346 North Main, St. George, Utah
Feb. 7, 1964

Dear Stanley:

I know that I'm a nuisance, but I'm still on this Babbitt-Rockwell problem, and if it's not too much trouble, I'd like the citation of Rockwell's pay for bringing in the Babbitt wagon train.[65] To me it seems very significant.

Harold says that he has full details of the murder: the three men all killed by Indians—one as he was trying to escape, the other standing his ground, but both filled with arrows; Babbitt, his back to the buggy shooting valiantly (no word of how many he killed!), and finally dispatched by a tomahawk from behind splitting his skull open. The Indians then taking his trunk and papers, firing the buggy, and driving off the animals, left all the bodies scattered.[66]

For me, some of this smells. Why would Indians take trouble to set the buggy on fire? There is not much of a buggy that would burn, and they would have no particular reason to want to burn it. John Jacques said that it happened some seventy yards from the road, yet passing companies could hardly have missed it, by the odor if nothing else, for some weeks.

This happened early in September—Hal has it dated for about Sept. 3, but I think probably about the 6th. Both dates have been given.

Now the returning group of Mormon missionaries from abroad and from the states made NO mention of Babbitt's death, but they came upon Rockwell with five wagons, at least one of which belonged to former Utahans trying to leave—Grimshaw, Cook, and Barnes, whom he had turned back to Laramie—This was on Sept. 16, and not far from where Babbitt had been killed. Here they camped with Br. Rockwell, accompanied him to Fort Laramie, where they arrived on the 19th.[67]

Could their camp have been near enough to the scene of the murder that the three "frontier missionaries"—William R. Kimball, George D. Grant, and James McGaw—could have gone with Rockwell to bury the bodies?[68] Or did later searchers find them? The dismembered skeletons would show the split skull and verify the story told to Babbitt's wife about a year later.

That the wagon train is mentioned, but not named as belonging to Babbitt, and the murder is NOT mentioned, seems evidence to me that the Mormons were aware of it. Those who wrote the final report for publication were, at any rate. It is signed by F.D. Richards and Daniel Spencer, and appeared in the Deseret News for October 22, 1856, even before Rockwell arrived with the goods. Hafen reprints it in his Handcarts to Zion pp. 218–221.

An official report of the unburied skeletons would prove me wrong in all this perhaps, but my feeling is that sometime during the three days spent by the missionaries and the Babbitt-Rockwell train, the frontier missionaries could have fixed the evidence for later reports.

Well, enough of this. I've always been a doubting, skeptical creature, perhaps too ready to question the official reports and to suspect them of being doctored to meet the circumstances. But when no teamsters of the Babbitt train are named, not even the survivors, and no testimonies taken from them regarding the first attack, I began to wonder. Our people usually name names unless there is some good reason not to.

It was good to see you even for a few minutes. I hope to get up for whatever is done to honor Dale, if he is there to accept it.[69] I wish I had a private plane or helicopter in which to make these trips. I can take the night bus rides, but not as well as it did years ago.

All good wishes,

To *Jack B. Shumate*,[70] February 25, 1964

346 North Main
St. George, Utah
February 25, 1964

Mr. Jack B. Shumate, Supervisor
U.S. Forest Service
Cedar City, Utah

Dear Mr. Shumate:

I am writing out of my deep interest in the monument at the Mountain Meadows. It is in such a state of dis-repair that it seems a disgrace to our southern communities. Members of the Utah State Parks Commission have urged me to talk to Mr. Ezra Lytle, the owner of the property, to see if I can help to persuade him to give or sell it to them, with the promise that they will make some improvements there.

I cannot do this if there is any chance at all that the place may be brought under the auspices of some Federal agency. The people whose bodies lie there were not from Utah, but from Arkansas and Missouri and other points east, so that the spot has national significance. It deserves the dignity and the continuity of planned program which would follow—access roads, landscaping, and up-keep, it should be available to the public without the commercialism which could attend a private enterprise or the danger of becoming the buffet of local political winds.

My friend, Mr. Howard Foulger,[71] was much interested in getting this into the Forest Service by some exchange of land, but was transferred before any arrangement was consummated. I know nothing of what went on, except that after he was in Washington, he wrote that it was a disappointment to him that the action had not been taken.

I have talked briefly to Mr. Lytle, and have a great respect for him as a man of integrity and honor. He keeps his own counsel—rightly—and as yet has had the courage to say "NO" to some rather heavy pressure.

I understand that as a representative of the Government, you or the other officials may make no advance or proposition for an exchange of property, but may give consideration only after the owner has made application. I have no assurance that Mr. Lytle wishes to do this, but if he does, I hope that you will give a sympathetic hearing. I am sure that the Fancher family of Arkansas and citizens generally would be pleased to have this spot properly honored and cared for.

Sincerely yours,

To *Fae Decker Dix*,[72] March 25, 1964

346 North Main, St. George
March 25, 1964

My dear Fae,

It was good to get your letter yesterday and I hasten to answer before it is lost in the shuffle here on my desk. I do remember your asking about the civil rights issue, and had an idea that I answered the questions, but am not sure.[73] In any event, I have never written about it because I have no experience from which to write. I saw my first colored person when I saw my first train—at about the age of eight. He was a porter on the train.

There has never been a colored family in St. George; there were NO colored students at the BYU while I was there; at Columbia there were some, but I did not become acquainted with them. I listened to the panel there in SLC a few years ago where the matter of discrimination was discussed—that is, discrimination in Utah.

I did call Mr. Doman when he was still head of scouting and ask if there were any colored boy scout troops in Utah and found that there were none. That troubled me, because I felt that if scouting would be good for white youngsters, it should be better for colored ones. And, after all, it is an international program, not just a local LDS one as we have made it in Utah.

I think it is something of a disgrace that we have never had a decent civil rights bill in Utah—the only state outside the deep south without one.

I'm glad that you heard Dr. Adamson[74] give his Joseph-sold-into-Egypt talk. I enjoyed it very much. I had hoped that he might become the president of the University. When I learned that Dr. Fletcher's wife and Dr. Olpin's wife are sisters, I understood better his appointment.[75] In Utah, so much depends upon WHO you are rather than WHAT you are.

I'm to be over-run by Easter vacation visitors mostly of the family, so am not sure when I'll pull out of here for a few days. Hope to sharpen up my thumb and make it before too long, though. And I'll get in touch with you.

In the meantime, it's good to know that you are finishing up strong and are soon to be out. You'll get a good position, never fear—one that will be satisfying as well as remunerative. And I hope that eventually—I said <u>eventually</u>—you'll team up with some fine man with whom you have much in common. It's too long a road to walk alone in loneliness.

Wait until I see you to scold me.

Love,

To *J. Wesley and Sana Williamson*, April 5, 1964

346 North Main, St. George, Utah
Sunday Morning, April 5/64

Dear Wes & Sana:

Sunday morning and conference is on. We are all supposed to stay home and listen on TV or radio. I've settled the question and my own problem by closing all doors and settling down to write a few short letters.

Yours first:

I liked your letter to Secretary Udall.[76] It states the case well. But I doubt that he will get time to read it or answer it at once. He is gone so much and in the midst of so many conflicting pulls that he simply MUST trust most of his correspondence to his office staff. I myself do not expect answers. One time he scribbled a one-sentence note "Bless you for writing as you did," and signed it.

He has had the arguments, all of them, on the MMMonument. The Forest Service is out of his jurisdiction entirely, since it is in the Department of Agriculture. I've wondered about going to the head there, but have not done it. I may write Howard Foulger again, since he is now stationed in Montana, and over a large district. He <u>really</u> wanted to do something about it, and may be in more of a situation now than before.

I have also written to Mr. Frank Oberhansley,[77] Supt. of Zion National Park. This, on the other hand, IS under the Sec. of Interior, and here we might be able to do something. I have promised to get into the Park in April sometime, but how or when I do not know.

Was the WATER! COOL, COOL WATER! Done with some magazine in mind, or was it also sent to Sec. Udall? I think it is fine. I did notice two words, though, which I think perhaps do not say what you mean: P. 2 end of line 5—<u>retribution</u>. Do you, perhaps mean <u>reprisal</u>? Also para. 3 line 2—<u>eminent</u>—you no doubt mean <u>imminent</u> or <u>acute</u>.

Re: the problem of de-salinating sea water. If and when that can be done economically, it should be much more feasible than converting whole river systems hundreds of miles. Forgive me—this is not my problem; I am ignorant in this area.

Now as to me: Never in all my long life have I found it so hard to "get into" a subject as I have the Nevada assignment, which is due to be finished and in on the 11th and is still like the earth at the end of the second day of Creation, "Without form and void." If I even get it done, it will be something of a small miracle.[78]

The reasons? The subject itself seems "Much Ado About Nothing" as Shakespeare would say, and the constant, beyond-my-control distractions. I hope that on this, The Lord's Day, He may help me to get off dead center.

Until a week from now—Adios or Adieuuuuu—

and my best love,

To *J. Wesley and Sana Williamson*, May 4, 1964

346 North Main, St. George, Utah
Monday morning early May 4

Dear Wes & Sana:

Things happen fast sometimes, even in an out-of-the-way place like this. But the MMMonument is a cause dear to my heart. The one thing which I have not done, and which I think I shall do today, is to write to Howard Foulger, and include in the letter your quote from the Chief of the Department of the Interior.[79] By the way—I have increased admiration for Stewart Lee Udall. He has nerve enough to stand calm between bitterly warring factions and to try to be just while both sides cry out against him.

I wrote to Mr. Oberhansley of the Park Service at Zion, but he was away. His clerk say that he would be glad to see me.

My Nevada paper was finished at last. While I'm not too proud of it, I think it does cover the subject adequately enough. I shall leave here early Wednesday morning, and travel up to Reno by car, which will give me an on-the-ground look at the area where our people settled. I shall be in the area until Saturday I presume.

Peg Gregory called the other night and was quite insistent that I come to Albuquerque for a couple of weeks. I told her that a couple of days would be more like it. Her husband is off on a world cruise in business for the Navy and will be away all month. So I toy with the idea of flying from Las Vegas out, and literally taking the long way home. I'd really like to see that area, especially Santa Fe and Taos and general back-ground where our earliest civilization took root.

Then, most importantly—I had a call from the President of the Utah State University at Logan that I was selected to receive an honorary PhD. Would I accept it? That will be on June 6th. And do you know who will occupy the stand with me and get one also? Apostle LeGrande Richards! I think I have never told you of my correspondence with him, in which I called his hand for condemning the MMM book when he had not even seen it. A rather heated correspondence followed, which he closed by saying that he was sorry he had ever become involved at all and wanted to hear no more of it. Life is full of paradoxes, certainly.

One other definite date I have. On May 28 I am to speak to the SUP at Provo. That is on Thursday night, and the date was set up six weeks ago. I should not have accepted it at all, but they were very insistent.

So now I must make some preparation to get off tomorrow night or in the early hours Wednesday. But I'll write to Foulger right now, before I eat my breakfast.

Hope Sana is all in good health again. Love to you both

To *Leonard J. Arrington*, May 6, 1964

346 North Main St.
St. George, Utah
May 6, 1964

Dr. Leonard J. Arrington
Department of Economics
Utah State University
Logan, Utah

Dear Leonard:

Thank you so much for your heart-warming letter.[80]

I certainly had no thought of such an award, but am happy to accept it—much happier that people such as you should think that I deserve it. For years I thought I would pitch in and earn myself a genuine, bona fide PhD., and then when I could see that I was not going to get it done, I rationalized that it wouldn't mean much to me anyway. Now I find that I am more than pleased to accept this.

I look forward to seeing you and all my friends in Logan. I've always had a warm spot for the school and the group there—seems that they combine the finest qualities of both the other universities of the state.

Thank you, too, for your invitation to stay at your home. I would certainly enjoy doing just that, but we have a son there who expects us, and two little grandchildren who look forward to our visit.

Until June 6, then,

Gratefully yours,

To *Ellvert H. Himes,*[81] June 27, 1964

St. George, Utah
June 27, 1964

Dr. Ellvert H. Himes
General Chairman
Commencement Activities
U.S.U., Logan, Utah

Dear Dr. Himes:

What with a progressive family reunion—where one family arrives just as another is leaving—along with a wedding and a funeral, I have been so occupied that all regular duties have been neglected. My correspondence has gathered dust for more than a week now. You're first on the list.

The Doctorate Hood did arrive, and had I timed it myself, it could not have come at a more dramatic time. I had eight members of the Lee family from Arizona and California in to lunch, and Will had to open the package and display it. Yes, I must even model it over my kitchen apron and a nephew pointed his camera at me. I didn't mean it to be a desecration; I wasn't being flippant, either. So I hope there was no film in the camera.

The far-reaching effect of your honor to me is certainly humbling. I did not realize at the time how many people outside the building were watching on TV, and how many others caught the story through the newspapers. But since no one here ever uses my new title, I am able to adjust.

The whole experience there was for me one of the rare "sun-bursts" of my life, the highest point to date, certainly. I shall always be grateful to the USU and especially to you for the kindness and courtesy you gave me. Those are not the right adjectives; they are too weak to express what I wish to say. But then all words are inadequate.

Accept my gratitude and do come here whenever you are in southern Utah.

Sincerely,

Source: WSU Levi Peterson Collection.

Chapter 10

1965–1966

Looking for Her Next Major Project

Again, in 1965, Brooks searched around for another major project on which to focus her efforts, though she was involved with a number of smaller endeavors including completing the biography of George Brooks and editing the diaries of Thomas D. Brown. At the first of the year she was floored with another movie proposal, this time for a movie on John D. Lee from author Samuel W. Taylor. As with the previous proposals, this one did not get off the ground. She again attempted to sell to her friends, Wesley and Sana Williamson, the possibility of publishing all of John D. Lee's diaries in a single edited series, an idea she had been pushing since the early 1950s. She also tried to drum up interest for the project in a letter to Ettie Lee in 1966. In a letter to Gladys Harrison, a friend in Logan, she even interpreted a dream as meaning that she needed to decide on a direction for her research and cut down on her speaking engagements, which were keeping her quite busy. She concluded this letter as she often did: "Please forgive this crazy letter, Gladys. It just oozed out of the machine."[1]

With the help of friends Leonard Arrington and Alfred Bush, she applied for and received a travel grant from the American Philosophical Society to conduct research on the pre-1848 John D. Lee diaries. This grant allowed her to travel to the Western History Association in Helena, Montana, to visit New Mexico to orient herself with the geography of John D. Lee's diary of his journey to Santa Fe, and to fly to Washington, D.C., to examine the papers of President James K. Polk at the National Archives.

In late 1965, she commenced on probably the most frustrating assignment of her career when she accepted the offer to research and write the history of the Jews in Utah sponsored by a Jewish organization represented, as coauthor, by Louis Zucker, an English professor at the University of Utah, and in conjunction with the University of Utah, supervised by University of Utah professor and administrator Sterling McMurrin. Though the original commitment was for eighteen months, the venture dragged on until 1973 when Sam Weller, of Zion Books and Western Epics, finally published it. She sent many letters to the participants in the project and to others, including Dale Morgan, explaining her challenges with Zucker over the content of the book and her writing and his inability to produce his agreed-upon portion. By September 1968, Juanita was so discouraged after Zucker announced he would rewrite her work that she notified the project committee she had "made a mistake when I accepted this assignment" proposing that either she could turn it over to Zucker to finish or she could take a six-month vacation from it and then continue.[2] In many amenable letters to Myrtle Friedman, the woman funding the book, Juanita confided her struggles and discontent, suggesting terminating the endeavor, as well as asking her thoughts on the schedule and manuscript. After enduring and finally bringing the writing to completion in 1972, she received a further blow when the committee contracted with Sam Weller under fantastic financial terms to publish the book while refusing to compensate her additionally for her efforts. She angrily protested these arrangements to several, including Friedman.

Brooks also renewed her objections to the Dixie National Forest concerning the condition of the Mountain Meadows Massacre site in 1966. She fired off several letters over a period of months demanding to know why the highway sign for the massacre site remained missing and wondered why it was taking five months to give the sign "a face-lifting."[3] She had heard the sign had been removed by orders from the LDS Church. She also questioned the claim that a flood had removed the picnic tables at the site, noting that she found no signs of a flood that could have removed the heavy tables and no evidence of the tables after walking downstream for two miles. The deplorable condition of the road leading to the site was also a concern, especially the deep tracks of a heavy truck that she believed was used to remove the tables.

As she did throughout her career, she continued her crusade for the truthful telling of Mormon history. One example in a letter to Ogden

Kraut was her alarm over the reversal of how the calling of the Mormon Battalion was portrayed through time. According to Brooks, the original reason, as given by Brigham Young, for the dispatch of the battalion—to get as many of the saints as possible across the plains at government expense—was switched after 1857–1858 to imply that the government recruited the men in an attempt to stamp out Mormonism.[4]

Her correspondence during these years continued to show her as a respected historian and member of the LDS Church. In a letter to LDS Church general authority Marion D. Hanks she declined his invitation to serve on the Advisory Council of "The Friends of the BYU Library" organization. Elder Hanks responded by saying that he had "long appreciated you and hope you live forever and keep influencing as many as you do with your courage and your solid brand of faith."[5] In 1965, she was also asked to review Harold Schindler's manuscript on Orrin Porter Rockwell for the University of Utah Press.

She also enjoyed discussing English literature and other books with friends. Upon receiving from J. Golden Taylor a copy of his analysis of Hawthorne's *The Gentle Boy*, she remarked that Hawthorne was an early favorite of hers and that his analysis added new dimensions to her thinking.

~

To *Samuel W. Taylor*,[6] January 10, 1965

St. George, Utah
January 10, 1965

Dear Sam:

Your talk of trying to film the John D. Lee story has rather knocked me off balance. I think, taken as a whole, with the MMM incident subdued somewhat, it would make as tragic a life as it actually was. I warn you of this one thing, however—the Church will fight you tooth and claw. The old fears, the old antagonisms are still there; this is still taboo, in so far as they are concerned

Re. the documentary film, I'm all for that. You can find innumerable cases where the Lee descendants were denied position because someone whispered, "You know who he (or she) is, don't you?"

Along with Miss Ettie, you must give recognition to Manetta Henry and to J. Wes Williamson, among others. Manetta compiled the family history, which you have no doubt seen, and collected the names of so many of the descendants as she could get to admit their connection.

Wes was influential in getting the Arthur H. Clark Company to publish the Lee Biography, he has sponsored the sales and advertised the book far and near, and when the Church (Specifically, Judge Jesse Udall under orders of Apostle Delbert Stapley) tried to get me to leave out the account of Lee's re-instatement into the church, Williamson was the ONLY one of the family that supported me and stood by me during the more than 2-hour grilling in which each in turn, and some the second or third time IMPLORED me not to do this. I called Wes long distance and asked him to make the trip from Whittier to Phoenix and bring his tape recorder, so that we might have an accurate account of what each one said. I refused to be brought before this inquisition otherwise; I wouldn't have them going out to try to repeat what I had said.

Miss Lee's stand at that time and under fire was with the family and the Church and against me. Because of this, I'm sure that she will not give you her blessing (if you think you need it) when the Church puts on the heat.

One other thing: I have at least a dozen pioneer incidents similar to those used in the Western Ads—authentic ones which I can document—dramatic, interesting, amusing. I've already given away too many for others to profit on—I mean, that I have furnished a number of incidents which have been presented. I think I might like to try one or two of these myself.

You are right about the Lee material being in the public domain. If you want to stir up a real hornet's nest, just make a preliminary sounding. My membership is not more valuable to me than yours is to you, I'm sure. If after some preliminary soundings, you think you want to go ahead with this, I'll go along. Does not the Arthur H. Clark own priority in all these things?

Better talk to them.

Sincere good wishes,

Source: Levi Peterson's Collection.

To *J. Wesley and Sana Williamson*, February 10, 1965

346 North Main
St. George, Utah
February 10, 1965

Dear Wes & Sana:

I look at the calendar and wonder where the last two weeks have gone, and then I wonder how I could have crowded so much into so short a time. But as the Chinese say "This will pass". Sometime, maybe, sometime I shall tell you about it, but not now.

To bring you up to date in case you are interested; I went to Logan to speak at two different places—the Cache Valley Hist. Society and the Associated Womens' Club of USU—but I was taken also to history classes and a Ladies' Literary Club. Every minute was full, so full that I did not get to visit with my grandson & wife and barely to see my son & wife.

Back home I've had my spring housecleaning done early in preparation for a general celebration honoring Will's oldest sister, on her 88th birthday. Two sisters and one sister-in-law came from the SLCity area and stayed with us. One is still here, and will stay until Friday, of this week.

NOW, my big idea—besides some article-length things—is this: to follow a line you have suggested before, and see if we can get together ALL of the John Doyle Lee writings and have them edited and fitted together chronologically. It will take three volumes, but I think they will be full of meat. The first step as I see it, will be to get family consent to publish what we have. Could all the warring factions combine on this, do you think? I have not written to Ettie or to Ewart, and shall not do so—at least not yet.

The task is really a big one. It will take at least two years of concentrated work. I have already written to sound out Lottinville of Oklahoma Press, but have had no answer. If the family will consent, we can proceed. Or maybe we can just proceed, whether or not they consent.

Part of my hesitation has been the fact that it will be such a big task, and I can hardly devote myself to it for just the honor and the glory. If I were officially attached to the State Historical Society, or if I were not already officially retired and on Social Security, it would be different. Well, these things are minor, and can be adjusted.

Let me know your thinking. In the meantime, I may call Lottinville to sound him out, and shall keep you posted. And as for you—DO TAKE CARE OF YOURSELF and you know what I mean.

Best love to Sana also,

Source: WSU Levi Peterson Collection.

To *Gladys Harrison*,[7] February 11, 1965

St. George, Utah
Feb. 11, 1965

I think maybe I have read too many of John D. Lee's dreams. Or is it that I am getting older and returning more to the folk-beliefs of my past? Anyway, last night I had one that seems significant, though I can pick most of the elements from recent experiences.

It seemed that I was about to board a plane for a trip East somewhere. I had my ticket purchased and in my purse. Then I looked down and saw that I had on a pair of boots—not the high, laced ones, but straight-up, rather tight legs almost to the knee. Not only were they awkward, but they were mis-matched. For a second I thought I only had them on the wrong feet; and then I saw that the top design was different. Sitting near was a third boot, but it did not match either of the others.

While I was trying to decide what to do about my foot-gear, the plane was called and the other passengers in the waiting room crowded into the elevator to go down. The door closed on me the instant I reached it. Turning, I started down the steps at the side, only to see the limosine pulling away as I reached the door.

There I stood in these silly boots, with my purse and my ancient black zipper bag. I opened it to find that it was empty! So it was well that—and a good thing I didn't get on the plane.

Crazy? Well, yes. Maybe. But I think I should get into some better shoes before I start to travel, and decide whether my major work from here on is to be editing other diaries or writing things of my own. My empty brief-case could have been a throw-back to my leaving my speech there; the identical boots were on a little teen-age girl who boarded the bus on my way up and rode only between two towns, but had such trouble to handle these unwieldy boots. So you see, I can rationalize it all away.

Only once before in my life did I have a dream to which I attached any significance, and that was when I had been asked to sell the MMM rights to the Warner Brothers for a movie. I saw a nest of about eight eggs, with one or two chickens hatched, and a third just pecking through the shell and cheeping loudly as if for help. I turned and walked away, saying that a chicken that could not peck its way out of its own shell would be too weak to live if I helped it out. So I told the family the next morning that the moving picture would die a-borning, as indeed it did.

I don't remember what I told you when I called, but somewhere along the line I have slipped up on my writing to good friends and instead answered letters asking for information or direction. After I called Tony in Ithaca and found him down with flu, I did take time to write him the usual cautions and reminders to stay down, keep warm, drink much liquid, especially juices, rub with Vick's or mentholatum, etc.etc.

Willa's birthday was Feb. 9, and we called to give the usual greetings, but found her and her family all down, too. I think the official title is "Executive Flu." So I repeated all my admonitions to her.

Our guests to the Brooks get-together left last Sunday morning, two of them, but Cornelia is still here until tomorrow. For her entertainment this morning I furnished some valentines for her to send to her grand-children and some stationery upon which she is supposed to write to her brother Lew, who was not here for the party. Having her thus occupied has given me a chance to write this.

For one reason her visit has been good. I have pretty well caught up on my mending and odds-and-ends of little chores that needed to be done and could be done to the accompaniment of a friendly chat.

I think I have decided not to accept any more invitations to go places to speak. I'm getting too old and forgetful, and then I don't have anything to say that would justify the time and the distance and the time it takes to get back into my own business after. I've just written as nice a refusal as I can to a Richfield group. There is no public transportation from here to there; I'd have to get off at Cove Fort with no way to get over; it would take a full day each way in order to speak twenty minutes. I think I'll keep a carbon of this refusal to use as a pattern for any others I may get.[8]

All of which only proves how old and crotchety I have become.

Please forgive this crazy letter, Gladys. It just oozed out of the machine. I did so enjoy seeing you and being in Logan and meeting so many wonderful friends. Ione[9] continues to amaze me with the things she gets done, the way she keeps alert and helpful in current, worthwhile activities, and the influence she shed around her. If ever a woman deserved a Purple Heart for service beyond the call of duty, she does. And you deserve it for courage in the face of adversity. I'm proud that women such as you two will be my friends.

Will you share this with her? I'm afraid I shall not get at another for a while.

My love and prayers,

Source: WSU Levi Peterson Collection.

To *Leonard J. Arrington*, April 13, 1965

346 North Main
St. George, Utah
April 13, 1965

Dear Leonard:

As I told you this morning, I am applying to the American Philosophical Society for a travel grant in order that I may visit the Library of Congress, the Coe Collection and the Princeton western collection, and stop at some of the mid-western depositories.[10]

I plan to edit a collection of the John D. Lee writings before 1848. These will consist of excerpts from his missionary writings (I think the long didactic poems and silly "acrostics" need not be preserved, nor the long arguments prepared for debate), most of his Nauvoo Journal (omitting the temple ordinance descriptions), all the day-by day account of the trek from the river to Winter Quarters, all of the Santa Fe Mission for the Mormon Battalion money, and just maybe, the journal which Kelly had printed in 1938.[11] You remember that there were only 250 of them.

Mr. Lottinville assures me that he will print such a volume. Pres. John Tucker[12] of Carbon College (now the College of Eastern Utah, I believe) wrote the Oklahoma Press suggesting that they re-do also the whole Mormon Chronicle, placing in order the scattered items of the present volume one, and completing volume two with an account of the second trial and execution. This would be a big, expensive undertaking, and though Lottinville was cordial and almost favorable, I doubt that he will do it.

What I want to do now is this one volume. The originals of the Kelly book are in Tucson and some new diaries purported to have been found at Farmington, so I would want to go that direction also. But mainly I need to become acquainted with the great depositories of the East.

The Library of Congress would let me see my own collection there made under WPA. I mean to get a list of originals photographed by Huntington and one of the copies bound and indexed at BYU as an extension of the little story you want me to do. I'd like to go into it at length while I am in Logan.

I didn't mean to go on so long. I enclose the form and a stamped, addressed envelope, and will appreciate anything you can say in my behalf. I'm building no hopes, but one can ask, anyway.

Sincere good wishes,

Dr. Leonard J. Arrington
Dept. of Economics
Utah State University

To *Richard Y. Thurman*,[13] May 19, 1965

St. George, Utah
May 19, 1965

Richard Y. Thurman, Director
University of Utah Press
University of Utah
Salt Lake City, Utah

Dear Mr. Thurman:
Re: Harold Schindler's ms. "Orrin Porter Rockwell"

I read this manuscript with much interest.[14] The subject had become a legend in his day, and through the years that have followed has been surrounded with more and more of folklore, until it is time that a definitive biography of his should appear.

I consider this manuscript to be a contribution to western history. The scholarship seems sound, the bibliography comprehensive. While I have questioned one or two of his sources as being not reliable, in the vain he has covered the ground well. Facts regarding the background and family life of this man have been carefully worked in, and he becomes a human being rather than an ignorant, indiscriminate murderer. Yet through his life, the reader gets the background of the society in which he lived.

I believe that there will be a good market for this book. Charles Kelley's Holy Murder[15] which purports to be a biography of O.P. Rockwell is not documented well and is grossly inaccurate.

In general the manuscript reads well. The author himself may wish to do some tightening up of the script.

I think this book would be a worthy addition to your list of publications.

Sincerely yours,

Source: Levi Peterson's Collection.

To *J. Golden Taylor*,[16] September 14, 1965

St. George, Utah
Sept. 14, 1965

Dear J. Golden,

I have spent a happy afternoon with your Hawthorne's Ambivalence Toward Puritanism.[17] Thank you very much for sending it to me; it has given me a new dimension in my thinking of Hawthorne.[18] He was early a favorite of mine, for in high school I read The Scarlet Letter, The House of Seven Gables, and such short stories as "The Great Stone

Face," "The Gray Campion," "Young Goodman Brown," and others. Even then I sensed the author's guilt-burden.

"The Gentle Boy" I did not know until today, and it is for your analysis of this that I say a special thanks. You have done a masterful piece of work here, a contribution to many, I am sure.

I miss seeing so many of my friends in Logan. I have done only a sort of trivia for some time now, but hope to get into action again on something more worthwhile. There are so many interesting things waiting to be done.

I'm going to be at the Historical Society's annual dinner program, which is now extended to a full day affair. Shall hope to get into a few other bits of research while I am in the area.

My love and gratitude to you and to Ethel, along with other Logan friends. I think so often of Ione as the embodiment of true religion and undefiled . . . "to visit the widows and the fatherless" or is it my own preferred on "To love the Truth, to deal justly with thy fellowmen, and walk uprightly before thy God."

Forgive me. My machine got out of hand, and I'm not a Scriptorian anyway.

Source: WSU Levi Peterson Collection.

To *Alfred Bush*, October 18, 1965

St. George, Utah, Oct. 18/65

My dear Alfred:

So I go to the Western Writers' conference at Helena[19] expecting to see you there and to talk things over with you at great length. I was disappointed in this, though I did see Klaus and the Utah People, as well as acquaintances from the convention two years ago in Salt Lake City. I came home all stimulated and renewed and eager to get on. I'm still tingling with it.

But the threads of my life become tangled and complicated—knotted, would be a better word perhaps. Let me back up a little: When you, bless you, helped me to get this travel grant, I wanted to do a third volume on the Mormon Chronicle to include the early writings of John D.

Lee. I talked to Dr. Pomfret,[20] who advised me to see what I could do to get access to the originals and suggested that the Huntington Library would be glad to cooperate in this. But at that time any chance of getting this seemed remote and hopeless indeed.

So I set myself to preparing the Thomas D. Brown "Journal of the Southern Indian Mission" for publication for the University of Utah Press.[21] This is now practically done, except for rounding out the biography of Brown, and the new director, Richard Thurman, assures me an early publication.

In the meantime I have finished the biography of Will's father, George Brooks, which I had done in June, and which the local printer assured me he could get out by Christmas. But he was involved with fairs and rodeos and school-opening material, and did not do too much. Now he has been taken to the hospital critically ill and his son wants to hand it all back to me. Which may, in the end, prove to be a good thing, I have decided. It does gum up things, though.

This would not count on any justification I might have for accepting travel money for research, of course. It's just one of these "asides" that I had taken on.

I had decided to make a trade with the LDS Church offices via Earl Olsen, by offering them a verifax copy of the John D. Lee missionary diary of 1841–1843. This contains the dates and names of all the baptisms he performed—most important items just now when the Church is in the midst of the program for full records of ancestors—especially of baptisms. I would trade it to Earl for a verifax of Lee's Santa Fe Mission, a document of about the same length. He agreed, but when I went to make the exchange, what does he hand me? The full 1846 account from the Mississippi River to establishment at Winter Quarters!!! SO—I shall re-open negotiations with Huntington, for I would be happy to have their backing and assistance in this. I had expected to do only the Santa Fe Mission as a travel account of the road during 1846, and would visit the area as a part of the preparation. I may still do this.[22]

Now, in the midst of all my uncertainty and blundering comes a telephone call from Salt Lake City: Louis Zucker[23] wondering if I might be interested in doing a history of the Jews in Utah.[24] Would I? Well, no, not particularly. In the first place, I know little of the Jews and care less. I do know little—just a very little—of the history of Utah. Would I meet with their committee and hear their plans?

I did that. Present were Attorney Roe,[25] who evidently controls the money bags, Louis Zucker, who represents the Jewish organization, Sterling McMurrin,[26] who represents the University. Seems that the Jews have pledged to raise $100,000. to help establish a Jewish department in the new Library, and that a small part of that is to go toward a history of the Jewish people in Utah. Dr. Jack Adamson had suggested that I be asked to write this, and Sterling had concurred. I should be paid for my service, the funds to be handle through the University, and the Press to print the book. I should have 18 months in which to produce a manuscript, after research—I mean the time should include research and writing, with the idea that, if necessary, the time should be extended.

I did not make a firm commitment further than to say that I think I may be interested to do this, but could not consider doing anything about it until after January 1st, by which time I hope to have these shorter items and perhaps one other brief one completed, with enough in print with others under way to justify the travel grant.

I have made one trip to Huntington and will go again soon; I expect to visit Santa Fe and the Arizona depositaries now soon while the fall and winter weather holds. My trips East must be after mid-winter and my research a combination of early Mormon items as well as Jewish references. I have a preliminary list of some of the things I should see in each depository.

I have been interested to see how many people are doing research on one or another phase of early Mormonism. Only the other day a long distance call to tell me that Bonney, author of Banditti of the Prairie was a baptized Mormon in Nauvoo and member of a counterfeiting group![27]

Enough for now. I'll try to muddle through my various family responsibilities and still not lose track of my work or my friends.

Love and gratitude,

Source: WSU Levi Peterson Collection.

To *Marion D. Hanks*,[28] November 20, 1965

St. George, Utah
November 20, 1965

Mr. Marion D. Hanks
47 East South Temple
Salt Lake City, Utah

Dear Mr. Hanks:

Thank you for your letter of November 16. I was pleased to hear from you, and glad you asked for the Derricks' address.[29] They live at 1716 Glenarm Drive, Clovis, New Mexico. Thales is due home from Viet Nam tomorrow or the next day, and be sure Willa will be glad to have him back. He has flown more than 125 combat missions.

As to my being an official "Friend of the B Y U Library," Chad Flake[30] or Brother Butt or any other member of the Special Collections Staff will tell you that I have been that for nearly thirty years. They are richer by some 142 original manuscripts which I have brought in, they have had copied, and brother Butt has indexed. Chad sent me a list a few months ago when I needed it for a report which Dr. Leonard J. Arrington of USU was making.

I have continued to direct Chad, Ralph Hansen,[31] and the new boy whose name I have forgotten to manuscript diaries known to be in private hands. I expect to continue to do this.

But just last week I signed for a position with the U of U in which I am to write a History of the Jews in Utah and Idaho, and to be financed by Library funds. In view of this, would it be appropriate to have my name on a list of those working actively for the BYU Library?

My chief interest has been that these historical sources be available to students and scholars, and with that in mind, I have taken journals to Henry E. Huntington Library, where they are put on microfilm and photographed, routed them back through BYU, where they have been copied and indexed, and passed some on to the Utah State Historical Society. Last week, for the first time, I took items in to Brother Earl Olsen upstairs so that he could make xerox copies.

So thank you again for considering me, but let me continue as I am doing, without my name on the list.[32]

Cordially,

Source: Levi Peterson's Collection.

To *Ogden Kraut,*[33] November 18, 1966

St. George, Utah
Nov. 18, 1966

Dear Ogden Kraut,

Thank you so much for the information concerning The Peacemaker pamphlet.[34] As you know, the diary of Norton Jacob is at the Utah State Historical Society, so is readily available. Since the only known copy of the controversial Chapter 18, I shall try to get a photocopy from there if possible

It is interesting, though, that Udney H. Jacob evidently lived his life out among the Mormons. Seems to me that a photostatic copy of The Peacemaker is somewhere available in the state. I'll make a double check.

There has been such a complete reversal of talk on the calling of the Mormon Battalion that it is hard to believe. Ray Luce, a graduate student in history at the BYU, did a seminar paper on Jessie C. Little in which he reproduced letters to and from Brigham Young urging that Little use every power at his command to have President Polk call 500 men or more to join the army of the west.[35] To get these people across the continent at government expense for food, clothing & shelter, and with a cash payment which might be used in part to finance the general migration would be a great lift to the Authorities. Luce lives at 710 North 6 West in Provo, and has mimeographed copies of this paper which you could get for the asking. He plans to do his Dissertation on a complete life of Little.[36]

This attitude that the Government called our men in an attempt to stamp out Mormonism grew up in the church after 1857–1858 when the army was on its way to Utah, and when our people were remembering all the persecutions they had undergone before coming to this barren land.

I myself spent time at the Library of Congress and examined the original papers of President James K. Polk, in which were the original letters written by Brigham Young and the other leaders to him.[37] There are several, all very long letters. One dated August 9, 1846 and written from their camp at Winter Quarters, was suggested by Col Thomas L. Kane, who had caught up with the company there. Excerpts of this follow:

> "a large portion of the Church of Jesus Christ of Latter Day Saints having passed from the nation of our nativity. . . . we were met by Capt. J. Allen of your army of the West proffering us the enrolment of 500 men, to be marched to California via Santa Fe, there to be discharged at the expiration of one year, receiving the pay of soldiers and other valuable emoluments, to this offer we promptly responded . . .
> "Resolved that the thanks of this people be presented to President Polk for his friendly offer of transferring 500 [missing]

This is the great difficulty of studying Mormon history. One must know not only who is speaking, but when he is speaking. In 1846 Brother Brigham was saying that he would have the 500 men if he had to take old men and women—which in the end, he did. "Father" Pettigrew[38] records his own call as an older man, and at least 23 women went along and many children. Jefferson Hunt[39] had two wives and about 11 children—though I am not sure whether this number was only children or whether it included the parents of his second wife.[40] Kate B. Carter put out a pamphlet on the women of the battalion.[41] (only four or five of whom went the full journey.)

What I started to say above is that in 1846 B.Y. had one story; in 1857 and 1858 he had another entirely. To read these speeches and compare them with his letters twelve years before makes one wonder if he took into account what these would do to later students and researchers. Perhaps he did not think the correspondence would be so carefully kept, both by Brother Little and Pres. Polk.

Is the Joseph Lee Robinson diary of the man who was president of the California Mission in the early 1900's?[42] I have seen a short biography of this man, but not a diary. I understand that he was one of the last to practice plural marriage in the Church—that he had three wives. Does the name of Miss Ettie Lee appear in it anywhere?

The subject of re-baptism in the Church is interesting. It was done sometimes as a renewal of covenants, as at the reformation of 1856. Sometime later it was used to re-instate people who had been cut off for moral offenses. When the 1847 pioneers arrived in the valley of the Great Salt Lake, there was a general baptismal day at which most of the teamsters and many of the other brethren were re-baptized. Do you remember the incident of J.D. Lee's wife, Emma? See A Mormon Chronicle Vo. 2 pp 100–101[43]

Well I have visited long enough this morning. I must get at my regular duties.

(Congratulations on your promotion! As a Seventy you are charged with preaching the true Gospel).[44]

Sincerely,

To *Jack B. Shumate*, November 23, 1966

St. George, Utah
November 23, 1966

Jack B. Shumate
Forest Ranger, Dixie National Forest
569 South 580 East
Cedar City, Utah

Dear Jack:

Within the last week two cars have stopped for direction to the monument at the Mountain Meadows, both saying that there is NO marker there of any kind. When we both knew that the sign was gone about the middle of July, we wondered if it might be the work of vandals, but I learn now—via the grapevine—that it was taken down by the ranger at Enterprise with the excuse that it needed re-finishing.

Now the road workers—or one of them—say that the sign was removed by orders from the LDS Church, and that it is not to be restored at all. In any event, five months should be long enough to have given it a face-lifting.

What do you know about this? Are we to assume that the spot is no longer to be marked on the road? Is the current whisper that the place itself will be closed to visitors founded in fact?

The St. George Chamber of Commerce say they are troubled daily by complaints, more especially because their literature had named it as a point of interest. Now the general attitude seems to be, "If the Church says NO, who are we to dispute it?"

Well, does the Mormon Church or any other church dominate the US Forest Service? If they want to build a wall around their 2 1/2 acres or put strong fences and locked gates around that, surely that cannot prevent a marker on a public road to point it out. Is not this an important spot in the line of historic places that are being marked?

I do not want to seem too out of line in this, but I am ashamed when a car of people en route from Denver to California detour here and waste almost a day trying to find an advertised point of interest and cannot find it.

Sincerely,

To *Ettie Lee*, November 23, 1966

Nov. 23, 1966

Dear Ettie:

I saw the account in last Sunday's paper of the moving picture which is being made of your life.[45] Wonderful! I'm sure it will be both beautiful and inspiring, and I hope it will get the wide circulation it should have.

I think I told you earlier that we have saved our Old Courthouse. There are those who would have torn it down to make room for another service station. Now we are converting it into a Civic Center where the Chamber of Commerce will have offices; there will be an art exhibit upstairs, and some rooms will be kept for pioneer collections.

I had the first County Record Book photographed in actual size to be displayed in a case with the picture of John D. Lee, who was the first Probate Judge and kept the first records.[46] We hope to give publicity also to the men who worked on the building, and other early officers, and in our book of records to have the autographs of as many of their descendants as we can. This program is just getting under way.

I expect to contact as many as I can to sign the pages following his name—at one dollar (or more) per signature.

The John D. Lee Diary covering his mission to Santa Fe will be published by the New Mexico Historical Quarterly this spring sometime. I still hope for the day when A Mormon Chronicle will be a 3-volume set which will include the earlier mission records and the trek from the Mississippi to Winter Quarters.

Congratulations again on the moving picture. It cannot do justice to all your life in a half hour, but it can give a glimpse into what you have accomplished.

Much Love,

To *Raymond Taylor*,[47] November 29, 1966

St. George, Utah
Box 303
Nov. 29, 1966

Mr. Raymond Taylor
645 North 7th East
Provo, Utah
P.O. Box 405

Dear Raymond:

Now that Thanksgiving is over and the multitude have all gone their devious ways, I try to pick up the pieces and catch up on my long-neglected correspondence.

I had no business coming up to speak about John Taylor without at least SOME preparation. I apologize to you privately for my ignorance. Since I have been more conscious of the man as a person, I have noted that I had not remembered Mrs. Ferris' description correctly.[48] It was Lorenzo Snow who "was a small, neatly-dressed, dapper-looking young man . . . accompanied by a tall six-footer, by the name of Cumming. . . . The one looked as if he never did anything wrong—the other, as if he never did anything else . . ."

She described P.P. Pratt, several of the wives of B.Y., and of those of Joseph L. Heywood, one of whom I was interested in, she gave a clear account. Of the first wife she said, "She is as pretty, well-informed, and accomplished as you will find anywhere in a thousand, and . . . exhibits . . . good taste in dress. . . . I was surprised to learn from Aunty Shearer, that he has two other wives; one known as Sister Very /Vary/ old enough to be his mother, (they call and act as mother & daughter). . . . The marshal keeps his third wife and her baby on his farming establishment in Juab, about 80 miles from here . . ." This last wife kept a most remarkable diary, which I may edit for the U of U press.[49] But Mrs. Ferris' account here is accurate.

She gives one line descriptions of many: B.Y. sitting at the theater with his hat on "according to his usual habit;" Elder Kimball with his harem, Amasa Lyman "a man of grossly sensual appearance," "John Taylor, a heavy, dark-colored, beetle-browed man, his wife on one arm, and on the other a wealthy widow from Tennessee," Parley P. Pratt "marched up with four wives and introduced them all as Sister P." Well, I could go on and on. I must include Bro Bullock . . . "too sleek and well fed; looks as if he lived near the tithing office where the good things are stored away for the benefit of the knowing ones. This man is short, round, dapper, and bustling, reminding one of a fussy, noisy little bumblebee . . ."—See what I mean?

NOW MY MAIN REASON FOP WRITING: Did you really mail "under separate cover" Sidney's Salt Sermon? I seem not to have seen it—which in the confusion of the past week, could be anywhere. If you mailed it, I feel sure I will come across it; if not, I'd very much like to see it. Was it from the 47 E South Temple office?

I have decided that Sidney must have given two very significant speeches about two weeks apart.[50] Reed Peck writes that:

". . . the Sunday following (June 17) /1838/in the presence of a large congregation—S. Rigdon took his text from the fifth chapter of Mathew "Ye are the salt of the Earth but if the salt have lost his savour wherewith shall it be salted, it is henceforth (p. 23) good for nothing but to be cast out and trodden underfoot of men" From this Scripture he undertook to prove that when men embrace the gospel and afterwards lose their faith, it is the duty of the Saints to trample them under their feet . . ." etc.etc.[51]

William Swartzell writes /July, 1838/:

"4 . . . A great crowd were assembled around a very high liberty pole, near the temple. Sidney Rigdon was the orator of the day; who, after singing and prayers were performed, read off his oration with considerable energy and eloquence. He declared that "we, as the chosen people of God, should be no more driven from place to place—and we swear by the great Jehoval, that we will take vengeance on the citizens of Missouri. We have borne more persecution than human nature is capable of bearing;" at which they all sung out with three loud cheers, "Amen! amen! amen!" . . . [52]

You are right about the number of wives of Joseph, Brigham, and Heber—who claims to have been the most-married with 75 to his credit.[53] But Pratt was like John Taylor, content with one for each day of the week.[54] I'm not sure about Orson Pratt; Mrs. Ferris said that Orson Hyde,[55] the Jew, had only one—as he might have had in 1852, when she wrote. Later he had at least two additional, perhaps without the knowledge of his first.[56] Bishop Hunter[57] and John Neff were others who took extras on command and neglected to notify their first families.

Well I have run on too long. Tell me about the "Salt Sermon" deal. Was it in a large manilla envelope or a letter size? I can't believe it would be set aside carelessly by anyone—yet I have not myself seen it.

Good wishes always,

I'm much interested in the movie of Miss Ettie Lee's life. I'm sure Sam did a better job on the script than Mrs. Stewart did on the "Biography."[58]

To *Dale Morgan*, December 1, 1966

St. George, Utah, Dec. 1, 1966

Dear Dale,

I have just returned from a different visit to the site of the Mountain Meadows massacre, and it set me remembering the time we two followed the old Spanish Trail[59] from Cedar City down to Lytle's ranch and then couldn't find the monument. Remember? We had to come in and get Will to take us back to it.

Well, since the Church purchased the property on which the monument stands, things are different in Zion. I had heard via the grapevine that the general policy was to be one of discouraging visitors, but I thought that would be like trying to gather up the scattered feathers of the pillow in the old folk tale. Now I wonder.

About mid-July I wrote to the district ranger, Jack B. Shumate at Cedar City, enclosing a xerox copy of a letter of complaint by a man from Berkeley. He reported that both the National Forest sign and the Western Trails sign were gone and only the supports left standing. Mr. Shumate seemed much surprised to get this word—at least he telephoned immediately and said that he would see that something was done at once.

The thing was put out of my mind until last week when a car stopped from Denver with another complaint that they had gone out and could not find the place because there was no sign. Again I wrote to Jack, suggesting that something be done to speed action. His reply included a foot-note to say that a recent flood had washed away the foot-bridge and the picnic tables! A <u>flood</u>, when all summer and fall the sky has been as brass over our heads? A flood? When? I began to inquire and learned that there truly had been a flash flood in the area sometime in August from a cloudburst that had hit only a small area.

Knowing that any flood large to carry off one of those heavy picnic tables would likely cut into the bank and undermine the monument itself, Will and I rode up there early this morning. Truly there had been a flood, but most of it had joined the stream <u>below</u> the picnic area. The rain had fallen heavily on the mountain to the east, so that there was plenty of evidence of erosion on the wash that paralleled us as we rode down. And some water had come down from the Lytle farm area, enough to dislodge the foot-bridge and carry it to just beyond the willow tree of the picnic area and drop it in a pile of debris. The long hand-rail was a few feet beyond. But in the picnic area where the table had been, the debris clinging to the willows (standing straight up) was not more than 18 inches high—certainly not enough to float a table. There was no disturbance of the cooking area, no sediment deposited—and yet the table was gone, as was the one on the bank above. This had been placed for the convenience of people who did not care to go down into the deep gulley.

Well, I followed the ravine down to the Lytle fence nearly two miles below the camp site, and there was NO table in evidence nor planks or remains of a table. There was some erosion of the banks, willow clumps were uprooted and tipped down, and light debris deposited on them. I followed a man's tracks—learned later from George Lytle that they were his, and that horsemen had followed the wash below the fence to where it opened and the flood water spread out over Henry Bowler's fields. But no table was in it.

I forgot to say that Jack said in his reply that the sign had been stolen on June 2—more than six weeks before I reported it. I suggested to Lytle that perhaps the two tables were "stolen." at the same time, but he said that they had been in use all summer. One other bit of evidence. A large truck of some kind had been on the ground before the cloudburst—at least there were no tracks double anywhere, and the one it made cut in so deep and was still so large (untouched by road leveler from August to December) that cars had to straddle it. Really it was a hazard. Yet from August to December it had remained, while the Washington County road equipment was working in the area part of the time. At first we thought of these deep, one-way tracks as only evidence that the road men had been advised NOT to touch this area because it was on Forest land. Then we wondered if perhaps the tables did not go out on this big truck and their extra load did not account in part for the depth of this muddy track and hoisting or wrecking equipment would be needed to get them out of the gully. A good Problem for the FBI!

***

December 7, 1966

So hectic is my life that this was left in the machine. I had to wait for the mid-night bus, and filled in my time writing my ideas to you.

Now it seems that the Lord is really on their side! This week there has been a storm of such flood proportions that it would carry things heavier than picnic tables through the town of Gunlock.[60] The fact that it did not damage the MMM area means nothing. From August 21 (the flash-flood which reportedly took them away, both being in the ravine at that time, I am told) to December 2 the place had remained un-marked, the road almost dangerous, the picnic facilities gone, and yet the local ranger at Enterprise had evidently not even reported it.

Well, I learn from Dr. Cooley that he is publishing in the next issue the Cordon Diary which tells of the location of the grave of the women and children, which is NOT on private land.[61] When the Senators from Arkansas and Missouri learn this, perhaps we can get action to have a monument placed there. It would seem fitting, since they were the innocent sufferers, and since the one now up is being made inaccessible. In the early days there were many myths, stories of wailing women searching for lost children or for missing bones of their own. Maybe these spirits did not want people picnicking in this area, and just "spirited" the picnic tables away.

To *Dale Morgan*, December 15, 1966

St. George, Utah
December 15, 1966

Dear Dale,

For more than a year now I have had this envelope stamped and addressed to you, but somehow could not bring myself to write. Now my natural Swiss thrift will not let me waste the 8¢, though the paper to fit has long been used up.

The last two years have been hard for me—or I have let myself get too discouraged. My time has been so much filled with trivia; I have been repeatedly frustrated. The T.D. Brown Journal took quite a time of honest work, and when it was practically done, Dr. Cooley told me it could not be published. Mortensen asked for a piece for The American West, and after it was done and all arranged to for his space, he lost the paper and sent the article back, etc. etc.[62] Dialogue urged me to send an item which they are sitting on.[63]

At first Dr. Cooley seemed unhappy at my appointment by Gov. Rampton; in fact, I felt for a time that I had suddenly turned black whenever I went there. The fact that I supported Hal in his study and recommended that the Society under write it, did not help. Now Everett is selling his books at cost to the staff![64]

I enclose the ad. from yesterday's Tribune. Hal and family were here—he came down on Sunday and went back Tuesday afternoon, spoke to a group at the Dixie College and to the SUP, where we had an excellent crowd. All the family enjoyed the warm sunshine, and, all in all, it has been very pleasant. But none of us ever thought we would live to see this.

Thurman called and said that when the Church asked for two or three copies, he sent them promptly, and added a personal copy for Brother Lund. This bit of generosity paid off, for Lund called Deseret Book and told them to go ahead and sell it. Sam Weller[65] was making such fabulous returns that they could not stand to be on the side-lines.

Now back to my problems: The University of New Mexico Press has the Lee Santa Fe Mission Diary which they will publish this year in their Quarterly. I am happy about this.

My work on the History of the Jews in Utah is suddenly easier since Dr. Zucker insisted that he write the bit for the Newsletter and then just could not get it out, so that they printed one that I sent in. In the deal, Dr. Zucker was to be my guide and helper, but we have found it hard to communicate, even on basics. He insists that only practicing Jews should be considered and the doings of the Jewish congregations be of chief concern, while I have felt that the contributions of Jews in civic and cultural areas, in medicine, education, business, etc. would be important whether or not the persons observed the Holy Days.

Also I have felt that living in Utah, especially during the early years, posed certain problems not common to Jews in other areas, and tried to bring this out, which made Dr. Zucker feel that I was more interested in the history of Utah than in the history of the Jews. But, as I said, the air seemed cleared at our last meeting. It will be a great relief to see this thing done. I'm now only to the completion of their first synagogue in 1881, after having rewritten the first chapters three times.

Dr. Zucker thinks I should close the book in 1948—that anything that is written after that time would be anti-climactic. I think that the Jews in Utah were not that profoundly affected by the establishment of Zion in Palestine, and that the last eighteen years have seen some important changes in the lives of Jews in Utah and in the group activities So we shall see what we shall see. I thought you might be interested in knowing my problems.

Your suggestion that I re-activate my interest in QUICKSAND and CACTUS came after I had committed myself to this assignment, through the encouragement of Dr. McMurrin and Jack Adamanson

This I must finish before I become too deeply involved with anything else.

Both Will and I are in good health—his could be called excellent. Our scattered family all are doing well also. I spend at least a week out of every month in Salt Lake City, traveling the mid-night bus up and returning on the six p.m. one that put me home at about 1:30 a.m.

I hope to be there sometime when you come in, as I understand you have done at times lately. If I knew, I would make my trips coincide with yours.

Have a happy holidays!

Chapter 11

1967–1969

Continual Insistence on Truth in Mormon History

Brooks started the year 1967 with a New Year's blessing to some of her children based in part on the Jewish observance of the New Year illustrating that she was deeply involved writing and researching her book on the history of the Jews. This history was still her major struggle and annoyance during 1967–1969, except for an agreed-upon needed break between September 1968 and July 1969. She even offered to revise her will giving Myrtle Friedman, the sponsor of the project, her papers concerning the history, after suffering a scary car accident in 1969 shortly after learning to drive. Through this time, she also dedicated her efforts on other projects including the autobiography of her husband, Will Brooks. She felt the need to complete this autobiography as Will's health was deteriorating. For much of 1969 Will was weak and had trouble getting around, limiting Brooks's travels. Her renown and popularity as a public speaker continued to keep her busy traveling throughout Utah to meet all the requests including invitations to speak at LDS Church ward sacrament meetings.

In a letter to Ettie Lee, she remembered back to the meeting with the Lee family held in Phoenix in July 1961 when they strongly demanded that she not publish the notice of John D. Lee's reinstatement in the biography. She reminded Lee that all those, including Lee herself, so emotionally against her at the time would probably thank her now for her stand. Having failed in her campaign to improve access to the Mountain Meadows Massacre site, she corresponded with J. Kenner Fancher of the Richard Fancher Society of America in Arkansas to encourage his organization to lobby their senators to get a monument erected at the site.

She continued her campaign especially against Brigham Young University for the honest portrayal of Mormon history regardless of the conclusions. She initiated a combative debate through a series of letters with Brigham Young University professor Richard L. Anderson, after receiving a reprint of one of his articles on Oliver Cowdery. Their dialog revolved around Oliver Cowdery and the Overstreet confession, a statement purported to have been written by Oliver Overstreet in 1857 and attested to by three witnesses, stating that he impersonated Oliver Cowdery in Kanesville, Iowa, in October 1848 when Cowdery reaffirmed that he had written most of the Book of Mormon as dictated by Joseph Smith. She fervently argued that the confession was not a forgery and that it should not be rejected without more detailed historical research. Regardless of whether the confession was actually a fraud, the main thrust of her argument was that historians should consider all data and not just write a faith-promoting version of history. She concluded one letter, "My own faith in the Church goes much deeper than incidents like these."[1]

She also singled out for criticism movies made by Brigham Young University for not picturing accurate history. One movie, *The True History of Las Vegas*, misrepresented the character of Dudley Leavitt, Brooks's ancestor, and presented the Indian girl, Janet Smith, as his only wife. She was especially dissatisfied with the movie *The Windows of Heaven*, which depicted Lorenzo Snow as a feeble, shaking old man delivering a dramatic public revelation on tithing in the St. George tabernacle. According to Juanita, Will Brooks, who was present at the meeting, asserted that "Lorenzo Snow walked up the aisle with a firm, quick step, that there was NO great moment such as was pictured." George E. Miles, the clerk on the stand during the meeting, supported Will's claim, calling the picture "Rubbish! Rubbish!"[2]

Throughout her career, she was regularly asked to summarize her current thoughts on the Mountain Meadows Massacre, to which she often responded, "Just read the book." However, in 1968 in answer to a request, she cited "a few items which throw a little different light upon the story as I see it," and went on with a few current thoughts. She felt that she had underestimated the Native American threat; she wished to emphasize that the participants were not normally thieves or murderers, but honorable citizens; and she had recently been able to obtain two additional documents. But, overall she maintained, "My own conclusion is still that the massacre was a result of the hysteria generated by the inflammatory speeches of Mormon leaders, of the war songs, of the whole attitude that 'we will not be driven again.'"[3] Again, in September 1969, she provided the University of Oklahoma Press her final written ideas on the Mountain Meadows Massacre that she had developed for an unaccepted *American West* article. These considerations were included in her "Author's Statement-II" published in the fourth printing of *The Mountain Meadows Massacre*, her final written statement on the massacre.

Ogden Kraut, who operated a Mormon fundamentalist press, Pioneer Press, regularly corresponded with Brooks for a few years after he sent her some copies of his booklets. In one letter she vented about the way polygamy could not even be mentioned in LDS Church classes or books; in another letter she mentioned, after receiving a copy of Kraut's *Jesus Was Married*, how the topic was much discussed during her early years in Bunkerville, but she had not heard much about it lately. These letters led her to have Kraut reprint her Dudley Leavitt book, first published in 1942.

~

To the *Brooks Family Children*, January 2, 1967

St. George, Utah, January 2, 1967

Kay & Jeannie & Brian
Tony & Janet, Mark & Kritson

Dear Children:

Your New Years letter is a day late, and you will notice from the poor typing up to this point that I have again put off writing it until I should be doing something else. A feeling of haste or pressure always reflects in errors in my work.

But I did want to crystallize my New Year's hopes for you, patterned in part from the Jewish observance of the New Year.

FIRST, I pray that you may have LIGHT in your homes—the light of God's spirit, the light of love for each other, the light that illuminates the mind to help you scc clcarly all the implications of your work, the extra, significant, little things that so often go unnoticed, called by some scientists "the inspired hunch." May you have light in making decisions to guide you in the patterns which will be important in your future work and placement.

SECOND, may you have good health that you may be able to perform at maximum capacity, that you may take pleasure in doing what you have to do, that you may face each day's duties with anticipation and pleasure. May you have care and foresight to avoid accidents which will impair your ability to do your work.

THIRD, may you know the sweetness of friendships, of accomplishment, of the lovely cultural things that give meaning and depth of life—the fine cultural things that represent the great achievements of man and set him above the rest of the Lord's creation. This should include a feeling of one-ness with the universe and your place in it—recognition of the father-hood of God and the brotherhood of man.

These are awkwardly put down, but they are some of the things for which I myself strive.

I see that it is nearly morning, and I have much to do before I catch the 11:30 bus tonight. I have been completely OFF my fork for more than two weeks now, and if I finish on schedule, I'll have to really double on it and shut out many other things.

Some thing's I can't shut out—such as the wedding [unclear] and the reception here at our home. This is January [unclear] of Gary Gifford, 22 years old and employed at Safeway.

Other things I will not shut out—my interest in and love for my family, for they are first.

So much more that I wanted to write to say to each of you, but the time is gone

My best love,

To *Leonard J. Arrington*, February 6, 1967

Box 303, St. George, Utah
February 6, 1967

Leonard J. Arrington
718 Radcliffe Avenue
Pacific Palisades, Calif.
90272

Dear Leonard:

Since before Christmas I have intended to write you, which is an indication of about how far behind I am in everything.

First, I want to tell you how useful I am finding your GREAT BASIN KINGDOM in my study of the Jews in Utah.[4] While it does not mention them as individuals, it does give me the kind of background for their coming into the state and remaining here—or shifting from one area to another in the state. Excellent!

Second, while I let the new history teacher at Dixie borrow my Dialogue so that I cannot make definite reference to your issue, and really have only dipped into it as yet, I am glad that you made such a good selection there.[5] Long ago I let one of the boys—his name escapes me at the present—take my little story of the "One Other Man."[6] I told him that it was not complete, as it was not. I have found some additional pertinent [*sic*] which I should like to add as a re-write. Several times I have asked about it, and at last someone said it had been handed to you. If you still have it, I'd like to get it back.

Third, I am very interested in your article "Inland to Zion, Mormon Trade on the Colorado River," published in Arizona and the West."[7] At first, I was troubled by the sentence in your opening paragraph, "For at least two seasons . . . thence six hundred miles upriver to a point near the Grand Canyon. . . ." Here I have been saying that of all that costly effort in building Callsville—costly in human time and strength—only ONE load ever arrived at this point. I had my information from a seminar paper written by my brother Francis Hale Leavitt and published in the California Historical Quarterly in two issues Vol. XXII nos 1 and 3, 1943.[8]

True, the Church established all the way-stations, prepared some roads, and made big plans and preparations. The first load was put off at Hardyvill. The second also was unloaded there, with varying reasons given in each case. The one and only to unload at Call's Landing after a trip from June to late October was the Esmeralda which was reported by the Alta California, for Nov. 16, 1866.

In his second half of the article "Steam Navigation on the Colorado River," he said that . . . "The expansion period had failed to establish trade with Callville, but trips to ElDorado Canyon, some forty miles below, were made with a semblance of regularity for the next twenty years."

I had listed this as just one more of the failures in Southern Utah, each of which had been attended by glowing advance stories, encouraging reports of the progress of the enterprise, long hard labor in high hope, and inevitable failure: the silk industry, the castor oil industry, the indigo plant, the cotton industry—the molasses industry is only recently stopping, and the wine was too successful. The artesian well in St. George's public square, another.

I read current diarists on Call's reports to and from Callville in 1864, and searched in vain for accounts of any goods being brought in from there. They seemed to be coming from San Diego or from San Bernardino. The "Colorado Landing" was at Hardyville or Hardy's Landing, not Calls, except for this one load when the Esmeralda "towed a barge 126 feet long by 27 wide, with between 90 and 100 tons of freight, and seems not to have encountered any difficulty in making the ascent. Her arrival at Callsville must have been the occasion for an enthusiastic welcome, although the only report of the event says tersely: 'Cannons were fired and other demonstrations of joy indulged in.'"

Well, this is a mere tempest in a teapot; what is a mere forty miles of Colorado River between friends? Or was it less even than that? The fact still remains that you are doing more than all the rest of us put together, and doing it better. I continue to be thrilled with your out-put.

I should not have taken time out to write at all, since I am pushing at my History of the Jews—sort of between enthusiasm and despair, and being kept too much from the latter by the material you provide in your Great Basin Kingdom.

And good wishes to the whole family. And do come to our house when you pass through St. George. Who knows, "If I know when you're coming, I'll bake a cake." Whether or not it will be edible is something else again. But come and see.

Many things I like to visit with you about.

Sincerely,

To *Willard Leroy Lee*, March 2, 1967

St. George, Utah
March 2, 1967

Mr. Willard Leroy Lee
4080 South 11 East
Salt Lake City, Utah

Dear Brother Lee:

Thank you for your letter of March 1, inviting me to speak in your ward. I shall be glad to do this if and when we can arrange a time. I am to be in your city on March 12, but I speak to a group out at Bountiful at 8 p.m. that night, so I could hardly make your meeting if it were later than 4 p.m. It would be a bit strenuous also perhaps, to have two on the same day.

I expect to be up again over the last of March and the first of April, but that will be Fast Day. I might make it for April 30—April 23 is my husband's birthday, and I'd hate to be absent then. Would it be better to wait until the middle of May?

I shall be at the Belvedere Apartment House[9] Tuesday through Sunday of next week, so perhaps we could discuss things by telephone, or visit a bit there.

Sincere good wishes,

To *Ettie Lee*, March 15, 1967

St. George, Utah March 15, 1967

My dear Ettie:

I was in Salt Lake City when your letter of March 7 arrived, with the xerox copy of the Authority given to Merrit Norton on April 26, 1961.

I am very glad to get this and especially glad for the note from Edna, telling of her experience with Vera. Privately, I think that Al and all the other members who that day were so strong and emotional against my putting it in the book would thank me now for standing out against them.

Wes said he made copies of the tape which he took of the meeting, and that I was to have one, but I never did get it. The original was supposed to have been put into a deposit box of some kind for safe keeping, but though I have asked a number of times about it, no one now seems to know anything. For me, it was quite an historic occasion, and one which I should like to preserve, mostly because it shows so clearly the fear that was in the family of displeasing any one of the Authorities. After my private conference with Bro. Stapley, I knew that this time I was right and he was wrong, for he had never seen any of the work I had done—he had heard of the Mountain Meadows Massacre book, but not seen or read it; he knew nothing of the Mormon Chronicle at all; he had rumors that I was writing a biography, but knew nothing about what it was to be like. Yet, ignorant as he was of the whole thing, he would presume to act as an expert just because he was an Apostle.

More and more as the years go on, I am conscious of the general change of opinion, both in the Church and out of it, regarding the character of John D. Lee.

I am deep in the middle of my work on the Jews in Utah, and hope to get a preliminary draft in their hands by July 1, though I must literally write around the clock. In the meantime, I should make one trip to the Henry E. Huntington Library to check on their attitude about the copyright to the Mormon Chronicle, which is in their hands.

I shall let you know when I am coming, and shall be glad to accept your hospitality. It warms my heart to see that you are getting some of the recognition due while you are still here to enjoy it.

Will joins in sending love and all good wishes,[10]

To *J. Kenner Fancher*, September 5, 1967

Box 303, St. George, Utah
Sept 5, 1967

Mr. J. K. Fancher
910 North Pine Street
Harrison, Arkansas

Dear Kenner:

It is always good to hear from you.

Re: the burial place of the women and children after the massacre at the Mountain Meadows, I have known all the time that they were in a separate grave from the men, for the reason that they were nearly a half mile away, walking behind the wagons. The men were held back on one pretext or another.

Anyway, the bodies of the men were put into the defense pits which they had prepared themselves and from which they shot at the approaching Indians, killing, so the account goes, seven of them. This trench was deep enough so that the bodies were well covered and none ever exhumed by animals. The first monument—the other later monuments too, for that matter—was placed upon this spot.

The women and children were first buried in a shallow grave in a narrow wash from which the animals dragged some and spring floods washed others. The soldiers from Camp Floyd, as told by Tommy Gordon, went down in the spring of 1859, a year and a half after the massacre, gathered up all they could find of the remains, and buried them deeply, covering them with a mound high enough to be easily discerned, but evidently unmarked then.[11]

As early as May, 1907, there were efforts made to have this spot properly marked and beautified. A speech by Senator James H. Berry in the Congressional Record of Feb. 12, 1907, refers to it.[12] I have Xerox copies of some early correspondence which I enclose, and which I would like back eventually. I think they might be used to advantage in finally getting permission to place a suitable marker at the site of the graves of the women and children.

Within the last two years—in April, 1966, the Mormon Church purchased from Mr. Ezra Lytle the 2 1/2 acres of land upon which the monument here pictured stands. It would seem that immediately the policy was to "discourage" visitors. On June 2. 1966, the Forest Service sign on the highway pointing to the place was "stolen." I learned of it from the enclosed letter of a stranger, Mr. L.T. Gremaux, and at once notified the forest ranger at Cedar City. No sign was placed until after Dec. 2, of that year, which means that no traveler could find the place without a guide.

Nor had any work been done on the road—no blade passed over it during the whole season, so that by early January, 1967, it was totally impassible for a car. There has been so much complaint that the worst places have been repaired, the largest gully filled in, and in dry weather a car can drive down to the spot where visitors have stopped for the last fifty years. But if there is any rain at all, cars may get down to the place, but cannot get out because of the clay road. Repeated complaints have not yet resulted in getting a hard surface of any kind.

This means that such a monument as stands is neglected and almost inaccessible, except by taking a three-mile hike down and back.

As for the other location, it lies on land purchased by the Lytle family and now owned by Mr. Ezra Lytle, who declines to sell it at any price. Though I have asked government officials and state officials, I learn that we are so concerned with the rights of the private citizen that nothing can be done about it. In other words, if Mr. Lytle chooses, he may level off this mound and farm over it, though he knows full well that here are buried some fifty bodies of women and children (probably a few less).

Our mutual friend, Caryl Holmes, when she visited here, thought perhaps the state of Arkansas or the Fancher Family, through their Senators, might secure permission to erect a monument to the memory of these people. If not on the actual spot, it might be put out on the public highway with the story told, including the refusal to put it where it belongs. After all, the State of Arkansas did give the Mormon Church permission to erect a monument to their Apostle Parley P. Pratt who was killed there.[13] Why should not the State of Arkansas erect one to their slain people in Utah????

I enclose the letter and four pictures from Mr. L. T. Gremaux. I should like these returned, though you may have them taken off if you care to. The Old Spanish Trail sign has not been replaced, nor has the one on the Forest Service posts. Instead, there is a long, low board carrying the words MOUNTAIN MEADOWS MONUMENT and an arrow pointing the direction.

This letter has grown longer than I had planned. In fact, one of the reasons why I have delayed writing was that I hated to tell you of these latest developments. I am much embarrassed about them myself, but have been able to do little to correct them.

Sincere good wishes always,

To *Truman G. Madsen*,[14] April 28, 1968

Box 303, St. George, Utah
April 28, 1968

Dr. Truman G. Madsen
165 Smith, BYU
Provo, Utah 84601

Dear Dr. Madsen:

Yes, indeed, I do remember our short conversation on B.H. Roberts at the State Historical Society. I knew so little about the man except as I knew his daughter, Georgia, the winter she taught school here in St. George.

Re: the events surrounding the assassination of the Prophet Joseph, I know little. My chief research into the period came through editing the Hosea Stout Journals, which began after the event some four months. Then I have had some correspondence with a Mr. Van Dan[15] who tried to convince me that one Edward William Bonney was a baptized Mormon, high in the Nauvoo Legion ranks and very close to the Prophet.

I think any psychologicals between the Mountain Meadows Massacre and these earlier happenings would be more near to the Haun's Mill massacre in Missouri, and the fact that a part of the emigrant train were from Missouri. Perhaps some rancor also toward the Arkansas group because of the death of Parley P. Pratt just previous.

There is an abundance of evidence that as the bodies of Joseph and Hyrum lay in state, men swore to avenge their deaths, and had their young sons also make such a pledge. Some young men placed the right hand on the chest of the dead prophet and took the oath with the left hand raised to the square, or vice-versa.

The avenging the blood of the Prophets came into many Patriarchal blessings, also. Brother Elisha H. Groves[16] used it, evidently often. When I first read his blessing to William H. Dame, Feb. 29, 1854, a little more than six months before the massacre, it seemed almost a command:

> . . . thou shalt be called to act at the head of a portion of thy brethren and of the Lamanites in the redemption of Zion and the avenging of the blood of the prophets upon them that dwell on the earth the angel of vengeance shall be with thee shall nerve and strengthen thee Like unto Moroni no power shall be able to stand before thee till thou hast accomplished thy work. . . . [17]

Then when I found another given to a boy not yet twelve years old, I decided that it must be a stock phrase of his. This blessing was on Nov. 22, 1857, a little more than two months after the massacre and in the vicinity:

> . . . for thou shalt be called in connection with many of thy brethren as an actor in the redemption of Zion, an avenger of the blood of innocence upon them that dwell upon the earth. The angel of Vengeance will be with thee and nerve thy sinews that no power will be able to withstand thee and will turn the darts of thy enemies from thee and thou shall not fall in the day of battle, but like the sons of Moroni . . . [18]

Well, I did not mean to go into this in detail, but there are many evidences of the pledge to avenge the blood of the prophets, taken by loyal members. It was written into the temple ceremony and down into the 1920's the Elders had an anointing of their right arm that it should be strong "to avenge the blood of the Prophets." I don't know when it was dropped. You yourself no doubt remember it.

A reading into any of the contemporary diaries shows the great love—almost adoration—that the people had for their Prophet. Many say they would gladly have given themselves up instead.

I hope you try to disentangle some of the folklore which sprang up immediately following, regarding the light from heaven, etc.

I simply do not have time to sift through to find these. Your own collection of diaries that include practically all that I have here.

More and more I find this early period interesting. As I suggested, I have made quite a collection of Patriarchal blessings, and the evolving of the pattern of blessings and promises through the years reflects the changing of attitudes on many subjects—the return to build up Zion, the Second Coming, etc. among them.

You have a dramatic story to tell, one that many before you have tried to picture. Success to you in this challenging assignment.

Cordially yours,

To *Richard L. Anderson*,[19] July 14, 1968

Box 303, St. George, Utah
Juiy 14, 1968

Mr. Richard L. Anderson
Brigham Young University.
Dept. of History & Religion
Provo, Utah

Dear Brother Anderson:

Thank you so much for the reprint of your article, REUBEN MILLER, RECORDER OF OLIVER COWDERY'S REAFFIRMATIONS, in the Spring, 1968, edition of the BYU STUDIES.[20] It has opened a whole new vista for me.

Aside from the one sentence on page 277: "The reality of the return of the former "Second Elder" does not rest alone on the Reuben Miller account,[21] since a <u>score</u> of solid historical references, disprove an <u>anonymous</u> "confession" describing the astounding feat of impersonating Cowdery before <u>hundreds of his former intimates</u>." I'll not argue with you, but try to present my views.

I agree with your appraisal of Reuben Miller's life and activity, of his devotion to the Church and his service in it, excepting, of course, the period during which he was preaching and writing in defense of the Strangites.[22] Miller certainly was acquainted with Oliver Cowdery, and had labored to get Cowdery to Winter Quarters in an effort to bring him back to activity in the Church.

I followed your lead and gained access to the Reuben Miller diary, made a number of notes, copying word-true and line-true the entries headed "Conference held on Mosquito Creek Council Bluffs October 21, 1848 Remarks of Bro Oliver Cowdrey:"

This remarkable document seems to me the initial copy of what was to be said, and what was actually said. Also the "Remarks of Bro Oliver Cowdrey before the high priests Quorum in the tabernacle November" actual date to be inserted later. This I also copied, and hope to get photostats of both.

I need not tell you how accurate these are with the printed accounts. Aside from the spelling of "gosple" and "he seen an angle" . . . "to every nation tunge and people," and a few other minor differences it is reproduced well indeed.

I must pause here to make myself clear: I think both Orson Hyde and Reuben Miller were loyal to the Church, both eager for prestige in it, both trying to impress the people with its truth and validity.

In my research in The Frontier Guardian[23] in an effort to do a biography of another man. I am impressed with evidence of discontent and disunion. The first issue front page article cautions the people "not to listen to tales . . . that someone has usurped a great deal of power . . . come to the High Council, or to the Twelve who are left here in charge of the Church, and ask advice before ensnare yourselves like the followers of Emmett and others. Some men proudly boast their ability to stand against the council and advice of their friends and consider it a disgrace to yield this position; but confidant in their own strength, they persist in stubborn self-will which is a sure precursor of disaster and ruin . . ."

Remember that the late 1847 emigration to the Valley took all the better-to-do, or a great many of them, and the great migration of 1848 drained off many more.

I was interested to see that Orson Hyde named 30 agents for his paper in as many little ranches or clusters of houses; I was also impressed with the various advertisements of services and goods. But it was a frontier village where several murders had already been committed in 1848, and where Hickman dared admit two "but not at his (Hyde's) instance"

As to Cowdery's "intimates" in Kanesville at this time, one wonders who and where they were. Orson Hyde and Reuben Miller, yes. George A. Smith was absent at the time, but came later. E. M. Greene[24] kept the minutes, and at the April 1850 conference named the officers. Many of the Saints were new arrivals from Europe and the East. Brother Dunn says that Oliver Cowdery arrived on October 24. The meeting was held on October 21. The confession was made, such a confession as would sound strange from this man, in the light of his past. Brigham Young, of course, knew nothing of this, but might be informed sooner or later. His name would be used to reassure Overstreet.

For the sake of argument, admit that the "reaffirmation" was by proxy. Where then was Overstreet??? I have not really started the search for him. His statement is attested to by three prominent men—not as to its veracity, but as to the fact that it is written by his hand.[25]

These men, according to the 1869 City Directory were living quite near each other, Jesse W. Fox, Territorial Surveyor, on 1st South between 1 and 2 West; Henry McEwan also on 1st South, but between 3 and 4th East. Both men were still listed there in 1873. The Bollwinkle home, occupied in 1869 by Frederick Bollwinkle was on 2nd North between 1st and 2nd West. Thus they were all in close proximity to each other, so that they could be quite easily assembled and taken at the same time to the office of Judge Elias S. Smith.[26]

I myself secured the Elias S. Smith Journals for copying by the WPA, but noted then—and found when I went to scan them again in microfilm—that the 1857 one was missing. At that time I assumed that there might be references to the Mountain Meadows Massacre, and that was the reason it was not found. Now I wonder.

Suppose that the Overstreet Confession is valid and true. What then? I think it is not any cause for apostasy or concern. It is only evidence of the zeal of some members who wished to place the Church in a better light. They did only what Bro. Stevenson did thirty years later in his attempt to "bring back" the Witnesses,[27] and what I am afraid you are having to do: Accept a point as TRUE, and assemble only facts to support it.

My own faith in the Church goes much deeper than incidents like these. But your own description of Miller's "pamphleteering" of his desire to vindicate the Priesthood, of his unbounded joy when that was done, make me feel that he had in it, really much remains to be done and eventually the truth will be found.

Good wishes,

To *Richard L. Anderson*, August 12, 1968

St. George, Utah
August 12, 1968

Mr. Richard L. Anderson
Dept. of History & Religion
Brigham Young University
Provo, Utah

Dear Brother Anderson:

Thank you for the fine article on "Oliver Cowdery's Non-Mormon Reputation" in the current Improvement Era.[28] It is very basic to an understanding of the integrity of this man, even as his letters from Missouri about the time he was "cut off" are enlightening as to his courage in opposing the policy of armed resistance at Far West. I expect to have photo-copies of all his writings at the Huntington Library.

I note your mention that "three Mormon periodicals" report his death. As you know, my discovery long ago of the one in the Deseret News filled me with many doubts and questions, some as yet unanswered. I located the general report in the Millennial Star with the wrong month in the death date and the ambiguous "sometime in 1847 or 1848" of his return to the church, which seemed to me a deliberate be-fogging the issue. They could as well have given the exact date of his baptism not two years before.

The other periodical was probably the Frontier Guardian. I did not notice it when I went through in search of information on Thomas D. Brown, but that does not mean that it isn't there. If you have it and care to send it, I'd be glad; otherwise I'll dig it out myself. Coming from Orson Hyde, it should be enlightening.

The article in the Era serves a good purpose for the Church membership, but if anyone ever undertakes to do a definitive biography of this man, he must take into account everything—all of Brigham Young's references, including the one on early polygamy, The "Defense,"[29] the Overstreet "Confession," and try to look at all and each in the light of history rather than faith-promoting. In the end, the whole story is better than any "slanted" version which will have to face the eventual disclosures. The idea that "if you don't look at it, it will go away," just will not hold up.

I realize your dilemma employed at the BYU and writing for a Church publication, you are forced to look at only what you know will build to the point you set out to prove, and carefully bury or ignore anything that will raise questions in the minds of the readers. Brother Gunn had the same problem, with the same result: his book is not history.[30] (My slip before is evidence that my fingers and my mind are not always coordinated, and that in the press of other [missing]

To *Richard Thurman and Others*, September 5, 1968

THE BELVEDERE,
SALT LAKE CITY, UTAH
September 5, 1968

TO:
Richard Thurman
Ben Roe
Dr. Louis Zucker

Gentlemen:

I choose to write what I want to tell you, because I'm afraid I cannot trust myself to speak without too much emotion.

First: I made a mistake when I accepted this assignment. I knew that I was ignorant of the subject; I did not guess how ignorant. But I was flattered that I had been asked, and determined to try. Now I find that I have wasted my time and your money, with little accomplished, and that little not accepted.

On March 12 last I wrote a letter to Mr. Thurman, giving details of the conversation in which Dr. Zucker announced that he would rewrite my work. This completely destroyed my desire to continue, but I did force myself to do two additions.

Now I have two alternatives to offer: First, I will close the deal once and for all, hand in my source materials and what I have done and permit Dr. Zucker and others to really do the book.

Second, I will accept a vacation or leave of absence or suspension of activities for six months, letting Dr. Zucker do all that he can in that time, and then I will pick it up again and devote FULL TIME—eight hours a day, five days a week until it is done. Let the date be tentatively April 1st.

This will free me to do one or two little things I have wanted to do for my husband, among them take him on a little trip while he is still well enough to travel and eager to go. Then I can give some attention to Thanksgiving and Christmas preparations, which in a family the size of mine, amount to a great deal.

As to financial part of this: I want no advance for travel and no pay checks. Perhaps I am too optimistic in thinking that, given a free rein, I can finish at full time in six to nine months.

I realize keenly that in all of this, we must take due consideration of that wonderful lady, Miss Myrtle Friedman.[31]

I shall be glad to consider such conditions as any of you gentlemen suggest.

Sincerely,

Source: MS 139, Marriott Library Special Collections.

To *Ogden Kraut*, October 6, 1968

Box 303, St. George, Utah 84770
Oct. 6, 1968

Dear Brother Kraut:

Thank you very much for the copy of the B.H. Roberts DEFENSE.[32] I am very glad to have this item. It is eloquent of the complete reversal which has taken place in our Church.

Only a few weeks ago after the wife of one of our high School Seminary teachers had discussed Emma Smith in our Sacrament meeting, I went up to speak to her about it, but before I could say a word, she told me, "I know, Sister Brooks. Emma's main problem was not the mobs or the sick children. But we are ordered not to even mention the word Polygamy to our students."

Have you examined the last book Brother Preston Nibley wrote before his death—I understand it was his last. My mother has a copy. It's entitled Lives of our Leaders or Lives of our Presidents.[33] Anyway, I have never seen Mother so out of patience before. She brought it to show me that in the life of Brigham Young only TWO women were mentioned—Miriam Works and Mary Ann Angell. Parley P. Pratt married only "The bride of his youth," John Taylor only Lenora Cannon, and so on. Only one wife each is mentioned. As the eldest daughter of the second wife of Bishop John G. Hafen[34] of Santa Clara, Mother thought this book was an insult to all who had entered into plural marriage. But that's how it is!

I notice your KRAUT'S PIONEER PRESS on the back. I wonder if you are reproducing other items. Only the other day I had an enquiry from a lady in Ogden about the John Pulsipher[35] Diaries which she saw at the DUP building.[36] Sister Carter would not tell her where she got it, but said a man brought it in and presented it to her. I too would like another copy. I have loaned my first volume once too many times, I guess.

To *Roger B. Mathison*,[37] November 21, 1968

Box 303, St. George, Utah 84770
Nov. 21, 1968

Mr. Roger B. Mathison
Gifts & Exchanges Librarian
The University of Utah Libraries
Salt Lake City, Utah

Dear Mr. Mathison:
When I first received your letter, I thought, "Well, of all the NERVE! Didn't he know what a mess my notes turned out to be?"[38] It was a windy, dusty day; we were far behind schedule; Dr. Ellsworth[39] had done a most remarkable back-ground presentation, both as to location and social.

Then I had long ago resolved that I would not tell this story again. When people corner me and say, "Just tell me briefly—in a nut-shell—what happened and who was responsible." Or if they say, "Was President Young at all responsible?" I would answer, "Listen, you—I Spent two full years writing that book after I had done all the research. It is available at any library or book store. You can read it in two hours (if you disregard the footnotes). Why don't you just read the book?"

But now there are a few items which throw a little different light upon the story as I see it. The first is the hand-written account as done by John S. Higbee, just after the first trial of John D. Lee in 1874.[40] This seems a fair and genuine attempt to tell the thing as it was, exactly. Since it is signed SNORT and is quite impersonal, I had just lined it up as another story. But it is more than that. It contains the words of the actual message which Dame had written—compare it with the later letter of Dame calling for the brethren to take the Indians off the road and to "... any property found among them should, if possible, be secured and returned to the owner which they have taken...." (MMM. P. 113)[41]

His adjutant, Martineau, worded his letters better. He would never have written "... but on no contitions you are not to precipitate a war with the Indians while there is an army marching against our people."

This seems to me to be an exact copy of the order, which Lee read and handed back.

I had earlier given little credence to the Indian threat—I mean, less than I now do. I also had made the local leaders more responsible though I knew of the council in Salt Lake City between Brigham Young and the Indian chiefs of southern Utah. Recently I saw a xerox copy of the diary of Brigham Young, which read: (under date of Sept. 1, 1857)[42]

> Kanosh the Pavaunt chief with several of his band visited me gave them some council and presents A spirit seems to be taking possession of the Indians to assist Israel I can hardly restrain them from exterminating the Americans

THIS IN BRIGHAM YOUNG'S OWN RECORD!

In view of the approaching army and the fact that just a week later—Sept.7—Brigham Young would tell Captain Stewart Van Vliet[43] of the army that, "I shall not hold the Indians by the wrist any longer,"[44] we may assume that the "council"—reinforced with presents—would be to the effect that the Mormons and "Mericats" are at war, and you are on our side—SEE?

Even in the letter carried south by Haslam telling them to let the emigrants go in peace, is the tell-tale sentence. "The Indians we expect will do as they please but you should try and preserve good feelings with them,"[45] might in an emergency be interpreted to mean to assist them in this undertaking.

At any rate, it does seem that Brother Brigham here admits his own responsibility in stirring up the Indians. That he should mention only one by name—Kanosh, the Pavant chief who was responsible for the murder of the Gunnison Party—may also be significant. And, further, the Americans are to be <u>exterminated</u>.

I noted in the book (MMM) that the various reports of the massacre differed as to the number of Indians present. Garland Hurt, Indian Agent, tells how he sent an Indian boy, "Pete, who speaks English quite fluently, with instructions to proceed to Iron County on a secret route, and to learn of the Piedes if possible, and also from the Utes, what the nature of the difficulties was, and who the instigators of it. He returned on the 23rd, and reported that he only went to Ammon's village, in Beaver County, where he met a large band of Piedes, who had just returned from Iron County . . ." (MMM, 252)[46]

Ammon was the brother of Chief Walker, who had died earlier, and of whom the Mormons of the south had been much afraid. A <u>large</u> band of Piedes in addition to Kanosh and his band would indeed have been formidable for the Mormons in the south. In Washington County at this time there were only 79 families widely scattered in 11 small settlements. Parowan and Cedar City were larger and protected somewhat by walls.

I go into this detail to show that I myself have come to feel that Brigham Young was directly responsible for this tragedy, since the company in question had already passed through Salt Lake City and was on its way south, and since the threat of the Indians on the southern settlements might have been more real than I had previously supposed.

The second point I wished to emphasize was that the participants were NOT normally thieves or murderers; they were honorable citizens, each trying to wrest a living from an unfriendly environment.

They were the strongest and best men in the area, selected especially because they were loyal and skilled in the needful trades to establish a community. They were mustered into an active militia only because of the word of the approaching army, or "Armed Mob", as they called it, and the rumored threat of another to approach from the west. Today they are ordinary citizens; tomorrow they are murderers. So heavily did this weigh upon them that within a very short time practically every one moved away—some north to Cache Valley, some out on the Paria, others across the Colorado into Arizona. They did not want their children to learn of this or to have their father's name connected with it.

Recently I have come into possession of two other documents. The first is the story of Samuel Knight as told to Abraham Cannon, Jr. on Thursday, June 13, 1895.[47] Brother Knight said he had told it to only one other person: Daniel H. Wells. This was probably much earlier. By 1895, the President of the Church, Joseph F. Smith, had asked that the testimonies of participants still living should be taken.

Knight tells that he was living at the upper end of the Mountain Meadows, near the present Burgess Ranch, where his wife had given birth to her first child. The road passed their place, and "Some of the emigrants were very boastful and seemed to be filled with a wicked spirit. The Territory was at that time under martial law, as the United States army was approaching from the East. These emigrants said that they would go to California and raise a company of soldiers, return to attack the Mormon people on the west, and thus destroy the people and their homes. These boastings they had expressed through the settlements of the people in the north, and it had a tendency to aggravate the Saints who had already suffered so much at the hands of mobs. After the emigrants had been located at the south end of the valley a day or two, a messenger came from the authorities in Cedar City…, commanded him to go to the South in the neighborhood of St. George and Santa Clara, and instruct the Indians to arm themselves and prepare to attack the emigrant train. This attack it was proposed to make at the junction of the Santa Clara and Magotsu.… Brother Knight did not return with the Indians, but remained to do some necessary work on the ranch … but after laboring there two days, he and his companion, feeling anxious to know what had occurred at the Meadows, mounted their horses and started for the place. While passing through the willows only a short distance south of the place, they were accosted by John D. Lee. He informed them that an attack had been made upon the emigrants, who formed a corral of their wagons and were defending themselves . . . As Brother Knight passed on the way to his ranch at the north end of the valley, he saw the militia camped at a place where Joseph Burgess's house now stands, and on reaching his home he heard considerable shooting. . . . but remained at his home until a message came requiring him to hitch up his team to his wagon, there being only one other team in the valley and proceed with it to the south end of the valley, where the arms of the emigrants were to be loaded into the wagon, together with the children who were unable to walk, the beseiged had surrendered. . . .

That same night Haight, Dame, and others took supper at Brother Knight's house and he learned from their conversation that none of the general authorities had sanctioned or encouraged in any way the dastardly deed of which these fanatics were guilty. . . ."

Knight's account gives the order of the march correctly: the wagons ahead, the women and children following behind, the men in the rear, and says that some white men assisted in the killing of the women and children, the bodies of whom were buried in a shallow grave.

He goes on to say that all the participants died miserable deaths in one place or another. According to the regular pattern, he stated that none of the general authorities of the church could be held in any way responsible.

One other item came into my hands recently—at the Folklore Conference in Logan. Dr. Don D. Fowler,[48] 1124 Manor Drive, Reno, Nevada, gave me a typescript of an anonymous account of the massacre at Mountain Meadows.[49] This was evidently written years later by a man who had lived at Harmony. He tells of Lee's coming to the fort with a band of Indians—he says 45 <u>about</u>—and of a statement concerning the massacre made in the Sunday meeting by Lee. This is similar to the statement made by Ben Platt.[50] (MMM ftnt. p. 75–76)[51]

The number killed, according to this report was 96, which seems more realistic than the 120–123 generally given, since the Arkansas Company numbered only 71 (MMM ftnt p 45–46),[52] and the group of horsemen called the "Missouri Wildcats," no where as yet found numbered, would hardly have exceeded twenty-five.

The writer claims that Lee himself told the story of his killing one of the emigrant herdsmen in the early morning—shooting him dead in his tent door—of the wounding of two Indian chiefs, one of whom later died, and of his own near escape with a bullet hole through his hat and another through his left sleeve.*

The account errs in insisting that Isaac C. Haight was on the ground and in command, and it also gives the order of the emigrants march in reverse: he says the men went ahead followed by the women and children. His account of the Indians killing three or four <u>hundred</u> of the emigrant's cattle is, of course, ridiculous. If they killed just one or two—at most three or four—that would be more than they would have ammunition for and more than they would want for food.

The narrator, while quoting Lee at first, adds that "it was said that" Lee took one of the young ladies into the brush for a half hour before he cut her throat. "Haight was the originator and cause of all the whites going out. I cannot say about Dane. I have heard that Dane was there, and also that he has proved his absence." The mis-spelling of Dame's name is another proof that either the writer or the typist was not familiar with the background.

His statement that "My son was employed by this second party to go with them through the Muddy as Interpreter. When he got to the Clara he was ordered back by Mormon authority," may give some lead as to the identity of the writer.

In general, it is, as many others have been, a mixture of folklore and fact.

***

My own conclusion is still that the massacre was a result of the hysteria generated by the inflammatory speeches of Mormon leaders, of the war songs, of the whole attitude that "we will not be driven again." Brigham Young, in his counsel to the Indians; George A. Smith, in his speeches to the settlers in the south, Elisha H. Groves, in the patriarchal blessings promising that the recipient would help "to avenge the blood of the prophets;" their own vows that, if the opportunity presented itself, they would do so; the rumored threat of an army approaching from the south—these and other things culminated in a deed that was tragic for all concerned, the participants as well as the victims.

*See MORMONISM UNVEILED: THE CONFESSIONS OF JOHN D. LEE, (St. Louis, 1882. Page 229)

... "So I ran with William Young and John Mangum to where the Indians were, to stop the fight. While on the way to them they fired a volley, and three balls from their guns cut my clothing. One ball went through my hat and cut my hair on the side of my head. One ball went through my shirt and leaded my shoulder, the other cut my pants across my bowels...."

Source: MS 486, Marriott Library Special Collections.

To *Dale Morgan*, December 16, 1968

Box 303, St. George, Utah 84770
Dec. 16, 1968

Dear Dale,

I don't want to impose too much on your time, but I must visit a bit with you—So don't feel called upon to answer.

You'll be glad to know that the reception honoring Everett was a signal success, with a very large crowd in the line for more than two hours. The Governor was impressed, especially after he learned that all these were members of the Society. We were all gratified, for feel that any honor was richly deserved.

But my reason for writing this early morning time is to let you in on my "one woman stand" against the policies of the "Mormon" Historians of BYU. I am sure I told you long ago of my protest at their picturing the marriage of Dudley Leavitt to the Indian girl, Janet Smith, as a significant part of THE TRUE HISTORY OF LAS VEGAS, and of the mis-representation of the character of Dudley Leavitt. Most of all, I was angry that they should represent this little Indian girl as the <u>only</u> wife of Dudley Leavitt.

Then in their moving picture "The Windows of Heaven,"[53] Will protested the presentation of a feeble, shaking old man, supported up the aisle by an attendant on each side, & of a dramatic public "revelation". He was present at the meeting, sat in the gallery, and said that Lorenzo Snow walked up the aisle with a firm, quick step, that there was NO great moment such as was pictured. George E. Miles, who was also present at the meeting—was clerk on the stand—also protested vigorously, calling the picture "Rubbish! Rubbish!" He refused to have a part in such a mis-representation.

Now my present protest is the effort to bring Oliver Cowdery back into the Church via a TV presentation, as dying with a testimony of the Gospel on his lips. They disregard entirely the one-line obituary which ran in the Frontier Guardian, the Deseret News and the Millennial Star, which called him Oliver Cowdery, Esq.

Stanley R. Gunn's OLIVER COWDERY, SECOND ELDER AND SCRIBE, makes no mention of the pamphlet, My Defence . . . , and Richard L. Anderson brands it as "spurious" and "fraudulent." This stand is unanimous among them, as is the stand toward the Oliver Overstreet "Confession." Even Leonard Arrington says he has concluded that there never was such a man. If there had been, some one would surely run across him somewhere.

I myself think that both are genuine. I believe the account of the Overstreet Confession was in the volumes which Miss Ethel Smith had, and which were not given in to be filmed at the time I got the other diaries. Then I believed that she held them out because they might have had damning information on the MMM, now I think that this Confession might have also figured.

I find that the men whose names were affixed to it were all prominent, reliable men. Judge Elias Smith had the reputation of honesty and fairness. I believe that somewhere the name of Oliver Overstreet will come to light, though he was too late for the 1850 census and died before the 1860 one.

Well, so what? Just that you know I am watching for this person, and if you run across him, at any time, let me know.

To *Ogden Kraut*, March 5, 1969

Box 303, St. George, Utah 84770
March 5, 1969

Mr. Ogden Kraut
163 East 4th Street
Dugway Utah 84022

Dear Brother Kraut:

Thank you so much for the copy of JESUS WAS MARRIED.[54] I am right glad to get it.

During my childhood and early adolescence this topic was much discussed, some of the men certain that Jesus was not only married, but that he had more than one wife. Interest in the subject waned, perhaps on orders from higher-ups, but I have heard little of it recently. Which makes the book all the more interesting.

I begin to wonder if you are operating a commercial Press. My little book, DUDLEY LEAVITT, published in 1941[55] has long been out of print. Since it is a family book and a whole new generation has grown up and married, I am getting more and more requests for copies.

I had thought that I would do a complete rewrite, but time is running out, and I figure that I might put in a page of introduction, insert foot-note numbers in ink on the pages, and add to the end the notes by Chapter and number. The sheets of Genealogy will all have to be re-typed, I believe. They will take eight pages.

IF you do this type of thing commercially, I should like to talk to you about possibilities. The book now is 120 pages.

My husband's health has been so poor that I have not been in to Salt Lake City for a long time. It is hard to get away at all.

I'd be glad to hear from you on this.

Continued success to you.

Sincerely,

To *Karl Keller*,[56] June 16, 1969

Box 303, St. George, Utah 84770
June 16, 1969

Mr. Karl Keller
Department of English
Division of Humanitics
San Diego State College
San Diego, Calif. 92115

Dear Karl Keller:

Thank you for your letter of June 12, and for the enclosure describing your Fall Issue of DIALOGUE. It looks very good to me; indeed, I should be proud to be in such company.

My reason for not being is NOT that I am angry, but that I am too involved otherwise. True, it has been hard for me to understand how a ms. could so completely disappear.[57] I have expected that Somebody, Sometime, when he is looking for something else, would run across it and send it home.

I cannot forget how, long-ago—in the 1930's—I did a story which I called "Old Grand-Daddy." I sent it to a well-known sports magazine, and when after a reasonable time, it was not returned and I wrote asking about it, I was told that it was lost. The next fall it appeared in the same magazine under the title "It Can't Happen Here."[58]

It was the story of a large, dun-colored Buck Deer that the cowboys and rangers of the Pine Valley had come to call "Old Grand-daddy," because year after year he had escaped the annual hunt. Wayne Gardner, who was a friend of ours, told how he hunted that year for only one animal—this deer with the giant horn-spread. He shot it; it fell; he dropped his gun and ran to cut its throat when it jumped up and attacked him. His bullet had just grazed the animals head behind the horns, leaving it stunned for a moment, but entirely unhurt.

In the new story the name was left out, along with a few other bits, but for pages it was identical with my carbon. So I expect to run across sometime, the essence of my story on "The One Other Man" under a different title.

I wonder if Gene England[59] has in mind the speech I made in Logan last fall regarding my experiences as a writer. It is supposed to appear in the UTAH HISTORICAL QUARTERLY sometime soon.[60] I have never had anything in the Nation, but Harper's used a couple of bits from me, as did Arizona Highways, The Pacific Spectator and a few other less well known magazines.

I have long thought that I would like to do a series of articles—perhaps only two or three—entitled "Saints are People," beginning with the Oliver Overstreet Confession. I have a great deal of material on this subject, and have kept up a sort of running battle with Brother Anderson of the BYU, who has history subordinated to proselyting.

To simply call publications "Fraudulent" and look the other way does not prove anything.

But enough of that.

I am currently struggling to get myself free of this book The History of the Jews in Utah or One Hundred Years of Judaism in Utah, which has been such a thorn in my side. I should never have started it in the first place, but now, being in, must see it to a conclusion.

During a "vacation" from it for six months I have put together an autobiography of my husband, "Uncle Will" Brooks to everyone in Dixie.[61] This is now only about 300 typed pages in rough draft, but since Will is in poor health, I must push it to a conclusion while he is still here to enjoy it.

So believe me when I say that I cannot take on anything else for a while. The American West is also pressuring me for an article on "The Mountain Meadows Massacre," which I should do in order to bring out some new material and changed insights on that tragedy. This is next in line after the Autobiography. All, EVERYTHING, must wait upon the Jews.

Then, if I live long enough myself, I'd like to shape a bit of a volume on my own background under the title "Quicksand and Cactus." This last may never appear, though I do have a whole box of stuff that I wrote about it long ago.

So now, after having visited most of my early morning hours for work away with you, I'll ring off, hoping that you will not carry any ill will because I cannot now do anything for DIALOGUE.

All good wishes,

To *Lyman F. Smart*,[62] June 29, 1969

Box 303, St. George, Utah
June 29, 1969
84770

Dr. Lyman F. Smart
Director of Development
Southern Utah State College
Cedar City, Utah
84720

Dear Lyman:

The official Certificate of my new PhD. arrived yesterday, and it is certainly with a grateful heart that I accept it.[63] Such a wonderful memento of a happy experience!

Thank you all very much.

I note also the new seal on the stationery, and am impressed with all the significant things it may come to mean in the lives of the students. Perhaps I should not say all the good things, for I cannot comprehend them all, but certainly many that appeal to me.

Will and I came into your town the other night to hear Bro. Albert R. Lyman speak to the Historical Society group. These two men had known each other in San Juan back in 1909–1912, and had been friends. Each recognized the other instantly after fifty years.

I should have visited with you by telephone then. I had plenty of time while I waited for Will to talk to old-time friends; it was really hard to get him to break away.

Thank you again for all your kindness to me.

Sincerely,

To MYRTLE FRIEDMAN, July 28, 1969

Box 303, St. George Utah 84770
July 28, Monday morning, 1969

My dear Myrtle,

I understood that I was not to communicate with you until you had settled your affairs with the University of Utah, but things have happened here which have changed my own outlook sharply

I don't remember that I told you this before: My Son Ernest Pulsipher, who lives in Las Vegas, had been told to get me a car. This he did, with a very nice 1966 Chrysler Newport 4-door, light colored car. I had finished the Drivers' Training Course and had my Learner's Permit & License. I have driven enough to feel quite secure, though not enough yet to go any distance on the highway.

On Friday morning July 25 I was coming home from a town errand just before eight o'clock. At the intersection of U.S. 91 and Main Street I waited for the red light to change, and then was just a little slow in coming into the intersection. This literally saved my life, for a car coming from west to east full speed struck the front edge of my bumper. The impact was such that his car spun into a right-angle curve and wrapped itself around a light pole, a complete wreck. My front fender was bent in, the chrome knocked loose, and the whole front part knocked a little out of gear.

I had my seat belt securely fastened, so came out without even a shock, that is, physically. I have been emotionally shaken, it is true, for it is clear that there was only a split second—one more turn of my front wheels—and it would have been flowers and slow music for me. No human being could have survived that head-on impact. He had not even seen a light!

The other driver got a citation, of course; I am covered with insurance, and after the business of getting out all the papers and waiting for the car to be repaired; can go on as usual.

I have taken this seriously as a warning. It would not be a bad time for me to leave now except for the one piece of unfinished business—the book on the Jews. I hope that I may stay to see that done. I have appended a handwritten note to my earlier hand-written WILL to say that all my books, magazines, xerox copies of material, notes, finished chapters on ONE HUNDRED YEARS OF JUDAISM IN UTAH belong to you, to be disposed of at your pleasure, probably to the University of Utah Library. But in the meantime, I must do all I can to actually get it done, and much remains, especially in the securing of pictures and current biographies.

Best love,

Source: MS 139, Marriott Library Special Collections.

To *Josephine B. Gregory*,[64] August 1969

Dear "Neighbor down the Hill"—

Your note arrived on Tuesday; I left that night on the bus for Salt Lake City, so I took it along to verify the quote.[65]

I found it in the Diary of Oliver B. Huntington,[66] Vol. 2, page 166 of the typed copy there in the Library.[67] The handwritten original is at the Brigham Young University, and is one of the most interesting, most revealing ones I have ever read. He began keeping a record when he was only a boy, and continued off and on all his life.

It doesn't disturb me greatly; it proves only his human limitations of the Prophet. Though he did receive inspiration and revelation, he had no way to be All-Wise. He himself admitted that there were times when he was in error, and this seems to be one. He evidently drew upon his own background and imagination and gave the best answer he could frame to the question. Of course, a simple "I really DON'T know" would have been better.

Don't let it trouble you unduly.

I look forward to seeing you

To *University of Oklahoma Press*, September 26, 1969

Box 303, St. George, Utah 84770
Sept. 26, 1969

Director, University of Oklahoma Press
Norman, Oklahoma

Dear Sir:

Since the retirement of Mr. Lottenville, I do not know just how to address this, but feel sure that it will come into the right hands.

I have two reasons for writing:

In January of this year I had a letter from Mr. T.H. Watkins of THE AMERICAN WEST, asking if I would do an article for them on the Mountain Meadows Massacre. He planned to use woodcuts from Leslie's Weekly[68] as a basis for his story, and thought it might appear in the July issue. Now it has been postponed, but the idea is not given up.[69]

As a result of my study, and more specifically of documents which came into my hands at the meetings of the History-Folklore Conference at Logan the fall before, I had modified somewhat my story of the Mountain Meadows Massacre. I felt that I should, in all honesty, report these to you or write them, perhaps, in a short monograph to be inserted in later printings. This, of course, after THE AMERICAN WEST had appeared.

This decision still holds: Mr. Watkins still expects to use the Lee material, he says, and after it is out, I will send a statement,

The basic changes are these:

1—The massacre was a part of the general War plan, determined upon by Brigham Young and carried to the South by George A. Smith.

2—The number of Indians involved was much larger than I had previously thought, and their gathering had started some time before the Fancher Train arrived at the Meadows.

3—The number killed was greatly exaggerated. Instead of 123 it was not more than 96. Twenty-seven human beings seem important to me.

Since no change in the present text is to be made, this material might be printed in a leaflet to be slipped in separately. It may be that I am unduly sensitive about this, but as of now, I think it should be done. After almost twenty years, one might be expected to get some new light on any subject.[70]

***

MY SECOND REASON FOR WRITING:

This year I entered a manuscript in the contest sponsored by the Utah Institute of Fine Arts, Prose Section, with an auto-biography of my husband, Will Brooks, and won first place.[71] Eighteen others were in competition.

This means little, I know. And I know, too, that biographies should be of nationally-known figures. The title should be changed, perhaps, to emphasize life on the desert frontier over the change of the century. St. George is only a small village, but it was—and is—a bottleneck through which all traffic to Southern California must pass, and Will Brooks was Sheriff MAYBE some of the incidents of growing up are worth saving.

I know that this may not be grist for your mill, even after we remove some of the chaff, but I want you to see it.[72]

I send it under separate cover, with postage for its return.

Sincerely yours,

To *Cornell Robinson*, October 14, 1969

346 North Main
St. George, Utah
Oct. 14, 1969

Mr. Cornell Robinson
Confederate Hall
Dixie College Campus
St. George, Utah

Dear Cornell Robinson:

Welcome to Utah's Dixie! We are glad that at last we have at least one negro student; we hope that before many years we will admit all who come and can qualify—the test being only past training, not skin pigment.

You are truly a pioneer here, so don't get discouraged if you meet some rough spots. I hope that you do not.

We live up the hill from the only semaphore in town, and have three college students here in a tiny apartment. I am a past faculty member, and interested in the school and proud of it. And I am glad that you are here.

My telephone number is 3-2752. I have tried to contact you by telephone, but somehow could not get through. I'd be glad if you care to call me, or to come up and visit in person. Better check first, to be sure I am in.

Sincere good wishes,

Source: Willa Derrick.

Chapter 12

1970–1971

Passing of Will Brooks and Back to Salt Lake City

Brooks suffered major losses during the first two years of the 1970s. First, her "husband friend," Will Brooks, passed away on March 28, 1970, while she was in Ogden giving an LDS Institute talk. Several letters document the circumstances surrounding this sorrowful event, including one thanking Russell and Dorothy Mortensen for driving her from Salt Lake City back to St. George during a snowy and windy night after she heard of her husband's death so she did not have to sit and wait for the midnight bus. She also thanked the governor of the state of Utah, Calvin L. Rampton, for his surprise attendance and speech at the funeral in St. George. In a letter to Ettie Lee, she detailed the last few months leading to Will's passing and the events of his last day and in typical fashion concluded the letter by disclosing that she needed to get busy on the three-volume production of the John D. Lee diaries. The other loss in her life was the death of her mentor Dale Morgan of cancer on March 30, 1971. One of her last communications to him reminisced on their many shared experiences, especially the several field trips to historic sites, and in appreciation for all he had taught her, she praised, "In my mind, you are the only true historian that Utah has yet produced. You stand like a Colossus among all the little people, your achievements like mountains in the midst of mole-hills."[1]

Following the passing of her husband, she moved back to Salt Lake City at the end of August 1970, first living at her house at 98 U Street and then buying a house at 1731 South 1400 East. In letters to friends she described the difficulties of sorting through collections of a lifetime, donating many of her and Will's books, and moving into a smaller house. She set up her work area in the bare basement of the new house and settled in until the end of 1976 when she returned to St. George for the last time.

In Salt Lake City, she sustained a busy schedule continually speaking to many groups throughout Utah including LDS Church seminary students, Institutes of Religion, and Sacrament meetings, history and writing workshops at the University of Utah and Brigham Young University, Utah State Historical Society meetings, other history organizations, and various study groups. A letter to her ward bishop in December 1970 provides a glimpse into her speaking schedule for late 1970 and early 1971. Among her listed upcoming talks or formal lectures were ones to an LDS Church MIA group, a study group, the public library, the women faculty of Brigham Young University, and two at the University of Utah, all within about a two-month period. She also mentioned that she was traveling to Provo to help with her aunt Ann Woodbury Hafen, who was in the hospital in the last stages of cancer. She concluded by saying that "I enjoy sacrament meeting and night Relief Society, but that must be the extent of my activity."[2]

These letters from her later years continue to illustrate her closeness to the faith, folklore, and stories of her rural Mormon roots in southern Nevada and Utah. In one, she remembered an experience as a child of an uncle in Bunkerville being possessed of the Devil and how her and her cousin's prayers helped free her uncle from the evil influence. In another, thanking Myrtle Friedman for a gift of almonds, she related that as a child she helped harvest the almonds from the Relief Society trees in Bunkerville and enjoyed eating those given her for her labors, either plain or included in candy or pomegranate salads. She always believed in the closeness of the hand of Providence in her life and work. In 1971, she reminisced, "I am more and more hesitant as I grow older, to put into words some of my experiences—some of the times when the way has been made smooth before me, when from unknown and unexpected sources vital material which I hadn't known enough about to be even looking for it, came into my hands, sometimes from strangers, sometimes from friends who just had a hunch that I might find this useful."[3]

Her battles over historic preservation are also evident in the letters from these years. What brought her especially to a rage was the

LDS Church's demolition of the historic and architecturally significant Coalville Tabernacle in 1971 against the protests of most of the adults of Coalville and vicinity. As always, she was also quick to question false statements based on folklore or express concerns over the rewriting of Mormon history. When Raymond Taylor proposed that Brigham Young was poisoned by one of John D. Lee's descendants she protested saying that it was "pretty far-fetched" and more likely he "ate himself to death," because of the gout that plagued him.[4] In another letter, she complained about the LDS Church's attempt to "present things as they want the people to believe they were, rather than they actually were."[5] Her correspondence and debate with Richard Anderson over the Overstreet confession continued into 1970.

Additional insights into her beliefs were expressed in a letter to Grace and Obert Tanner in 1971 after receiving their gift of a book on John Milton. She remembered reading and memorizing lines from a number of Milton's works, and especially liking the sonnet "On His Blindness," which she felt should be memorized by every student. This discussion led her into some thoughts on God and the universe and her feelings "that man's little mind cannot conceive the whole of God's worlds and works. The universe is vast beyond our comprehension endless in time and space. And yet here in our little personal worlds there does seem to be a power outside ourselves which helps to shape our destinies."[6]

Brooks completed and started a number of writing projects during these years. In the fall of 1971, she submitted to Myrtle Friedman a revised manuscript of the history of the Jews, finally liberating her mostly from that project. Her *Uncle Will Tells His Story* came off the press in December 1970. Two of her stories appeared in *Lore of Faith and Folly*, edited by Thomas E. Cheney with her and Austin Fife's assistance. Among her published articles was one she contributed to the special women's issue of *Dialogue*, where she described raising a "Compound-Complex Family" while at the same time pursuing her writing efforts in a small space reserved for her in each house. She was especially excited to see on page 92 of the issue a photograph of her family taken by Dorothea Lang in 1953. She again pitched her two-decades-old idea to combine all of John D. Lee's diaries into a single set, working "like a doodle-bug, hind side first."[7]

To *David S. King*,[8] January 15, 1970

Box 303, St. George, Utah 84770
Jan. 15, 1970

Hon. David S. King
9614 Dewmar Lane
Kensington, Md.
20795

Dear David & Rosalie King:

I have read this manuscript with much interest, and appreciate very much the comparisons with some contemporary happenings.[9]

You will notice, if you get the last edition of my MMM, that I have been permitted to add in the foreword some items recently acquired which illuminate just a little the story of the massacre.

I think your presentation was well made for the time and audience, and for your position in the Church, perhaps. Only a minor change or two need to be made.

PAGE 12—Paragoonah[10] was evacuated in 1853—on August 2, to be exact. I wish I had time to give the full citation as written by Gwinn Harris Heap in his Journal for E. F. Beale, Superintendent of Indian affairs in California, and published in 1854.[11]

> Paragoona . . . contains about thirty houses, which, although built of adobies, present a neat and comfortable appearance. The adobes are small and well pressed, and are made of a pink-colored clay. The houses are built to form a quadrangle, the spaces between them protected by a strong stockade of pickets . . .

> . . . soon after our arrival, the inhabitants, in obedience to a mandate from Governor Brigham Young, commenced moving to the town of Parowan,. . . . It was to us a strange sight to witness the alacrity with which these people obeyed an order which compelled them to destroy in an instant, the fruit of two years' labor; and no time was lost in commencing the work of destruction. Their houses were demolished, the doors, windows, and all portable woodwork being reserved for future dwellings and

> wagons were soon on the road to Parowan, loaded with their furniture and other property . . .

I should add that most of them returned in a year or so and rebuilt their deserted village.

The only really SERIOUS error is on page 20. You have the line of travel so completely wrong, it is hard to believe. I think every man who was on the ground testified to the fact that the two wagons left first, the lead one driven by Samuel Knight, carrying the small children—eighteen of them—who were saved. To the Mormons these represented "innocent blood," which they must not shed. The wagon contained also some clothing, hastily gathered, and some bedding.

The second wagon, driven by Samuel McMurdy,[12] carried the guns of the emigrants, additional bedding, upon which three wounded were lain, presumably from all accounts, two men and one woman. This came out most clearly in Lee's second trial when the only point to be established was that John D. Lee committed murder that day, by killing one person. Some witnesses said it was a man, others a woman; some had him shoot a rifle from the ground, others had him step up onto the wheel and shoot at close range with a pistol. One saw him making motions as if he were cutting a throat. <u>None of this is relevant to your story</u>, but you must get the idea that the children in the lead wagon were more than a half mile in advance, and over a knoll where they could not possibly witness the killing.

The women and older children walked in a loose group some distance behind the second wagon. This procession had proceeded about a half a mile before the order to fire was given. This was by Higbee, who commanded the troops on horseback. The Mormon men, armed, marched beside an un-armed emigrant, and each was required to shoot only once. At the signal to fire, the Indians leaped from their places in the only heavy thicket along the road, and killed the women and older children.

To leave the women in the rear would be to discredit your whole story.

There were enough affidavits made independently by participants, all of whom agreed in the essentials, to bring the whole into focus. We have now identified the "missing child" about whom so many folk tales were told, and know that she grew up in a Mormon home, married a Mormon husband in the Mormon temple.[13] Her descendants are even now searching out their genealogy.

I should add that the fourth printing of the MMM book is not off the press yet. I'm sure that Oklahoma will give publicity when it does appear. Essentially it is not changed.

With all good wishes,

To *David E. Miller*, February 19, 1970

Box 303, St. George, Utah
February 19, 1970

Dr. David E. Miller, Director
Center for Studies of the American West
THE UNIVERSITY OF UTAH
Salt Lake City, Utah
84112

Dear Dave,

Thank you so much for your letter of February 17, inviting me to become a member of your Advisory Board. I'm much flattered, but hesitate because I already belong to three Boards: The State Department of History (as they now call the Utah State Historical Society), The Utah Heritage Foundation, and the Folklore Society. Each expects me to come in to meetings.

The main problem is TIME. It takes a day to get ready and off, and after it is over, to get back, unwind, and pick up where I left off. Even so, I'm foolish enough to say yes.

You have guessed, of course, that my chief interest is to get my little "Uncle Will Tells His Story" into print. When Mr. Thurman said he would like to do it, but it must wait its turn, I was somewhat disheartened, for in this case "time is of the essence" truly. I like the way the Porter Rockwell book was done, though, and thought I could wait.

Strangely, not two hours after I had talked to Mr. Thurman, Brent Crosby[14] came to my home bringing Mr. Charles A. Taggart,[15] who was looking for something to print. I said nothing about "Uncle Will," but suggested that I should like to see the Mormon Chronicle re-done, expanded into three volumes, and set up with the footnotes on the bottom of the page. But the Huntington Library had the Copyright and would not release it.

Two days later Mr. Taggart telephoned that he had flown to San Marino, cleared the Copyright, and is ready to go. Well, I'm not. I have some work to finish the Jewish book. The parts I have ready of the Lee biography will come near the end of volume one. Unless we go into it backwards like a doodle bug, I'll have to have some time.

But "Uncle Will" is ready. It's not an earth-shaking thing, no matter who does it. It's just a collection of incidents as told by an old man. Should I let Mr. Taggart start off on this, I wonder? Anyway, all my cards are on the table, face up.

Source: WSU Levi Peterson Collection.

To *A. Russell and Dorothy Mortensen*, April 3, 1970

Box 303, St. George, Utah
Friday, April 3, 1970

Dr. & Mrs. A.R. Mortensen
1408 Perry Avenue
Salt Lake City, Utah

Dear Rus & Dorothy:

First things first! Karl & family have just pulled away, the last of the family to leave.[16] On the table are boxes of cards taken from floral offerings, stacks of sympathy cards, a book with a list of the names of those who brought food. Everywhere are things that need doing, kindnesses that need acknowledgment. But nothing, NOTHING that has ever happened to me in my life quite equals your impulsive, generous offer to bring me home. And at night in bad weather.

As I look back, it seems that things could not have gone better had we planned them. Will was really feeling better; Clair was down to share the responsibility with Walt. I had given Will a hot bath in the night and spent quite some time on his neglected feet, I hadn't noticed how long his nails had grown.

At breakfast I couldn't get through the prayer, but had to break off in the middle of the sentence, cry a bit, and say "Amen." And I ran back for a second good-bye after to the door: I left with a sense that all would be well with him—as it was. Clair came early and took him to the Post Office for the mail, where he had a couple of letters from the children. Walt picked him up about ten o'clock and took him to Hurricane——

This represents a break of an hour and five Callers. Just as well. You know all the rest. The funeral was beautiful. Such a profusion of flowers! And some good music, and Governor Rampton[17] to give the closing speech. I was surprised that he came, and much pleased with his talk.

We have taken flowers to both the rest homes and the hospital—three pieces each. Every child had one to take home, and we have planted a row of azaleas and also chrysanthemums. Still the grave was more than covered and the house is still full.

NOW TO BUSINESS: Chapter 11 page 10, just above the last paragraph cut the sentence which refers to Wabash.[18] It begins "The situation here was entirely different.... and wouldn't throw it if they had. To me it seemed dramatic to see how quickly the whole climate of the room was changed."

What I really wanted to say is that life may give me an opportunity to pay in a small part the things you have done for me. I'm grateful beyond words.

Best love,

Source: MS 201, Marriott Library Special Collections.

To *Calvin L. Rampton*, April 6, 1970

Box 303, St. George, Utah 84770
April 6, 1970

Gov. Calvin L. Rampton
1270 Fairfax Road
Salt Lake City, Utah

Dear Governor Rampton:

I was never more surprised or more pleased than when I saw you in St. George for Will's funeral. I certainly had not expected any such honor, but then I hadn't expected anything about it to be as big as it actually was—the long lines at the mortuary, the crowded Tabernacle, the flowers!

So many said, "He was the first man I got acquainted with when I came to St. George," or "He always had a special interest in me." The girls he had to take to the Reform School, the boys he disciplined, even his prisoners came to see him.

Your presence said volumes. Your talk was very impressive: appropriate, sincere, eloquent. Everyone in the audience was gratified that you came, pleased and impressed.

Thank you very much. Give our love to your sweet wife and to her mother if she is there. Will thought Uncle Tony Ivins was the personification of the real "Spirit of Dixie."

Gratefully,

Source: Levi Peterson's Collection.

To *Ettie Lee*, April 15, 1970

Box 303, St. George, Utah
April 15, 1970

Miss Ettie Lee
℅ Neil Howard
Box 339, Baldwin Park
California, 91706

My Dear Ettie:

I wonder if you have heard of the passing of my fine husband, Will Brooks. I have been so involved since that I have done little more than write "Thank You" notes to friends who sent flowers, food, or money. I'll go back a little:

On the 5th on last November I was impressed to take him to see our sons, Kay at Washington, D.C. and Antone at Albuquerque. I called Ernest at Las Vegas; he arranged for the flight, got the tickets, came and took us to his home in the evening, and the next morning put us on the plane. It was a delightful trip out. Will enjoyed it thoroughly, saying later that the pretty stewardess acted as if he was the only passenger she had—or at least the most important one.

Kay met us at the airport at 5 p.m. We stayed rather close to his home, except for the Relief Society bazaar & dinner and the Sunday church activities. Kay took Monday and Tuesday off to be with us. Then he put us on the plane again and Antone met us in mid-morning at Albuquerque. Here we spent another happy three days.

Will lived and re-lived this trip; remembering details, telling all who had time to listen about it.

Then just before Thanksgiving he began having what he called "The Smothers," when he had difficulty breathing. We took him to the hospital, where he also developed urinary complications. We brought him home for Thanksgiving, and he spoke well to the family assembled. (Our home could not accommodate the crowd, so we rented the DUP hall).

Our young doctor—a classmate of Tony's and a family friend—told me to keep him home, keep him up, keep him walking some every day. This I did, and he gained strength until he was soon at his normal activities, Church, Ward Teaching, Sons of Utah Pioneers, N.A.R.C.E., and the basket-ball games for the high school. He didn't miss a game here, sitting always in the midst of the Pep Club—with his hearing aid turned off!

It was during this time that I wrote his Autobiography, starting with tape recordings he had made for Clair during the Christmas holidays. It was finished by March 20, submitted to the State Institute of Fine Arts in its annual competition, and won first place. With the prize money I made a down payment on a car. I saw that I MUST learn to drive, which I did. Though I shall never be an expert, I could take Will out twice each day—once at 9 a.m to take Mother to the Temple and to get the mail, and again at about 3:30 p.m. to send out any mail, and just to ride around a little so that he could get out of the house.

In the meantime, I couldn't get my story published. I offered it to two places, each of which held it for <u>ten weeks</u>, and then returned it saying that the subject-man was not well enough known for national markets.

Then suddenly—on March 2—I had two offers in less than two hours. The first was a telephone call from Mr. Richard Thurman of the University Press, who said that they were ready to begin immediately. The next was from a Mr. Charlie Taggart, who came to my home with Brent Crosby, a local boy the age of Karl, who has "made good" evidently.

Mr. Taggart had recently come into possession of a printing press at Kaysville, Utah, and was looking for something to print—or re-print. I told him of the MORMON CHRONICLE, The Diaries of John D. Lee, and how Huntington Library would not re-print themselves or sell the copyright to someone who would. I told him we want a 3-volume set, Volume one to be the early writings of John D. Lee—missionary diaries and the Nauvoo period—Volume 2 to be the present volume ONE but with the material which has been printed in other places put in where it belongs in time. The last volume is quite complete, but we would change the format of all, putting the footnotes at the bottom of the page.

WELL, believe it or not, Mr. Taggart has purchased the copyright from Huntington, and is ready to start work at once. That is, he was ready within the week. But I felt that I must see Will's story through first.

In the meantime, Will was failing until I wrote the children that I doubted that we could keep him until his birthday, April 23. I had a speaking engagement since way last fall to speak to the LDS Institute group at Ogden on March 28. This was Spring Vacation week-end; Will felt as well as usual; Clair was down from Salt Lake City; Walt was off for the day, too. So I left with a light heart, flying up to Salt Lake City at 8:20 a.m., and to return the next day at 1:30 p.m., in the meantime checking on the book after the lecture was over. I would call him at 7 p.m. and again at 8 a.m. the next morning. Walter would have charge of him during the day, and Clair sleep in the room with him at night. He was in exceptionally high spirits.

I carried out my schedule: engaged a room by telephone at the Belvedere for 6 p.m., went with the people from Ogden to visit some old book stores, had lunch, rested, delivered my talk, back to the Belvedere, to meet Will's sister, Edith, there with the word of his death!

I called Rus Mortensen to tell him and cancel my appointment for the next morning, and he—Bless him!—said I was not to wait at a bus depot to ride down at midnight. He and Dorothy would take me in their car! It was a stormy night. We fought high winds and snow all the way, and arrived here at 3:30 to find the family up and waiting for me. Karl & Kay had both arrived before I did. Tony & Willa came the next day.

This is what happened here in my absence:

My grand-daughter Susie Brooks, came up to run the vacuum and generally dust and clean up, which kept her a couple of hours.

Clair came at 8:30 and took his father to the Post Office for the mail. He had two family letters, which Clair read to him, and stayed to visit until about 9:30, when Walt came to take him to Hurricane, on a trip for some building items. Will always enjoys going to Hurricane and passing the Will Brooks Home for Boys.

As they returned, Walt mentioned that it was time for the viewing and funeral of Rodney Leaney. Will said, "Yes, I want to go to that, too. Rodney was our neighbor and Ward Teacher for several years, and I think I should go. You let me out, and I'll get dressed and be ready as soon as you are."

So Walt just let him come on into the house unaided, saying he'd be back in just a few minutes. Will had had a good bath and clean underwear much earlier, before I left—so he put on a clean white shirt, a tie (complete with tie-clasp) and his Sunday suit. Only his shoes were not tied. This is a chore which I have done for many months.

Ernest Judd, working on his lawn across the street, said that he waved at Will through the big front window not three minutes before Walt drove up. Will was all ready and waiting. When Walt came in, he noticed that Daddy was not in his chair, so he hurried into the bath room, and back to find him on the floor on his side, as if he had been sitting on the edge of his big chair and leaned down to tie his shoes, blacked out, and slipped to the floor. Walt called the doctor, picked him up and carried him to the bed and started a heart massage, since he was still warm. The doctor came at once, but advised against trying to bring him back. I am glad that he did.

What to do next? They could not get in touch with me, since no one knew exactly where I was speaking. The Belvedere told them I had checked in for 6 P.M. Actually, I was in the car on my way to Ogden, as near as I can tell.

The whole thing was a complete surprise to everybody. The line at the Mortuary extended to the street, around the corner and a half block down—more than 600 at the evening viewing and about as many the next morning. The Tabernacle was packed; even the Governor came down.

Well, I go into all this detail because I know you loved him as we all love you.

I want to come and visit with you as soon as I can get things here squared away a little. In the meantime have Neil write or call me. I want to get this 3-Volume MORMON CHRONICLE under way. This will be the most perfect monument to John D. Lee, for it will be known and read for years and by thousands. I always said that he writes better for himself than anyone else can ever write for him. Remember? So be of good cheer.

I'll try to keep in better touch, and keep you posted as to how the work progresses on THE CHRONICLE.

To *Richard L. Anderson*, July 11, 1970

Box 303, St. George, Utah
July 11, 1970

Richard L. Anderson
132 JS Bldg, B.Y.U.
Provo, Utah
84601

Dear Brother Anderson:

By the strangest coincidence, I received a letter from Francis Adam van Dan in the same mail with yours—the first I have had in more than two years, But this was different: only two single-spaced pages. Seems some friend told him that Bonney was mentioned in the Utah State Historical Quarterly, so he searched out the issue in which my little talk at Logan was printed. So now he knows all about me. . . .

I sent the packet just to show how some correspondence was gummed up. It's really only a fraction of what went back and forth from 1965 to 1968, and I didn't really expect that you would take it too seriously. Still there might be a little wheat in all that chaff!

Re: Overstreet. He is only in the periphery of my interest. I have very detailed biographies of the three men who signed the paper: John Bollwinkle, (sometimes Bollwinkel) Henry McEwan, and Jessie W. Fox, and find them all really respected members of the Mormon society. You yourself did most to convince me that this is just the kind of thing Reuben Miller would do—all with the best intentions of strengthening the testimonies of the Saints, nearly all of whom were new arrivals from Britain. He sought approval & promotion.

I have found also two new references to the confession, but both were of people who came into the Church after Cowdery had left it. Actually the juggling of dates after the fact is also a very important consideration. The report to SLC & the one to the Mil. Star so different!

From past experience, I think I shall find additional evidence, but not when I am searching for IT. Like my puzzle over Nathaniel Thomas Brown, The Pagan Prophet, and others, it will be there plain and clear, perhaps when I least expect it. This sounds a bit demented, I know, but sooner or later someone will give it away. The natural thing then, as now, was to fail to look at items or happenings which might in any way shake the faith of the Saints.

I hope you get a xerox of the Bathsheba Smith[19] entry. I have seen the printed one.

Immediately ahead I have the publication of Uncle Will Tells His Story, which is due by September, Additional material for the new fourth printing of my M. M. Massacre, completing an article of about 20 pages on A PLACE OF REFUGE,[20] the mission to the White Mts. In the spring of 1858, and a book review of Taylor's URANIUM BOOM.[21]

I'll be on the BYU campus on July 31 & August 1st and perhaps a day earlier and later. I'm participating in the Youth Conference that is being held there.

All good wishes,

To *B. Don Taylor and High Priest's Quorum*, July 17, 1970

Box 303, St, George, Utah
July 17, 1970

Brother B. Don Taylor
and all Members of the High Priest's Quorum
of the St. George Third Ward

Dear Brethren;

I'm sorry to have missed you when you called, for I would have enjoyed very much visiting with you in my home. I did make a trip of several days into Salt Lake City, and last week was from Tuesday to Saturday to Albuquerque and back.

I do thank you from the bottom of my heart for this contribution, not that I need it so bad, but that it is a recognition of my husband. He was so proud to be a High Priest. He was first made one at Monticello, before he was married, as I remember. He has served as counselor to Bishop Miles and Karl N. Snow here in St. George, and was for a time in the Stake Presidency of the quorum here.

I thank especially Brother Burgess and all of the others who let him continue his Ward Teaching during his last years. He wanted so much to be used.

He always enjoyed the Sunday morning meetings; the dinners and social activities were truly special events to him.

He was grateful to Brother Matthew M. Bentley that at one time he was asked to speak to the meeting of all the High Priests of the Stake. Some of you will remember that he spoke on the history of the Salt Lake Tabernacle Organ.

A few times he prepared talks on various subjects to use in his home teaching or on Fast Sunday. While these were good, he felt that they didn't fit, since our testimonies today seem only expressions of gratitude for parents, wives, husbands & opportunities to serve. He wanted to give some faith-promoting stories.

I feel that he was a loyal member of the church and a great Christian. He has been a great influence for good wherever he has been, And he had a very special love, for each of you, his Fellow High Priests,

Thank You again,

Sincerely,

Source: WSU Levi Peterson Collection.

To *Claudia Bushman*,[22] August 25, 1970

98 U Street, Salt Lake City, Utah
84103
August 25, I believe, 1970

Dear Sister Bushman,

Thank you for your letter of August 19. It caught me in the midst of a move from St. George to here.[23]

I'll be glad to contribute to the Women's issue of DIALOGUE,[24] and will want to know about dead-line dates, space limitations, and any other specifications.

I'll make it a part of my chapter "I Married a Family" of my projected QUICKSAND AND CACTUS, which may never appear.

Tell your good husband that I am not at all angry at DIALOGUE; in fact, I was not surprised that the manuscript was "lost."[25] I'm glad that it was. You see, I set out to learn the identity of the "One Other Man, whose name was not of the record." That was very easy. It was the Notorious Tom Brown, who a few months before had been involved with a robbery-murder at Montrose. The two Hodges brothers, the younger still in his teens, were apprehended, tried and hanged in short order. Their older brother, Ervin Hodges, evidently protested too much or talked too much. Anyway, he was murdered in Nauvoo, not far from the home of Brigham Young. This was by a member of the police; I feel that it was Hosea Stout himself, . . . BUT, Tom Brown, the real instigator, took refuge in Nauvoo and went with the first company to the Valley.

My article ended with another question: What was the reason that the historian, Andrew Jenson,[26] dismissed him, with one brief sentence in the first listing of the company; added month of the year and place of his murder in the next account; and then thirty years later wrote a real eulogy of this man, stating that Brother Brigham much deplored this as "the old boots of the man who was killed were worth more than the whole body of the man who killed him?"

Another puzzle to figure out. Well, now it is solved, and it is easy to understand the <u>why</u> behind it. I'll not divulge the secret here. I want to do a series of perhaps three articles under the title SAINTS ARE PEOPLE.[27] We are over eager to make them demi-Gods, and to refuse to look at what we do not want to see.

Enough, enough.

All good wishes,

Source: WSU Levi Peterson Collection.

To *Ralph H. Lee and Counselors*, December 2, 1970

STATEMENT OF Juanita Brooks
1731 South 1400 East
Salt Lake City, Utah
December 2, 1970

Dear Bishop Ralph H. Lee & Counselors
Sunday School Superintendent & Counselors:

I think I should explain why I am unable to accept a definite responsibility in the Ward.

I moved to Salt Lake City for one reason: to finish a book on History of the Jews in Utah. In 1966 I accepted an assignment to do this, and for more than two years I worked at it diligently. At the end of that time, I had ten chapters done, which I handed to Dr. Louis Zucker for an appraisal. He did not like it. After we discussed it for some time, I took it back and re-wrote a great deal of it.

Again I handed it to him, as he said he would rewrite it, and I turned my attention to doing an Autobiography of Will Brooks, my husband. This I finished. It won first place in the State Institute of Fine Arts competition for the best book length prose. It is now in the press and due to appear this week.

Then I turned to complete this earlier work, moving here to be near the library facilities and the Jewish congregations. I am having a hard time to concentrate on it and get it done.

I have already spoken in two Sacrament meetings, and two study groups. My immediate schedule is about like this:

Dec.8—evening at a teen-age MIA group, the sponsor a young man who wants me to repeat the talk I gave to the youth group at BYU this summer.

Dec. 10—Meet with a study group at the home of Mary Ada Gardner.

Jan. 8—lecture at the Public Library for the U. of U.

January 28—Lecture before the Lady Faculty of the BYU on Eliza R. Snow.

March 3—University of Utah The Western Frontier.

March 10—" " " The Western Frontier of John D. Lee.

These last four must be written out and prepared for printing.

***

I have taken some week-ends and must take more going to Provo to help at the hospital with Ann Woodbury, who is in the last stages of cancer. Dr. LeRoy Hafen is my uncle—my Mother's baby brother. We grew up as neighbors in Bunkerville, he almost like an older brother to me. His only son is in Washington, D.C. He has been out and stayed as long as he could, but had to return to his job. A half-sister, Mrs. Ella Hafen Perkins, stayed more than a month, but she, too, needs time at her home in Salt Lake City. So I feel a strong obligation to lend a hand there.

***

In addition to all these, the Jewish book MUST be done. I enjoy sacrament meeting and night Relief Society, but that must be the extent of my activity

Source: Levi Peterson's Collection.

To *Dale Morgan*, December 31, 1970

1751 South 1400 East
Salt Lake City, Utah
December 31, 1970

My dear Dale,

I must not let this year pass without writing letters of appreciation to a few of the people who have meant so much to me throughout the years.[28] You head the list, for of them all, you have done more for me and meant more to me than any other person, for you have helped me to keep some perspective. Always I could turn to you for guidance.

Remember our trip south from Cedar City on the Old Spanish Trail,[29] past the old Iron mines and coke ovens?[30] I had come up by early morning bus to meet you in your car. Remember how we got lost in the mazes of the Lytle corrals and stock-yards, and in the almost shoulder-high sage, and had to go all the way to St. George to get Will Brooks to come back with us? Approaching from that direction, he took us right to it?

Remember the trip with Vesta Crawford along to the top of Little Mountain and the view of the Salt lake Valley from the point where the first group of Mormon pioneers had stood? For me, that was another event worth storing away.

Remember the climb from Rockville[31] up the old wood road to the Canaan ranch and plateau? Brother Brigham had named it this because at that time it was a sea of waving grass—a land of milk and honey. There are just so many shared experiences to remember, the last one out in the Hebron–Terry's Ranch area[32] one of the very best, even though we didn't find the cave we were looking for. You know, of course, that Todd Berens[33] did find it and photograph it.

I must thank you, also, for encouraging me to begin my "Quicksand and Cactus" bit. If it ever is finished and published, it will be because of your reaction to it. You understood early that I am more of a Folk-loreist than a true historian, and you were so right.

In my mind, you are the only true historian that Utah has yet produced. You stand like a Colossus among all the little people, your achievements like mountains in the midst of mole-hills.

I enjoyed so much our brief time together this fall when Fawn Brodie made her brilliant presentation.[34] That whole evening was one to remember up to the time the Tanners took us home. Did you know that my house is just across the street from the one they lived in during the early years of their marriage, before he went to California for further study? An interesting coincidence.

Well, like Tennyson's Brook, I could babble on forever. I just wanted to remind you that "the youngest of your Old friends and the Oldest of your new friends" still counts you as the best of all her friends.

God bless you,

Love,

Source: Levi Peterson's Collection.

To *Raymond W. Taylor*, January 7, 1971

1731 South 1400 East
Salt Lake City, Utah 84105
Jan. 7, 1971

Raymond Taylor
Suite 216 13 West Center
Provo, Utah 84601

Dear Raymond:

Thanks for your too, too extravagant praise of Uncle Will. It is a simple story, told in his own vernacular—in so far as I could stay true to it—a rambling account of a man who loved people. For his own family it is truly significant, for it puts into permanent form stories they have heard many times before. For the younger generation in general, it is a picture of times long past. I think, though, that those over sixty will relate to it better than will those under sixteen.

I am much interested in your suggestion that Brigham Young was poisoned by one of John D. Lee's descendants.[35] That's pretty far-fetched, it seems to me.

Was it DeVoto or Stegner who said that Brigham Young ate himself to death? This would seem to be true, for when he came to the dedication of the Temple at St. George, he was so obese and so plagued with gout that he couldn't walk through the rooms. A special chair had been made by Thomas Cottam[36] large enough to fit his portly frame, and he was carried through the rooms by two (or was it four) men. James C. Bleak gives the particulars, I think. Lee was executed March 23, 1877; temple was dedicated April 6 following; Brigham Young died August 29 following that. Folklore says that someone suggested to Lee that he affront Brigham and declare his innocence, but Lee answered, "He will not out live me six months. I'll settle with him on the other side."

Lee's descendants were numerous, it is true, but few if any were in the Holy City during these years. Panguitch, yes; Arizona, New Mexico, and the far out places sheltered most of them. I think it most unlikely that any would get near enough to Brother Brigham to have poisoned him. Why don't you give me some hint as to how, when, or where this might have taken place—or by whom.

There was so much of folklore and fabrication concerning the whole MMM affair that it is difficult to sift out the truth. But there was no carelessness about the care Brother Brigham received, or the people who prepared his food and medicine.

In another envelope I'll give you the details as well as I can, on my review of URANIUM FEVER.

Thank you again for your patience with me.

Sincerely,

Source: Levi Peterson's Collection.

To *Austin and Alta Fife*,[37] March 6, 1971

1731 South 1400 East
Salt Lake City, Utah
March 6, 1971

Dear Austin & Alta,

Thank you so much for the xerox copy of the Mormon and Anti-Mormon Pamphlets which came out in the late 1870's and all through the 1880's. They make a valuable addition to what I have.

I have—in St. George—Cradlebaugh's Speech in full, and also the one called "Nuggets of Truth" as well as Penrose's speech in pamphlet form.[38] This item was very hard for Lee's grandson, David Lee, on a mission in England, to take.

It is hard to believe the bitterness of the Editorials in the Tribune during those years, the accusations, the ridicule and scorn. On the other hand, we did put out a booklet justifying "Blood Atonement" which would trouble even the most loyal Member of today, I think.[39]

More and more I am convinced that the idea of the Second Coming being imminent shaped many of our policies and spurred people to excesses. To compare the Patriarchal Blessings of this period with the modern ones is certainly an exercise in change and abandonment, and reversal even, of some of the early promises.

My own feeling is that "Saints are People" steeped in the concepts of their time, and gullible enough to believe the Prophet when he said that the Ten Tribes might even be on a distant star. Only last week my Mother sang through all five verses of Eliza R. Snow's hymn picturing the Last Days when . . . "the stars from Heaven shall fall; the moon be turned into blood, the water into gall . . . the sun in blackness shall be clothed, all Nature look afright, while Men, Rebellious, wicked men, gaze trembling at the slight . . ." and so on and on.[40]

Our great problem in the Church is the fact that we cannot accept these early teaching, and our leaders are trying to work up shows and slide sequences to present things as they want the people to believe they were, rather than they actually were.

Oh, well, after the Coalville incident my own faith of our present leaders is almost shattered.[41] Perhaps if I could shake off this bad throat and hacking cough so that I could manage this machine better, I'd be more charitable toward some of them.

I think it was better that I didn't come on over this week end. I'd overdone until must just "hole in" for a while.

My best love to you all, and my gratitude for your kindness.

Source: Levi Peterson's Collection.

To *Fawn Brodie*, May 4, 1971

1731 South 1400 East
Salt Lake City, Utah 84105
May 4, 1971

Dear Fawn:

I was in Washington, D.C. visiting my son who lives there, hence my delay in answering.

I cannot express my own grief and feeling of personal loss at the passing of Dale.[42] You may remember that we were together when you spoke to us in October. (I was delighted with that speech!) I sat at Dale's left and explained the reactions of the audience by pointing out in his printed copy where you were and what the ad-lib happened to be. He seemed in good health and high spirits.

He let me read his last letter from the Lady Friend—a warm, pleasant letter in which she expressed her love for him, but which ended with "but NO wedding bells, please." He seemed confident that he could change her mind.[43]

I had known of this courtship for about two years. He bought a car and had her daughter drive him through the West. They had along two of her girl-friends, one of whom occasionally changed off at the wheel. All three were girls facing their first teaching experience in the fall, and Dale thought it would be fine to introduce them to the West as a part of their general education.

We left St. George early and spent a long day following trails west of Enterprise, returning via Cedar City in the evening. The young lady driver was so kind and considerate and pleasant that I almost wondered why he didn't propose to her rather than to her mother. She seemed to have a high regard for him.

I have wondered if the cancer developed thus quickly as a result of her definite negative answer. It was a cancer of the kidneys, and I didn't learn about it until some time after they knew of it here—Dr. Cooley had word first, I believe, as he and others were all trying to see what was to become of all Dale's possessions, especially manuscripts. I have no idea where they finally were put.[44]

Like you, I have a large folder of personal letters, which I have not had the heart to go through yet. I kept every line I ever got from him—he was so perceptive, and understanding and accurate.

I personally would like to read his letters to you, though I doubt that I'll ever attempt any serious writing about the Church. If you have already given the University of Utah your private collection, I see no reason why these letters should not be added. They would be invaluable, I think.

I have long since ceased trying to figure out the WHY'S of the Universe. I can only accept these tragedies with what grace I can muster. The cause of Utah History suffers greatly from his loss, as I was reminded when I went to the viewing for Charles Kelly.[45]

Source: Levi Peterson's Collection.

To *Sana Williamson*, July 12, 1971

1731 South 1400 East
Salt Lake City, Utah 84105
July 12, 1971

My dear Sana,

I look at the calendar and wonder when it was that I last wrote to you. Life presses in on me—demands here when I ought to be somewhere else. Trying to move all the collections of a life-time, to dig out a big house and transfer to a small house—furniture, books, letters, bills, income-tax files—I wonder how we had accumulated so much.[46]

My son Karl & family are moving into the Big House at St. George. It is good to know that the Brooks Home will still be the Brooks Home instead of being—as it was all last winter—a dormitory for College Boys. But the business of moving is slow and painful and never done.

I now have my files here and some of my books. I gave to the Public Library a large number; to the English Department of Dixie College a great many more. I think that if we had put all of Wes's in the History Department they might have had more public notice, but at the time there was not a place in that Department because the building wasn't finished. But they are really appreciated where they are, and in every volume is his stamp, large and clear.

I still hope to live long enough to get the tape of the meeting held in the home of Jess Udall, when Wes saved the day for us all. There was I saying NO! again and again, every time one of the 23 Lee family members pled with me NOT to print the restoration of John D. Lee to all his former power and blessings. And there was Wes squatted on the floor operating his recording machine. When he could see that the situation had got to be most tense, he spoke up. How I should like to hear that voice and that presentation! Never was a man more clear, more lucid, more effective! I wish I could quote him <u>verbatim</u>, but it went about like this:

> "I have not been asked to participate here, but I am of the same relation to John D. Lee that you are: his great-grandson from his wife Lavina Young, and her daughter Lavina Clark. . . .
>
> I want you all to know that this has already appeared in print. I sent out more than a hundred copies of the family newsletter in which I told it. And I went to Salt Lake City, stopping at Harmony on my way, and telling every one I knew about it. I think we should all be so glad that we should shout it from the housetops! It's time the world knew the character of this man!"

Well—that's about as I remember it, and not half as effective as it actually was. I'm sure Wes kept that tape. Where in the world has it gone to? But if it is never found, the incident will never be forgotten by some twenty-four to twenty-five people, of that I'm sure. It was Wes at his keenest, [unclear] best.

***

Dear Sana—I was stopped by some little girls selling cherries—then by the telephone.

I needed only to say that I do love you, that I'd like to live near enough to see you occasionally. Oh, yes, and that Aunt Ettie Lee is now at the Home at Hurricane, which has been changed from a home for boys to one for retired people. She is the first guest of the oldsters, and is bright and rational, though she walks with a cane and is quite feeble. The Lunts are buying the place from the Corporation, I understand. It is fixed up now for boys, but that will be changed as they change their program.

I wish you could get set up here somewhere, but I'm sure that nothing in Utah can be nicer than what they have in California, and I hope to keep in better touch either by letter or telephone.

My best love,

Sana Williamson
3952 Katella Ave
Los Alamitos, Calif
90720

Source: WSU Levi Peterson Collection.

To *Asael C. Lambert*, August 29, 1971

1731 South 1400 East, SLC, Utah
August 29, 1971

Dear A. C.,

I have just finished scanning your note-book on THE DEVIL,[47] and I must say that it appealed to me less than anything else of yours that I have read. It comes through as an eloquent picture of your early rural raising, with its chores and folkways. It is much like my own, except that in our home THE DEVIL was never mentioned. To us, he did not exist. Our neglect of chores, or sins of stealing melons were not prompted by Him, but by our own laziness or the heat and the thirst and the nearness of the melon patch.

Among some of Pa's odder sisters there was an occasional reference to someone or other in Hebron who had been possessed of the Devil, and that when he was cast out of one, he was apt to go into another, but my parents always played this down, passed it off, and changed the subject, as though they themselves took no stock in such tales.

I had only one experience in which I saw a person who was "possessed of the Devil"—and this is the first time that I have attempted to put it down on paper. The room was full of witnesses, and I understand that members of the family have passed it on by word of mouth. The man who shared this experience with me is still alive, and perhaps I should get his version of the incident—or at least see if he remembers it after all these years.

UNCLE CULL

Uncle Cull was Orange D. Leavitt, son of Lemuel Leavitt.[48] He was married to two of my father's sisters, Aunt Lena and Aunt Mary Ellen.[49] Cousin marriages were rather common in the isolated villages. At his death he had seven living children from his first wife and nine from his second, had filled two missions for the church, and was still in full vigor of life—a large man, big-boned and broad, but not fat. He was stricken with what the local people called cholera morbus.[50]

I don't remember that I even knew he was sick until one evening when one of the boys came galloping up to our place on a horse, asking for Pa to please came up quick, for Uncle Cull was possessed of the Devil. I had just come in from MIA or choir practice—anyway, I was up and "cleaned up" so that Pa said to me, "Wouldn't you like to come along with me?" I would like to go anywhere with my Father.

I waited for him to give himself a thorough washing of head, face, and hands, for he never went out to administer to the sick without this physical cleansing. I had the bottle of Olive Oil, and we walked the nearly six blocks. The weather was mild and pleasant, and I don't think we exchanged a word in the whole distance. This was no time for talk.

We entered a room in some confusion: wives, children & two brethren who had been trying to Administer to Uncle Cull. He paid no heed to us, but his son Elmer[51] followed close upon us and went directly to the bed, stooped, took his father's hand, and squatted down to be on a level with his father.

"Why, Elmer," his father said in a clear, natural voice, "You shouldn't have run so hard all that way! You'll kill yourself! I'd a-waited." Elmer was seventeen years old; Uncle Cull's oldest by Aunt Mary Ellen.[52]

For a minute the room was quiet. Then as Elmer stood and moved back so that the brethren could administer, he started to curse and rave. Pa had the oil and stepped up close to begin, but Uncle Cull started to laugh. I don't know how the Devil would laugh, but this curdled my blood. Then he started to repeat a part of the prayer about the Power of the priesthood and would swear and threaten them. "Bull Shit!" I can handle you all, one at a time or all together! Wanna take me on?"

I was standing just inside the door, horrified, of course. Elmer pushed through those around the bed and over to where I stood. Taking my hand, he motioned to come along, so I went with him across the dooryard and the street, up a trail to the top of the Big Ditch bank, to a willow tree growing there. Together we kneeled beside it, and he offered a short prayer beseeching a blessing for his father, that he might be freed from the evil influence which surrounded him.

I followed in the same vein. Short, earnest prayers, both of them. We did not linger, but returned and slipped in as quietly as we could.

Uncle Cull was quiet and relaxed, breathing deeply, and evidently asleep. After a few minutes the crowd decided that all should go home except two to remain at the bedside, and two to sleep in a room adjoining, in case they needed to go for help.

We left the house with several others, all mostly in silence, and one after another with a "good-night" as they came to their own gates. We walked the last block alone.

"Where did you and Elmer go?" Pa asked. I didn't think he knew we had gone.

"Up to the willow tree on the ditch bank."

"Oh." No more comment than that.

Uncle Cull died at midnight that night.

Later as people gathered at the home before the funeral, I heard Theodosia[53] tell several times how her father was possessed of the Devil until he didn't even look like himself, how he laughed and cursed and raved, and then suddenly said, "'All right! All right! I'll go now! But it's not you guys here with that oil; it's them two kids up by the willow tree!" and from that minute he was quiet, passing away after a few hours with hardly a struggle.

***

A second case where it seemed that the person was possessed of the Devil was Leo A. Snow's oldest daughter.[54] She had been a student of mine, and a more refined, lovely girl I never knew. She was married to a Judd boy from Kanab, and they had three children: a girl and two boys.

She died at the home of her parents in St. George, and her Mother told me that the hardest thing she had to take was this time just before when she was Possessed: She looked wicked, ugly, mean, vengeful—swearing such oaths as she never had even heard in her life.

The Doctor gave this a name, and said that was a rare thing, but not unknown in the medical world. The family felt that when the girl was so sick and weak, Satan could truly get possession, and did!

A third case is recorded by Hosea Stout in connection with the death of his son June 28, 1846./On the Mormon Frontier: 170–171/[55]

I'll not copy it out; it's too long. It does follow the pattern, though.

I have no solution. I think that IF the spirit of man is eternal, evil spirits will continue to be evil in the next life—that is, if we continue to be ourselves. And in the whole over-all plan there must be evil as well as good. I confess my ignorance. I can only bumble along the best that I can here, taking such experiences as come to me and interpreting them as I can. My sons all think I have ESP—I won't be specific now, as I could, but it has seemed that many times a power OUTSIDE MYSELF was working in my behalf, opening the way, bringing into my hands materials that I could never have found otherwise, or opening my mind to a new vision of some of the materials I already had in my files. I'm sure that I could not have done as well as I did by John D. Lee without some extra help from someone or something outside myself, silly as this may sound to you.

Well, it will not be too long before we both will be launched on our next new adventure, and can compare notes there, wherever we are.

All good wishes,

To *Thomas E. Cheney*,[56] September 6, 1971

1731 South 1400 East
Salt Lake City, Utah 84105
Sept. 6, 1971

Thomas B. Cheney
1720 North Lambert
Provo, Utah 84601

Dear Tom:

Congratulations! Congratulations to everybody!! It's a beautiful book we have produced.[57] Of course, you have been the one who has done the work, filled in the necessary information, and pushed the thing along. Your name should be done in gold somewhere in the volume.

One criticism only do I find. Nowhere is the sale price listed. I can't think of a nicer present for each of my children than this book. I assume that Zion Book will carry it, maybe Deseret Book also. But to an old lady in my situation, the price is important to know, so that I can begin saving my "Sunday Eggs" toward building up a bit of fund enough to purchase as many as I will need.

I forgot that I was not still down on the farm. Excuse the slip.

I'm pleased, too, that the riddles and rhymes are added, and I know nearly every one. Fact is, I'd like to have added a few. Oh, well, I'll work them in somewhere in my own writing—maybe.

As you see, I'm writing before I have read some parts carefully. I must get into the stories of Sam Brannon and O P Rockwell. Already I have written in and marked this one up so much that I'll have to keep it for myself, so I'll begin tomorrow to see what I can do about extra copies.

I read this letter through and know that I should rip it apart and start over, but it's late and I'm already tired and confused. After 11 p.m. I have to take a recess. So forgive it, but don't forget that I am sincere when I say that I am pleased and proud to have been just a little part of this venture.

Cordially and gratefully,

Source: Levi Peterson's Collection.

To *Grace and Obert C. Tanner*, October 5, 1971

1731 South 1400 East
Salt Lake City, Utah
October 5, 1971

Dear Grace and Obert:

I just received the book BRIGHT ESSENCE, STUDIES IN MILTON'S THEOLOGY[58] and hasten to say my thanks and appreciation. I'm flattered that you should think I may be able to read this with some understanding and appreciation.

I have not specialized in the works of John Milton, but in my senior high school year we spent more time with him than with any other except Shakespeare. I remember my delight in memorizing lines from L'Allegro and Il Penseroso, Comus, and Lycidas. Then his sonnet On His Blindness[59] which is so extra special, should be memorized by every student.

I thought as I sat through a meeting in our ward recently of the line, "The hungry sheep look up and are not fed," as being typical of too many of our gatherings—dry husks and fodder instead of nourishing food.

I am glad to get into the philosophy of the relationship between God the Creator and Jesus Christ the human. I've read enough of the Jewish concept that I find myself repeating the Psalm, "The Heavens declare the glory of God and the firmament shewith His handiwork . . ."[60] and on to the end, with the feeling that man's little mind cannot conceive the whole of God's worlds and works. The universe is vast beyond our comprehension endless in time and space.

And yet here in our little personal worlds there does seem to be a power outside ourselves which helps to shape our destinies. I am more and more hesitant as I grow older, to put into words some of my experiences—some of the times when the way has been made smooth before me, when from unknown and unexpected sources vital material which I hadn't known enough about to be even looking for it, came into my hands, sometimes from strangers, sometimes from friends who just had a hunch that I might find this useful.

I have not studied into the doctrines of Arius, the Alexandrian theologian.[61] This book will be my introduction to some of that. I think that my role for the few years I have left will be to get added breadth of vision for myself, and in some small way put into words on paper some of the stuff of life as I have observed and experienced, something of what it was to grow up in an isolated rural village.

I know that this is not very coherent, but it is late at night and I am waiting a call from a hospital in Albuquerque giving a report on a very serious ear operation which my youngest son underwent today.

Thank you again for your consideration of me, and for all your many kindnesses.

Sincerely,

Source: WSU Levi Peterson Collection.

To *Winifred (Peg) Gregory*, October 21, 1971

1731 South 1400 East
Salt Lake City, Utah 84105
Oct. 21, 1971

Dear Peg:

I'm too shaken up to write. I just learned via Alfred Bush of Princeton that Sam Weller is to print the Jewish book! I couldn't believe it! Seems that he is connected in some way with Publisher's Press, and had bid to put out 1000 of the books for $3000. With size of page, type, hard cover & jacket specified. . . .

So—that is that. In a way, I'll be glad just to have it out and done with, especially if by some magic we could sell a new issue of the enlarged MORMON CHRONICLE to Oklahoma Press. If we could work like a doodle-bug, hind side first—and Huntington would sell the copyright for $1000. Or less, we could put out a really worthwhile publication, one that would dwarf everything else in print on early Mormon History. Lee is so frank. He writes in more detail than many—or most—others. He tells so casually happenings which the Church now is trying hard to forget.

The more I think about it, the more I am glad that this Jewish book can soon be set aside. While I have a minor item or two in the mill, NOTHING ever can compete with a 3-volume MORMON CHRONICLE.

Anyway, that is the way things are falling into place right now. And I'm going nowhere fast.

Best love,

By "hind-side-first" I meant to begin with Volume 3, where few changes need to be made, and those chiefly in the footnotes.

Source: Levi Peterson's Collection.

To *Myrtle Friedman*, December 21, 1971

1731 South 1400 East
Salt Lake City, Utah
Dec. 21, 1971

Dear Myrtle:

I was so surprised and pleased to get your wonderful gift of almonds. Almonds have always been my favorite nut, maybe because the Relief Society of Bunkerville had a quarter of a block of almond trees. My Mother was Secretary and Treasurer, and we children helped to harvest the nuts. We were given some for our work, and could glean after the sacks had been hauled away.

But we never did anything with them except store and eat them, put them in candy and pomegranate salads. They tasted so good to us that we hadn't an idea that they could be improved.

I'm a co-hostess next week at a Study Group here, and I'll be proud to "show off" a bit with these wonderful almonds. But I'll be a bit stingy, too, in that I shall save out some of each kind for myself. I can treat myself for some time on a few of these each day. Thank you again, very much!

Last week Sam Weller sponsored me as speaker before the Exchange Club at Hotel Utah. I'm sending one of his Programs. I don't know where he got his Biography, but it's a bit sloppy. In his typed Introduction he stated that my "The Jews of Utah and Idaho" would be off the press in early 1972. He insists that I shall help with it—which I shall be glad to do—but I've seen not a thing so far as general lay-out or plans are concerned.

My little gift to you may seem unusual. I told my son, when I gave him one, "There's nothing in this thing except what <u>you</u> put there.

It may mean much or little. For me, it is a sort of stabilizer. If I get to feeling important, I immediately see myself in perspective."

A man in Dixie makes a business of sawing out pictures in stone, ranging from six or seven inches in length to that many feet. They are used often to face fireplaces and planters. Some folks frame them, others set them in wire holders, and some just prop them on a shelf. And many, of course, consider them trash.

It occurs to me that I just might have sent you one of these before; I've been quite interested in them myself. So if you have one already, pass this on to someone else or dispose of it.

We've had a few clear days, but it's so cold that the snow is still piled high everywhere. I may go South for a few days during the holidays.

Best love to you. I hope your health is good, for good health is one of life's greatest blessings.

Thank you again for this generous gift.

Source: WSU Levi Peterson Collection.

To *Claudia Bushman*, December 21, 1971

1731 South 1400 East
Salt Lake City, Utah 84105
Dec. 21, 1971

Mrs. Claudia Bushman
28 Oak Street
Belmont Mass. 02178

Dear Claudia:

Congratulations on your Ladies' issue of Dialogue![62] I've read it from cover to cover, and find it interesting and stimulating.

Thank you especially for the picture on page 92. I suppose you know that it is a family group—our family—in front of the Old Brooks Home in St. George. Mother has the guitar, Clair is sprawled on the step, I am holding my little nephew, Bernie Leavitt.[63] The little girl with the curly top is his sister Kathy; the girl with the pig-tail is Clair's daughter Katie. Mother is still alive and going strong at 94; Katie is expecting her first baby in January; Kathy will be married Jan. 15 in the St. George Temple; Bernie is an athlete at the University here. A historic picture, this, for us.

Dorothea Lang was at our place many times, as was her husband, Paul Taylor.[64] Her son was also in the area that summer, as was also Ansel Adams,[65] who was photographing the Canyons for advertising for International airlines, I believe.

Dorothy Lang took many pictures of Mother, some of which she put into a booklet for her. It's really beautiful & now belongs to me.

I'll not comment on any except Almera Anderson Romney.[66] How I would like to know that lady! She's one of the truly great—a Savior on Mount Zion in the highest sense. Would that we had more like her.

I understand perfectly the position of "A Widow in the Church;"[67] for thirteen years I was one, and at that time there was truly NO place for her anywhere. Married couples did Not want her; single groups had even less use for her. Now that the Church has so changed its policy re: Temple Work, friends and family think that I should be sealed to Will Brooks, the father of four of my children. I am already sealed to Ernest Pulsipher. I feel that with this lax a policy, neither sealing will mean much.

Forgive me. That last slipped out. Mother still goes to the temple two sessions a day for five days a week; she has a careful record of every one of the 5,000+ that she has ushered into the Celestial Kingdom. It keeps her alive and happy and going strong, so I'm most happy for her. I prefer to try to help "save" people still alive on this earth, as does Mrs Romney.

Congratulations again. And thanks for letting my name be on the list.

Sincerely,

Source: Levi Peterson's Collection.

Chapter 13

1972–1978

Her Final Letters

These years mark the deterioration of Brooks's mental capabilities, necessitating her move back to St. George at the beginning of 1977. As the years passed, she was less and less able to focus on her research, with others picking up the slack and helping with some of her unfinished work, including especially her autobiography, *Quicksand and Cactus*, originally started in the 1940s. This decline is evident in her letters and actions. One example is her conflict with her neighbors over dog droppings on her lawn. After leaving the mess on her neighbor's porch and calling the animal control, she wrote an irritable letter to the neighbor saying she came from a family of guns, threatening to buy one and use it on the dog. Her letters became more disjointed and less clear as time passed.

As her intellectual competence diminished, her acceptance throughout the region and renown continued to surge. Among her honors during this period were an honorary life membership in the Western History Association, honorary doctorate from the University of Utah, honorary membership in Phi Beta Kappa at the University of Utah, and the Charles Redd Prize in Humanities and Social Sciences from the Utah Academy of Sciences, Arts and Letters. Even some leaders of the LDS Church praised her writing abilities and courage, such as Wendell J. Ashton, director of the public communications department, who wrote: "I have long admired your fairness, your thoroughness, your courage, and your skill as a writer in giving to us some of our finest literature in Utah history."[1] She was able to report in December of 1974 that Deseret Book had asked her to autograph one hundred copies of her Mountain Meadows

Massacre book, which would have been unheard of in previous decades. She also maintained an ongoing correspondence with authors such as Samuel Taylor, Rodello Hunter, and Fawn Brodie, as well as budding writers asking for advice. Her final failed attempt to promote interest in a three-volume edition of the John D. Lee diaries came in a letter to Elaine McPhie, a Lee descendant, in April 1976.

Her letters during this period reveal someone concerned about the excellence of the final product of her publications. In one such case, she was critical of the illustrations of the desert plants drawn for her book *The Christmas Tree.* She fired off a letter to the illustrator complaining that he should get in touch with the author at least once during the process and if he was "to illustrate stories in the desert setting, he should spend sometime in the desert to get to know the plants."[2] In another incident, she was dissatisfied with the poor reproduction of the photograph of Janet Smith Leavitt, the Native American wife of Dudley Leavitt, in her book *On the Ragged Edge: The Life and Times of Dudley Leavitt.* To solve this problem, she sent many of the descendants of Janet Leavitt an improved copy of the photo, which she had made at her own expense, with a note apologizing and asking them to replace the one in the book.

Several books or monographs authored or edited by Brooks came off the press during these years. Her edited journal of Thomas D. Brown was finally printed in July 1972 after years of delay over permission to publish from the LDS Church. Two small efforts, *Frontier Tales* and *The Christmas Tree,* containing her stories, appeared near the end of 1972.[3] The History of the Jews was finally available from Sam Weller's Western Epics in the summer of 1973. In late 1972 and into 1973, she produced a revised version of her Dudley Leavitt book, originally published in 1942. A short biography of Emma Lee came out in 1975, after the review help of Charles Peterson from the Utah State University Press, where her friend Mary Washington was the director. The important diary of Martha Spence Heywood was published in 1978 with the editorial help of Miriam Murphy of the Utah State Historical Society.

One of her last letters in the collection vividly expressed her confusion and anguish as her condition worsened. She exclaimed, "Do you know what it is to be in HELL? Well, I'll tell you: It's being in a confusion, where nothing seems important, where there are so many THINGS and nothing seems important, but is to somebody else. It's being in the midst of all kinds of unrelated Things."[4] In the final extant letter Juanita responded to a request for her to escort some friends to the Mountain Meadows Massacre site and for any new information on the massacre. She replied that she could not take them and concluded her letter, "So come along, and I'll do the best I can—which will be to look through my books," and thus ended the amazing career of the pioneer Mormon historian, Juanita Brooks.

~

To *Myrtle H. Friedman*, January 3, 1972

1731 South 1400 East
Salt Lake City, Utah
Jan. 3, 1972

Myrtle H. Friedman
Box 186
Hailey, Idaho, 83333

Dear Myrtle:

I have just had a conference with Mr. Diston,[5] and have come home so upset that I can hardly control my hands.

He is working on an agreement with Sam Weller which makes you finance THREE THOUSAND copies of The Jews of Utah and Idaho, instead of the ONE thousand which you were to have sponsored.[6] This brings Sam out with all the money. There would be $700.00 left for me.

Through all our meetings with the University people, the number of books was one thousand, with additional printings later as the demand justified.

After all the time and labor that I have put in on the project, the night trips up and back on the bus, the digging in libraries and old magazines, the writing and re-writing, I think he is not the one to make the profit. Not all of it, at least.

Oklahoma Press would have put it out without any subsidy unless you wanted the first thousand in extra fine binding and paper. They have made enough off my book to take anything I write. They have just issued the Fourth Printing of 10,000; my 15% commission came to just less $500.00. It came just about ten days after my SOS to you for that amount. I should have had more faith and waited, I guess. And they are a Nationally known press.

According to the records, my salary at $125.00 per month totaled $3750. My travel and lodging were another $3095.54. Those night rides on the bus to save the daylight to work, and to cut down the room rent!

For the last nearly two years, I have paid my own travel & hotel expenses, and worked just as hard. The $700. would not cover the expenses. It hasn't been a full two years, either, for I took six months off, and I sent the manuscript with Mr. Diston to you a few months ago.

I think your gift of $15,000. was most liberal. Not for anything would I ask you to increase that. I just don't like this deal with Sam Weller. There are other personal reasons which I shall talk to you about later.

Very sincerely,

Source: WSU Levi Peterson Collection.

To *Gibbs M. Smith*,[7] January 18, 1972

1731 South 1400 East
Salt Lake City, Utah
January 18, 1972

Mr. Gibbs M. Smith
PEREGRINE PUBLISHERS, INC
P.O. Box 8084 Salt Lake City Utah
84108

Dear Mr. Smith:

Thank you for yours of January 12.

I'm glad you liked the little Christmas Tree story.[8] I have a son in Las Vegas, and a nephew in Mesquite, both of whom know a Mescrew bush,[9] and could get pictures. I'll make a project of getting one—or perhaps two or three from which you might choose.

Bless you, I had no printed card this year. I had only the story as it was sent to you, with a bit of Christmas sticker on the top. This three-page bit was a substitute for a card. So if you print it, you'd have a full opportunity for added art work. You would know better than I. A fireplace with the Yule log? The wooden candy-bucket stand? Maybe only the Mescrew tree, with a close-up of its tightly twisted seedpod on a small branch would help.

But I'll work a bit at this photography project right away, within a couple of weeks or so.

NOW Re: the Indian Stories and Jacob Hamblin: During the middle 1940's I was working on a biography of Jacob Hamblin, had gone to Arizona to look over the area where he spent his last years, and contacted members of the family for their folklore. Then the Church assigned Brother Pearson Corbett to do a definitive study, and at the same time Paul Bailey was working at one.[10] I felt that it would be idle for me to continue, so I finished off what I had and shelved it.

Brother Corbett's book was little more than a change from First to Third person of Brother Little's,[11] with much genealogy. Mine may not seem much, either, but I'm sending it that you may consider how best we might handle it. I'd be glad if you would prefer to take it—with additions—and send the other back for good. Or it might be that we could combine some parts with one or the other.

The scribbling on this was put there by my sweet husband to parts that he enjoyed. He read and re-read it, and passed it around his little circle. I'm sending it only because you suggested that we bring Hamblin into it.

I'll take time to write another letter about the first mss.

Be patient with me, but I've had this for [missing]

Source: WSU Levi Peterson Collection.

To *William Wise*,[12] February 17, 1972

It might interest you to know that
Mr John Cronin, P.O. Box 1409,
Jackson, Wyoming, 83001, is now
engaged in a novel centered in the MMM;
his pages of questions match yours.

1731 South 1400 East
Salt Lake City, Utah
17 February 1972

Mr. William Wise
129 East 62nd Street
New York, N.Y. 10021

Dear Mr. Wise:

I have had no conversation with Mr Melvin Smith[13] with regard to your project, as I understand that Mr. Smith is out of town for a few days.

So far as my study goes, there are some modifications in this last Fourth Printing. I was given some fifteen pages as an addenda in the introductory pages, in which I explained some new material secured since the first printing, which did modify some of my earlier conclusions. These you would do well to get and study.

Since Oklahoma Press holds the Copyright to this publication, you would do well to deal with them.

A new printing of the John D. Lee BIOGRAPHY is also to appear soon. It contains some little new material. It is published by the Arthur H. Clark Company, Glendale, California.[14]

As for the basic causes, I think you must go back to the Mormon expulsion from Missouri, and then their later forced evacuation of Nauvoo. You should read their diaries, the minutes of some of their meetings. For example, Thomas D. Brown's History of the Southern Indian Mission (now in press at the Utah State University, Logan, Utah) records testimonies in 1854—three years before the approach of the army—which speak of avenging the blood of brothers and sisters slain in Missouri at Haun's Mill.[15]

Since the death of Mr. Kenner Fancher, I have had no communication with any of the family. The seventeen surviving children could have left no historical material, since the oldest was about ten years old, and without any knowledge except the distant firing of guns to report.

In the new material mentioned in paragraph 2 above is a letter from a lady who came as far as Salt Lake City with the Fancher train.[16] Her parents, some younger brothers and sisters, a married sister and her husband were all killed in the massacre. Three of the surviving children belonged to this sister.

Another letter asks the names of the eleven men who were a part of the company for a short time, though they were independent packers, who became known as "The Missouri Wildcats."[17] They did not stop at the Meadows longer than overnight. They pushed on and learned of the massacre after they arrived in San Bernardino. But you should get this from the Fourth Printing of the MMM.

I feel that the whole truth may never be found; there are so many, many things in the background of individual characters and of the whole Mormon Movement that to learn and evaluate them all impossible.

Sincerely,

Source: WSU Levi Peterson Collection.

To *Gay and Sam Taylor*, February 22, 1972

1731 South 1400 East
Salt Lake City, Utah
84105 Feb. 22,/72

Dear Gay: (and Sam too, of course)
1954 Stockbridge Ave
Redwood City, Calif.
94061

Dear Lady,

I'm sorry about the lack of address on the book. I had none here at the house, so went to the store to have it wrapped and mailed. The lady who took me down couldn't find a parking place, but was riding around the block until I should come out. I should have let her make another trip, I guess, but since the clerk had my home address, I supposed she would use it. Evidently she did not.

I'm thoroughly enjoying Nightfall,[18] but how I wished that I had talked to Sam on a few points. For example: He did not even name Tom Brown in the book; he told of the hanging of the two Hodge boys, William & Stephen, but not mention the fact that Tom Brown, older than they, was the leading actor in that tragedy. They didn't catch him.

When I read the THIS IS THE PLACE marker and saw the names listed, with the phrase, "and one other man, whose name is not of the record," I had my curiosity aroused. I set out to find the "one other man." It took a little doing, but I found him as "The Notorious Tom Brown," in Bonney and "Nathaniel Thomas Brown" in the official list of the 1847 pioneers, one of the few horsemen who owned his own horse. He was quite heroic in many places, killing game, facing up to Indians, finding the lost binoculars. He was re-baptized along with others; and was finally shot and killed by Bill Hickman, there at Kanesville. Without going into details, he was Brigham Young's step brother. When the LDS story says that Brigham baptized "his parents" and other members of the family, it means his father and step-mother, Hannah Dennis Brown[19] and her two sons Thomas and Alanson. I notice that you have listed him often, though, though I'm not sure that you noted his appointment as a High Councilor, or the ride in which he ran his horse to death in an effort to save the Prophet.

This lady and her two sons were dropped from the record, as was her son by John Young, Edward by name, who returned with her to New York soon after the death of her husband. Some energetic researcher has a page for this son, all completely filled out. I believe he might have been baptized on the same date as the others; he would have been old enough.

So much for this. It is just exciting to probe a little beneath the surface. But when the Mormons <u>wipe out</u> a name the blot is pretty black and final.

You know so many things that I didn't know, and showed so many angles; but I could have given you a few real honies—though you really didn't need them. Thank you for doing this book.

All good wishes,

Source: Levi Peterson's Collection.

To *Rodello Hunter*,[20] June 23, 1972

1731 South 1400 East
Salt Lake City, Utah 84105
June 23, 1972

Dear Rodello Hunter,

Thank you for A DAUGHTER OF ZION![21] I couldn't put it down; the minute I got it everything else just melted away. I knew just what you meant about the Church and the lives of its women members. For a while, I was submerged in it, too, but never so completely or for such a long time. My daughter's activities almost match yours: she was Relief Society President at the Branch in England; again in Clovis, New Mexico (where they cleared some $1500 at their bazaar; and in Hawaii . . .) During her nine months in the St. George 5th Ward, she managed the Road Show.

The only incident that I could question at all was the recovery from polio of LEONE. I worked with Ross Eager,[22] who was paralyzed from his neck down, except for his left arm and its index finger. I helped him with reading; that is, I read to him. He couldn't breathe, but was in a rocking chair device which forced the air into his lungs. Clearly, Leone was not as bad as Ross, but even so, her walking at all was a major miracle.

I, too, have used the palm-reading trick a time or two. It's amazing how effective it can be sometimes.

I see nothing in the book to take much exception to. The Church won't like it, but I don't see how they can criticize it. The whole picture is just too true. "The highest tithe-payer in the Stake" is a case in point, but altogether too typical of our respect for money and the people who have it.

And the Patriarchal Blessings! Such a chapter as might be done on that! I gave a young man working on his Masters enough promises of the Last Days, the Return of the Ten Tribes, The Return to the Center Stake, the calamities to Befall the Wicked, for a fair sized volume. I think he may abandon his subject.

Really, I think you have been kind and understanding. I see not a thing that is exaggerated, not one that cannot be matched with another fully as bad.

And a condemnation just might stimulate sales. The thing will go like wildfire, once it takes hold. My own writing is not nearly so effective.

Under separate cover I am sending a reprint of the three little items that appeared in AMERICAN FOLKLORE.[23] Re-written and separated, they will appear in my QUICKSAND & CACTUS, along with the two that earlier appeared in Harpers. In all these, it is the desert that is important—and the isolation.

Thanks again for a most delightful couple of days, and Congratulations.

In Ross Eager's case, he relied upon promises of his recovery, and married a fine Mormon girl whose Mother preferred him, crippled as he was, to another Mormon boy who smoked tobacco!!! Contrary to all the general expectations, Ross did father a child or two—girls.[24] He died soon after the second child was conceived, as I remember it. I'll get the facts and set the record straight.

Source: Levi Peterson's Collection.

To *My Neighbors*, [August 10, 1972]

TO MY NEIGHBORS NEXT DOOR

Please read this through before you destroy it.[25]

I'I1 probably fry in HELL, anyway, regardless of your curse upon me.

But hear me out: I like DOGS. My best friend and childhood companion was a Dog: old Briz, and his memory is a bright spot in my life. I still like dogs, but I am unaccustomed to have to clean up after them.

I called the officer the other morning to ask chiefly what I could do to locate the owner of the dog whose last three deposits were right in the same place—the middle of the lawn nearest you.

Here I must apologize to you. I was wrong in putting this last mess on your porch. I let myself react too strongly to the frustration of the whole situation—this shadow-boxing with an animal that has a set pattern of returning to the same spot to do his chores. I'M sorry.

I wanted advice about getting a hand pistol with which to shoot whatever dog it was that persisted in coming here for his bathroom duties. As a girl at home, I used a .22 and a shot gun; NOBODY touched Dad's rifle.

In the Brooks family I found a gun-minded crew. Will was County Sheriff; many of the Saturday afternoon sports consisted in target practice with 22's. Here boxes of bullets were shot in an afternoon. I participated once or twice.

I told the officer that I had serious intentions of lying in wait for that dog and killing it. My son in the FBI here might not let me use anything of his, but I would buy a small pistol of my own.

How else could I do away with this??? I could not lasso the animal and tie it up until its master could claim it. I might catch it with a long whip, but that was a slim chance, too, and it needed to be hurt bad enough to avoid the place hereafter. Maybe one lash in the right place would do it.

I did not know of the City Ordinance restricting the number of dogs to a household. I only know that if people were going to make a business of breeding dogs and raising puppies it should not be it a residential district—but that was my own idea.

I did not see the officer until after he had walked up to the fence and been greeted by the three dogs that were there. He asked me if their barking annoyed me, and I told him No, not especially. My only gripe was this sanitation problem that I never had before your dogs were brought there.

He asked if there were other dogs, and I told him that the blonde boy seemed to have a little brown lap-poodle. I was out when he turned it loose. I waved it away from my lawn, so it turned and made three brief stops on your place, and in just a minute or two he took it back inside. I had the idea that he probably took in in his car.

I did not know any names; I had no idea of your business, where or whether you worked. I'm too involved in my own projects to leave this corner of my basement, and have felt that at my age I might have better employment than cleaning up after dogs.

I should add that this is the first time in all my life that I have had trouble with a neighbor. For much of it I must take the blame of being perhaps too old, too impatient.

Again, I apologize.

Source: Levi Peterson's Collection.

To *Mary Hafen Leavitt*,[26] November 5, 1972

1731 South 1400 East
Salt Lake City, Utah 84105
November 5, 1972

Dear Mother:

I've been remembering my earliest childhood days, now that you are 95 years young and I am almost 75 years old. If my little booklet

QUICKSAND & CACTUS, ever comes out, you will be the heroine, especially in the first part when we lived in the little one-roomed adobe house.

You always wanted nice things, not just cobbled-up ones, and you wanted our home to be nice. I remember how we peddled cloverine salve[27] at 15¢ a can to get the premium of ten mounted pictures. We ended up with most of the salve on our hands, but we gave free cans to the grand-parents and some of the other relatives, until after a long time the salve was all gone. But we paid for the lot and got our pictures. How proud we were! How we experimented to find the best place for each one, putting them up and taking them down to find a better place.

Then the problem of dishes. The store carried only tin-ware, so you got a catalogue and took orders, starting up at Uncle Nephi Hunt's and calling at every home. The women looked at the pictures, and ordered items that appealed to them, knowing that they might not want them or be able to pay for them when the order arrived. For a twenty-dollar order you would get a basic set, with extra pieces if you had a larger order. By the time you got your premium and paid for all extra we were well supplied.

What excitement when the big barrel of dishes came in on the mail! The neighbor kids swarmed around until you had to send us all away.

The rag carpet—what a labor that cost! And the throw rugs as well. The annual house-cleaning with the whitewashed walls, the new straw to crackle under foot, the lace curtains starched stiff and stretched on the quilting frames, made our front room just delightful!

What I am trying to say is that you took seriously the saying, "Thou shalt not live by bread alone!" You wanted music and art and beautiful things. You wanted us to memorize and make our own the Articles of Faith, The Ten commandments, "The Beatitudes," and poems and songs of all kinds.

Don't forget our orchestra, with Mel and Laurel on the violins and Aura at the piano—later with Francis & Dudley on trumpets. The walls fairly echoed.

Best of all was you and your guitar, on summer evenings on the porch and bermuda-grass lawn, when everyone sang whether they could carry a tune or not. Of course, the Christmas Serenades were the most fun, and were most enjoyed by all.

May you fill out your full one-hundred year span, and keep as sharp and interesting as you are today. And may our children and their children appreciate the wonderful heritage you are leaving them

My best love,

To *David Crockett*,[28] December 7, 1972

1731 South 1400 East
Salt Lake City, Utah 84105
December 7, 1972
Telephone 484-8110

Dear David Crockett:

I assume that you, like Mr. Gibbs Smith, are young and talented and relatively new in the game of illustrating stories. At any rate, this is just a suggestion: Do get in touch with the Author, at least by telephone. Just one time, at least. And when you don't know, ASK.

It is clear that you know little of the desert or the desert plants. If you are to illustrate stories in the desert setting, you should spend one day and night, at least, in the desert.

Then in the matter of the frontier of the turn of the century: B.C., Before Cars, things were different.

Specifically—in this story, when I said that we had a candy bucket, A WOODEN CANDY BUCKET, I was saying something wonderful! What could be nicer than a wooden candy bucket to hold our tree? Of course the tree couldn't be too large. The bucket would be 18 to 20 inches high, the slats larger at the top, and held together with two shining copper bands—the wood itself varnished. In my book—as yet unpublished,—I tell about our getting this special bucket. That's why the rocks & sand.

Here the container looks like a 20 gallon swill barrel or open-headed pickle barrel! And holding a one-sided. . . .

Forgive me. I'm just grieving because we just might have had some communication over the telephone. But Gibbs Smith dropped off the earth—with no telephone to call—and no David Crockett in my telephone book, either. I had absolutely NO way to find either of you.

Well, I'm relatively new at this game, too, in spite of my great age. Pray God for me that I will learn.

Whatever this one little, unimportant publication may mean to anyone else, I hope it will mean to all three of us that people who are sharing the responsibility for bringing out a book should have some communication with each other. A voice over the telephone, if nothing else.

Source: Levi Peterson's Collection.

To *Charles S. Peterson*,[29] July 5, 1973

1731 South 1400 East
Salt Lake City, Utah
July 5, 1973

Dr. Chas. S. Peterson
Utah State University
Logan, Utah

Dear Charles:

Thank you so much for your letter. I'm so pleased to have you go over that Emma Lee manuscript.[30] I always tell my classes, and remind myself often that: "There is No such thing as good writing; there is only good rewriting."

In this case I worked with too much haste, for while in one sense, this is a re-writing, it needs much in the way of clarification and fill-in. I must not only go through many parts of the manuscript again, especially in the last section: Emma's life as "Dr. French," but I must visit the area, Winslow, at least, and the cemetery there.[31]

I imagine the best depository for history in all parts of the state would be at Phoenix. Do you know whether or not newspaper files were kept there?

There is such a wealth of material on Emma while she was married to John D. Lee, but after she left the ferry it is largely folklore.

I think this manuscript is a good beginning, but there remains much to be done. Perhaps I was "slightly teched" to think I could turn out any kind of a monograph in such a short time. It's a beginning, however, and I'll make time to come back to it again within a relatively short time.

I'll have to impose upon you for much information on the Arizona background, however, and shall appreciate all the help you can give me.

I'll always be deeply indebted to you for giving me the opportunity of being on your campus this last summer.[32] I hope to find a time rather soon when we may go over this little monograph together.

All good wishes, to your wife and family as well,

Source: Levi Peterson's Collection.

To *Editor, Washington County News*, August 28, 1973

1731 South 1400 East
Salt Lake City, Utah
August 28, 1973

Editor, Washington County News
St. George , Utah

Dear Sir:

A few weeks ago I started a letter to you, complaining because you told about a Golden Wedding, and pictured a very beautiful couple, but gave only the man's name. I'm sure that I know the wife, but you didn't give her maiden name at all! She was just his Mrs. Now I feel that a woman's name should be given in full; fact is, I was about to telephone and ask for it. Surely if a person deserves space in your columns and a picture, your readers have a right to know her name!

Now, here this week Mrs. McAllister has a birthday! Fine! But why don't you tell us her name? And the name of the lady who baked the cake, and of at least some of her children. Being Mrs., she must have had a husband sometime. What if he is dead? Certainly she might have a first name by which her friends know her. Why sell us short? Why not reveal her identity?

I enjoy these pages from the past, as I am sure that many of your readers do, and I like to be current on who in doing what in the old home town. Funerals and obituaries seem very important to me, because they usually DO name the family.

I don't mean any offense, but I do think your readers are entitled to know the names, of the full names—or at least a nick-name by which a character may be identified, just in case absent friends would like to extend sympathy, or perhaps congratulations. If no address is given, one might route a letter in care of the Washington County News.

Don't be offended; just have your news people get all the news. We watch for it.

Sincerely,

Source: Levi Peterson's Collection.

To *Josephine B. Gregory*, May 2, 1974

1731 South 1400 East
Salt Lake City, Utah 84105
May 2/74

Dear Jo,

Thank you so much for the xerox of WHY THE COALVILLE TABERNACLE <u>HAD</u> TO BE RAZED.[33] I had already scanned it in my own copy, but was so blazing mad that I threw the magazine aside and would not support it in its plea for funds. For me, this was treason!

So the Coalville Tabernacle HAD to be razed! Of the 2131 members of the Summit Stake only 733 voted to tear the building down. Of the 500 members of the Coalville Ward which had always used the building, 123 voted to tear it down. (The <u>Deseret News</u> reported that 85% of the people wanted it destroyed)

When the local unit of the Daughters of the Utah Pioneers took down a petition to save the Tabernacle, signed by most of the adults of Coalville and vicinity, they were told that Pres. Harold B. Lee was out of town, and were sent to Mark Garff's[34] office, where they were told that "There is nothing I can do for you; you don't hold the Priesthood."

A price was finally set of the value of the building, and the full sum was collected to put on the line at eight o'clock in the morning; to avoid that, the destruction began before daylight. I wonder if the Church can ever live down the shame of this act! And then to argue that it HAD to come down! Why? To give the Building Board another highly remunerative job? To prove the POWER OF THE PRIESTHOOD?

The moving pictures taken as the work continued will stand as evidence against our leaders while time lasts. In early Christendom, it was the savages who destroyed their shrines?!!!!

How can our children read the Dedication Services of that building, in which they were promised that it would stand until the Second Coming! The same promise was made in St George for the Tabernacle on which men labored ten long years. The temple went up in less than half the time, but the same promise was pronounced on both.

An investigation of the activities of the Building Board would show that some families are making fortunes in the "Service of the Lord." But don't let me start on that.

I'm waiting with some anxiety the fate of the most beautiful one at Spring City. If that one goes, I'm through! There can be NO reason of space; it's the only building on the large block, and its beauty is of symmetry of line and beauty of hand-done wood carving in the interior. There's nothing to compare it with. I wish you'd make your next trip to Zion to this far north, and we'd go to see it. It's a real experience.

Thanks for your patience; and thanks for being my friend. I may need someone to say a good word for my salvation. I need to come to the Huntington Library in the near future, but am behind in my schedule so far now that I can't tell when it will be. See you in Dixie sometime!

Best love to you both,

Source: Levi Peterson's Collection.

To *Zina Barnum*,[35] May 18, 1974

1731 South 1400 East
Salt Lake City, Utah 84105
May 18/74

Zuna Barnum
1908 Elm Avenue
Las Vegas, Nevada
89101

Dear Zina:

Dear Zina again—I'm so glad to hear from you, or from any of Grandma Janet's descendants. I was so whopping MAD when that ugly thing came out that I had enough made up of these others to go in every book that has been printed.[36]

But many books were sold before the pictures were finished. I'm sending approximately 50 here—maybe nearer 60—I didn't count them. But you know Grandma Janet's family better than I do, and all I ask is that you give them to her descendants, to all of Grandpa Dudley's descendants who do not have them.

I think it is better to lay them cross-wise on the bottom of the page, so they wont cover the print on Uncle Lister's family picture. It fits into the space well, and is certainly nicer than that one.

I'd appreciate it if you would give these all to people who will appreciate them. When they are gone, write me, and I'll send some more.

Thank you for your help in this.

Sincerely, your Cousin

Source: Levi Peterson's Collection.

To *Lowry Nelson*, July 25, 1974

1731 South 1400 East
Salt Lake City, Utah
July 25, 1974

Dr. Lowry Nelson
80 North 200 East
Provo, Utah 84601

Dear Lowry:

I feel like the Morning of the First Resurrection to get a letter of my own written a quarter of a century ago! Twenty-five whole years![37]

And here I am in Salt Lake City, happily situated in a little house with a dungeon-room in which to keep this machine. And You back in Provo—the very heart of Zion, along with our common friend, Gus Larson.

I had hopes that the atmosphere in Zion would clear a little, but after the experience of our friend, Tom Cheney, I have serious doubts; so much made of so little![38]

Do the "Senior Citizens of the BYU" ever hold jam sessions in which to measure the distance they have come in the last twenty years? Or have we really made any headway at all?

I'll be right eager to see your article in the CHRISTIAN CENTURY.[39] Let me know when it appears.

I think this deal of featuring me in DIALOGUE is a joke, no matter which way you look at it.[40]

Thanks again for writing,

Source: Levi Peterson's Collection.

To *Mary Washington*, August 26, 1974

1731 South 1400 East, Salt Lake City, Utah
84105 August 26/74

Millie Washington,

I'm so thrilled and excited that I just have to tell you. Last night Jeff Johnson[41] brought a couple of researchers in to visit with me, and with them a letter in the handwriting of Emma,[42] dated May 17, 1879, in which she sends to John Nuttall a draft from John W. Young[43] on John Taylor for the sum of five hundred dollars in payment for her interest in the ferry.[44] She writes a beautiful hand. The signature on the attached receipt is so full of flourishes that it is hard to decode, but the last two letters seem to be WY. /JWY/

This is doubly important, since our friend from Arizona insists that Emma got nothing from her sale of the Ferry. In one sense, he is right, because after the driving of the stock such a long distance, they were scattered and many stolen in the Indian uprising. But she did get a check from John Taylor for the $500.00.

I think that I may be able to take time off now, or within the next few weeks, if we really feel that we should go. It may be that we can get some of the items we need for just writing for them, and save ourselves the trip, though there is an advantage in actually being there. I leave the decision on this up to you. I'll cooperate.

I may value this letter too highly, but to me the handwriting is almost as important as the words . . . Emma had a good education.

Called away by people at the front door, then by the dear Relief Society Sisters. Now that I've got my calendar from the wall, I find a commitment on Sept. 1 and one on Sept 7th—Nothing in between. and nothing after.

Drop me a note—call me collect. Or I'll give you a ring on Sunday, Sept 1. . . . . I shouldn't get so high over just a letter, I guess, but that's the way I am. Old & slightly demented. Eager to get this into print before I kick-off. Maybe not all printed & bound, but ready for the printers and binders.

Best love,

Source: Levi Peterson's Collection.

To *David S. Grow*,[45] December 16, 1974

1731 South 1400 East
Salt Lake City, Utah 84105
December 16/74

Dr. David S. Grow
P.O. Box 202 373-4000
Provo, Utah 84601

Dear Bro. Grow:

Your letter of Dec. 8 caught up with me here yesterday. For a number of years now, Salt Lake City has been my home. My Mother was in Idaho visiting with the family there, so evidently nobody did much about the mail.

About a month ago the Deseret Book Store had me come down and autograph one hundred copies of the Mountain Meadows Massacre, as it seems that the purchasers prefer them signed by the author. I keep none at home for sale, so I'm going in to the store and will have the books mailed out immediately; I'm sorry for the delay.

I'm pleased that more members of the BYU Faculty are no longer calling me "An apostate." I had a daughter and son graduate from there when feeling against me was very strong, and more than one time they stood up in class to tell a Professor that their Mother was NOT an apostate.

I'm very sorry for this delay. I take the bus when I go into town, but we've had another heavy snow last night and this morning so that I haven't ventured out onto it.

All good wishes, and a Happy Christmas to you!

Sincerely,

Source: Levi Peterson's Collection.

To *Editor, Washington County News*, May 26, 1975

1731 South 1400 East, Salt Lake City
May 26, 1975

Editor, Washington County News
St. George, Utah 84770

Dear Sir: You have probably received several letters of protest over the story of ST. GEORGE TEMPLE. . . . TO BE REDEDICATED. The statement, "It was dedicated April 6, 1877, just four months AFTER the death of Brigham Young," is so totally false that I am sure Mr. A. Karl Larsen, Elizabeth Beckstrom,[46] or some other local persons have written to set the record straight.[47]

The diary of Charles L. Walker records the doings in great detail.[48] The ceremony took place on New Year's Day—Jan. 1, 1877. Walker tells of going early to help move benches in. At 12 o'clock noon the doors were opened to the public; he attended one and Bro Charles Smith[49] the other. He listed carefully the songs, the prayers, the speeches with a short summary of each, giving the full four verses and chorus which he himself had composed for this service.

He noted also that "The President had to be carried in a chair owing to his infirmities." We had already learned that Bro. Cottam had built a special chair for this occasion, large enough to be comfortable, and with two braces underneath extending out so that four men could carry it from room to room.

"Brother Brigham was carried up to the Sealing Room . . ." "Here Brigham Young Jr.[50] offered the dedicatory Prayer."

The full minutes take up several pages, but when President Young himself arose to speak at the pulpit . . . "he smote the stand with his walking stick and made the room ring again, and the marks are on the stand and will remain there a testimony to the truth and the great power by which he spoke. . . ." About 1349 people were present.

Another bit of folklore has been passed down in the John D. Lee diaries. Lee was in prison at Fort Cameron[51] when President Young stopped over night, and one of the guards asked if he would not like to face up to him. Lee is reported to have said: "No. Brother Brigham will not out-last me more than six months. I'll settle with him on the other side." Lee was executed on March 13, 1877. Brigham Young died Aug. 29, 1877.

I'm sure that A. Karl Larson will verify this, as well as any of the students of Utah History.

Very sincerely yours,

Source: Levi Peterson's Collection.

To *Ruth Louise Partridge*,[52] December 7, 1975

1731 South 1400 East
Salt Lake City, Utah 84105
December 7, 1975

Ruth Louise Partridge
195 East 400 North
Provo, Utah 84601

Dear Ruth:

I was surprised to receive your wonderful book, NIGHTFALL IN NAUVOO,[53] but I am right in the middle of a project of my own, so I thought I'd let my neighbor read it first. I would just sample it.

Well, I started to read, and I found that I could not just sample it; I must read it all and read it with undivided attention, which I did.

I myself have been interested in the Love-life of Joseph Smith; my copy of the early HISTORICAL RECORD[54] pp 233–234 names twenty-seven wives,[55] so that is the number I have accepted, and since both of my grandfathers had plural families, I knew a little of the everyday problems. My own father predicted the return of the Practice.

Now, when I am asked to speak to the "Special Interest Groups" in our Church, and face an audience of women and older unmarried girls, I wonder if it might not be a good thing. The ratio is about 8 to 1, of lovely single girls and widows, every one of whom would prefer to have a husband, a home of her own, and children.

You have done a masterful presentation of life in the homes of your Partridge family, a picture above price. By the way, I saw no price on the book. That isn't fair, for many people will feel as I do—that they MUST have an extra copy or two to use for gifts.

I'm just guessing, but I'm enclosing a check for $10.50, hoping that will help cover the book you have already sent. I'll gladly pay that much for an extra copy—yes, I'd go $12.50.

But regardless, accept my hearty congratulations for the production of an excellent book.

All good wishes,

Source: Levi Peterson's Collection.

To *Mary L. Bradford,*[56] January 23, 1976

1731 South 14th East
Salt Lake City Utah 84105
January 23, 1976

Mary L. Bradford
4012 North 27th St
Arlington, Va., 22207

My dear Mary Bradford:

As you can tell by my writing, I'm on the down-hill drag. A short, sharp illness has left my fingers less certain. As you know, I never have had a course in typing, but used the "Columbus Method" in my work. "Discover the Key; then land on it!"

There was a time in my life when I often said, "I need only a corner of my own," a place where I can write unmolested, and when necessary, can leave at a moment's notice and return to as I could.... to find everything as I left it. The children all understood that "Behind that door, there is NOTHING for you. Stay out!"

Then in a family there is always the matter of the home pattern being adhered to: prayers, meals, clearing up after, checking each child as he or she leaves for school. Then the blessed silence after 8:30–to last until 11:30. My writing time was best for a two to three-hour period. After that, I'd busy myself with the home duties.

Likewise, if I managed well, I could work-in another stretch of two to 2 ½ hours again. But I found that the wee hours were best of all when I was not nursing a baby, and all were in good health. In periods of sickness or trouble I could not work at all—NOT at all.

As to your question: I was not from Utah; I lived in Nevada, but the geography made little difference: the society was solid Mormon.

I think it is easier now to write in the Church and about the Church now than it was in the early '40's when I began. I kept very quiet about my work. Even pulled the shade down in the East window; the home across the street had many eyes.

As to whether the society helps or hinders—to me it did neither; that is after the MMM appeared. It took more than a year for the dust to clear away from that. Nothing after that made any difference.

I think I lack the creative genius of a novelist; I have tried only biography. Here I believe one must be acquainted with the local mores, the social patterns, the folkways, the family backgrounds—In Utah FAMILY must be spelled in capital letters. In our area everyone took it for granted that if you have the right name, don't worry. If you don't have the right name, marry into it. I'll not name them; you know them yourself.

Only one time in my life have I talked back to an Apostle—told him outright that "Here's where I know, and you do NOT Know, and I will NOT do as you tell me to do:"[57] I wonder if he'll ever forgive me. Probably not, because I still do the same again.

Now, my dear, I know that this is not much help. I believe we must each step to the music of our own inner instrument.

Source: Levi Peterson's Collection.

To *Elaine McPhie*, May 16, 1976

1731 South 1400 East
Salt Lake City, Utah 84105
May 16, 1976

Mrs Elaine McPhie
4302 Snow Mountain Road
Yakima, Wash. 98904

My dear Lady:

I've had quite an experience with these J.D. Lee diaries. I left them in the box, thinking that I had spent so many years of my life with this man that I'd let him rest in peace. Then I picked up his first missionary Diary and started to read. I had read it before and found it interesting, but when I came to write my book, it just wasn't available. I believe the excuse was that one of officials had it, intending to use it himself. Now the going through it this time was a real awakening. This is really something NEW!

I mailed it to my good friend, Peg Gregory, with the remark that she sample it. She was much moved, and her new husband was more enthusiastic than she. Now the idea that we begin at the beginning and gather together all that he wrote, place it in its proper sequence with the proper annotations seems a MUST with them. He even worked out a plan of sorts of how it could be done. While I think his estimated costs are too low if we use first quality paper & binding, I'd be willing to risk a full new edition of three volumes. He thinks that we should have some pledges from members of the family that they support the undertaking by buying copies. It might be necessary to have a deposit in order to get it out.

I enclose a xerox copy of his suggestions. He evidently knows more about publishing than I do, but I think we should consider the plan seriously, and if the different branches of the family have organized, that we talk about this and get their various reactions.

How I wish our good friend Wes Williamson were still here! He would love this.

Why don't you sound out such members as you know might we interested and willing to lend a hand in the sales, a signature, and maybe a small down payment. I'm awkward at this, but I do think that if we undertake it, we should assurance of support.

So-well, God Bless us All !

Source: Levi Peterson's Collection.

To *Fawn M. Brodie*, December 29, 1976

1731 South 1400 East
Salt Lake City, Utah 84105
December 29/76

Dr. F. M. Brodie
Department of History
University of California
Los Angeles, Calif. 90024

Dear F. Brodie

Thank you! Thank you for your generous and scholarly letter to Cynthia Vartan, Editor.[58] It was generous to me, and a thing to her. And in no way could she refute it. I had begun to lose confidence in myself; I'm growing old at too fast a gait; I sometimes think I should lock up this machine, and perhaps talk into a proper device and have someone pick it up on paper.

My little QUICKSAND AND CACTUS was never designed to be anything very exciting or important, but the girls at the Press want me to fill in places before I hand in in. It's just the desert background.

I continue to get material in the mail from the Lee family. Evidently a number of items in Lee's handwriting are in the Historical Society in Tucson, Arizona. I have copies which you may take if you are interested.

His first missionary Diary has also come into my hands. It is interesting and ties right into the years that follow, and are very revealing. None of these have been printed.

As I said, Lee is unlettered, and unlearned, but what he writes comes through well.

For me, this Pulsipher original is as reveling and valuable as any.

I must stop. I'm invited to honor former Senator Frank Moss. I and a few others like me might have got him re-elected. But we didn't.

I myself felt that he represented us well, but that's all water under the bridge now.

Thank you again for taking time out to write to me, I appreciate it very much.

Sincerely,

Source: Levi Peterson's Collection.

To *Trudy McMurrin*,[59] early 1977

Dear Trudy:

Do you know what it is to be in HELL? Well, I'll tell you: It's being in a confusion, where nothing seems important, where there are so many THINGS and nothing seems important, but is to somebody else

It's being in the midst of all kinds of unrelated Things.

When we razed Mother's home to make a place for Karl's new house, they brought everything here and stacked it in the old kitchen and back porch.[60] Gradually, we have been able to get some of it distributed. Mother was out for nearly a month; then when Charity took her over she became lucid and remembered—not things in the immediate past, but those from earlier years. We have tried to distribute her "Things" among the 10 children by having them draw lots for numbered items, and then exchanging between each other. Even so, there is still many.

Then she has become lucid—as clear in her mind as she has ever been. Except for the the two or three months at the YOUNG REST HOME, she remembers everything clearly: birthdays of the grandchildren, the few married out of the Temple, all of whom are remembered in her prayers.

My family decided that it was time for me to get home, too—and in my heart I know they are right. So the Salt Lake City house was sold and the furniture loaded into a block-long van, brought here and unloaded. Beautiful, lovely things cometing wto fill the place. I'm just telling you: I don't want you to comc and see.

Do you have the story of Will's passing? Seems to me that I did for you. If not, Say so, and I'll get it done. After that we can make a brief accounting of the the various members of the family

If you have the story of Will's passing, we can make a quick of everything else. Call me sometime in the wee hours when it wou't cose your shirt.

Source: Levi Peterson's Collection.

To *Guy and Pamela Walker*, September 1, 1978

You NEVER gave your MAILING

346 North Main
St. George, Utah
Sept. i/78

Dear Guy & Pamela Walker, wherever you are:

I owe you more than any apology: An extended trip to Homedale, Idaho, which extended for more than a week.[61] Then a Air trip to Las Vegas which got all stretched to more than a week again, mostly running around in search of shoes and a new dress. Home again by plane, a little "puddle-jumper," which gave me—if not exactly fear, a great feeling of gratitude for the solid earth under me.

Youre interested in THE Mountain Meadow Massacre, I think new material, I take. Well, I can't promise you there. I've had three sets of missionaries come and urge me to take them to to the place and rehearse the whole thing. This, of course, I cannot do. The years of weathering have changed a little, though the general landscape is much the same. And I have written it as well as I can. I'll only refer the person to that.

I thought the thing would die of its weight, but it seems to to do.

But come along, by all means, and I'll do the best I can. I saw lately a review of Fawn Brodie of a writer who criticized my book. She literally tore his work to shreds: he copied from my book verbatim

I don't want to discourage you, but I have Nothing that you cannot find there.

So come along, and I'll do the best I can—which will be to look through my books.

Cordially,

Source: Levi Peterson's Collection.

Notes

Editorial Procedures

1. Levi S. Peterson, *Juanita Brooks: Mormon Woman Historian* (Salt Lake City: University of Utah Press, 1988).
2. These individuals are introduced more fully in the following chapters.

Introduction

1. Juanita Brooks, *The Mountain Meadows Massacre* (Stanford: Stanford University Press, 1950).
2. Juanita Brooks, *John Doyle Lee: Zealot–Pioneer Builder–Scapegoat* (Glendale, CA: Arthur H. Clark, 1961). John D. Lee was a prominent Mormon pioneer to southern Utah, who was eventually the sole individual convicted of mass murder for his role in the Mountain Meadows Massacre and executed by firing squad in 1877.
3. Brooks's life is detailed in Peterson, *Juanita Brooks: Mormon Woman Historian*. Other works that discuss her life and work include Davis Bitton and Leonard J. Arrington, *Mormons and Their Historians* (Salt Lake City: University of Utah Press, 1988), and Gary Topping, *Utah Historians and the Reconstruction of Western History* (Norman: University of Oklahoma Press, 2003).
4. JB to Donald P. Bean, July 11, 1949, Operational Files, Stanford University Press.
5. JB to Charles Kelly, August 27, 1941, MS 100, Marriott Library Special Collections.
6. JB to Austin and Alta Fife, March 6, 1971, Levi Peterson's Collection.
7. Leonard Arrington to JB, December 23, 1955, Juanita Brooks Papers.
8. Emeritus Club Luncheon Program, April 23, 1981.
9. Brooks added to the confusion by asserting in 1974, during her disjointed interview with Davis Bitton and Maureen Ursenbach, as her memory was fading, that neither she nor Will had been asked to do anything in church meetings up to the Sunday before he died, a period of twenty years. She mentioned that he was asked to speak to his priesthood quorum the Sunday before he died, the first time in seven years. Davis Bitton and Maureen

Ursenbach, "Riding Herd: A Conversation with Juanita Brooks," *Dialogue* 9, no. 1 (Spring 1974): 11–33.

10. JB to David S. Grow, December 16, 1974, Levi Peterson's Collection.
11. JB to Hansen, February 6, 1956, Juanita Brooks Papers.
12. JB to A. Russell Mortensen, December 14, 1953, Juanita Brooks Papers.
13. LDS Church institutes are religious-education auxiliaries serving students at higher education institutions.
14. JB to Savoie Lottenville, October 25, 1963, Juanita Brooks Papers.
15. Marion Hanks to JB, November 16, 1965, Juanita Brooks Papers.
16. JB to Marba C. Josephson, April 17, 1962, Juanita Brooks Papers.
17. JB to Ralph H. Lee, December 2, 1970, Levi Peterson's Collection.
18. Melvin C. Johnson, "Just a Housewife? Juanita Brooks," *Journal of Mormon History* 42, no. 2 (April 2016): 214–23.
19. Levi S. Peterson, "In Memoriam: Juanita Brooks," *Sunstone* 13, no. 5 (October 1989): 6–8.
20. JB to Rodello Hunter, June 23, 1972, Levi Peterson's Collection.
21. JB to Ettie Lee, November 28, 1947, Juanita Brooks Papers.
22. JB to Thomas Cheney, September 6, 1971, Levi Peterson's Collection.
23. Bitton and Arrington, *Mormons and Their Historians*; Topping, *Utah Historians.*
24. Topping, *Utah Historians*, 336.
25. Gary Topping, "Women of Letters, A Unique Literary Tradition," in *Women in Utah History*, ed. Patricia Lyn Scott and Linda Thatcher (Logan: Utah State University Press, 2005), 295–323.
26. Douglas D. Alder, *Honoring Juanita Brooks: A Compilation of 30 Annual Presentations from the Juanita Brooks Lecture Series, Dixie State University* (St. George, UT: Dixie State University, 2014).
27. Patty Limerick, "Quicksand, Cactus, and the Power of History in Polarized Times: Bringing Juanita Brooks and Dale L. Morgan Back into the Conversation" (Keynote Address, Utah State Historical Society Conference, Salt Lake City, September 30, 2016).
28. Johnson, "Just a Housewife? Juanita Brooks," 215.
29. Will Bagley, *Blood of the Prophets: Brigham Young and the Massacre at Mountain Meadows* (Norman: University of Oklahoma Press, 2002), 348–64.
30. Ronald W. Walker, Richard E. Turley Jr., and Glen M. Leonard, *Massacre at Mountain Meadows: An American Tragedy* (Oxford: Oxford University Press, 2008). Turley is currently the LDS Church managing director of Public Affairs.
31. Richard E. Turley Jr., *Juanita Brooks "Ahead of Her Time,"* delivered to Alta Club Forum, January 24, 2017 (Salt Lake City: Alta Club, 2017), 27.
32. Brooks, *Mountain Meadows Massacre*. Brooks, *John Doyle Lee: Zealot–Pioneer Builder–Scapegoat*; Juanita Brooks, *Quicksand and Cactus: A Memoir of the Southern Mormon Frontier* (Salt Lake City: Howe Brothers, 1982).

33. Juanita Brooks, "The Outsider," in *Great Western Short Stories*, ed. J. Golden Taylor (Palo Alto: American West Publishing, 1967), 393–404; Juanita Brooks, "The Outsider," in *Westward the Women: An Anthology of Western Stories by Women*, ed. Vicki Piekarski (New York: Doubleday, 1984), 158–67.
34. Juanita Brooks, "The Christmas Tree," in *A Dixie Christmas: Stories of Christmas Past*, ed. Lyman Hafen and Roland Lee (St. George, UT: Publishers Place, 1988), 34–44; Juanita Brooks, "Home Reminiscences of Uncle Will Brooks," in *A Believing People: Literature of the Latter-day Saints*, ed. Richard H. Cracroft and Neal E. Lambert (Provo, UT: Brigham Young University Press, 1974), 94–102.
35. Juanita Brooks, "The Land That God Forgot," in *A Zion Canyon Reader*, ed. Nathan N. Waite and Reid L. Neilson (Salt Lake City: University of Utah Press, 2014), 201–6.

Chapter 1

1. Dale L. Morgan (1914–1971) was one of the preeminent historians of the West and author and editor of numerous books and articles. The bibliography of his published writings is Richard L. Saunders, *Eloquence from a Silent World: A Descriptive Bibliography of the Published Writings of Dale L. Morgan* (Salt Lake City: Caramon Press, 1990). His efforts at Mormon history are included in Richard L. Saunders, *Dale Morgan on the Mormons Collected Works*, parts 1 and 2, *Kingdom in the West, The Mormons and the American Frontier*, vols. 14 and 15 (Norman: Arthur H. Clark, 2012 and 2013). Some of Morgan's letters have been published in John Phillip Walker, *Dale Morgan on Early Mormonism: Correspondence and a New History* (Salt Lake City: Signature Books, 1986).
2. Dale L. Morgan, *Introduction to the Inventory of State Archives of Utah: The State of Deseret* (Salt Lake City: Utah Historical Record Survey, Work Projects Administration, 1940).
3. Brooks is probably referring to the diaries of William Lang (1826–1896), who moved to St. George in 1861.
4. Jacob Hamblin (1819–1886) was a Mormon colonizer, missionary, and liaison to the Native Americans in southern Utah and northern Arizona. An important biography is Todd M. Compton, *A Frontier Life: Jacob Hamblin, Explorer and Indian Missionary* (Salt Lake City: University of Utah Press, 2013).
5. Morgan wrote the recommendation for the fellowship and offered to help her track down sources for the biography. She did not receive the fellowship and after working on the biography for a couple of years it was not completed, though a partly fictionalized biography of Jacob Hamblin based on her 1952 movie script was published as Juanita Brooks, *Jacob Hamblin: Mormon Apostle to the Indians* (Salt Lake City: Westwater Press, 1980).
6. Brigham Young (1801–1877) was president of the LDS Church from 1847 until his death, first governor of Utah Territory, and superintendent of Indian Affairs.

7. Heber C. Kimball (1801–1868) was one of the original members of the Quorum of Twelve Apostles and first counselor to Brigham Young in the First Presidency of the LDS Church from 1847 until his death.
8. Parley P. Pratt (1807–1857) was an early member of the Quorum of Twelve Apostles of the LDS Church and the writer of many early church books and tracts.
9. John D. Lee (1812–1877) was a prominent Mormon pioneer to southern Utah, who was eventually the sole individual convicted for mass murder for his role in the Mountain Meadows Massacre and executed by firing squad in 1877. Juanita Brooks's biography on John D. Lee is *John Doyle Lee: Zealot–Pioneer Builder–Scapegoat.*
10. Maurine Whipple (1903–1992) was a novelist best known for her novel *The Giant Joshua* (Boston: Houghton Mifflin, 1941) about southern Utah and polygamy. She was living in St. George and was a friend of Juanita Brooks at the time. Whipple's biography is Veda Tebbs Hale, *"Swell Suffering": A Biography of Maurine Whipple* (Salt Lake City: Greg Kofford Books, 2011).
11. Charles Kelly (1889–1971) was a historian, writer, and first superintendent of Capitol Reef National Monument.
12. George A. Smith (1817–1875) was a member of the Quorum of Twelve Apostles and First Presidency of the LDS Church. He toured the settlements of southern Utah and gave speeches just prior to the Mountain Meadows Massacre, adding to the war hysteria.
13. Sarah Priscilla Leavitt Hamblin (1841–1927) married Jacob Hamblin as his third wife on September 11, 1857, in Salt Lake City.
14. Albert was from the White Knife band of Shoshonis and Hamblin adopted him in February 1853 when he was about ten years old. He died in 1863. Compton, *A Frontier Life*, 487.
15. Isaac C. Haight (1813–1886) was the LDS Church stake president in Cedar City and conspirator in the Mountain Meadows Massacre.
16. B. H. Roberts actually gives the date of September 11 for the massacre in *A Comprehensive History of the Church of Jesus Christ of Latter-day Saints Century I*, vol. 4 (Salt Lake City: Church of Jesus Christ of Latter-day Saints, 1930), 153–57.
17. Santa Clara is a town in southern Utah near St. George first settled in 1855 as part of the Southern Indian Mission.
18. Samuel Knight (1832–1910) was an early settler in Santa Clara, who served as a counselor with Dudley Leavitt to Jacob Hamblin, president of the Southern Indian Mission.
19. This event occurred on May 25, 1861, during Brigham Young's first visit to southern Utah following the massacre. Brooks, *Mountain Meadows Massacre*, 133.
20. The Journal of Discourses is a twenty-six-volume collection of public sermons by early leaders of the LDS Church published from 1854 to 1886.

21. David H. Morris (1858–1937) was an attorney and judge in St. George who had affidavits concerning the Mountain Meadows Massacre that Brooks failed to see after several attempts. After Morris's death in 1937, the affidavits were donated to the LDS Church where Brooks was again turned away from examining them. The affidavits have been published as Richard E. Turley Jr. and Ronald W. Walker, *Mountain Meadows Massacre: The Andrew Jenson and David H. Morris Collections* (Provo: Brigham Young University Press, 2009).
22. James Godson Bleak (1829–1918) kept a diary of his activities in the St. George area from 1863 to 1901. He also wrote manuscripts on the history of St. George and the Southern Utah Mission.
23. Brooks is probably referring to Lorenzo H. Reid, "Early History of Utah's Dixie" (Master's thesis, Brigham Young University, 1931).
24. Brooks is referring to Whipple, *The Giant Joshua.*
25. James A. Little, *Jacob Hamblin: A Narrative of His Personal Experience, as a Frontiersman, Missionary to the Indians and Explorer, Fifth Book of the Faith-Promoting Series* (Salt Lake City: Juvenile Instructor Office, 1881).
26. Bernard DeVoto (1897–1955), born in Ogden, Utah, was a historian and author of the American West.
27. Short Creek was a small ranching town settled by Mormon fundamentalists in the 1930s. Straddling the state line, it is now known as Colorado City, Arizona, and Hildale, Utah.
28. Joseph Walker (1878–1964) was a doctor in Los Angeles who corresponded with Brooks for a number of years. He was a native of St. George.
29. Brooks visited Morgan in Salt Lake City near the end of March 1942. He took her on a tour of local libraries and archives. Peterson, *Juanita Brooks: Mormon Woman Historian*, 124.
30. George William Beattie and Helen Pruitt Beattie, *Heritage of the Valley: San Bernardino's First Century* (Pasadena: San Pasqual Press, 1939). Morgan wrote of the book, "I now have a copy of that book. I've wanted a copy ever since I first saw it, since it is a definitive study of its kind—and there are precious few of those in Mormon history. Beattie was given access at the Church Historian's office to the official mission journals kept by Richard Hopkins, and also the journals of Lyman and Rich, hence the thirteen chapters he devotes to the Mormons are authoritative." (Morgan to JB, January 1945, Dale L. Morgan Papers.)
31. The biography of her grandfather was published as Juanita Brooks, *Dudley Leavitt: Pioneer to Southern Utah* (St. George: Printed by the author, 1942). Upon receiving a copy of the Leavitt biography, Morgan in typical fashion wrote her a page-long list of comments.
32. Joseph Fish (1840–1926) wrote an autobiography based on his journals that was published in part as John H. Krenkal, *The Life and Times of Joseph Fish, Mormon Pioneer* (Danville, IL: Interstate Printers and Publishers, 1970).

33. This letter was written as Morgan was moving to Washington, DC, to look for employment.
34. M. Wilford Poulson (1884–1969) was Brooks's psychology professor at Brigham Young University and a cocollector of pioneer diaries with Brooks. He had many early diaries transcribed and indexed for the BYU library.
35. Ray B. West, *Rocky Mountain Reader* (New York: E. P. Dutton, 1946).
36. James Farmer (1825–1908) kept a diary of his immigration to Utah in 1853 and his missionary activities.
37. Myron Abbott (1837–1907) recorded his farming activities at Bunkerville, Nevada, in a diary.
38. Henry W. Bigler (1815–1899) wrote of the events of the Mormon Battalion and the discovery of gold in California in his journals.
39. Levi Savage Jr. (1820–1910) recorded his mission to Burma, his travels with the Willie handcart company in 1856, and his life in Utah and Arizona in his journal.
40. Nephi Johnson (1833–1919) attempted to provide Juanita Brooks his account of the Mountain Meadows Massacre before he died, but she arrived at his bedside too late and some of his last words he yelled to her were "Blood! BLOOD! BLOOD!"—the start of Brooks's interest in the massacre.
41. Heber J. Grant (1856–1945) was president of the LDS Church from 1918 to 1945.
42. Brigham or Mormon Tea (*Ephedra nevadensis*) is used as a beverage and a medicine.
43. Priddy Meeks (1795–1886) was a Mormon pioneer and the first doctor in southern Utah.
44. William R. Palmer (1877–1960) was a stake president in Cedar City, a historian who wrote about the Paiute, and a local authority on the Mountain Meadows Massacre.
45. Hurricane is a town in Washington County near St. George founded in 1893.
46. The Brookses traded their house for the Hurricane fruit farm and moved back into their small house on the hill at 346 North Main Street, which would require remodeling. Will's son Walt would live on the farm and manage it. Peterson, *Juanita Brooks: Mormon Woman Historian*, 135.
47. Even with the remodel the house was still small for the Brooks family.
48. Pearson H. Corbett (1900–1964), an LDS Church Institute teacher, was also writing a biography of Jacob Hamblin as a master's thesis at Brigham Young University with a guarantee that it would be published. It was eventually published as Pearson H. Corbett, *Jacob Hamblin, the Peacemaker* (Salt Lake City: Deseret Book Company, 1952).
49. Oose, or yucca, root was used as a substitute for soap.
50. The Slough of Despond is a deep bog in John Bunyan's *The Pilgrims Progress*, into which the Christian sinks under the weight of his sins and his sense of guilt for them.

51. Rachel Judd Page Henderson Hamblin (1821–1865) was a widow who married Jacob Hamblin at Council Bluffs, Iowa, on September 30, 1849. She also had previously been married to John E. Page.
52. Mary Adams Judd Page (1818–1907) was Rachel Hamblin's older sister, who wrote the LDS Church hymn *Ye Who Are Called to Labor.*
53. John E. Page (1799–1867) was a member of the Quorum of Twelve Apostles of the LDS Church and was excommunicated from the church in 1846.
54. Joel E. Johnson (1817–1882) moved to St. George in 1864 or 1865 and was a newspaper proprietor, politician, and businessman.
55. The Native Americans killed at Pipe Spring refers to an incident that occurred in January, 1866, when the local settlers killed seven Paiutes in retaliation for the deaths of James Whitmore and Robert McIntyre, who may have been killed by Navajos.
56. Brooks's Indian article that was so heavily edited by Morgan was published as Juanita Brooks, "Indian Relations on the Mormon Frontier," *Utah Historical Quarterly* 12, nos. 1–2 (January–April 1944): 1–48.
57. This article was published as Juanita Brooks, "Jacob Hamblin: Apostle to the Indians," *Arizona Highways* 19, no. 4 (April 1943): 31–55.
58. Brooks is probably referring to Dale L. Morgan, *The Humboldt: Highland to the West* (New York: Farrar & Rinehart, 1943).
59. Her "Utah Historical piece" is her Indian Relations article.
60. Richard G. Lillard, *Desert Challenge: An Interpretation of Nevada* (New York: Alfred A. Knopf, 1942).
61. Bernard DeVoto, *The Year of Decision: 1846* (Boston: Little, Brown, 1943). Morgan replied, agreeing that *The Year of Decision* was DeVoto's new book, commenting that DeVoto's "account in general of the Mormon migration from Nauvoo is sympathetic, an admirable picture of the facts, and a beautiful job of writing." Morgan to JB, April 21, 1943, Juanita Brooks Papers.
62. The Hamblin-Lee feud was partly over Jacob Hamblin testifying at the second John D. Lee trial that Lee had admitted having cut the throat of a young woman during the Mountain Meadows Massacre. Compton, *A Frontier Life*, 433.
63. Brooks made a trip to Phoenix and Mesa, Arizona, to meet with members of the Hamblin family in March 1943. Peterson, *Juanita Brooks: Mormon Woman Historian*, 136.
64. Members of the Lee family had hard feelings over LDS Church president Heber J. Grant's protest before the Arizona legislature that resulted in the name of the Lee's Ferry Bridge being eventually named the Navajo Bridge.
65. Isaac Morley (1786–1865) was among the first converts to the newly organized LDS Church in Kirtland, Ohio. He immigrated to Utah in 1848 and was the founder of Manti, Utah.
66. Hyrum Smith (1800–1844) was the older brother of Joseph Smith and assistant president of the LDS Church, who was killed with his brother in 1844.

67. Morgan wrote Brooks complaining that Whipple had written him about locating photographs for her picture book on Utah. Morgan told her she could not use the photos from the WPA photo collection since it was still an ongoing project. Whipple turned around and went to the Utah State Historical Society and asked for those photos saying that Morgan had given her permission to use them. Morgan called her "nothing but a dirty doublecrosser." Morgan to JB, July 20, 1943, Juanita Brooks Papers.
68. Whipple's picture-book project was eventually published as Maurine Whipple, *This Is the Place: Utah* (New York: Alfred A. Knopf, 1945).
69. Zion's Cooperative Mercantile Institution.

Chapter 2

1. JB to Hugh Nibley, November 7, 1946, Juanita Brooks Papers.
2. George Washington Brimhall (1814–1895) wrote an autobiography published as *The Workers of Utah* (Provo City, UT: Printed by Enquirer Co., 1889).
3. Chief Walker or Walkara (c. 1808–1855) was the prominent Native American chief of the Timpanogos Band at the time the Mormon pioneers arrived in 1847.
4. Parowan is the county seat of Iron County, Utah, founded in 1851.
5. St. Thomas, Nevada, was located near where the Muddy River flows into the Colorado River, an area now within Lake Mead. It was founded by Mormon settlers in 1865 and then abandoned in 1871.
6. Morgan wrote Brooks that "the frontier is right inside you in a way it never has been, and maybe never will be, in me." Morgan to JB, December 28, 1943, Juanita Brooks Papers. This comment and Brooks's response led Morgan to suggest she write her autobiography. Brooks dropped her other projects and started writing about her childhood in Bunkerville, which became known as *Quicksand and Cactus.*
7. William P. McIntire (1813–1881) was a settler in St. George.
8. Fawn Brodie (1915–1981) was the author of several books and articles including *No Man Knows My History: The Life of Joseph Smith* (New York: Alfred A. Knopf, 1945).
9. Eliza Hamblin was a Shivwits Paiute, who married Jacob Hamblin sometime before October or November 1860 and then was sealed to Hamblin for eternity in the Endowment House on February 14, 1863. She later left Hamblin and married a Shivwits Paiute. Compton, *A Frontier Life*, 487. Members of the LDS Church believe that marriages sealed in the Endowment House or a temple will last an eternity.
10. Marguerite Sinclair was the secretary and treasurer of the Utah State Historical Society and was helping with the editing of Brooks's "Indian Relations on the Mormon Frontier" article.
11. The reference to the Endowment House record of the sealing was included in Brooks's article "Indian Relations on the Mormon Frontier," 42n75.

12. Bunkerville is an unincorporated town across the Virgin River from Mesquite in Clark County, Nevada, where Juanita Brooks was born and raised.
13. The Huntington Library, located in San Marino, California, consists of a large research library, art collection, and botanical gardens established by Henry E. Huntington. Among its holdings is a large collection of Utah and Mormon documents and books. Morgan had informed Brooks that the library had the transcripts of the John D. Lee trials.
14. Morgan's friend was Madeline Reeder McQuown (1906–1975), at the time in San Francisco convalescing from a heart problem.
15. The material she sent Morgan with this letter was the start of her biographical essays. Morgan and Brooks attempted to get the essays published for a number of years in the 1940s. They were not published until 1982, as Brooks, *Quicksand and Cactus.*
16. This letter was the first written to the library, which led to their long relationship with her collecting pioneer diaries and evidently the grant for writing the book on the Mountain Meadows Massacre. Leslie Bliss of the Huntington Library immediately responded to her letter granting her access to the transcripts and asking her about collecting diaries. They had acquired a copy of her biography on her grandfather, Dudley Leavitt, and were impressed. Bliss to JB, February 18, 1944, Juanita Brooks Papers.
17. The trials of John D. Lee concerning his role in the Mountain Meadows Massacre were held at Beaver, Utah, in 1875 (first trial) and 1876 (second trial). The library had the transcripts for both trials.
18. Leslie E. Bliss (1889–1977) was the head librarian at the Huntington Library until his retirement in 1958. This letter represents Brooks's first of many providing the Huntington Library materials to be copied under her appointment to collect diaries as part of the Rockefeller Foundation grant.
19. The handwritten newspaper was *The Vepricula*, published twice a month from May 1864 to June 1865. The four editors were Orson Pratt Jr., George A. Bergen, Charles Lowell Walker, and Joseph Orton.
20. Mark Whiz was the pseudonym for Charles Lowell Walker (1832–1904), who settled in St. George in 1862 where he lived most of his life. His diary was published as A. Karl Larson and Katharine Miles Larson, *Diary of Charles Lowell Walker*, 2 vols. (Logan: Utah State University Press, 1980).
21. The *Millennial Star* was an LDS Church periodical published in England from 1840 to 1970.
22. All letters are from the Juanita Brooks Papers, MSS B103, Utah State Historical Society, unless otherwise noted at the bottom of the letter.
23. John David Pulsipher (1861–1944) was the father of Leonard Ernest Pulsipher, Brooks's first husband.
24. Milkweeds (*Asclepias* spp.) consist of over 140 species.
25. Squawbush or skunkbush sumac (*Rhus trilobata*).
26. The picture book was Whipple's *This Is the Place: Utah.*

27. Harold S. Snow (1897–1972) was the St. George Temple president from 1937 to 1963. He became president during the remodeling of the temple.
28. John M. Higbee (1827–1904) was a counselor to Cedar City Stake president Isaac C. Haight, a major in the Iron County Militia, and one of the leaders at the Mountain Meadows Massacre.
29. Brooks discusses the petition in Brooks, *Mountain Meadows Massacre*, 61.
30. Joel W. White (1831–1914) of Cedar City was a participant in the Mountain Meadows Massacre who testified at both of the John D. Lee trials in 1875–1876.
31. John Wesley Powell (1834–1902) led the 1869 and 1871–1872 expeditions down the Green and Colorado Rivers and adjacent areas in southern Utah. Jacob Hamblin facilitated the expeditions' dealings with the Native Americans.
32. Brooks is referring to the Judge David H. Morris collection consisting of affidavits concerning the Mountain Meadows Massacre that were donated to the LDS Church after Morris's death in 1937. She made several unsuccessful attempts to view these documents.
33. David O. McKay (1873–1970) was the Second Counselor in the First Presidency of the LDS Church at the time of this letter and later the president of the LDS Church from 1951–1970.
34. Joseph Fielding Smith (1876–1972) was a member of the LDS Church Quorum of Twelve Apostles and Church Historian and Recorder at the time of this letter and later the president of the LDS Church from 1970–1972.
35. Robert G. Cleland (1885–1957) was a professor of history at Occidental College from 1912 to 1943 and then research associate at the Huntington Library in charge of the Rockefeller Foundation grant.
36. Brooks evidently wrote a narrative for a movie on Jacob Hamblin in 1952 and submitted it to Warner Brothers for consideration with negative results. It was published as *Jacob Hamblin: Mormon Apostle to the Indians* in 1980.
37. The history of the movie industry in Utah is detailed in James V. D'Arc, *When Hollywood Came to Town* (Layton, UT: Gibbs Smith, 2010). The Parry brothers—Gronway, Chauncey, and Caleb Whitney—were instrumental in bringing the movie industry to Utah.
38. The *Improvement Era* was an LDS Church official magazine from 1897 to 1970.
39. The *Relief Society Magazine* was the official periodical of the Relief Society of the LDS Church from 1915 to 1970.
40. Marba C. Josephson was managing editor of *Improvement Era.*
41. Thomas Dunlop Brown (1807–1874) kept the journal for the Southern Indian Mission, which Brooks eventually published as *Journal of the Southern Indian Mission: Diary of Thomas D. Brown* (Logan: Utah State University Press, 1972).

42. Thales Hastings Haskell (1834–1909) served as part of the Southern Indian Mission and Brooks edited his diary as "Journal of Thales H. Haskell," *Utah Historical Quarterly* 12, nos. 1–2 (January–April 1944): 70–98.
43. Brooks did produce several articles for the *Improvement Era* in the mid- to late 1940s, including a series on Thomas D. Brown and the Southern Indian Mission published as Juanita Brooks "The Southern Indian Mission," *Improvement Era* 48, nos. 4–6 (April, May, and June 1945): 188, 212–15, 262–63, 342, 368–69.
44. This manuscript was what became Brooks, "The Southern Indian Mission."
45. Rufus C. Allen (1827–1915) led the Southern Indian Mission in 1854.
46. Brooks's *Arizona Highways* article on Jacob Hamblin had been reprinted as Juanita Brooks, "Jacob Hamblin: Apostle to the Indians," *Improvement Era* 47, no. 4 (April 1944): 210–11, 249, 251–55. She also published a story about Jacob and Rachel Hamblin's experiences during the Southern Indian Mission as "Ye Who Are Called to Labor," *Improvement Era* 51, nos. 8, 9 (August, September 1948): 498–99, 532–33, 564–65, 593–94, 596–97.
47. Brooks responds to Cleland's offer of a Rockefeller Foundation grant to write the Mountain Meadows Massacre book, but without an increase in her fifty-dollar-per-month stipend that she already received for diary collection.
48. LeRoy R. Hafen (1893–1985), a historian of the American West, was the Colorado state historian and then taught at Brigham Young University.
49. Cleland offered to increase Brooks's stipend from fifty to one hundred dollars per month for diary collection and writing the Mountain Meadows Massacre book.
50. Helen Forsha Hafen was the adopted daughter of David H. Morris. She was the individual who donated the Mountain Meadows Massacre affidavits to the LDS Church in 1938.
51. George Albert Smith (1870–1951) was president of the LDS Church from 1945 to 1951.
52. It was probably the January–April 1944 issue of the *Utah Historical Quarterly* she sent Cleland, which contained her "Indian Relations on the Mormon Frontier" on pages 1–48 and her edited "Journal of Thales H. Haskell" on pages 69–98.
53. Glenn E. Snow (1900–1984) was president of Dixie College in St. George from 1938 to 1950.
54. Daryl and Anna McConkey were Morgan's close friends. Daryl McConkey (1905–1961) spent six months working with Morgan for the Utah Writers' Project, editing *Utah: A Guide to the State* (New York: Hastings House, 1941). Daryl McConkey and Fawn Brodie reviewed Brooks's *Quicksand and Cactus* manuscript.
55. Morgan's review article was "They Happened to Be Mormons," *Saturday Review of Literature* 28, no. 33 (April 18, 1945): 16. The review was of Richard

Scowcoft, *Children of the Covenant* (Boston: Houghton Mifflin, 1945). The review is reprinted in Saunders, *Dale Morgan on the Mormons* 1:247–49.

56. Helen Hafen never wrote the requested letter, which caused a breach between her and Brooks. Turley and Walker, *Mountain Meadows Massacre,* 293.
57. Mabel Jarvis (1888–1955) was a St. George writer, local historian, and a friend of Brooks, who had assisted Brooks with the collecting and copying of pioneer diaries during the 1930s.
58. Jonreed Lauritzen (1902–1979) was an author of several books including *Arrows into the Sun* (New York: Alfred A. Knopf, 1943). His wife was Verda Lauritzen.
59. Zora Smith Jarvis (1881–1969) was a local St. George family historian.
60. Brooks is referring to Charles Kelly's proposed book on the Mountain Meadows Massacre which was never produced.
61. President Smith graciously replied and Brooks met with him. President Smith said he knew nothing about the affidavits and that she would need to visit with David O. McKay.
62. Dale Morgan's review of Fawn Brodie's biography of Joseph Smith appeared as "A Prophet and His Legend," *Saturday Review of Literature* 28, no. 47 (November 24, 1945): 7–8. The review is reprinted in Saunders, *Dale Morgan on the Mormons* 1:251–54. Morgan praises the biography as "the finest job of scholarship yet done in Mormon history and perhaps the outstanding biography in several years—a book distinguished in the range and originality of its research, the informed and searching objectivity of its viewpoint, the richness and suppleness of its prose, and its narrative power."
63. Parley P. Pratt and Orson Pratt (1811–1881) were both original members of the Quorum of Twelve Apostles of the LDS Church and writers. John Taylor (1808–1887) was president of the LDS Church from 1880 to 1887. Willard Richards (1804–1854) was Second Counselor in the First Presidency of the LDS Church from 1847 until his death. Wilford Woodruff (1807–1898) was president of the LDS Church from 1889 to 1898.
64. Thomas Carlyle (1795–1881) was a Scottish philosopher, satirical writer, and historian.
65. Zina Diantha Huntington Jacobs Smith Young (1821–1901) was a president of the Relief Society of the LDS Church and wife of Joseph Smith and later Brigham Young. Eliza Roxcy Snow Smith Young (1804–1887) was a president of the Relief Society of the LDS Church, a poet, and wife of Joseph Smith and later Brigham Young.
66. Emma Hale Smith Bidamon (1804–1879) was the first wife of Joseph Smith. She did not approve of her husband's polygamy.
67. The three Nephites were three disciples of Christ in the Book of Mormon who were blessed by Christ to never taste death so that they could minister to the people. Stories about modern encounters with one or more

of them abound in Mormon folklore. Two publications concerning them are Hector Lee, *The Three Nephites: The Substance and Significance of the Legend in Folklore* (Albuquerque: University of New Mexico Publications in Language and Literature 2, 1949), and Ogden Kraut, *The Three Nephites* (Dugway, UT: Pioneer Press, 1969).

68. She probably retold this story numerous times, and it was published at least twice: once in the interview with Davis Bitton and Maureen Ursenbach in "Riding Herd," 15, and again in Brooks, *Quicksand and Cactus*, 236–37. Another version, dated February 1940, exists in the Juanita Brooks Papers.
69. Milton Reed Hunter (1902–1975) was an author, historian, and a member of the LDS Church's First Council of the Seventies from 1945 to 1975. He received his PhD in history from the University of California, Berkeley in 1935.
70. J. Reuben Clark (1871–1961) was the First or Second Counselor in the First Presidency of the LDS Church from 1934 to his death in 1961.
71. University of Utah.
72. Brigham Young University.
73. J. H. Beadle, *Western Wilds and the Men Who Redeem Them: An Authentic Narrative* (Cincinnati: Jones Brothers, 1877).
74. The first edition of the book was actually in 1877. It went through several printings with various publishers in the late 1870s and early 1880s.
75. Samuel Knight (1832–1910) was a member of the Southern Indian Mission, helped build the early fort at Santa Clara, was a participant in the Mountain Meadows Massacre, and testified in John D. Lee's second trial of 1876.
76. C. P. Lyford, *The Mormon Problem: An Appeal to the American People* (New York: Phillips & Hunt, 1886).
77. Philip Klingensmith (1815–1881) was one of the first settlers in Iron County, Utah, was the bishop of Cedar City 1852–1859, and was a participant in the Mountain Meadows Massacre. He testified in John D. Lee's first trial in 1875. An account of his life is given in Anna Jean Backus, *Mountain Meadows Witness: The Life and Times of Bishop Philip Klingensmith* (Spokane: Arthur H. Clark, 1995).
78. Milo Andrus (1814–1893) was an early leader in the LDS Church. He was bishop in Nauvoo, stake president in St. Louis, and a member of the Quorum of Seventy. He eventually settled in St. George.
79. Jesse Gove, *The Utah Expedition, 1857–1858* (Concord: New Hampshire Historical Society, 1928), 284–85. Gove records that Milo Andrus cut the "throat from ear to ear" of his third wife in 1857. However, Andrus's third wife was Lucy Loomis Tuttle Andrus, who was born in 1822 and died in 1890.
80. Charles Kelly and Hoffman Birney, *Holy Murder: The Story of Porter Rockwell* (New York: Minton, Balch, 1934), 137. They note that a Milo Andrews cut the throat of his third wife with the help of Orrin Porter Rockwell

during the Reformation of the mid-1850s. They reference Fanny Stenhouse, *Tell It All: The Story of a Life's Experience in Mormonism* (Hartford: A. D. Worthington, 1874), and note that virtually every account of the Reformation period cites the Andrews affair. The "Milo Andrews" in these accounts is probably a misspelling of "Milo Andrus."

81. William Hickman, *Brigham's Destroying Angel* (New York: Geo. A. Crofutt, 1872).
82. Waddington L. Cook (1860–1949) was a court reporter whom Judge Jacob Boreman of the Lee trials asked to transcribe the Adam Patterson shorthand notes of the two John D. Lee trials. Cook completed the transcript with the help of Josiah Rogerson. The various transcripts of the two Lee trials are published as Richard E. Turley Jr., Janiece L. Johnson, and LaJean Purcell Carruth, *Mountain Meadows Massacre Collected Legal Papers*, 2 vols. (Norman: University of Oklahoma Press, 2017).
83. Albert E. Miller (1873–1967) was the mayor of St. George and an author and historian.
84. Brooks is referring to Morgan's negative review of Maurine Whipple's book *This Is the Place: Utah*, which appeared as "Scenic Backdrop with People" in the *Saturday Review of Literature* 28, no. 45 (November 10, 1945): 17. The review is reprinted in Saunders, *Dale Morgan on the Mormons* 2:249–51. Morgan writes that the book "is a reflection of Miss Whipple's lusty, gusty, sometimes bumptious personality." He accuses her of lifting lines from McConkeys' volume *Utah: A Guide to the State*, and Nels Anderson's *Desert Saints: The Mormon Frontier in Utah* (Chicago: University of Chicago Press, 1942) without acknowledgment, copying the good as well as "a number of their errors." In a response to a letter he received from Whipple complaining about the review, Morgan carefully documented page by page where she plagiarized from *Utah: A Guide to the State*. Morgan to JB, December 15, 1945, Dale L. Morgan Papers.
85. B. H. Roberts made a study of the parallels between the Book of Mormon and Ethan Smith's *View of the Hebrews* (Poultney, VT: Smith and Shute, 1825). It has been printed in Brigham D. Madsen, *B. H. Roberts Studies of the Book of Mormon* (Urbana: University of Illinois Press, 1985), 323–44.
86. Clark gave the speech at the installation of Howard S. McDonald as the new president of BYU. Morgan in his letter quoted from the speech: "He wounds, maims and cripples a soul who raises doubts about or destroys faith in the ultimate truths. God will hold such a one strictly accountable." Morgan to JB, December 15, 1945, Juanita Brooks Papers.
87. Samuel Stucki (1824–1910) emigrated from Switzerland and settled in Santa Clara in 1861.
88. Her book *The Great Joshua* was originally planned to be a trilogy. She wrote about two hundred pages of the sequel entitled *Cleave the Wood*. Veda

Tebbs Hale, "In Memoriam, Maurine Whipple," *Sunstone* 88 (August 1992): 13–15.

89. E. P. Dutton and Company was a book publishing company in Boston that appears to have turned down Brooks's *Quicksand and Cactus* manuscript.
90. Hugh Nibley, *No Ma'am That's Not History: A Brief Review of Mrs. Brodie's Reluctant Vindication of a Prophet She Seeks to Expose* (Salt Lake City: Bookcraft, 1946).
91. "Appraisal of the So-Called Brodie Book" (Salt Lake City: Church News, May 11, 1946).
92. Albert Ernest Bowen (1875–1953) was a member of the Quorum of Twelve Apostles of the LDS Church from 1937 to 1953. Henry A. Smith was the editor of the *LDS Church News* from 1931 to 1968 and press secretary to the First Presidency. John A. Widtsoe (1872–1952) was a member of the Quorum of Twelve Apostles of the LDS Church from 1921 to 1952.
93. Daryl Chase (1901–1984) was director of the LDS Church's Logan Institute of Religion and president of the Utah State University from 1954 to 1968.
94. Utah State Agricultural College.
95. J. Earl Arrington (1895–1986) lived many years in New York City and collected over forty thousand books, emphasizing American history from 1800–1860 and the early years of the LDS faith. He donated his collection to BYU.
96. It was published as J. Cecil Alter, "Journal of Captain Albert Tracy, 1858–1860," *Utah Historical Quarterly* 13 (1945): 1–128.
97. Brooks is discussing the *Utah Historical Quarterly* editorial policy.
98. Samuel Whitney Richards (1824–1909) was a member of the State of Deseret Constitutional Convention, Salt Lake City Council, and Utah Territorial Legislature, and was president of the European Mission for the LDS Church in 1857–1858.
99. Claire Noall (1892–1971) was the author of several books.
100. Several versions of the Henry W. Bigler journals exist. This copy was probably the ledger version which consists of his journals that he copied into a ledger in 1898.
101. Franklin Dewey Richards (1821–1899) was a member of the Quorum of Twelve Apostles of the LDS Church from 1849 until his death.
102. Brooks made another failed attempt to see the Morris affidavits concerning the Mountain Meadows Massacre. She got only as far as Joseph Anderson who turned her down.
103. Joseph Anderson (1889–1992) was the secretary to the First Presidency of the LDS Church from 1921 to 1970 and then an assistant to the Quorum of Twelve Apostles and a member of the First Quorum of the Seventy.
104. The telegram was actually from R. C. Lund, a prominent southern Utah politician and mayor of St. George, to Isaac C. Macfarlane, dated February 16, 1896, requesting that the recipient work with Morris on dismissing

charges against John M. Higbee. Turley and Walker, *Mountain Meadows Massacre*, 295.

105. The Morris affidavit collection as published by Turley and Walker contains documents related to the campaign to dismiss the twenty-year-old indictment against Higbee; an affidavit by Lucy Walker Smith Kimball citing her plural marriage to Joseph Smith; the Samuel Knight affidavit; and the two Nephi Johnson affidavits. Ibid., 292–334.
106. Virginia Sorensen, *On This Star* (New York: Reynal & Hitchcock, 1946).
107. L. M. McQuarrie, *Half Angel* (Garden City, NY: Doubleday, 1946).
108. Charles Kelly, "Lee's Lost Gold Mine," *Desert Magazine* 9, no. 10 (August 1946): 9–11.
109. John Cradlebaugh (1819–1872) was a United States associate justice who convened a grand jury in Provo, Utah, concerning the Mountain Meadows Massacre and then continued his investigations at the site of the massacre in 1859.
110. James G. Bleak kept the official records of the Southern Utah Mission known as the *Annals of the Southern Utah Mission, Books A and B*, which cover happenings in southern Utah to 1877.
111. Jacob Forney (1829–1865), superintendent of Indian Affairs for Utah, gathered the children surviving from the Mountain Meadows Massacre that were living with Mormon families and united them with extended families in Arkansas and other states.
112. *Journal History of the Church of Jesus Christ of Latter-day Saints*, LDS Church Archives, Salt Lake City, is Andrew Jenson's extensive compilation of LDS Church historical information.
113. William H. Rogers (1824–1907) was the federal deputy marshal who assisted Jacob Forney in gathering the surviving children.
114. The *Valley Tan*, an alternative newspaper to the predominantly Mormon press, was published from 1858 to 1860.
115. The record Brooks is referring to is probably the journal of George Mayer (1805–1895), who was a resident of Spanish Fork, Utah, most of his life.
116. The manuscript written in 1839 by Reed Peck (1814–1894), a disaffected Mormon, contains a firsthand account of the Mormon settlement in Missouri, 1836–1839.
117. Brodie followed her advice and submitted the manuscript to the Huntington Library for photostating.
118. Besides being a poet and a teacher, Vesta Pierce Crawford (1899–1983) was editorial secretary in 1945 and then associate editor in 1947 of the *Relief Society Magazine*.
119. Brooks and Vesta Crawford are mentioned in the acknowledgments of Brodie's Joseph Smith biography for allowing her to view Mormon documents.
120. Newburn Isaac Butt (1890–1980) was a researcher and assistant professor at the Brigham Young University library, who produced many indexes to LDS Church periodicals and histories.

121. Hugh Nibley (1910–2005) was an author, Mormon apologist, and professor at Brigham Young University.
122. Brigham Henry Roberts (1857–1933) was a prolific writer, historian, politician, and member of the First Council of the Seventy of the LDS Church.
123. The United Order was an organization through which the early members of the LDS Church sought to live the law of consecration, a form of communalism. It was begun in 1831 and terminated after a few years, then attempted again in Utah Territory mostly in the 1870s.
124. Anthony Woodward Ivins (1852–1934) was a member of the Quorum of Twelve Apostles of the LDS Church beginning in 1907 and a member of the First Presidency from 1921 until death.
125. Ettie Lee (1917–1974) became wealthy through the buying and selling of real estate and founded the Ettie Lee Youth and Family Services. Her biography is Ora Pate Stewart, *Tender Apples: A Biography of Ettie Lee* (Salt Lake City: Deseret Book Company, 1972). This first letter from Brooks to Ettie Lee, a descendent of John D. Lee, was the start of a long and fruitful relationship.

Chapter 3

1. JB to Donald P. Bean, July 11, 1949, Operational Files, Stanford University Press.
2. JB to Stanton Schmutz, January 18, 1949, Juanita Brooks Papers.
3. Harold B. Lee to JB, January 24, 1949, Juanita Brooks Papers.
4. Geneva Day Larsen (1885–1975) and Bent Franklin Larsen (1882–1970) were friends of Brooks in Provo. She had lived with Geneva while attending Brigham Young University in the mid-1920s. Bent was an art professor and head of the art department at the university.
5. Dale Morgan, *The Great Salt Lake* (Indianapolis: Bobbs-Merrill Company, 1947).
6. The last chapter of *Great Salt Lake* is entitled "Door Upon the Future" and briefly discusses the Mormon people and the LDS Church.
7. George Laub (1814–1880) kept a diary from his days in Nauvoo through his life in southern Utah, a source used by Brooks for her Mountain Meadows Massacre book.
8. Parley P. Pratt was killed by the estranged husband, Hector McLean, of his twelfth wife, Eleanor McLean, on May 13, 1857, near Van Buren, Arkansas. Some researchers think his murder played a role in events leading to the Mountain Meadows Massacre a few months later.
9. Roberts, *Comprehensive History*, 155.
10. Andrew Love Neff, *History of Utah 1847–1869* (Salt Lake City: Deseret News Press, 1940).
11. John Stillman Woodbury (1825–1914) recorded in his diary for July 2, 1857, that he had read the news in the paper while in Carson Valley on his way to the Hawaiian Islands. Brooks, *Mountain Meadows Massacre*, 37.

12. Andrew Sproul (1816–1886) was on the plains in charge of the LDS Church cattle when he wrote the quote in his pocket diary on May 26, 1857. Brooks, *Mountain Meadows Massacre*, 37. Erastus Snow (1818–1888) was a member of the Quorum of Twelve Apostles of the LDS Church from 1849 until his death and was in charge of the southern Utah settlements. James A. Little (1822–1908) was author of several books on the Mormons.
13. Enterprise is a small town in Washington County about forty miles north of St. George, Utah. La Verkin is a small town in Washington County about twenty-four miles northeast of St. George. Hurricane is a small town in Washington County about twenty miles northeast of St. George and about four miles south of La Verkin.
14. The "Centennial activities" were for the Washington County celebration of the Utah Centennial 1847–1947 held April 9–15, 1947. Brooks wrote the text for the *Souvenir Edition, Washington County Program* that was prepared by the Washington County Centennial Committee.
15. Croesus (595 BC–c. 546 BC), the king of Lydia, was renowned for his wealth.
16. Jesse N. Smith (1834–1906) was a Mormon pioneer, colonizer, and LDS Church stake president in Arizona.
17. LeRoi C. Snow (1876–1962), a son of LDS Church president Lorenzo Snow, wrote a number of articles for the *Improvement Era*, including one of his father's experience of seeing Jesus Christ in the Salt Lake Temple, "An Experience of My Father's," *Improvement Era* 36, no. 11 (September 1933): 677, 679.
18. Brooks was frustrated over the slow progress of the review of her Mountain Meadows Massacre manuscript by the Huntington Library.
19. The John L. Ginn manuscript, *Early Perils of the Far West: The Mountain Meadows Massacre and Other Tragedies Incident to the Mormon Rebellion and Indian Wars of 1857–1858*, is listed in Brooks's *Mountain Meadows Massacre* bibliography, with copies at the LDS Church History Department and in the Coe Collection, Yale University Library.
20. A version of the Nephi Johnson affidavit was included as Appendix I in Brooks, *Mountain Meadows Massacre*; the John M. Higbee account was included as Appendix II. The Jacob Hamblin "Journal" is listed in Brooks's *Mountain Meadows Massacre* bibliography as being located at the LDS Church History Department.
21. Kate Bearnson Carter (1891–1976) was an editor, historian, and longtime president of the Daughters of Utah Pioneers. Brooks wrote her after Carter sent letters to those in her organization discouraging them from sharing original diaries with non-Utah archives such as the Huntington Library.
22. Brooks is probably referring to Cheever's grandfather, George Laub (1814–1880).
23. Hector Lee (1908–1992) established the Utah Humanities Research Foundation at the University of Utah and was a collector and analyst of Mormon folklore.

24. The play *Promised Valley* was performed for the Utah Centennial from July 21 through August 10, 1947. The Broadway playwright Arnold Sundgaard (1909–2006) wrote the dialogue and lyrics.
25. Helen Cortez Stafford, *Sweet Love Remembered* (Salt Lake City: Deseret Book Company, 1946).
26. Mabel Harmer, *The story of the Mormon Pioneers* (Salt Lake City: Deseret News Press, 1944).
27. Works Progress Administration.
28. Historic Records Survey of the Works Progress Administration.
29. Wallace Stegner (1909–1993) was a novelist, short-story writer, and historian who won the Pulitzer Prize and U.S. National Book Award. Stegner offered to help Brooks find a publisher for her Mountain Meadows Massacre manuscript.
30. Manetta Prince Henrie (1884–1986) was a granddaughter of John D. Lee and an author of several genealogy books.
31. "Record of Seventies, Book B, 1844–1848" is now located at the LDS Church History Library.
32. These John D. Lee diaries were typically closed to research at the LDS Church Historian's Office.
33. Nancy Bean Lee (1826–1903), Louise Free Lee (1824–1886), Sarah Caroline Williams Lee (1830–1907), Abigail Woolsey Lee (1786–1848), and Rachel Andora Woolsey Lee (1825–1912) were wives of John D. Lee.
34. Sidney Rigdon (1793–1876) was the First Counselor in the First Presidency of the LDS Church under Joseph Smith. He later competed with Brigham Young for the leadership of the LDS Church following the murder of Joseph Smith.
35. Mary Vance [Polly] Young Lee (1817–1893) and Lavina Young Lee (1820–1883) were sisters who married John D. Lee on February 27, 1847.
36. Joseph Hyrum Woolsey (1826–1886) came to Utah in the Pioneer Company of 1847.
37. A. William Lund (1886–1971) was assistant LDS Church historian for almost sixty years.
38. Stanton Eugene Schmutz (1928–2016) served an LDS mission to the North Central States. Brooks taught him in Sunday School prior to his mission.
39. Joyce Nielsen Schmutz (1931–2014) was Stanton Schmutz's wife.
40. Howard Egan (1815–1878) traveled with John D. Lee to Santa Fe to bring back pay for the Mormon Battalion families. He also brought ammunition from California during the Utah War, was a Pony Express rider, and was a special guard to Brigham Young. His diary was published as William M. Egan, *Pioneering the West, 1846–1878: Major Howard Egan's Diary* (Richmond, UT: Howard R. Egan Estate, 1917).
41. John D. Lee and William Egan actually traveled to Santa Fe in 1846 and received $2,447.32 from battalion members. Norma Baldwin Ricketts,

The Mormon Battalion: U.S. Army of the West, 1846–1848 (Logan: Utah State University Press, 1996), 70–71.

42. Lee gracefully responded to her letter saying that her conclusions of what happened at Mountain Meadows were "obtained from hearsay and rumor rather than from any historical source." He also questioned her inference that John D. Lee was given all the blame to "close the incident once and for all" and that it would be best to avoid any unnecessary discussion of the subject. Lee to JB, January 24, 1949, Juanita Brooks Papers.
43. Lowry Nelson (1893–1986) was a professor of sociology at the University of Minnesota and previous teacher at Brigham Young University, who completed studies of rural communities including various Mormon villages.
44. Juanita Brooks, "The First One Hundred Years of Southern Utah History," *Proceedings of the Utah Academy of Sciences, Arts and Letters* 24 (1946–1947): 71–79. In this paper, she criticized the editorial procedures of the Daughters of Utah Pioneers, whose policy encouraged the removal from edited diaries of anything considered provocative. Brooks insisted that the past needed to be studied in an objective manner and pioneer journals should be reproduced without modification or deletion.
45. Nelson corresponded with the LDS Church First Presidency concerning blacks and the priesthood in 1947. In response to his inquiry, the First Presidency claimed that "from the days of the Prophet Joseph Smith" the doctrine of the church has been that blacks "are not entitled to the full blessings of the Gospel." They were also against the possibility of interracial marriage. First Presidency to Lowry Nelson, July 17, 1947, MS 0115, Marriott Library Special Collections.
46. Gustive Olaf Larson (1897–1978) was an LDS Church Institute teacher, a professor at Brigham Young University, and an author of many books and articles.
47. Donald Bean was director of the Stanford University Press from 1945 to 1956.
48. Brooks is responding to a letter from Bean saying that her Mountain Meadows Massacre study was approved for publication, but the press lacked funds and a guaranteed purchase of a thousand copies would facilitate its publication. Bean to JB, March 10, 1949, Juanita Brooks Papers.
49. Ettie Lee had agreed to the Stanford University Press requirement of a $3,000 advance to publish the Mountain Meadows Massacre book. She devised a plan to put Brooks on her payroll and pay her a monthly stipend to be banked until the press required the money for publishing the book, allowing Lee to claim the payment as a business expense. Peterson, *Juanita Brooks: Mormon Woman Historian*, 197.
50. Brooks attended an *Improvement Era* writing seminar in Salt Lake City where she was the featured speaker on June 16, 1949. Ibid., 199.

51. Mary Moselle Norton Bickley (1901–1973) was a granddaughter of John D. Lee and her sister was Olive Mae Norton LaFevre (1880–1971) of Panguitch, Utah.
52. Memorial Day, the last Monday in May.
53. Bickley's sister, who owned the diary, somehow left it on her sister's bed after she had refused to let her see it.
54. Panguitch, Utah, is the county seat of Garfield County and is about sixty-five miles north of Kanab, Utah.
55. Brooks is responding to the Stanford University Press request for the entire $3,000 payment in advance from Ettie Lee before the publication of her Mountain Meadows Massacre study. Bean to JB, July 8, 1949, Juanita Brooks Papers.
56. Nels Anderson (1889–1986) was a sociologist who worked for various agencies of the federal government in Washington, DC, and abroad including the Works Progress Administration during the 1930s. He first met Brooks in 1933 while he was in St. George working on his book on the history of the Mormons, *Desert Saints: The Mormon Frontier in Utah.*
57. The Arthur H. Clark Company was a publisher of books on the history of the Western United States founded by Arthur Henry Clark (1868–1951). They eventually produced Brooks's biography of John D. Lee, *John Doyle Lee.*
58. Pamela Faust was assistant to the editor at Stanford University Press.
59. Faust proposed deleting two pages that discussed the "analogy drawn between the Mormon emotions and actions of September 1857, and the behavior of American soldiers in the recent war." Faust to JB, November 2, 1949, Juanita Brooks Papers. In her next letter Faust proposed a compromise of deleting about four paragraphs, which Brooks finally accepted. Faust to JB, November 23, 1949, Juanita Brooks Papers.
60. Daniel S. Macfarlane (1837–1914) was a participant in the Mountain Meadows Massacre who prepared an affidavit in 1896, which was published in Brooks's *Mountain Meadows Massacre*, 64.
61. William H. Dame (1819–1884) was the regimental commander of the Iron Military District, who approved the order authorizing attacks at Mountain Meadows.
62. Brooks is responding to a letter from Stanford University Press asking her for the index for her book.
63. Herbert E. Gregory (1869–1952) was a Yale University geologist, who studied and wrote several major monographs on the geology of the Colorado Plateau of Utah and Arizona.
64. James Henry Martineau (1828–1918) was a settler in Parowan, who was off on a scouting expedition in the mountains east of Parowan at the time of the Mountain Meadows Massacre. His journal was published as Donald G.

Godfrey and Rebecca S. Martineau-McCarty, *An Uncommon Pioneer: The Journals of James Henry Martineau, 1828–1918* (Provo: Religious Studies Center, Brigham Young University, 2008).

65. Brooks is probably referring to Charles W. Willden (1806–1883), who was in Cedar City at the time of the Mountain Meadows Massacre and testified in an 1882 affidavit that he witnessed events surrounding the immigrant company's arrival in Cedar City. The affidavit is printed in Turley and Walker, *Mountain Meadows Massacre*, 134–40.
66. Levi Stewart Udall (1891–1960) served on the Arizona Supreme Court, including as Chief Justice from 1947 until his death. He was a member of the LDS Church.
67. *Improvement Era*.

Chapter 4

1. JB to Robert G. Cleland, April 29, 1951, Juanita Brooks Papers.
2. Albert R. Lyman to Charity Rowley, January 17, 1951, Juanita Brooks Papers.
3. JB to Albert R. Lyman, February 12, 1951, Juanita Brooks Papers.
4. JB to Charles Kelly, January 5, 1952, Juanita Brooks Papers.
5. Dale Morgan to JB, April 26, 1951, Juanita Brooks Papers.
6. Joseph Fielding Smith to Frank H. Jonas, January 24, 1951, MS 508, Marriott Library Special Collections. Vardis Fisher and Maurine Whipple were authors of novels about Mormons. Only Brodie's work was historical nonfiction.
7. Milton R. Hunter to Frank H. Jonas, February 2, 1951, MS 508, Marriott Library Special Collections.
8. Stephen L. Richards to JB, January 7, 1952, WSU Levi Peterson Collection.
9. JB to Stephen L. Richards, January 15, 1952, WSU Levi Peterson Collection.
10. Irvin P. McQuarrie (1891–1961) was the chair of the Department of Pediatrics at the University of Minnesota from 1930 to 1955. He was a native of St. George and one of Brooks's teachers in Bunkerville.
11. Joseph Walker.
12. Michael Harrison (1897–2005) of Sacramento, California, was a private book collector of Western Americana, who formed the Michael and Margaret B. Harrison Western Research Center at the University of California at Davis library.
13. January 28, 1951.
14. The *Western Humanities* review panel consisted of LeRoy Hafen, Robert Athearn, Myrl V. Walker, and L. H. Kirkpatrick and appeared in the *Western Humanities Review* 5, no. 2 (Spring 1951): 209–15.
15. Heinrich Lienhard was a Swiss who wrote a journal of his overland trail experiences across the Hastings Cutoff in 1846. A portion of his reminiscences was published as a section in John Paul von Grueningen, *The Swiss in the United States* (Madison, WI: Swiss-American Historical Society, 1940).

16. Dale Morgan's editing of the Heinrich Lienhard journal was published in J. Roderick Korns, "West from Fort Bridger: The Pioneering of the Immigrant Trails Across Utah, 1846–50, edited by Dale L. Morgan," *Utah Historical Quarterly* 19 (1951).
17. The two Harvard students were probably Thomas F. O'Dea and Irving Telling. O'Dea spent five months living in Ramah, New Mexico, and produced a PhD dissertation, "Mormon Values: The Significance of a Religious Outlook for Social Action" (Harvard University, 1953), and later *The Mormons* (Chicago: University of Chicago Press, 1957). Irving Telling wrote the PhD dissertation "New Mexico Frontiers: A Social History of the Gallup Area, 1881–1901" (Harvard University, 1952). Their studies are discussed in Howard M. Bahr, *Saints Observed: Studies of Mormon Village Life, 1850–2005* (Salt Lake City: University of Utah Press, 2014), 178–79.
18. Will Brooks retired as postmaster of St. George on May 1, 1951, after serving seventeen years. Peterson, *Juanita Brooks: Mormon Woman Historian*, 212.
19. "Thou shalt not covet." Exodus 20:17.
20. Albert Robison Lyman (1880–1973), from Blanding, Utah, was the author of several historical fiction and nonfiction books.
21. Charity Leavitt Rowley (1899–1999) was a sister of Juanita Brooks living in Blanding, Utah. Lyman wrote the review at the request of Charity.
22. Procter Hancock Robinson (1842–1857) died on September 21, almost a month after the Arkansan immigrants camped at Corn Creek, where he was allegedly poisoned.
23. Colonel Albert Sidney Johnston (1803–1862) led the U.S. troops into Utah in what is known as the Utah War in 1857–1858.
24. Brooks met with Cleland on Saturday, May 5, after an all-night bus ride, to discuss the possibility of publishing all the John D. Lee diaries. She returned with typescripts of the Lee diaries held at the Huntington. Peterson, *Juanita Brooks: Mormon Woman Historian*, 212. This attempt was the first in a lifelong quest to publish all the Lee diaries together.
25. The Brookses moved to their Hurricane fruit farm for the summer. Peterson, *Juanita Brooks: Mormon Woman Historian*, 212.
26. Brooks was unable to locate an official record of the date of Lee's excommunication. Brooks, *John D. Lee*, 294. Several apostles' journals mention the excommunication of John D. Lee on October 8, 1870.
27. Escalante is a city in Garfield County in south-central Utah.
28. Her visitors included Edward Banfield, a professor at the University of Chicago, and Henri Mendras, a graduate student at the University of Paris, who were conducting sociological studies of the Mormon villages of Gunlock and Virgin. The study of Washington County was apparently not published. Bahr, *Saints Observed*, 176–77.

29. Tuweep is along the north rim of the Grand Canyon in the Arizona Strip.
30. The Towers of Tumurru are at Colorado City.
31. G. Homer Durham (1911–1985) was president of Arizona State University, member of LDS Church Presidency of the Seventy, LDS Church historian, and author and editor of many books.
32. Howard Driggs (1873–1963) was an English professor at the University of Utah and author and editor of over fifty books.
33. Albert E. Miller, *The Immortal Pioneers* (St. George, UT: Privately published, 1946).
34. Jesse Wentworth Crosby (1820–1893) was a pioneer to Utah in 1847, who settled in St. George in 1861. He conducted a freighting business between California and St. George and may have brought the cannon to St. George during these activities.
35. George Washington Bean (1831–1897) was a pioneer to Utah in 1847, a Native American interpreter, and a prosecuting attorney and probate judge. In 1849, he had an accident with a cannon, which caused his left arm to be amputated three inches below the elbow.
36. Mormon apostle Parley P. Pratt led an exploring expedition to southern Utah near the future town of St. George during the winter of 1849–1850. The documents resulting from that expedition are published as William B. Smart and Donna T. Smart, *Over the Rim: The Parley P. Pratt Exploring Expedition to Southern Utah, 1849–1850* (Logan: Utah State University, 1999).
37. Levi Edgar Young (1874–1963) was one of the first seven presidents of the Quorum of Seventy of the LDS Church and a history professor at the University of Utah.
38. Urim and Thummim is an instrument prepared of God through which revelation may be received. Joseph Smith said he used an Urim and Thummim consisting of a pair of stones set in a silver bow fastened to a breastplate to translate the Book of Mormon.
39. Warren Foote (1817–1903) came to Utah in 1850, eventually settled in St. Joseph and St. Thomas as part of the Muddy Mission in 1865, and then moved to Glendale in Long Valley, Kane County, Utah, in 1871 when the Muddy Mission was discontinued.
40. Elias Smith (1804–1888) came to Utah in 1851 and was the editor of the *Deseret News* and probate judge of Salt Lake County.
41. Brian Foy (1896–1977) was an American film producer and director, producing 214 films between 1924 and 1963.
42. James Holt Haslam (1825–1913) was the express rider who delivered a message from Isaac Haight at Cedar City to Brigham Young in Salt Lake City and returned to Cedar City with a message from Brigham Young during the Mountain Meadows Massacre.

43. William Henry Reeder Jr. (1884–1961) was a municipal judge in Ogden, Utah. Some general authorities of the LDS Church including Milton R. Hunter claimed that Reeder gave them a negative review of Brooks's Mountain Meadows Massacre book in response to a questionnaire from Frank H. Jonas of the University of Utah.
44. Frank Herman Jonas (1906–1982) was a professor of political science at the University of Utah. He sent a questionnaire to general authorities of the LDS Church requesting their comments on Brooks's Mountain Meadows Massacre book.
45. Caxton Printers or Caxton Press is a book publisher in Caldwell, Idaho, founded in 1925. Caxton Press appears never to have produced a book on the Mountain Meadows Massacre.
46. John A. Widtsoe (1872–1952), Spencer W. Kimball (1895–1985), Delbert L. Stapley (1896–1978), and Harold B. Lee (1899–1973) were all members of the Quorum of Twelve Apostles of the LDS Church at the time.
47. Stephen L. Richards (1879–1959) was the First Counselor in the First Presidency of the LDS Church. He was originally called to the Quorum of Twelve Apostles in 1917 and then to the First Presidency in 1951.
48. Mary Leavitt Frehner (1915–2003) was Juanita Brooks's youngest sister.
49. Samuel W. Taylor, *Family Kingdom* (New York: McGraw-Hill, 1951).
50. Olive Woolley Burt (1894–1981) published at least forty-six books including many children's books. She was also a teacher and newspaper editor.
51. Mark E. Petersen (1900–1984) was a member of the Quorum of Twelve Apostles of the LDS Church from 1944 until his death.
52. Preston Nibley (1884–1966) was an assistant LDS Church historian for a few years and an author of several books on the history of the LDS Church.
53. Paul Dayton Bailey (1906–1987) was the owner/publisher of Westernlore Press and the writer of many books focusing on the Western American experience, including *Jacob Hamblin: Buckskin Apostle* (Los Angeles: Westernlore Press, 1948).
54. Mexican Hat is a small town on the San Juan River in south-central San Juan County, Utah, near the northern edge of the Navajo Reservation.
55. Finlay McDermid (1905–1987) was a television series writer.
56. The Brookses moved into the Lyn Mor motel, which was renamed the Lee Motel, during the Christmas holidays of 1951 to manage the motel for Ettie Lee. Peterson, *Juanita Brooks: Mormon Woman Historian*, 220. The hotel was located at 420 East St. George Boulevard in St. George.
57. The bridge was named the Navajo Bridge. It crosses the Colorado River at Marble Canyon near Lee's Ferry; the original bridge was constructed between 1927 and 1929.
58. Leonard H. Kirkpatrick (1907–1962) was the head librarian at the University of Utah in the 1940s and 1950s.

59. Russel Swensen (1902–1987) was a professor of history at Brigham Young University specializing in ancient and medieval history.
60. Ralph James Hafen (1925–2012) was a native of St. George who practiced law in Salt Lake City for fifty years.
61. In early September 1951, Brooks and Palmer spoke at the Mountain Meadows Massacre monument to a group attending the Utah Conference on Higher Education at Cedar City. Peterson, *Juanita Brooks: Mormon Woman Historian*, 213.
62. Brooks mentions in footnote 4 on page 122 of the 1950 edition of *Mountain Meadows Massacre* that George Wood killed Olive Coombs and was not brought to civil trial. Footnote 4 on page 164 of the second edition of *Mountain Meadows Massacre* (University of Oklahoma Press, 1962) says he was convicted and sentenced to the Territorial Penitentiary.
63. The Bull Valley Snort story was actually written by John M. Higbee in Salt Lake City in February 1894. Brooks included it as Appendix II in *Mountain Meadows Massacre.*

Chapter 5

1. Robert Glass Cleland and Juanita Brooks, *A Mormon Chronicle: The Diaries of John D. Lee, 1848–1876* (San Marino, CA: Huntington Library, 1955).
2. J. K. Fancher to JB, September 10, 1955, Juanita Brooks Papers.
3. Leonard Arrington to JB, December 13, 1955, Juanita Brooks Papers.
4. JB to Leonard Arrington, December 28, 1955, Juanita Brooks Papers.
5. Anthony I. Bentley to JB, January 28, 1956, Juanita Brooks Papers.
6. JB to Anthony Bentley, February 2, 1956, Juanita Brooks Papers.
7. Brooks is accepting the offer from the Huntington Library of a stipend of $150 per month for twenty-four months to edit four of the John D. Lee diaries.
8. Brooks is describing the Short Creek raids on the polygamists by Arizona officials in July 1953.
9. Sterling Moss McMurrin (1914–1996) was a theologian and University of Utah administrator and professor of philosophy. He also served as US Commissioner of Education in 1961–1962.
10. His other book was *Hyrum Smith: Patriarch* (Salt Lake City: Deseret Book, 1963).
11. Brooks describes her near-death experience that occurred in St. George in the spring of 1930. Another letter dated September 11, 1939, detailing this experience was published in Lee Nelson, *Beyond the Veil* (Orem, UT: Cedar Fort, 1990), 3:59–63. Another version that appears to have been written in 1940 exists in the Juanita Brooks Papers.
12. Lumpy dick is a boiled pudding made of milk, flour, salt, and cream.
13. A. Russell Mortensen (1911–1995) was the director of the Utah Historical Society and editor of the *Utah Historical Quarterly*, director of the

University of Utah Press, and professor of history and library science at the University of Utah, and then chief historian for the National Park Service in Washington, DC.

14. Evans Coleman (1874–1954) lived in Thatcher, Arizona, and served an LDS Church mission to South Carolina.
15. Hyrum Lorenzo Reid (1884–1973) was the author of a thesis and a book on the early history of Utah's Dixie. Andrew Karl Larson (1899–1983) was an English and history teacher at Dixie College and author of several books and articles on the history of Utah's Dixie.
16. This journal was published as "Journal 1, First Mission to Tennessee, December 7, 1840–July 31, 1841," in Verne R. Lee, *The Early Journals of John D. Lee* (privately printed by Verne Lee, n.d.), 1–87.
17. This journal was published as "Journal 5, Fifth Mission to Kentucky, May 28, 1844–August 20, 1844" in Lee, *The Early Journals of John D. Lee*, 191–235.
18. This journal was published as "Journal 7, Brigham Young's Departure of Nauvoo, February 1, 1846–August 28, 1846" in ibid., 259–380.
19. This journal was published as Juanita Brooks, "John D. Lee: Diary of the Mormon Battalion Mission," *New Mexico Historical Review* (July and October 1967): 165–209 and 281–332.
20. Charles Kelly, *Journals of John D. Lee, 1846–47 and 1859* (Salt Lake City: Western Printing Company, 1938).
21. Brooks attended a reunion of the John D. Lee family at Lee's Ferry on the first weekend in June 1954. Peterson, *Juanita Brooks: Mormon Woman Historian*, 234.
22. Gus and Ramona Griffin purchased the ranch in 1940 and settled there full-time in 1958.
23. Warren Marshall Johnson (1838–1902) and his two wives, Permelia Jane Smith and Samantha Nelson, permanently ran Lee's Ferry from 1876 to 1895.
24. Brooks was using some edition of John D. Lee, *Mormonism Unveiled; or, The Life and Confessions of the Late Mormon Bishop, John D. Lee, Written by Himself* (St. Louis: Bryan, Brand, 1877), while Cleland was quoting from the later John D. Lee, *Mormon Menace: Being the Confessions of John Doyle Lee Danite—An Official Assassin of the Mormon Church Under the Late Brigham Young* (New York: Home Protection Publishing, 1905).
25. Rachel Andora Woolsey, Sarah Caroline Williams, Emma Louise Batchelor, Polly Ann Workman, Lavina Young, Terressa Morse, and Ann Gordge were wives of John D. Lee.
26. Little, *Jacob Hamblin*.
27. Alexander Findlay Macdonald (1825–1903) moved to St. George in the early 1870s to help with temple construction and manage the Erastus Snow mansion. He eventually settled in Colonia Juarez.
28. Bellevue, now called Pintura, is a small, unincorporated community in northern Washington County.

29. Pahreah, or Paria, is on the Paria River in central Kane County. Brooks, in her published Lee biography, *John D. Lee*, p. 334, mentions Kanarra instead of Pahreah when discussing this event. Kanarra (now called Kanarraville) is located north of Bellevue in southern Iron County at the southwest edge of Cedar Valley.
30. Martha Elizabeth Berry (1827–1885) married Lee in Nauvoo in 1845 and divorced him about 1857 or 1858.
31. William Orson Lee (1852–1908), Harriet Josephine Lee (1850–1922), and Thurza Jane Lee (1855–1894) were the children of Martha Elizabeth Berry.
32. William Shanks Berry (1828–1884) was the brother of Martha Elizabeth living in Kanarraville.
33. Dennis Dorrity (1819–1894) married Martha Berry as his third wife in 1859.
34. Ann Gordge Lee (1848–1915) was John D. Lee's last wife, probably being married around 1863.
35. Ann Gordge had three children—Samuel James Lee (1867–1937), Merabe Emma Lee (1868–1945), and Albert Doyle Lee (born 1871).
36. Samuel Gordge apparently drowned on Christmas Eve in 1853. Merab Gordge and her small family immigrated to America from Australia in 1854, arriving in California later that year, where they remained until 1857. During that time, Ann Gordge's mother, Merab, married a man named John Phillips. The family moved to Utah in 1857.
37. Ann Gordge married a mining engineer, Frank Kennedy.
38. John Lawson (1805–1884) came to Utah with the Mormon Battalion detachment. Brooks details this story in *John D. Lee*, 282.
39. Emma Louise Batchelor Lee French (1836–1897), a wife of John D. Lee, lived at Lee's Ferry in the 1870s and then later married a prospector named Franklin French and moved to Arizona.
40. Morgan's books had been stored in his mother's damp basement.
41. This journal was published as "Journal 7, Brigham Young's Departure of Nauvoo, February 1, 1846–August 28, 1846" in Lee, *The Early Journals of John D. Lee*, 259–380.
42. Kimball Young, *Isn't One Wife Enough?* (New York: Henry Holt, 1954).
43. Virginia Sorensen, *The House Next Door* (New York: Charles Scribner's Sons, 1954).
44. The "Strength of the Union" series included historical novels from different states written for young adults. They were published by Charles Scribner's Sons and edited by Erick Berry. A book on Nevada appears not to have been published. Brooks wrote Erick Berry on the same day saying, "I was most presumptuous to suggest that I should like to do a book on Nevada before I had seen one of your series." JB to Erick Berry, October 15, 1954, Juanita Brooks Papers.
45. Erick Berry (1892–1974) was an award-winning author and illustrator. Erick Berry was a pseudonym and the author was actually female, Allena Champlin.

46. Virginia Sorensen, *Many Heavens* (New York: Harcourt Brace, 1954).
47. Virginia Sorensen, *The Evening and the Morning* (New York: Harcourt, Brace & World, 1949).
48. Fae Ollerton Tarlock (1897–1989) wrote several stories for the LDS Church *Relief Society Magazine.*
49. In June 1954, Utah officials, as a test case to see if they could separate children from their parents if the parents did not disavow polygamy, rounded up seven of Vera Black's children and transported them to Provo for placement in foster homes. Judge Dunford overturned the order of separation and the children were reunited with their mother. However, in January 1956 Utah officials with a refined case again separated Black's children from their mother. Brooks wrote four angry letters to the *Deseret News* against separating the children, which were eventually published in *Truth* 21 (March 1956): 310–13.
50. William Stanley Dunford (1893–1955) was a judge in the Fourth Judicial District in Provo from 1945 to 1955.
51. LeGrand Richards (1886–1983) was a member of the Quorum of Twelve Apostles of the LDS Church from 1952 until his death.
52. Donald P. Seegmiller (1914–2000) was a resident of St. George.
53. Brooks spoke at the dedication of a monument to the victims of the Mountain Meadows Massacre in Harrison, Arkansas, where the Fancher train had assembled before heading west.
54. Juanita Brooks, "Speech Given at the Dedication of a Monument Honoring the Victims of the Massacre at Mountain Meadows," *Utah Historical Quarter*ly 24, no. 1 (January 1956): 72–77.
55. Brooks responds to LeGrand Richard's letter that cautioned it would have been in the Church's interest not to bring up the history of the Mountain Meadows Massacre, even if her statements were correct. He mentions a story of a mother instructing her son not to inform a man that he had a big red nose as an example of why the truth is not always the best. Elder Richards replies that he has defended the church all his life and would rather the topic would just die. He agrees to read the book. His final letter on the topic negatively reviews her book, questioning her deductions and again saying that she should have followed repeated counsel to keep it quiet.
56. Leonard Arrington (1917–1999) is considered the father of the New Mormon History, a more open and truthful portrayal of Mormon history, and was the LDS Church historian for ten years, a professor at Utah State University from 1946 to 1972, and the author of many books and articles.
57. Brooks responds to Arrington's comments on her *Mormon Chronicle* volumes.
58. In his letter, Arrington corrects a note in Cleland and Brooks, *A Mormon Chronicle* 2:253n44, by saying that church officials began to promote the silk industry in the middle 1860s and not in 1874 as stated by Brooks.

59. Anthony Ivins Bentley (1908–1986) was a religion professor at Brigham Young University from 1954 to 1973.
60. Brooks answers Bentley's questionnaire requesting her opinion on "the place of creative thinking in the Church" for a BYU discussion group he was heading.
61. Brooks refers to her letters to the editor that appeared in the *Salt Lake Tribune* regarding the polygamist Vera Black and her children.
62. Turnley Walker (1913–1997) was an author of books, a TV book reviewer, and a writer of TV series. Walker was the person who interviewed Brooks for the Los Angeles television show *Cavalcade of Books* and had an interest in producing a movie script for the Mountain Meadows Massacre.
63. Stanley S. Ivins (1891–1967), a friend of Brooks and son of Anthony W. Ivins of the First Presidency, studied Utah and Mormon history and wrote a series of articles.
64. Greenville is an unincorporated community in eastern Beaver County, Utah.
65. Immediately following Lee's sentence to death, petitions were circulated in the towns of Beaver and Panguitch begging Governor George W. Emery for clemency for Lee. Emery asked Col. Henry Douglass, commander of Fort Cameron at Beaver, for his opinion. It was decided that if Lee made a full statement concerning the massacre, his life would be spared. Lee never made this public confession. Brooks, *John D. Lee*, 365–66.
66. Arthur F. Bruhn (1916–1964) was president of Dixie College from 1954 to 1964 and was also a member of the Utah State Parks and Recreation Commission.
67. This booklet appears not to have been published.
68. This article was never published by *Colliers*. However, Brooks did publish a book on Emma Lee, *Emma Lee* (Logan: Utah State University Press, Western Text Society Series, 1975).
69. Asael Carlyle Lambert (1893–1983) was a friend of Brooks, who was a professor of education administration and dean at Los Angeles State College (now California State University at Los Angeles). In addition to his numerous publications on education, he wrote several manuscripts on the history of early Mormonism. His papers, along with many of his manuscripts and notebooks, are housed in the Marriott Library Special Collections at the University of Utah.
70. According to Lee's autobiography, he "became a member of the order and received three degrees" in Nauvoo. Lee, *Mormonism Unveiled*, 144.
71. Leon E. Seltzer (1919–1988) was director of Stanford University Press from 1956 to 1983.
72. In May 1956, the new director of the press, Leon Seltzer, rescinded the copyright to Brooks. Peterson, *Juanita Brooks: Mormon Woman Historian*, 250.

Chapter 6

1. Leonard Arrington to JB, May 5, 1958, Juanita Brooks Papers.
2. JB to O. Boyd Mathias, May 27, 1957, Juanita Brooks Papers.
3. Ibid., February 8, 1959.
4. Oral Boyd Mathias (1926–2009) was a friend and correspondent of Brooks, who was a student at Kansas City University and later an instructor at colleges in Stockton, California. He was interested in the LDS Church's policy of blacks in the priesthood and wrote a graduate paper on the topic.
5. Esaias Edwards (1812–1897) kept a diary of his experiences in Nauvoo, Salt Lake City, Tooele, Cache Valley, and St. George.
6. Joseph Fielding Smith.
7. Utah State Agricultural College, now Utah State University.
8. Brooks refers to the *Symposium on Mormon Culture*, sponsored by the Utah Academy of Sciences, Arts and Letters in Logan in 1952. Her talk was titled "St. George, Utah: A Community Portrait," and included in pp. 1–8. Mimeographed copies of the talks were distributed.
9. John Kenner Fancher (1899–1968) was key organizer and leader of the Richard Fancher Society of America and descendant of some of the Mountain Meadows Massacre victims. Daisy Florence Fanshier Fancher (1899–1988) married John Kenner in 1956.
10. Nicholas Groesbeck Morgan (1884–1971) was president of the Sons of Utah Pioneers, on the board of trustees of the Utah State Historical Society, and author of several books.
11. Kit Carson Wilson (1886–1976) was a resident of Carroll County, Arkansas.
12. Summer Quarters refers to a farm established about thirteen miles north of Winter Quarters in Nebraska by Brigham Young in 1847 to provide food supplies for later emigrant wagons. John D. Lee was asked to help with the farming activities, while most of the others continued west.
13. Kelly, *Journals of John D. Lee.*
14. These individuals were thirty-eight of his adopted sons called together to discuss who was going to stay and farm.
15. John Vance (1794–1882) was a bishop at Winter Quarters and came to Utah in October 1847.
16. David Isom Young (1826–1847) was the child of David Young and Elizabeth Vance.
17. Kelly, *Journals of John D. Lee*, 197n160.
18. Edith L. Neale (1891–1980) was a historian, teacher, and director of the Washington County (Nebraska) Historical Museum where Fort Calhoun is located.
19. This journal is published in Cleland and Brooks, *A Mormon Chronicle.*
20. Most likely Omer James Smith (1914–1982), who was a resident of Graham County, Arizona, and the grandson of Lot Smith.

21. Hosea Stout (1810–1889) was a bodyguard of Joseph Smith, the chief of police in Nauvoo, first attorney general of Utah, and U.S. attorney. He kept an extensive diary, which was published in Juanita Brooks, ed., *On the Mormon Frontier: The Diary of Hosea Stout, 1844–1861* (Salt Lake City: University of Utah Press, 1964).
22. The YTFIF or Council of Fifty was a council organized by Joseph Smith on March 11, 1844, in Nauvoo. Thought to be the start of the literal kingdom of God on earth, the council ran parallel with the ecclesiastical structure of the LDS Church and continued until January 1846. The minutes of their meetings are published in Matthew J. Grow et al., *The Joseph Smith Papers, Administrative Records, Council of Fifty Minutes, March 1844–January 1846* (Salt Lake City: The Church Historian's Press, 2016).
23. *Pilgrim's Progress from This World to That Which Is to Come; Delivered Under the Similitude of a Dream*, written in 1678 by John Bunyan.
24. Dale L. Morgan, "The Reminiscences of James Holt: A Narrative of the Emmett Company," *Utah Historical Quarterly* 23, no. 1 (January 1955): 1–33. James Emmett (1803–1952) led an advance party of about one hundred Latter-day Saint followers from the vicinity of Nauvoo to present-day Vermillion, South Dakota, in 1845–1846.
25. William Decatur Kartchner (1820–1892) was a member of the Emmett Company, who left and continued to Utah arriving on July 28, 1847.
26. *Journal of Discourses Volume 2 by Brigham Young . . . Reported by G. D. Watt* (Liverpool: F. D. Richards, 1855).
27. In mid-June 1843, Joseph Smith was arrested and held prisoner in Dixon, Illinois. As he was being conveyed to the Fifth Circuit Court in Quincy, he was rescued by a large party of Mormons and taken safely back to Nauvoo.
28. Sons of Utah Pioneers.
29. Nancy Bean Lee Decker (1826–1903) married John D. Lee on February 5, 1845, and was sealed to him in the Nauvoo Temple on January 14, 1846.
30. Cornelia (Eliza) Lee (1846–1937) was born on January 15, 1846.
31. Wives of John D. Lee.
32. Louisa Beaman (1815–1850) was sealed to Joseph Smith on April 5, 1841, as the first documented plural marriage in Nauvoo.
33. Lucy Ann Decker (1822–1890) was sealed to Brigham Young on June 14, 1842, as his first plural wife.
34. Brooks responds to Arrington's request for advice on how he should have handled Isaac Haight, one of the Mountain Meadows Massacre participants, in his article "Planning an Iron Industry for Utah," *Huntington Library Quarterly* 21, no. 2 (May 1958): 237–60. In this article, Arrington argued that many moved away from the area following the massacre as a reason for the termination of the iron mission.
35. Brooks, *Mountain Meadows Massacre*, 122.

36. Laban Morrill (1814–1900), William Bateman (1824–1869), William Rufus Slade (1811–1871), William Slade Jr. (1834–1902), Elliott Wilden (1833–1920), Harrison Pearce (1818–1889), and James Pearce (1839–1922).
37. William Cameron Stewart (1827–1895).
38. The last two sentences of the paragraph in which Arrington requested Brooks's thoughts were: "The general manager of the iron company, Isaac Haight, was the person who reputedly gave the order that resulted in the killing. He was one of those who left the county after having been dropped from his position as president of the Iron County Mormons." Arrington to JB, May 5, 1958, Juanita Brooks Papers.
39. George Miller (1794–1856) was the second bishop of the LDS Church from 1844 to 1846 when he was dropped from the church due to opposition to Brigham Young.
40. Under May 4 and 5, 1842, Joseph Smith writes that he met with Hyrum Smith, Newel K. Whitney, George Miller, Brigham Young, Heber C. Kimball, and Willard Richards and instructed "them in the principles and order of the Priesthood." Andrew Jenson, *The Historical Record* (Salt Lake City: Andrew Jenson, 1888), 7:493–94.
41. The minutes of the Council of Fifty for April 10, 1880, are published in Jedediah S. Rogers, *The Council of Fifty: A Documentary History* (Salt Lake City: Signature Books, 2014), 258. Note 4 on p. 258 says, "The Council of Fifty did not officially meet for two years after the date mentioned here for the revelation that allegedly called for its organization."
42. Winifred (Peg) Gregory (1911–1987) was a friend of Brooks and an editor. They first met when Gregory was editing the John D. Lee diaries for Cleland in the early 1950s. Gregory then became an editor at the University of New Mexico Press in Albuquerque.
43. They traveled from Hurricane, Utah, southeast on Utah State Highway 59 through Short Creek (now called Colorado City/Hildale), into Arizona on State Highway 389 to Fredonia, and then north to Kanab. Pipe Spring was a settlement founded by Mormons in the 1860s and is now a U.S. national monument.
44. Brigham Young led a party to explore the area east of Kanab for an approach to the Colorado River in September 1870. John D. Lee located the road and selected the campsites.
45. In October 1870, John D. Lee moved from New Harmony to Skutumpah Valley outside of Kanab to set up and operate a mill.
46. Levi Stewart (1812–1878) founded Kanab in 1870 and served as its first LDS Church bishop. He ran the sawmill with John D. Lee.
47. Art Green's Cliff Dwellers Lodge at Marble Canyon.
48. Jacob's Pools is located at the base of the Vermilion Cliffs between Marble Canyon and Jacob Lake just north of Highway 89A. Rachel Lee, one of Lee's wives, moved into a willow shelter at Jacob's Pools in 1872.

49. On June 2, 1872, Lee notes that members of the John Wesley Powell expedition stopped at Jacob's Pools and took the photograph. Cleland and Brooks, *A Mormon Chronicle* 2:200.
50. Peter Shirtz (1808–1882) settled in the Paria River valley about thirty-five miles east of Kanab, building a fort and grist mill.
51. Albert King Thurber (1826–1888) settled in Spanish Fork where he served as LDS Church bishop, mayor of the city, and delegate to the territorial legislature, and then moved to Richfield, eventually being LDS Church Sevier Stake president.
52. Nancy Ann Vance Lee Wordsworth (1824–1851), daughter of John Vance, married John D. Lee in the fall of 1845 and then later divorced him and married William Shin Wordsworth or Wadsworth.
53. Frank Esshom, *Pioneers and Prominent Men of Utah* (Salt Lake City: Utah Pioneers Book Publishing, 1913). The description is on p. 1264 and the photograph is on p. 65.
54. Hannah Lee Wordsworth Harris (1846–1917) was the daughter of Nancy Ann Lee and John D. Lee, born at Winter Quarters in 1846. She later adopted the name of Wordsworth or Wadsworth.
55. Brooks was on the Utah State Historical Society board for twenty-four years.
56. Dale L. Morgan, "The Changing Face of Salt Lake City," in special issue, *The Valley of the Great Salt Lake, Utah Historical Quarterly* 27, no. 3 (Summer 1959): 209–32.
57. Nellis Air Force Base is a United States Air Force installation in southern Nevada.
58. O. Boyd Mathias, "Mormon Church and Its Negro Doctrine," was a term paper for a graduate social science seminar at the University of Kansas City (Missouri).
59. Rulon W. Doman (1905–1997) was the chief professional Scouter in the Greater Salt Lake Council from 1952 to 1964 and Scout executive emeritus from 1964 to 1970.
60. James Hamilton Gardner (1888–1964) was a former speaker of the Utah House of Representatives and a historian who wrote several articles and books.
61. Hamilton Gardner, "Report of Lieut. Col. P. St. George Cooke of His March from Santa Fe, New Mexico, to San Diego, Upper California," *Utah Historical Quarterly* 22, no. 1 (January 1954): 15–40.
62. Robert L. Ashby (1880–1970) was an educator, architect, poultry man, historian, and author of several books.
63. Robert L. Ashby, *Holden, Utah: Early History Compiled by Robert L. Ashby at the End of 100 Years, 1855–56—1955–56* (privately printed, 1956).
64. Maiben Ashby (1913–2005) was a resident of St. George.
65. William Stevens (1799–1876) was a pioneer of the town of Holden, Millard County, Utah. Brooks in *John Doyle Lee* 375–76, mentions that Stevens gave

Amos Milton Musser, as traveling bishop for the LDS Church, $4,000 in gold coin for temple-building purposes in 1876. She discusses the possibility that the gold coin may have been the $4,000 in gold supposedly carried by the Fancher train at the time of the Mountain Meadows Massacre, but she was skeptical of this idea and even that the Fancher train had that amount.

66. Brooks discusses the *Deseret News* excerpting her "The Land That God Forgot," *Utah Historical Quarterly* 26, no. 3 (July 1958): 207–19, in their newspaper without notifying her. It appeared as "'*Dixie*'—*Land of Enchantment*" in the August 1, 1959, issue.

Chapter 7

1. JB to Ida Hamblin, August 7, 1961, Juanita Brooks Papers.
2. Gregory A. Prince and Wm. Robert Wright, *David O. McKay and the Rise of Modern Mormonism* (Salt Lake City: University of Utah Press, 2005), 54–55.
3. JB to Stewart Udall, September 7, 1961, Juanita Brooks Papers.
4. Dean Robertson Brimhall (1886–1972) was Utah director of aviation for the Civil Works Administration and director of research for the Civil Aeronautics Administration, among his many other positions in aviation. After retirement, he moved to a farm near Fruita, Utah, where he became interested in photographing Native American rock art.
5. Brooks is referring to an essay by Fawn Brodie, "A Lincoln Who Never Was," *Reporter* 20 (June 25, 1959): 25–26, which reviews a letter written to President Eisenhower protesting the Supreme Court decision on integration.
6. *The "Epistole" of Liberty Jail* study by A. C. Lambert is located in the Marriott Library Special Collections.
7. Everett L. Cooley (1917–2006) was Utah state archivist from 1954 to 1960, associate professor at Utah State University in 1960, the director of the Utah State Historical Society from 1961 to 1969, and then the director of the Marriott Library Special Collections at the University of Utah until 1985.
8. Utah State University.
9. Alexander McRae (1807–1891) was with Joseph Smith in jail at Liberty, Missouri. In Nauvoo in 1845, he was a captain in the Nauvoo Legion and a member in what was referred to as the "Fur Company." The Fur Company, first named in 1838–1839 during the troubles in Missouri, consisted of groups of men who guarded the city and made nightly trips to enemy lines.
10. The biography was finally published in November 1961.
11. Alfred L. Bush (1933–) is the retired curator of Western Americana at the Princeton University Library. He was the editor of the papers of Thomas Jefferson and author of numerous books and articles.
12. *Let Every Sluice of Knowledge be Open'd and Set a Flowing: A Tribute to Philip May Hamer on the Completion of Ten Years as Executive Director*

(New York: National Historical Publications Commission, 1960). The book reproduces several documents including those by Adams, Hamilton, Jefferson, Madison, and Franklin.

13. National Education Association.
14. Thomas Carlyle wrote that a "critic fly" finds fault in the minutiae while failing to see the beauty of the whole.
15. Brooks's articles for the Cotton Mission issue were "The Face of the Land," "The Cotton Mission," "Early Buildings," "Silver Reef," and "Vignettes." *Utah Historical Quarterly* 29, no. 3 (July 1961): 193–97, 201–21, 241–53, 281–87, and 289–302.
16. Will Brooks was a member of the honorary Mormon Battalion that paraded during the inauguration of John F. Kennedy on January 20, 1961. Peterson, *Juanita Brooks: Mormon Woman Historian*, 268.
17. The notice of John D. Lee's reinstatement did not appear in the first edition of her biography of Lee, which consisted of just 209 copies, but in the second edition, printed simultaneously with the first edition.
18. Merritt Lee Norton (1891–1981) was a grandson of John D. Lee and the one who facilitated the reinstatement of John D. Lee.
19. Jesse Addison Udall (1893–1980) served in the Arizona House of Representatives and was Chief Justice of the Arizona Supreme Court from 1960 to 1972. He was married to Lela Lee Udall, granddaughter of John D. Lee.
20. Address of the Utah State Historical Society where Brooks was employed.
21. The address of the LDS Church headquarters.
22. Vardis Fisher (1895–1968) was an author of historical novels of the West including his most famous, on the Mormons, *Children of God* (New York: Harper & Brothers, 1939).
23. Kaskaskia is a small, incorporated town in Randolph County, Illinois, on the Mississippi River.
24. Manetta Price Henrie, *Descendants of John Doyle Lee, 1812–1877* (Provo: Privately printed, 1960). Brooks wrote a thirteen-page biography of John D. Lee for the book.
25. Attorney Reed Albert Stout (1911–2002) edited his great-grandfather's autobiography, which appeared as "Autobiography of Hosea Stout," reprinted from *Utah Historical Quarterly* 30 (1962): 1–88.
26. Brooks summarizes some of her editorial procedures.
27. George Wilcken Romney (1907–1995) was president and chairman of American Motors, the governor of Michigan, secretary of Housing and Urban Development, and a 1968 United States presidential candidate.
28. *Utah Historical Quarterly* 29, no. 3 (July 1961).
29. The biography is Tom Mahoney, *The Story of George Romney: Builder, Salesman, Crusader* (New York: Harper, 1960).
30. Miles Romney (1806–1877) was an early settler of St. George. He served as superintendent of construction of the St. George Temple and designer of the St. George Tabernacle, among other buildings.

31. Miles Park Romney (1843–1904) was a chief of police, attorney, newspaper editor, and architect. Along with his father, he designed the St. George Tabernacle. He later settled in St. Johns, Arizona, and then in Colonia Juarez, Chihuahua, Mexico. His biography is Thomas C. Romney, *Life Story of Miles Park Romney* (Independence, MO: Zion's Printing and Publishing, 1948).
32. Lorenzo Brown (1823–1902) settled in St. George in 1862 and later moved to Nutriosa, Arizona.
33. The Winsor Castle Stockgrowing Company was formed in 1873 on the basis of the LDS Church cattle herd at Pipe Spring with Brigham Young as president of the board of directors.
34. David H. Cannon (1838–1924) was called to the Cotton Mission in St. George in 1861, served as an LDS Church bishop and counselor in an early St. George Stake presidency, and was the St. George Temple president from 1893 until his death.
35. Henry W. Miller (1807–1885) was a member of the Utah Territorial Legislature, led a group of Mormons to found the settlement of Millersburg (now Beaver Dam, Arizona), and later settled in St. George.
36. Adolphus Rennie Whitehead (1841–1895) kept a diary of his life in St. George.
37. Ida Lee Hamblin (1884–1977) was a granddaughter of John D. Lee and Agatha Ann Woolsey Lee and an attendee at the meeting in Phoenix.
38. Brooks's replies to Ettie Lee's letter that again tries to convince her not to publish the John D. Lee reinstatement notice in the Lee biography. Lee writes that she is "certain" that the reinstatement will be rescinded if word of it leaks out. She also apologizes for the way Brooks was treated at the Phoenix meeting, noting that she was the Lee family's "defender and liberator so to speak being pressured and almost castigated by those who love and admire her deeply and know you are our savior and best friend." Lee to JB, August 17, 1961, Juanita Brooks Papers.
39. J. Wesley Williamson (1903–1966) was a great-grandson of John D. Lee living in Whittier, California, and a friend of Brooks. Williamson attended and recorded the Lee family meeting in Phoenix as the only one in support of Brooks.
40. Wesley Williamson designed the monument that was going to be dedicated to John D. Lee at a Lee family reunion to be held at Navajo Bridge in mid-October. Brooks along with Peg Gregory and Williamson attended the event and were totally ignored by the family. Peterson, *Juanita Brooks: Mormon Woman Historian*, 280.
41. Stewart Lee Udall (1920–2010) served three terms as a member of the U.S. House of Representatives and as secretary of the Interior from 1961 to 1969.
42. Lydia Lemira Hall (1905–1960) was a resident of St. George. Her poems include "Where the Sego Lilies Grow," published in 1936; "Little Quails Take

A Walk," published in 1946; and "No Mountains," published in February 1950, all in the *Relief Society Magazine*.

43. Hazel Bradshaw, *Under Dixie Sun: A History of Washington County by Those Who Loved Their Forebears* (St. George, UT: Washington County Chapter, Daughters of Utah Pioneers, 1950), 116, 213, 267, 333, 344.
44. Marion George Romney (1897–1988) was a member of the Quorum of Twelve Apostles and the First Presidency of the LDS Church.
45. Ezra Lytle (1904–1988) was the owner of the land containing the Mountain Meadows Massacre site.
46. Brooks previously wrote Stegner, then serving as assistant to Secretary of Interior Stewart Udall, concerning possibilities of employment.
47. Everett L. Cooley became the director of the Utah State Historical Society in 1961.
48. In response to his request, Brooks offers to help Stegner compile a bibliography of Mormon Trail journals that could be used for his book on the Mormon Trail. The book was evidently published as Wallace Stegner, *The Gathering of Zion* (New York: McGraw Hill, 1964).
49. LeRoy R. Hafen and Ann W. Hafen, *Handcarts to Zion: The Story of a Unique Western Migration, 1856–1860* (Glendale, CA: Arthur H. Clark, 1960).
50. Burton White Musser (1886–1974) was the son of Amos Milton Musser, who was the son of Anna Barr Musser Bitner Starr. Mary Barr Neff (1801–1875) immigrated to the Salt Lake Valley in 1847 with the third party to enter the valley. Anna Barr Musser Bitner Starr (1803–1893) came to the Salt Lake Valley in 1849 and was the great-grandmother of Gordon B. Hinckley, a president of the LDS Church, 1995–2008.
51. Klaus J. Hansen (1931–), a retired professor of history at Queens University, wrote books and articles on Mormon history, especially focusing on the Council of Fifty, including *Quest for Empire: The Political Kingdom of God and the Council of Fifty in Mormon History* (East Lansing: Michigan State University Press, 1967).
52. Jonathan Calkins Wright (1808–1880) was a member of the Utah Territorial Legislature from Box Elder County from 1857 to 1881, as well as first counselor in the LDS Church Box Elder Stake presidency under Apostle Lorenzo Snow.
53. Everett L. Cooley, "Journals of the Legislative Assembly: Territory of Utah Seventh Annual Session, 1857–1858," *Utah Historical Quarterly* 24, nos. 2–4 (April, July, and October 1956): 107–22, 237–60, 339–57.
54. The first-edition copies of the John D. Lee biography, limited to just 209 copies, were issued without printed dust jackets and had only a plain brown wrapping-paper cover. These first-edition copies are now valuable collector's items. The second edition had a printed dust jacket, which she wanted to put on her first-edition copies.

55. The first edition was issued in a blue cloth binding and the second edition had a red cloth binding. The first and second editions were printed and released simultaneously. Robert A. Clark and Patrick J. Brunet, *The Arthur H. Clark Company: An American Century, 1902–2002* (Spokane, WA: Arthur H. Clark, 2002).
56. The Arthur H. Clark Company responded to her previous letter saying only booksellers qualify for the maximum 40 percent discount while authors receive a 25 percent discount. They also mentioned that they had not heard from Deseret Book yet with orders for the book. Paul Galleher to JB, November 28, 1961, Juanita Brooks Papers. Deseret Book finally wrote the Clark Company saying they would not order the book because it was controversial. Axel Andresen to Paul Galleher, December 27, 1961, Juanita Brooks Papers.
57. The letter dated April 27, 1860, lists those from Arkansas that were massacred at Mountain Meadows. It was in the files of the Office of Indian Affairs, Utah Superintendency. The "Senate Document No. 42" is *Message of the President of the United States, Communicating, in Compliance with a Resolution of the Senate, Information in Relation to the Massacre at Mountain Meadows in Utah Territory*, 36th Congress, 1st Session, Ex. Doc. 42 (Washington, DC: Government Printing Office, 1860).
58. Sarah Caroline Williams Lee (1830–1908) was the fourth plural wife of John D. Lee, being sealed to him in 1846.
59. Ewart Tyler Lee (1920–2005) served as LDS Church bishop of the Thatcher, Arizona, First Ward for fifteen years.
60. *Blood: A Private Notebook* and *A Private Notebook about the Serpent*, manuscripts by A. C. Lambert, are located in the Marriott Library Special Collections.
61. According to Quinn, the "Committee of Seven" was an executive committee within the Council of Fifty that consisted of seven members with unclear functions. D. Michael Quinn, "The Council of Fifty and Its Members, 1844 to 1945," *BYU Studies* 20, no. 2 (1980): 163–97.
62. Brooks, *On the Mormon Frontier*, 21. The "Living Constitution" Stout discusses is probably a special board of the trade association called the Mercantile and Mechanical Association.
63. Lee, *Mormonism Unveiled*, 173. The "Living Constitution" that Lee mentions is probably another name for the Council of Fifty.
64. Alpheus Cutler (1784–1864) was a member of the Council of Fifty and served as captain of Joseph Smith's bodyguard. He broke away from the LDS Church led by Brigham Young and founded his own church in 1853 called the Church of Jesus Christ (Cutlerite).
65. In this context "Celestial Law" refers to the practice of plural marriage.
66. Samuel Bent (1778–1846), Charles C. Rich (1809–1883), and John Taylor (1808–1887) were members of the Council of Fifty prior to June 27, 1844.

Edward Hunter (1793–1883) and Theodore Turley (1801–1871) were not members until after the death of Joseph Smith. Grow et al., *Joseph Smith Papers*, 648–49.

Chapter 8

1. JB to Dale Morgan, January 15, 1962, Juanita Brooks Papers.
2. Dale Morgan to JB, January 16, 1962, Juanita Brooks Papers.
3. JB to Winifred (Peg) Gregory, February 2, 1962, Juanita Brooks Papers.
4. Dale Morgan, *Jedediah Smith* (Indianapolis: Bobbs-Merrill, 1953).
5. JB to George T. Boyd, December 11, 1962, Juanita Brooks Papers.
6. The Brookses moved from their house at 1295 Crystal Avenue in Salt Lake City to one at 98 U Street in Salt Lake City. Peterson, *Juanita Brooks: Mormon Woman Historian*, 286.
7. Brooks was using the typescripts consisting of eight volumes created under the direction of Morgan for the WPA. She was comparing these typescripts with a microfilm copy of the original journals.
8. Morgan responds saying "nepoed" actually means "opened," such as opening "a man's belly, filling it with rocks, and sinking it in a river." Morgan to JB, January 16, 1962, Juanita Brooks Papers.
9. Savoie Lottinville (1906–1997) was the director of the University of Oklahoma Press for thirty years.
10. Morgan recommended that she go with the University of Oklahoma Press if the finances were similar, because of the possibility of reprints and a wider distribution. Morgan to JB, January 16, 1962, Juanita Brooks Papers.
11. Newspapers in Utah that reviewed her John D. Lee biography included the *Salt Lake Tribune* (December 10, 1961) and the *Washington County News* (April 5, 1962).
12. January 21, 1962.
13. Obert Clark Tanner (1904–1993) was a professor of philosophy, philanthropist, and founder of the O. C. Tanner Company.
14. The Brigham Young quotation for which Larson wanted a source was, "This present race of Indians will never be converted. It mattereth not whether they kill one another off or Some body else do it & as for our sending Missionarys amoung them to convert them, it is of no use." Brooks, *A Mormon Chronicle* 1:108. Larson to JB, April 2, 1962, Juanita Brooks Papers.
15. The "b'hoys" were Brigham Young's inner circle of rough operatives that included Howard Egan, Ephraim Hanks, and Orrin Porter Rockwell.
16. Brooks, *On the Mormon Frontier*, 653.
17. William Henry Kimball (1826–1907) was the oldest son of Heber C. Kimball and a general in the Utah militia. He settled in Parley's Park where he owned a stage station and hotel.
18. Brooks, *On the Mormon Frontier*, 653n21, says the 1853 letter was from James Ferguson.

19. Brooks sent Josephson a copy of a photograph taken by Wesley Williamson.
20. Locations in northern Arizona along the trail to St. George. It was called the "Marriage Trail" because settlers in Arizona traveled to St. George as the location of the nearest LDS Church temple to marry.
21. Lee's Ferry.
22. Earl Eidswold Olson (1916–2010) worked at the LDS Church Historian's Office for fifty-two years including serving as assistant church historian to Joseph Fielding Smith.
23. Each of these individuals wrote or had someone write a journal of their experiences on the pioneer trek to the Salt Lake Valley. Heber C. Kimball's journal written by William Clayton had been published as "The Pioneer Journal of Heber C. Kimball," *Utah Genealogical and Historical Magazine* 30 and 31 (1939 and 1940). Wilford Woodruff's journal of the pioneer trek is included in Scott C. Kenney, *Wilford Woodruff's Journal*, vol. 3, *1846–1850* (Midvale, UT: Signature Books, 1983). Thomas Bullock (1816–1885) was the clerk who kept the official daily journal of the initial Mormon pioneer company as they traveled to the Salt Lake Valley in 1847. Bullock's 1846 and 1847 journals were published as Will Bagley, *The Pioneer Camp of the Saints: The 1846 and 1847 Mormon Trail Journals of Thomas Bullock* (Spokane: Arthur H. Clark, 1997). George A. Smith's journal written by Albert Carrington has not been published. The LDS Church History Department has only a transcript, with the original journal in private hands. Craig S. Smith, "The 1847 Mormon Pioneer Trek: A View from the Unpublished Journal of Albert Carrington Written for George A. Smith," *Overland Journal* 27, no. 1 (Spring 2009): 3–17.
24. Matthias F. Cowley, *Wilford Woodruff: History of His Life and Labors as Recorded in His Diary Journals* (Salt Lake City: Deseret News, 1909).
25. Thomas Edgar Lyon (1903–1978) was a historian and educator who wrote his master's thesis at the University of Chicago in 1932 on Orson Pratt.
26. Portions of Orson Pratt's 1846 and 1847 journals were originally included as "Interesting Items Concerning the Journeying of the Latter-day Saints from the City of Nauvoo, until Their Location in the Valley of the Great Salt Lake," *Millennial Star* 11 and 12 (1849–1850). Orson Pratt's journals have been published as Elden J. Watson, *The Orson Pratt Journals* (Salt Lake City: Privately published, 1975).
27. William Clayton (1814–1879) was a clerk and scribe for Joseph Smith, who kept a daily journal of his activities, wrote a number of Mormon hymns, and is credited with designing a version of the odometer during his trip across the plains.
28. Brooks is referencing William Clayton's journal for April 11 and 13, 1847. William Clayton, *William Clayton's Journal* (Salt Lake City: Deseret News, 1921).
29. This quote and the following are from Brooks, *On the Mormon Frontier*, 239–41.

30. Phineas Howe Young (1799–1879) was the brother of Brigham Young and a member for the initial Mormon pioneer company to the Salt Lake Valley in 1847.
31. William L. Knecht was the author or editor of several books and articles.
32. Brooks is referring to her speculation in her previous letter that William Clayton was the unnamed person that Stout caught being delinquent in performing his guard duties. Despite Brooks's concerns, Stegner included reference to the incident in his book. He wrote, "But Hosea was in bad with many, and he himself had his passionate dislikes, one of whom was William Clayton. Toward spring, apparently because Clayton had been careless about his police duties, he assured Clayton that he would kill him as soon as the Twelve started west." Stegner, *The Gathering of Zion*, 104.
33. Stegner was confused which Joseph Smith he needed to contact for permission to use the LDS Church Archives.
34. Stegner eventually wrote that "there was an indeterminable number, reported variously as anything from two to six, who were not members of the Church at all." Stegner, *The Gathering of Zion*, 112.
35. The black slaves were Oscar Crosby (1815–1870), Green Flake (1828–1903), and Hark Lay (1825–1890). Each was a baptized member of the LDS Church. Stegner noted that "there were three Negro 'servants,' technically baptized but doctrinally of a secondary status as Church members because of God's curse on the sons of Ham." Ibid., 112.
36. Nathaniel Thomas Brown (1787–1848) was involved with Stephen and William Hodges in the murder of members of the Miller family in Iowa on May 10, 1845, and then was a member of the 1847 Mormon pioneer company. He was killed at Winter Quarters in 1848.
37. Edward William Bonney (1807–1864) wrote about the murder in his book *Banditti of the Prairies; or, The Murderer's Doom!!: A Tale of the Mississippi Valley* (Chicago: T. B. Peterson and Brothers, 1850).
38. The horsemen arriving from Winter Quarters while the 1847 pioneer company was stopped for their midday rest included Jesse C. Little, Orrin Porter Rockwell, Jackson Redden, and Nathaniel Thomas Brown. They brought letters and gifts from Thomas L. Kane for members of the Quorum of Twelve.
39. Norton Jacob (1804–1879) was one of the individuals of the initial Mormon Pioneer Company of 1847 that wrote a journal of their daily activities. Jacob's journal has been published as Ronald O. Barney, *The Mormon Vanguard Brigade of 1847: Norton Jacob's Record* (Logan: Utah State University Press, 2005).
40. Howard Egan (1815–1878) also kept a diary during the initial journey to the Salt Lake Valley and his life after arriving in Utah. It has been published as William M. Egan, *Pioneering the West, 1846 to 1878: Major Howard Egan's Diary* (Richmond, UT: Howard R. Egan Estate, 1917).

41. Orrin Porter Rockwell (1813–1878) and Return Jackson Redden (1817–1891) were both bodyguards of Joseph Smith and later Utah deputy marshals. The notorious Rockwell was reputed to have killed many men as a gunfighter, religious enforcer, and deputy.
42. Brooks accepted temporary employment in October 1962 with Assistant U.S. Attorney Parker M. Neilson to research the history of the upper Green River to counter a suit by the State of Utah to gain possession of the riverbed.
43. Elizabeth Lawrence was with Harper & Brothers in New York City.
44. John Whipple (1874–1966) was a resident of Washington County, Utah.
45. Brooks enclosed her manuscript "Clear, Cool Water" for Lawrence's consideration. It included stories of water in the desert as told partly by the old man, John Whipple. Lawrence eventually rejected the manuscript because it was not "dramatically effective enough to be successful." Lawrence to JB, October 15, 1962, Juanita Brooks Papers.
46. Ferdinand Monjo was an editor at Harper & Brothers over books for boys and girls. Brooks submitted him some portions of her manuscript *Quicksand and Cactus* for his consideration.
47. The story of this expedition is told in Clifford L. Stott, *Search for Sanctuary: Brigham Young and the White Mountain Expedition* (Salt Lake City: University of Utah Press, 1984).
48. Conway B. Sonne (1917–1995) was the financial officer of Standard Oil and author of several books on the history of the Mormons.
49. Conway B. Sonne, *World of Wakara* (San Antonio: Naylor, 1962).
50. Conway B. Sonne, *Knight of the Kingdom* (Salt Lake City: Deseret Book, 1949), is about Richard Ballantyne.
51. Karl F. Brooks, *The Life of Amos Milton Musser* (master's thesis, Brigham Young University, 1961). Amos Milton Musser (1830–1909) served a mission to India in the 1850s, wrote several pro-Mormon pamphlets, and held positions with the Deseret Agricultural and Manufacturing Society, among a number of other associations.
52. Richard Ballantyne (1817–1898) was the founder of the LDS Sunday School in 1849 and served a mission to India in the 1850s.
53. Floy L. Turner, *While the Desert Blossomed* (Provo, UT: J. Grant Stevenson, 1962).
54. Mary Ann Stucki Hafen (1854–1946) was the second wife of four married to Johann Georg Hafen. Her first husband was Johannes Reber.
55. Morgan, *Jedediah Smith*.
56. Dale Morgan edited the William H. Ashley papers as *The West of William H. Ashley: The International Struggle for the Fur Trade of the Missouri, the Rocky Mountains, and the Columbia, with Explorations Beyond the Continental Divide, Recorded in the Diaries and Letters of William H. Ashley and His Contemporaries, 1822–1832* (Denver: Fred A. Rosenstock, Old West

Publishing, 1964). William Henry Ashley's (1778–1838) Rocky Mountain Fur Company conducted several large-scale trapping expeditions in the American West.

57. Thomas "Broken Hand" Fitzpatrick (1799–1854), James Pierson Beckwourth (1798–1866), William Lewis Sublette (1798–1845), and Warren Angus Ferris (1810–1873) were trappers and fur traders, who played a major role in the exploration of the American West. Hiram Martin Chittenden (1858–1917) and Ray Allen Billington (1903–1981) were historians of the American West and the fur trade.
58. The second edition was published as *The Mountain Meadows Massacre*, 2nd ed. (Norman: University of Oklahoma Press, 1962).
59. Samuel Brooks (1886–1962).
60. Carrick Dudley Leavitt (1942–1991) was the son of Brooks's younger brother, Dudley Maurice Leavitt (1913–1999), and Eva Rene Cox (1917–1950).
61. George T. Boyd (1909–2004) was an LDS Church seminary and institute teacher and director. At the time, he was the University of Southern California Institute of Religion instructor.
62. Brooks writes this letter after returning from giving invited talks in Southern California.
63. Grace Atkin Woodbury (1889–1964) was a proponent of education, a poet, and author of two books. She and her husband, Angus M. Woodbury, were killed in an automobile collision on August 1, 1964.

Chapter 9

1. JB to Alfred Bush, January 17, 1963, Juanita Brooks Papers.
2. JB to Washington County Commissioners, January 24, 1963, Juanita Brooks Papers.
3. JB to Jack Shumate, February 25, 1964, Juanita Brooks Papers.
4. JB to Fawn Brodie, December 30, 1963, Juanita Brooks Papers; JB to Ogden Kraut, October 6, 1968, Juanita Brooks Papers.
5. The three stories were published as "Memories of a Mormon Girlhood," *Journal of American Folklore* 77, no. 305 (July–September 1964): 195–219.
6. JB to Ellvert H. Himes, June 27, 1964, WSU Levi Peterson Collection.
7. JB to J. Wesley Williamson, May 4, 1964, Juanita Brooks Papers.
8. Brooks just received her five copies of the second edition of her Mountain Meadows Massacre.
9. Miguel Leon-Portilla, *Aztec Thought and Culture* (Norman: University of Oklahoma Press, 1963).
10. Brooks discusses the possibility of writing to see if she could edit the Territorial Papers of Utah at the National Archives. She wrote Wayne C. Grover, archivist for the United States, and sent copies of the letter to Senator Frank E. Moss and Secretary of Interior Stewart L. Udall. Grover responded to her letter saying that the project was put on hold following the death of

Clarence Carter, the general editor, and a committee of experts was going to advise the National Archives on their future course of action. Grover to JB, January 25, 1963, Juanita Brooks Papers.

11. Clarence Edwin Carter, *The Territorial Papers of the United States* (Washington, DC: US Government Printing Office).
12. Wayne C. Grover (1906–1970) served as the third Archivist of the United States from 1948 to 1965.
13. Frank Edward Moss (1911–2003) was a U.S. senator from Utah from 1959 to 1977.
14. Juanita Brooks, *George Brooks: Artist in Stone* (St. George, UT: By the author, 1965).
15. Brooks assisted in editing the ward biographies that were published as Evan P. Wright et al., *Biographies: Federal Heights Ward* (Salt Lake City: Federal Heights Ward Genealogical Committee, 1963).
16. A. Russell Mortensen was the editor of the University of Utah Press at the time.
17. Evan John Woodbury (1910–2001) was associated with the St. George and Washington Canal Company and organized the Dixie Rural Electric Association. Woodbury was chairman of the Washington County Commissioners.
18. This letter is one of several Brooks wrote in the successful attempt to save the St. George Court House.
19. Jack Mormon refers to an inactive or lapsed member of the LDS Church who still maintains a positive feeling toward the church.
20. Hannah Louise Leavitt Terry (1855–1939).
21. The story was published in a somewhat different version in Juanita Brooks, *On the Ragged Edge: The Life and Times of Dudley Leavitt* (Salt Lake City: Utah State Historical Society, 1973), 95–96.
22. Dudley Leavitt's wives included Mary Huntsman Leavitt (1836–1922), her sister Mariah Huntsman Leavitt (1841–1922), Thirza Hale Riding Leavitt (1843–1927), and the Native American woman Janet (Jeanette) Smith Leavitt (1845–1911). He later also married the widow Martha Hughes Pulsipher (1843–1907).
23. It appears that this novel was never published. This letter is an example of the many manuscript reviews she wrote for prospective authors.
24. William Weeks (1813–1900) was the first LDS Church architect and was the architect for the Nauvoo Temple. He came to the Salt Lake Valley with the Jedediah Morgan Grant Company, arriving on October 2, 1847. He soon became disaffected with Mormonism and moved his family back to the Midwest. He eventually settled in San Bernardino, California, by 1857.
25. Easton Kelsey (1813–1899) led a company to the Salt Lake Valley in 1851 and eventually settled in New Harmony and St. George.
26. John Hyde, *Mormonism: Its Leaders and Designs* (New York: W. P. Fetridge, 1857).

27. Kolob is a star or planet nearest to the throne of God according to the LDS Church scripture, *Book of Abraham.*
28. Brooks provides comments on Stegner's book on the Mormon Trail, *The Gathering of Zion.*
29. Kate Carter, *Heart Throbs of the West: A Unique Volume Treating Definite Subjects of Western History*, vol. 12 (Salt Lake City: Daughters of Utah Pioneers, 1951).
30. Stegner included the 46,972 figure, as well as the 68,028 number from the LDS Church Historian's Office discussed by Brooks later in this letter, in the note on p. 9 of *The Gathering of Zion.*
31. The sentence Brooks wanted deleted referred to Brigham Young superintending the evacuation of the Saints from Missouri in 1838. Stegner kept the sentence in his book, but qualified it by saying that contemporary records do not bear it out. He also included some of the information on the whereabouts of Brigham Young that Brooks details in the following two paragraphs of the letter without referencing Brooks, but mentioning Stanley Ivins. *The Gathering of Zion*, 21–22.
32. Amos Milton Musser was an assistant LDS Church historian from 1902 until his death in 1909.
33. John Smith (1781–1854) was the uncle of Joseph Smith, assistant counselor in the LDS Church First Presidency under Joseph Smith, presiding patriarch of the LDS Church, and president of the LDS Church stake in Lee County, Iowa, during the Nauvoo period.
34. Elias Smith (1804–1888) was a cousin of Joseph Smith, a member of the Council of Fifty, and a bishop in the LDS Church stake in Lee County, Iowa, during the Nauvoo period.
35. Thomas L. Kane (1822–1883), a Philadelphia attorney, helped the Mormons by using his political connections in Washington, D.C., on several occasions including when the Saints were fleeing Nauvoo, becoming a close friend of Brigham Young. He was given a patriarchal blessing by LDS Church patriarch John Smith on September 7, 1846. Stegner mentioned the speculation that Kane had been baptized. Stegner, *The Gathering of Zion*, 22.
36. Lucien Woodworth (1799–after 1860) was the architect of the Nauvoo House, aide-de-camp in the Nauvoo Legion under Joseph Smith, and a member of the Council of Fifty. Prior to him being baptized into the LDS Church, he was nicknamed the "Pagan Prophet" by Joseph Smith. Stegner wrote that Woodworth was sent to negotiate a grant with the Republic of Texas in 1844 as a possible settlement place for the Saints. Stegner, *The Gathering of Zion*, 32.
37. Lorenzo Brown (1823–1902) assisted in the settlement of Las Vegas in 1856. In 1862, he and his family were called to St. George, and then in 1883 he and his wife moved to Arizona to be near their sons.

38. George Washington Braffitt (1801–1887) was tried and convicted of adultery in Parowan in July 1854 for his relationship with Margaret Woodworth and ordered to pay a fine of $1,000 resulting in the sheriff selling all his property. Brigham Young in Salt Lake City pardoned him with the help of John D. Lee. Brooks, *John D. Lee*, 188–89.
39. The biography was published as Harold Schindler, *Orrin Porter Rockwell: Man of God, Son of Thunder* (Salt Lake City: University of Utah, 1966). Stegner kept the reference to "a hundred holy murders" but qualified it by noting, "his most scrupulous biographer guesses twenty." *The Gathering of Zion*, 37–38.
40. Kelly and Birney, *Holy Murder*.
41. Zina Dianthah Huntington Jacobs Smith Young married Henry Bailey Jacobs on March 7, 1841, after turning down proposals from Joseph Smith. She then married Smith on October 27, 1841, while seven months pregnant with her son Zebulon William Jacobs. She continued to live with Jacobs and they had a second son, Henry Chariton Jacobs, on March 22, 1846. She married Brigham Young on February 2, 1846, and they had one daughter, Zina Prescinda Young, in 1850. Albert Carrington (1813–1889) was counselor in the LDS Church First Presidency and a member of the Quorum of Twelve Apostles from 1877 until 1885, when he was excommunicated for adultery.
42. John Neff (1794–1869) crossed the plains to the Salt Lake Valley in Jedediah Grant's Company of 1847 and upon arriving in the valley built the East Mill Creek mill. Rockwell married Mary Ann Neff in 1851.
43. Rockwell has been accused for attempting to murder Missouri governor Lilburn W. Boggs on May 6, 1842. Rockwell shot Frank Worrell on the Warsaw Road on September 16, 1845, to protect Hancock County sheriff Jacob Backenstos, who was in the process of raising a posse to capture the raiders who had burned some of the Mormon settlements.
44. The "Miracle of the Quail" occurred on October 9, 1846, when flocks of quail flew into the so-called "Poor Camp" of the starving Nauvoo refugees on the bank of the Mississippi River. They were probably not pigeons, as Brooks suggests, because the pioneers could probably identify quail from pigeons.
45. Pansy Leavitt Hardy (1910–1997) was born in Bunkerville, Nevada, and was Brooks's cousin. She taught English and folklore at Dixie College.
46. Brooks responds to Pansy Hardy's request for information for her master's thesis discussing her and LeRoy Hafen, which appeared as Pansy Hardy, "The Influence of Southern Nevada and Southern Utah on the Writings of Dr. Juanita Brooks and Dr. LeRoy R. Hafen" (Master's thesis, Brigham Young University, 1965).
47. Israel Abbott (1896–1966) and Marion Bradley Earl (1897–1988) were both born in Bunkerville, Nevada, at about the same time as Brooks.
48. Catarrah is excessive discharge or buildup of mucus in the nose or throat, associated with inflammation of the mucous membrane.

49. Harrison Reuben Merrill (1884–1938) was a member of the English faculty at Brigham Young University and then the first chair of the journalism department. He was selection chairman of the Utah Academy of Sciences, Arts, and Letters.
50. Virginia Sorensen, *Where Nothing Is Long Ago: Memoirs of a Mormon Childhood* (New York: Harcourt, Brace, & World, 1963).
51. Juanita and Will Brooks moved back to St. George on September 21, 1963. Peterson, *Juanita Brooks: Mormon Woman Historian*, 301.
52. Deseret Book had refused to carry the book earlier.
53. Susan M. McDonald of St. George wrote a letter to the Salt Lake Tribune criticizing the people of St. George on their behavior when President John F. Kennedy was killed. "St. George Criticized," *Salt Lake Tribune Public Forum Page* (November 30, 1963): 18.
54. Andrew Karl Larson (1899–1983) and Katherine Walker Miles Larson (1901–1975).
55. Stewart Udall, *The Quiet Crisis* (New York: Holt, Rinehart and Winston, 1963).
56. Stewart Udall, "The Quiet Crisis," *Saturday Review* (November 23, 1963): 19–22, 52–54.
57. Ernest H. Linford, "Conservation in Perspective: Udall Pens Persuasive, Moderate Book," *Salt Lake Tribune* (Saturday, November 30, 1963): 18.
58. "Home parents" were a married couple who lived with and taught the boys at Ettie Lee's ranches for at-risk boys.
59. Fawn Brodie, "Who Won the Civil War Anyway?" *New York Times Book Review* (August 5, 1962).
60. Dale L. Morgan, *Overland in 1846: Diaries and Letters of the California-Oregon Trail* (Georgetown, CA: Talisman Press, 1963).
61. Fawn Brodie, *Richard Burton's City of the Saints and across the Rocky Mountains to California* (New York: Alfred A. Knopf, 1963).
62. Frank Robertson, *Fort Hall: Gateway to the Oregon Country* (New York: Hastings House, 1963).
63. John Greenway (1919–1991) was a folklorist and professor of English at Denver University and later professor of anthropology at the University of Colorado, Boulder.
64. The three stories were published as Brooks, "Memories of a Mormon Girlhood." These stories were also later included in Brooks, *Quicksand and Cactus*.
65. Almon W. Babbitt (1812–1856) was the first secretary and treasurer of Utah Territory and as the federal government representative had frequent clashes with Brigham Young. Babbitt was killed in September 1856 on the overland trail near Ash Hollow as he was returning from Washington, DC. Brooks is questioning the official story of the killing and is speculating on the possible role of Orrin Porter Rockwell.

66. Schindler's account of Babbitt's killing is provided in *Orrin Porter Rockwell*, 238.
67. This encounter of the returning missionaries with Rockwell and the wagons is noted in the report provided by F. D. Richards and Daniel Spencer appearing in the *Deseret News* (October 22, 1856). Grimshaw, Cook, and Barnes were three families mentioned in the report that were turned back to Fort Laramie by Rockwell.
68. William H. Kimball, George D. Grant, and James McGaw were among the returning missionaries traveling from Florence, Nebraska, to the Salt Lake Valley who encountered Rockwell east of Fort Laramie on September 16, 1856.
69. Dale Morgan was honored as a University of Utah Distinguished Alumnus.
70. Jack B. Shumate (1920–2011) was at the time supervisor for the US Forest Service, Dixie National Forest.
71. Howard Reese Foulger (1914–1998) was the former supervisor of the Dixie National Forest.
72. Fae Decker Dix (1906–2002) was coordinator of the Adult Education Program for the Iron County Schools and then for the program in the Department of Education at Utah State University until 1960. She later was the associate director of women's programs, Division of Continuing Education, University of Utah. Her husband had passed away in 1961.
73. Fae Dix wrote Brooks on January 15, 1964, and then again on March 23, 1964, asking her if she had written anything on the Mormons and blacks.
74. Jack Hale Adamson (1918–1975) was professor of English at the University of Utah, as well as serving in administrative positions including academic vice president.
75. James C. Fletcher was the president of the University of Utah from 1964 to 1971, when he became the administrator of the National Aeronautics and Space Administration in 1971. A. Ray Olpin (1898–1983) was the president of the University of Utah from 1946 to 1964.
76. Wesley Williamson wrote a letter to Secretary of Interior Stewart Udall asking for his help with the Mountain Meadows Massacre monument.
77. Francis Reid (Frank) Oberhansley (1896–1967) was the superintendent for the National Park Service at Hawaii Volcanoes, Grand Teton, and lastly at Zion. He authored several books and articles.
78. Brooks was preparing a paper to be given at the first annual Nevada History Conference in Reno in May 1964. The paper was published as Juanita Brooks, "The Mormons in Carson County, Utah Territory," *Nevada Historical Society Quarterly* 8, no. 1 (Spring 1965): 3–23.
79. Williamson received a response from his letter to Secretary Udall signed by Charles W. Potter, chief historian of the National Park Service, stating that it was their understanding that the US Forest Service had plans to recognize and mark the site.

80. Brooks is thanking Arrington for his letter congratulating her on the award of an honorary doctorate degree from Utah State University on June 6, 1964.
81. Ellvert H. Himes (1909–1996) was a professor of English at Utah State University. He was also president of Dixie College from 1951 to 1954.

Chapter 10

1. JB to Gladys Harrison, February 11, 1965, WSU Levi Peterson Collection.
2. JB to Richard Thurman and others, September 5, 1968, MS 139, Special Collections, Marriott Library, University of Utah.
3. JB to Jack B. Shumate, November 23, 1966, Juanita Brooks Papers.
4. JB to Ogden Kraut, November 18, 1966, Juanita Brooks Papers.
5. Marion D. Hanks to JB, December 8, 1965, Levi Peterson's Collection.
6. Samuel Woolley Taylor (1907–1997) was a novelist, scriptwriter, and historian, who wrote several biographies and histories on the Mormons.
7. Gladys Harrison was a friend of Brooks in Logan.
8. Brooks continued a busy schedule of speaking to a wide range of groups throughout Utah.
9. Ione Spencer Bennion (1908–1997) was a friend of Brooks from Logan. She was Dean of Women at Utah State University until 1952 and then worked with disadvantaged and disabled students for the Logan City School District.
10. Brooks was awarded the travel grant from the American Philosophical Society, which allowed her to travel to the Western History Association in Helena, Montana, to visit New Mexico to orient herself with the geography of John D. Lee's diary of his journey to Santa Fe, and to fly to Washington, DC, to examine the National Archives and the papers of President James K. Polk. Peterson, *Juanita Brooks: Mormon Woman Historian*, 315.
11. Brooks is referring to Charles Kelly, *Journals of John D. Lee*, which included Lee's journals for 1846–1847 and 1859.
12. John W. Tucker (1926–2001) was president of the College of Eastern Utah from 1962 to 1970, the executive vice president of the University of Utah, and then chancellor of Purdue University from 1972 to 1979.
13. Richard Y. Thurman (1921–2017) was director of the University of Utah Press.
14. She is reviewing Harold Schindler's manuscript *Orrin Porter Rockwell* for the University of Utah Press.
15. Kelly and Birney, *Holy Murder*.
16. J. Golden Taylor (1912–1982) was a professor of English at Utah State University and the author of several books and articles.
17. *Hawthorne's Ambivalence Toward Puritanism* (Monograph Series 12, no. 1; Logan: Utah State University, 1965).
18. Nathaniel Hawthorne (1804–1864) was a novelist and short story writer.

19. Western History Association conference in Helena, Montana.
20. John Edwin Pomfret (1898–1981) was the director of the Henry E. Huntington Library and Art Gallery from 1951 to his retirement in 1966. From 1942 to 1951, he was president of the College of William & Mary.
21. The Thomas D. Brown journals were eventually published as Brooks, *Journal of the Southern Indian Mission: Diary of Thomas D. Brown*.
22. These diaries were published as Brooks, "John D. Lee: Diary of the Mormon Battalion Mission."
23. Louis Clement Zucker (1895–1982) was a professor of English at the University of Utah and was involved with the Salt Lake City Jewish community.
24. This proposal to write the history of the Jews was the start of probably her most frustrating assignment of her career, which dragged on until 1973.
25. Benjamin M. Roe (1898–1960) was a leader in the Salt Lake City business and Jewish communities.
26. Sterling Moss McMurrin (1914–1996) was a professor of philosophy and history, the academic vice president, and dean of the graduate school at the University of Utah. During the John F. Kennedy administration, he served as Commissioner of Education.
27. Edward Williams Bonney was a member of the Council of Fifty, one of the three LDS Church non-members, and also aide-de-camp to Joseph Smith in the Nauvoo Legion.
28. Marion Duff Hanks (1921–2011) served in the Presidency of the Seventy and as an assistant to the Quorum of Twelve Apostles for the LDS Church.
29. Willa and Thales Derrick. Willa is Brooks's daughter.
30. Chad John Flake (1929–2003) was curator of the L. Tom Perry Special Collections of the Brigham Young University Harold B. Lee Library.
31. Archivist Ralph Hansen (1927–) established the first archive at the Brigham Young University Library and was in charge of manuscript collecting for the library.
32. Elder Hanks responds by thanking her and noting that he "long appreciated you and hope you live forever and keep influencing as many as you do with your courage and your solid brand of faith." Hanks to JB, December 8, 1965, Levi Peterson's Collection.
33. Author and publisher Ogden Kraut (1927–2002) produced books through his Pioneer Press concerning his independent Mormon fundamentalist beliefs.
34. The *Peacemaker* pamphlet was written by Udney Hay Jacob and published in Nauvoo in 1842 with Joseph Smith listed as printer. The pamphlet advocated polygamy and was denounced by Joseph Smith later in 1842. Jacob was not a member of the LDS Church when the pamphlet was published but became a member in 1843.
35. Ray Luce's work was eventually published as "The Mormon Battalion: A Historical Accident?" *Utah Historical Quarterly* 42, no. 1 (Winter 1974): 29–38.

36. Ray Luce wrote a master's thesis, "Samuel Brannan: Speculator in Mexican Lands" (Master's thesis, Brigham Young University, 1968).
37. Brooks was able to fly to Washington, DC, as part of her travel grant from the American Philosophical Society.
38. David Pettigrew (1791–1863) enlisted in the Mormon Battalion and marched to California at the age of fifty-five. He then came to Utah in 1848 and was an LDS Church bishop in Salt Lake City.
39. Jefferson Hunt (1803–1879) was a captain in the Mormon Battalion and with his entire family journeyed with the battalion to California. Hunt settled in Salt Lake City in 1847, helped create the Mormon settlement of San Bernardino, California, in 1851, and founded Huntsville, Utah, in 1860.
40. Jefferson Hunt's two wives (Celia Mounts Hunt and Matilda Nease Hunt), eleven children (two of these children had enlisted under Hunt's command), and in-laws Peter and Ellen Nease traveled with the battalion.
41. Kate Carter, *The Mormon Battalion* (Salt Lake City: Daughters of Utah Pioneers, 1956).
42. Joseph Lee Robinson (1811–1893) came to Utah in 1848, settled in Iron County in 1850–1851, and then returned to Farmington where he remained. He supported the Manifesto of 1890. Joseph Eldridge Robinson (1867–1941) served as California Mission president from 1901 to 1919. He was sealed to two plural wives, Willmia Brown and Harriet Spencer, in 1901, which created later legal problems.
43. In April 1868, the bishop E. D. Pace sentenced Emma Lee to be rebaptized in freezing water for defending the rights of her husband against George Hicks. Cleland and Brooks, *A Mormon Chronicle*, 100–102.
44. Kraut was set apart as a "Seventy" by Joseph W. Musser, a leader of the early Mormon fundamentalist movement.
45. The movie *The Little Red Hen*, produced by Brigham Young University in 1967, is a dramatization of Lee's life and her role in setting up eleven ranch homes for boys in California and three in Utah.
46. John D. Lee was made Washington County probate judge, clerk, and assessor on February 7, 1856, when the county government was set up at Harmony. Brooks, *John D. Lee*, 185.
47. Raymond Woolley Taylor (1904–1972) was a developer, author, and entrepreneur in Utah, and with his brother, Samuel W. Taylor, researched and wrote *Uranium Fever* (New York: Macmillan, 1970). He also helped his brother with the research for *The Kingdom or Nothing: The Life of John Taylor, Militant Mormon* (New York: Macmillan, 1976).
48. Mrs. B. G. Ferris, *The Mormons at Home* (New York: Dix & Edwards, 1856).
49. Heywood's diary was eventually published as Juanita Brooks, *Not by Bread Alone: The Journal of Martha Spence Heywood, 1850–1856* (Salt Lake City: Utah State Historical Society, 1978).
50. One of Sidney Rigdon's significant speeches, known as the "Salt Sermon," of which a complete text is not extant, was given on June 17, 1838, when he

pronounced his hatred for dissenters. The other speech was his July 4, 1838, oration threating the local Missourians, published as *Oration Delivered by Sidney Rigdon on the 4th of July, 1838 at Far West, Caldwell County, Missouri* (Far West: Printed at the Journal Office, 1838).

51. This quote is from Peck's manuscript written in 1839 providing a firsthand account of the Mormon settlement in Missouri, 1836–1839.
52. This quote is from William Swartzell, *Mormonism Exposed: Being a Journal of a Residence in Missouri from the 28th of May to the 20th of August, 1838: Together with an Appendix, Containing the Revelation Concerning the Golden Bible, with Numerous Extracts from the "Book of Covenants"* (Pekin, OH: Published by the author; Printed in Pittsburg, 1840).
53. Heber C. Kimball had forty-five wives. Stanley B. Kimball, *Heber C. Kimball: Mormon Patriarch and Pioneer* (Urbana: University of Illinois Press, 1981), Appendix A.
54. Parley P. Pratt had twelve wives. Terryl L. Givens and Matthew J. Grow, *Parley P. Pratt: The Apostle Paul of Mormonism* (Oxford: Oxford University Press, 2011), Appendix 2. John Taylor had at least sixteen wives. J. Lewis Taylor, "John Taylor: Family Man," in *Champion of Liberty: John Taylor*, ed. Mary Jane Woodger (Provo: Religious Studies Center, Brigham Young University, and Salt Lake City: Deseret Book, 2009): 193–217.
55. Orson Hyde (1805–1878) was an original member of the LDS Church Quorum of Twelve Apostles and in 1841 traveled to Jerusalem and on the Mount of Olives dedicated Jerusalem for the gathering of the Jews.
56. Hyde ultimately had eight wives. Myrtle Stevens Hyde, *Orson Hyde; The Olive Branch of Israel* (Salt Lake City: Agreka Books, 2000), Appendix 4. Hyde actually had two wives in 1852, Marinda Nancy Johnson and Mary Ann Price, and a third, Charlotte S. Quindlin, whom he married in November 1852. He also had married Martha Rebecca Browett in 1843, but they were divorced in 1850.
57. Edward Hunter (1793–1883) was the third presiding bishop of the LDS Church.
58. Ora Pate Stewart, *Tender Apples: A Biography of Ettie Lee* (Salt Lake City: Deseret Book, 1965).
59. The Old Spanish Trail was a trade route between the northern New Mexico settlements near Santa Fe and Los Angeles that was most extensively used from 1829 through the mid-1850s.
60. Gunlock is an unincorporated community in western Washington County on the Santa Clara River.
61. The Gordon diary was published as A. F. Cardon, "Mountain Meadows Burial Detachment, 1859: Thomas Gordon's Diary," *Utah Historical Quarterly* 35, no. 2 (Spring 1967): 143–46.
62. The article was rejected by *American West*, but a revised version appeared as Juanita Brooks, "The Mountain Meadows: Historic Stopping Place on the Spanish Trail," *Utah Historical Quarterly* 35, no. 2 (Spring 1967): 137–43.

63. The manuscript on Nathaniel Thomas Brown was lost and Brooks was unable to retrieve it after repeated requests to *Dialogue.*
64. Brooks is referring to Harold Schindler's book, *Orrin Porter Rockwell: Man of God, Son of Thunder.*
65. Sam Weller (1921–2009) was the owner of Sam Weller's Zion Bookstore in Salt Lake City.

Chapter 11

1. JB to Richard L. Anderson, July 14, 1968, Juanita Brooks Papers.
2. JB to Dale Morgan, December 16, 1968, Juanita Brooks Papers.
3. JB to Roger B. Mathison, November 21, 1968, MS 486, Marriott Library Special Collections.
4. Leonard Arrington, *Great Basin Kingdom: An Economic History of the Latter-Day Saints, 1830–1900* (Cambridge: Harvard University Press, 1958).
5. Brooks is referring to an issue of *Dialogue* in which Leonard Arrington served as guest editor, "Reappraisals of Mormon History," *Dialogue* 1, no. 3 (Autumn 1966).
6. Brooks is asking about a manuscript on Nathaniel Thomas Brown that she had submitted to *Dialogue.*
7. Leonard Arrington, "Inland to Zion: Mormon Trade on the Colorado River, 1864–1867," *Arizona and the West* 8, no. 3 (Autumn 1966): 239–50.
8. Francis Hale Leavitt, "Steam Navigation on the Colorado River," *California Historical Society Quarterly* 22, nos. 1–2 (March and June 1943): 1–25, 151–74.
9. Brooks stayed at the Belvedere Apartments at 29 South State Street while in Salt Lake City working on the history of the Jews.
10. Ettie Lee responded saying that she believed that Delbert Stapley "just acted on his own in fear of a bit of criticism" and not with the direct guidance of "God our Father." Lee to JB, March 17, 1967, Juanita Brooks Papers.
11. A. F. Cardon, "Mountain Meadows Burial Detachment, 1859: Tommy Gordon's Diary."
12. James Henderson Berry (1841–1913) was the US senator from Arkansas from 1885 to 1907. The referenced speech was *Speech of Hon. James H. Berry, of Arkansas, in the Senate of the United States: On the Question of Excluding Hon. Reed Smoot, of Utah, from the United States Senate, Monday, February 11, 1907* (Washington, DC: U.S. Government Printing Office, 1907).
13. The Parley P. Pratt monument placed at the spot where he was killed on May 13, 1857, is near Alma, Crawford County, Arkansas.
14. Truman Grant Madsen (1926–2009) was a professor of religion and philosophy at Brigham Young University for over thirty years and the author of many books including a biography of B. H. Roberts and several on Joseph Smith.
15. Francis Van Dan wrote long letters to Brooks in his search for information on Edward William Bonney.

16. Elisha H. Groves (1797–1867) was the patriarch of the LDS Church stake in Iron County and a member of the Utah territorial legislature.
17. The patriarchal blessing was given by Elisha H. Groves to William Horne Dame on February 20, 1854, three and a half years before the massacre. It is reproduced in H. Michael Marquardt, *Later Patriarchal Blessings of the Church of Jesus Christ of Latter-day Saints* (Salt Lake City: The Smith-Pettit Foundation, 2012), 108–9.
18. The patriarchal blessing was given by Elisha H. Groves to Horatio Morrill on November 22, 1857. A copy of the blessing is in the Juanita Brooks Papers. Groves used the phrases "Angel of Vengeance" and "avenge the blood of innocence" in a number of his blessings included in Marquardt, *Later Patriarchal Blessings.*
19. Richard Lloyd Anderson (1926–2018) was an emeritus professor of LDS Church history and doctrine at Brigham Young University and author of a book on the Book of Mormon witnesses.
20. Richard L. Anderson, "Reuben Miller, Recorder of Oliver Cowdery's Reaffirmations," *BYU Studies* 8, no. 3 (Spring 1968): 277–93.
21. Reuben Miller (1811–1882) recorded the only known contemporaneous account of Oliver Cowdery's testimony in Kanesville in October 1848. Miller later printed his account in the *Deseret Evening News* (April 13, 1859): 48.
22. Miller was a follower of James J. Strang for a few months in 1846.
23. The *Frontier Guardian* was published in Kanesville, Iowa, from February 1849 to February 1852 with Orson Hyde as editor.
24. Evan Molbourne Greene (1814–1882) was the first postmaster for Kanesville and recorder and treasurer for Pottawattamie County, Iowa, until leaving to emigrate to Utah in 1852.
25. The Overstreet confession is a statement purported to have been written by Oliver Overstreet in 1857 stating that he impersonated Oliver Cowdery in Kanesville, Iowa, in October 1848 when Cowdery reaffirmed that he had written most of the Book of Mormon as dictated by Joseph Smith.
26. Elias Smith (1814–1882) was a probate judge in Salt Lake City from shortly after he arrived in the Salt Lake Valley in 1851 until 1882 and editor of the *Deseret News* from 1856 to 1862. Judge Smith signed a statement that the three signers (Jesse W. Fox, Henry McEvan, and Fredrick Bollwinkle) of a document appended to Overstreet's confession attesting to Overstreet's handwriting had appeared before Smith on April 7, 1857.
27. Edward Stevenson, *Reminiscences of Joseph the Prophet and the Coming Forth of the Book of Mormon* (Salt Lake City: published by the author, 1893).
28. Richard L. Anderson, "Oliver Cowdery's Non-Mormon Reputation," *Improvement Era* 71, no. 8 (August 1968): 18–19, 22, 24, 26.
29. Oliver Cowdery's *Defence in a Rehearsal of My Grounds for Separating Myself from the Latter Day Saints* is a document critical of Joseph Smith

purported to have been published in 1839 by Cowdery. The earliest known copies are dated 1906 and published by R. B. Neal.

30. Stanley R. Gunn, *Oliver Cowdery: Second Elder and Scribe* (Salt Lake City: Bookcraft, 1962).
31. Myrtle Friedman (1893–1990) was a lifelong resident of Hailey, Idaho, and the one who sponsored the book on the history of the Jews.
32. *B. H. Roberts Defense Before Congress* (Dugway, UT: Pioneer Press, n.d.). The pamphlet includes part of Roberts's defense during the proceedings on whether he was eligible for his seat in the House of Representatives that he won in 1898. The members of the House decided against him.
33. The Preston Nibley book she was probably referring to was the 1968 edition of *Presidents of the Church* (Salt Lake City: Deseret Book), first published in 1941.
34. John George Hafen (1838–1928) immigrated to Utah from Switzerland in 1861 and then was called to southern Utah as part of the Swiss Company. He was bishop of the Santa Clara ward from 1884 to 1912.
35. John Pulsipher (1827–1891) traveled overland to Utah in 1848, was eventually called to the Cotton Mission in 1862, and settled in Shoal Creek at Hebron, Utah, in 1868.
36. Brooks appears to be referring to a Pioneer Press printing of the John Pulsipher diaries; however, the press records show that these diaries were not published until 1970 suggesting that an earlier, unrecorded edition was also produced. Earlier, Brooks edited an extract from the diaries of John Pulsipher as "From the Journal of John Pulsipher," *Utah Humanities Review* 2, no. 4 (October 1948): 351–79, and *Western Humanities Review* 3, no. 1 (January 1949): 38–55.
37. Roger B. Mathison was head of the Gifts and Exchange Department of Marriott Library at the University of Utah. He was an attendee at her speech given at Mountain Meadows on September 14, 1968.
38. She spoke to a group of Utah Academy members on September 14, 1968 at Mountain Meadows. Peterson, *Juanita Brooks: Mormon Woman Historian*, 334.
39. George Samuel Ellsworth (1916–1997) was a professor of history at Utah State University from 1951 to 1983.
40. John M. Higbee's account was included as Appendix II in Brooks, *Mountain Meadows Massacre*.
41. Brooks, *Mountain Meadows Massacre*, 2nd ed., 113.
42. Brigham Young's 1857 diary is published as Everett L. Cooley, *Diary of Brigham Young, 1857* (Salt Lake City: Tanner Trust Fund, University of Utah Library, 1980) and the September 1 entry is on p. 71.
43. Stewart Van Vliet (1815–1901) was of the quartermaster's corps of the army, who traveled ahead of General Albert Sidney Johnston's expedition to communicate with Brigham Young in 1857.

44. Quoted in Brooks, *Mountain Meadows Massacre*, 2nd ed., 139.
45. The letter that Haslam carried from Salt Lake City was from Brigham Young to Isaac Haight dated September 10, 1857. It is fully reproduced in Brooks, *Mountain Meadows Massacre*, 2nd ed., 63.
46. Ibid., 252. The quote is from Garland Hurt's report included as Appendix 8 in Brooks's book.
47. Abraham Hoagland Cannon (1859–1896) was a member of the Quorum of Twelve Apostles of the LDS Church. His journals were published as Edward Leo Lyman, *Candid Insights of a Mormon Apostle: The Diaries of Abraham H. Cannon, 1889–1895* (Salt Lake City: Signature Books and Smith-Pettit Foundation, 2010). The June 13, 1895, entry is found on pp. 671–73.
48. Don D. Fowler (1936–) is an anthropologist and archaeologist working in the southwestern United States and emeritus professor at the University of Nevada, Reno.
49. This manuscript is referenced as "BAE Ms #3141—Historical Notes—Rept. On Mountain Meadows Massacre, Anonymous" in the fourth printing of Brooks, *Mountain Meadows Massacre* (Norman: University of Oklahoma Press, 1970), xiii.
50. Benjamin Platt (1833–1918) emigrated from England to Utah in 1856 and then settled at Fort Harmony and worked for John D. Lee.
51. Brooks, *Mountain Meadows Massacre*, 2nd ed., 75–76n2.
52. Ibid., 45–46n13.
53. *The Windows of Heaven* is a movie about Lorenzo Snow and his speech and prophecy in St. George on May 18, 1899, produced by Brigham Young University in 1963. The film was directed and produced by Wetzel Whitaker with the screenplay by Scott Whitaker and Richard Neil Evans. The inaccuracies in the movie are detailed in Dennis B. Horne, *Latter Leaves in the Life of Lorenzo Snow* (Springville, UT: CFI, 2012), 324–27.
54. Ogden Kraut, *Jesus Was Married* (Dugway, UT: Pioneer Press, 1969).
55. It was actually published in 1942.
56. Karl Keller (1933–1985) was in the English department at San Diego State College and on the *Dialogue* board of editors for literature.
57. Brooks is referring to the manuscript on Nathaniel Thomas Brown that was apparently lost at *Dialogue*.
58. *It Can't Happen Here* is also the title of a novel by Sinclair Lewis (New York: Doubleday Doran, 1935).
59. George Eugene England Jr. (1933–2001) was a Mormon writer, teacher, and scholar, and one of the founders of *Dialogue*.
60. Her speech given in Logan was published as "Jest a Copyin'—Word f'r Word," *Utah Historical Quarterly* 37, no. 4 (Fall 1969): 375–95.
61. It was published as Juanita Brooks, *Uncle Will Tells His Story* (Salt Lake City: Taggart, 1970).

62. Lyman Francis Smart (1925–1986) was a Brigham Young University English professor and then director of development at Southern Utah State College.
63. Brooks received an honorary doctor of humanities degree from the College of Southern Utah in Cedar City at the end of May 1969. Peterson, *Juanita Brooks: Mormon Woman Historian*, 341.
64. Josephine B. Gregory (1920–) was a neighbor of Brooks in St. George. Gregory also lived in Los Angeles.
65. Gregory in her note asked Brooks for the original source of Joseph Smith's quote concerning men on the moon, which was included in an article in the *Los Angeles Times*, August 23, 1969. Gregory to JB, August 25, 1969, Juanita Brooks Papers.
66. Oliver Boardman Huntington (1823–1909) kept a diary of experiences in Missouri, Nauvoo, his mission to England, and various places in Utah.
67. The quote from vol. 2, p. 166 of the typescript of the Huntington diary is, "The inhabitants of the moon are more of a uniform size than the inhabitants of the earth, being six feet in height. They dress very much like the quaker style and are quite general in style or the one fashion of dress. They live to be very old; coming generally, near a thousand years. This is the description of them as given by Joseph the Seer, and he could 'See' whatever he asked the father in the name of Jesus to see." This quote was included as one of several "curious and miraculous events in the Church that I have taken some time and pains to pick up" (p. 160) listed by Huntington in his diary in February 1881. Oliver B. Huntington Papers, MSS A858-3, Utah State Historical Society.
68. The illustrations of the execution of John D. Lee appeared in "Justice at Last! Execution of John D. Lee for Complicity in the Mountain Meadows Massacre," *Supplement Frank Leslie's Illustrated* (April 14, 1877): 109–11.
69. The article never appeared in *The American West.*
70. Edward A. Shaw of the press responded saying they could include her revised ideas on the Mountain Meadows Massacre as a new preface to the book. The revised ideas were included as "Author's Statement—II" in Brooks, *Mountain Meadows Massacre,* Fourth Printing, vii–xviii.
71. Brooks's *Uncle Will Tells His Story* won first place in the long prose narrative category of the Utah Arts Council competition. Peterson, *Juanita Brooks: Mormon Utah Historian*, 342.
72. Brooks sent the *Uncle Will Tells His Story* manuscript to several publishers and all declined publication.

Chapter 12

1. JB to Dale Morgan, December 31, 1970, Levi Peterson's Collection.
2. JB to Ralph H. Lee and Counselors, December 2, 1970, Levi Peterson's Collection.

3. JB to Grace and Obert Tanner, October 5, 1971, WSU Levi Peterson Collection.
4. JB to Raymond Taylor, January 7, 1971, Levi Peterson's Collection.
5. JB to Austin and Alta Fife, March 6, 1971, Levi Peterson's Collection.
6. JB to Grace and Obert Tanner, October 5, 1971, WSU Levi Peterson Collection.
7. JB to Winifred Gregory, October 21, 1971, Levi Peterson's Collection.
8. David Sjodahl King (1917–2009) was a Democrat member of the House of Representatives from Utah from 1959–1963 and 1965–1967.
9. It was published as David King, *Mountain Meadows Massacre: A Search for Perspective* (Washington, DC: Potomac Corral of the Westerners, 1970).
10. Paragoonah or Paragonah is a town on Red Creek in Iron County, Utah, near Parowan.
11. Gwinn Harris Heap, *Central Route to the Pacific, from the Valley of the Mississippi to California: Journal of the Expedition of E. F. Beale, Superintendent of Indian Affairs in California, and Gwinn Harris Heap, from Missouri to California, in 1853* (Philadelphia: Lippincott, Grambo, 1854), 89–90.
12. Samuel McMurdy (1830–1922) immigrated to Utah in 1853 and settled in Cedar City in 1857. On the morning of the massacre, he and Samuel Knight drove wagons to the immigrant wagon circle and then transported the wounded and young children away from the circle.
13. It was thought that Priscilla Klingensmith Urie (1855–1924) was a massacre survivor raised by Philip Klingensmith and Betsy Cattle Klingensmith; however, mtDNA evidence provides a strong indication that Betsy Cattle Klingensmith was Priscilla's biological mother. Ugo A. Perego and Scott R. Woodward, "Mountain Meadows Survivor? A Mitochondrial DNA Examination," *Journal of Mormon History* 32, no. 2 (October 2009): 53–61.
14. Brent Crosby (1939–2015) was a resident of St. George and a friend of Brooks.
15. Charles Welch Taggart (1932–1996) was an entrepreneur, businessman, and rancher active in real estate, manufacturing, and publishing. He published *Uncle Will Tells His Story.*
16. Brooks writes the Mortensens following the passing of her husband on March 28, 1970, thanking them for driving her from Salt Lake City back to St. George.
17. Calvin Lewellyn Rampton (1913–2007) was the governor of the state of Utah from 1965 to 1977.
18. The Mortsensens were helping with the copyediting of the *Uncle Will Tells His Story* book.
19. Bathsheba Wilson Bigler Smith (1822–1910) was the fourth president of the Relief Society of the LDS Church, a leader in the woman's suffrage movement, and wife of George A. Smith. Anderson had written that he was on

his way to see the memoir of Bathsheba Smith written in her handwriting that included mention of seeing Oliver Cowdery at his return in 1848. Anderson to JB, July 7, 1970, Levi Peterson's Collection.

20. Juanita Brooks, "A Place of Refuge," *Nevada Historical Society Quarterly* 14, no. 1 (Spring 1971): 13–14.
21. It does not appear that this review was published.
22. Claudia Marian Lauper Bushman (1934–) is emerita professor of American studies at Columbia University, a historian of domestic women's history and Mormon history, and the author of many books.
23. At the end of August 1970, Brooks moved back to Salt Lake City, first living at her house on U Street and then buying a house at 1731 South 1400 East. Peterson, *Juanita Brooks: Mormon Woman Historian*, 355.
24. The article appeared as Juanita Brooks, "I Married a Family," *Dialogue* 6, no. 2 (Summer 1971): 15–21.
25. Brooks again mentions the previously submitted manuscript on Nathaniel Thomas Brown.
26. Andrew Jenson (1850–1941) was a Danish immigrant and an assistant LDS Church historian from 1897 and until his death. He was a prolific writer and compiler of Mormon history.
27. This series was never published.
28. This letter is one of the last Brooks wrote to Morgan before his passing on March 30, 1971.
29. The Old Spanish Trail was a seven-hundred-mile trade route that connected the northern New Mexico settlements with those of southern California.
30. The area west of Cedar City has a long history of iron mining starting in the 1850s when Brigham Young sent settlers to the area.
31. Rockville is a town in Washington County. It is located along the Virgin River near the mouth of Zion Canyon.
32. Hebron was located on Shoal Creek, six miles west of Enterprise, in the very northwest corner of Washington County. Thomas S. Terry and his family were early ranchers in the area.
33. Todd Berens was an innovative teacher of history at Walker Junior High School in La Palma, California, who brought students to southern Utah to trace the California and Spanish pioneer trails. He would often bring his students to Brooks's home during his field trips.
34. Fawn Brodie spoke at the ballroom of the Hotel Utah in October 1970. Peterson, *Juanita Brooks: Mormon Woman Historian*, 357.
35. Samuel W. Taylor, in collaboration with Raymond Taylor, suggested that Brigham Young was poisoned with arsenic, in Samuel W. Taylor, *The Kingdom or Nothing*, 3.
36. Thomas Cottam (1820–1896) immigrated to Utah in 1852, settled in St. George in 1862, and worked as a furniture maker and sexton.
37. Austin Edwin Fife (1909–1986) and Alta Stevens Fife (1912–1996) were pioneering Utah folklorists, who spent much of their time collecting and

preserving Mormon folklore. Austin taught folklore and French at Utah State University.

38. The speech by John Cradlebaugh was reproduced in the pamphlet, *Utah and the Mormons: Speech of Hon. John Cradlebaugh* (Washington: L. Towers, 1863). The pamphlet was probably *Nuggets of Truth and Gems from the Speeches and Letters of the Leading Minds of Utah (Past and Present)* (N.p.: 1895). The speech by Charles W. Penrose was first published as *The Mountain Meadows Massacre: Who Were Guilty of the Crime?* (Salt Lake City: Juvenile Instructor Office, 1884).
39. Charles W. Penrose, *Blood Atonement as Taught by Leading Elders of the Church of Jesus Christ of Latter-Day Saints: An Address Delivered in the Twelfth Ward Assembly Hall, Salt Lake City, October 12, 1884* (Salt Lake City: Juvenile Instructor Office, 1884).
40. Brooks is quoting from verse 3 of "Let Zion in Her Beauty Rise," by Edward Partridge. The hymn was included as Hymn 66 with seven verses in the first LDS Church hymnbook, Emma Smith, *A Collection of Sacred Hymns for the Church of the Latter Day Saints* (Kirtland, OH: F. G. Williams, 1835). The hymn was reduced to just three verses leaving out those about the last days for the 1948 hymnbook, *Hymns: Church of Jesus Christ of Latter-day Saints* (Salt Lake City: Church of Jesus Christ of Latter-day Saints). It is in the current (1985) LDS Church hymnbook with three verses.
41. The Summit Stake Tabernacle in Coalville, Utah, was razed by the LDS Church on March 5, 1971.
42. Dale Morgan passed away on March 30, 1971.
43. Morgan's "Lady Friend" was Louise North of Accokeek, Maryland. Morgan moved to her house in February 1971 and died there the following month.
44. Many of his papers are housed in the Dale L. Morgan Papers.
45. Charles Kelly died on April 19, 1971.
46. Brooks moved to 1731 South 1400 East in Salt Lake City in October 1970.
47. "*The Devil,*" *A Private Notebook*, manuscript by A. C. Lambert, is located at the Marriott Library Special Collections.
48. Orange Decatur Leavitt (1859–1918) and his father, Lemuel Sturdevant Leavitt (1827–1916), who was born in Quebec, Canada, immigrated to the Salt Lake Valley in 1849, settling in Santa Clara in 1856.
49. Thirza Helena Leavitt (1863–1953) and Mary Eleanor Leavitt (1866–1954) were the sister wives of Orange Leavitt. They were residents of Bunkerville.
50. Cholera morbus is a historical term that was used to refer to gastroenteritis characterized by cramps, diarrhea, and vomiting.
51. Elmer Leavitt (1893–1973) was the son of Orange and Mary Eleanor Leavitt.
52. Elmer was the oldest living son (he had older sisters) and would have been twenty-five years old if the event took place at the death of Orange Leavitt in 1918 and Brooks would have been twenty years old.
53. Theodosia Leavitt Bowman (1895–1971) was the daughter of Orange and Thirza Helena Leavitt.

54. Leo Alva Snow (1881–1963) and his daughter was Esther Snow Judd (1914–1941).
55. Hosea Stout's son William Hosea Stout (1843–1846) died while they were crossing Iowa on June 28, 1846. Stout records, "His looks were demoniac accompanied by the most frightful gestures I ever saw in a child." Brooks, *On the Mormon Frontier* 1:170.
56. Thomas Edward Cheney (1901–1993) was a folklorist and English professor at Utah State University and Brigham Young University.
57. Brooks and Austin Fife assisted Thomas Cheney on the publication of his edited volume, *Lore of Faith and Folly* (Salt Lake City: University of Utah Press, 1971), which included two articles by Brooks, "Our Annual Visitors" and "Pranks and Pranksters."
58. B. H. Hunter, C. A. Patrides, and J. H. Adamson, *Bright Essence: Studies in Milton's Theology* (Salt Lake City: University of Utah Press, 1971).
59. On His Blindness:

    When I consider how my light is spent,
    Ere half my days, in this dark world and wide,
    And that one Talent which is death to hide
    Lodged with me useless, though my Soul more bent
    To serve therewith my Maker, and present
    My true account, lest he returning chide;
    "Doth God exact day-labour, light denied?"
    I fondly ask. But patience, to prevent
    That murmur, soon replies, "God doth not need
    Either man's work or his own gifts; who best
    Bear his mild yoke, they serve him best. His state
    Is Kingly. Thousands at his bidding speed
    And post o'er Land and Ocean without rest:
    They also serve who only stand and wait."

60. Psalm 19.
61. Arius (250 or 256–336) taught about the nature of the Godhead, emphasizing the Father's divinity over the Son. Perceived as heterodoxy by some, the "Arian Controversy" led to the First Council of Nicaea.
62. *Dialogue* 6, no. 2 (Summer 1971).
63. Brooks is commenting on a photograph taken by Dorothea Lange in 1953 of her family that was included in the *Dialogue* issue on page 92. Dorothea Lange and Ansel Adams photographed Mormon towns in southern Utah in August 1953 for a *Life* magazine article. They appeared in Dorothea Lange and Ansel Adams, "Three Mormon Towns," *Life* 37 (September 6, 1954): 91–100. Additional photographs are reproduced in Mary Ellen Mark, Harry Reid, and Mark Hedengren, *Ansel Adams and Dorothea Lange's Three Mormon Towns* (Oakland: Oakland Museum of California, Utah Arts Council, 2012).

64. Dorothea Lange (1895–1965) was a documentary photographer and photojournalist, best known for her Depression-era work for the Farm Security Administration. Paul Schuster Taylor (1895–1984) was a professor of economics at the University of California, Berkeley from 1922 until his retirement in 1962.
65. Ansel Easton Adams (1902–1984) was a photographer well known for his black-and-white landscape photographs of the American West, especially Yosemite National Park.
66. Almera Anderson Romney (1903–1980) was a teacher and principal at a school with a predominantly African American and Hispanic student body from 1946 to 1963 in Southern California. She wrote the article for the *Dialogue* issue, "All Children Are Alike unto Me."
67. Brooks is probably referring to the article "Single Voices" in the *Dialogue* issue.

Chapter 13

1. Wendell J. Ashton to JB, June 5, 1973, Levi Peterson's Collection.
2. JB to David Crockett, December 7, 1972, Levi Peterson's Collection.
3. Juanita Brooks, *Frontier Tales: True Stories of Real People*, Western Text Society Special Publication (Logan: Utah State University Press, 1972).
4. JB to Trudy McMurrin, early 1977, Levi Peterson's Collection.
5. Frank Diston (1920–1999), Friedman's agent, was an attorney and executive vice-president at Tracy-Collins Bank and Trust.
6. It was eventually published as Juanita Brooks, *History of the Jews in Utah and Idaho* (Salt Lake City: Western Epics, 1973).
7. Gibbs Morgan Smith (1940–2017) was president and founder of Gibbs Smith book publishing.
8. Gibbs Smith published the story as Juanita Brooks, *The Christmas Tree* (Salt Lake City: Peregrine Smith, 1972). Brooks originally wrote the story as a 1971 Christmas gift for her family and friends. She distributed copies of the three-page typed version with Christmas stickers.
9. Mescrew bush or screwbean mesquite (*Prosopis pubescens*) is a flowering shrub or small tree that can grow to seven meters in height and is the bush used as the Christmas tree in Brooks's story.
10. The Jacob Hamblin biographies were published as Paul Bailey, *Jacob Hamblin: Buckskin Apostle*, and Pearson H. Corbett, *Jacob Hamblin*.
11. James A. Little, *Jacob Hamblin*.
12. William Wise (1923–) is an author of many children's and young adult books. He was the author of *Massacre at Mountain Meadows* (New York: Thomas Y. Crowell, 1976).
13. Melvin T. Smith (1928–) was a professor of history at Dixie College, director of the Utah State Historical Society, and editor of the *Utah Historical Quarterly*.

14. The new edition with corrections was published as Juanita Brooks, *John Doyle Lee: Zealot–Pioneer Builder–Scapegoat* (rev. ed., Glendale, CA: Arthur H. Clark, 1972).
15. In testimonies given on Sunday, May 14, 1854, John Lott stood and bore: "We suffered from damned Sectarians in Missouri driven, robbed and murdered. I hope to see the day when the blood of the martyrs will be avenged, and these damnable rebels make restitution, or the children suffer for the wickedness of their Fathers." Next, Preston Lewis agreed, saying, "All the scenes Bror Lott has recounted I shared in, my Bror Benjamin was killed in Missouri, and I am alive to avenge his blood when the Lord will." Brooks, *Journal of the Southern Indian Mission*, 25. Haun's Mill refers to the event on October 30, 1838, where some of the Missouri militia attacked a Mormon settlement in eastern Caldwell County, Missouri, killing seventeen Mormons. Benjamin Lewis was one of those killed. Beth Shumway Moore, *Bones in the Well: The Haun's Mill Massacre, 1838* (Norman, OK: Arthur H. Clark, 2006).
16. Brooks is referring to a claim made by Malinda Cameron Thurston referenced and discussed in Brooks, *Mountain Meadows Massacre*, Fourth Printing, xv–xvii.
17. This letter was dated July 17, 1932, and signed by Mrs. Frances Haynes. It is discussed in Brooks, *Mountain Meadows Massacre*, Fourth Printing, xv.
18. Samuel Taylor, *Nightfall at Nauvoo* (New York: Macmillan, 1971).
19. John Young (1763–1839), Brigham Young's father, married Hannah Dennis Brown (1780–1867) in 1815 and had a son, Edward Young (1823–1900).
20. Rodello Hicken Hunter (1920–2005) was the author of several books and magazine articles.
21. Rodello H. Hunter, *A Daughter of Zion* (New York: Alfred A. Knopf, 1972).
22. Ross Eager (1933–1962) was stricken with polio in 1952 at the age of nineteen.
23. The three stories were included in "Memories of a Mormon Girlhood," *Journal of American Folklore* 77, no. 305 (July–September 1964): 195–229.
24. Eager married Zelda Fish and they had two daughters.
25. Brooks writes her neighbors about a continuing problem of dogs leaving deposits on her lawn that she has to clean up. She had called animal control and an investigating officer found that the neighbors had four or five dogs in violation of city ordinance, forcing them to remove some of their dogs and making them quite angry with Brooks. Peterson, *Juanita Brooks: Mormon Woman Historian*, 376.
26. Mary Hafen Leavitt (1877–1980) was the wife of Dudley Henry Leavitt (1870–1944) and Brooks's ninety-five-year-old mother.
27. White Cloverine brand salve is a petrolatum product for chapped and dry skin. The company offered premiums for selling their product.
28. David Crockett was the illustrator of Brooks's book, *The Christmas Tree*.

29. Charles S. Peterson (1927–2017) was professor of history at Utah State University and previously director of the Utah State Historical Society and editor of the *Utah Historical Quarterly.*
30. The manuscript was published as Juanita Brooks, *Emma Lee* (Logan: Utah State University Press, Western Text Society, 1975).
31. Following the death of John D. Lee, Emma Lee French married Franklin French, lived in several locations in Arizona, and finally settled in Winslow, Arizona, where she died and is buried. She served as a midwife and had the ability to cure the ill, so she was known as "Dr. French."
32. Brooks was a full-time instructor for the spring quarter (March 9–June 9, 1973) at Utah State University. Peterson, *Juanita Brooks: Mormon Woman Historian*, 384–85.
33. Mark Leone, "Why the Coalville Tabernacle Had to Be Razed: Principles Governing Mormon Architecture," *Dialogue* 8, no. 2 (Summer 1973): 30–39).
34. Mark B. Garff (1907–1995) was chairman of the LDS Church building committee from 1965 to 1971 and a member for eighteen years of the LDS Church welfare committee.
35. Zina Barnum (1921–2008) was a great-granddaughter of Janet Smith Leavitt, the Native American wife of Dudley Leavitt and Brooks's cousin.
36. Brooks provides Barnum with copies of the photo of Janet Smith Leavitt to replace the poor-quality one published in her *On the Ragged Edge: The Life and Times of Dudley Leavitt.* She included in many copies of the book a copy of a note explaining the problem with the illustration and a replacement photograph of Janet.
37. Brooks wrote the letter to Nelson on January 25, 1949, mentioning his correspondence concerning blacks and the priesthood. See chapter 3.
38. Brooks is referring to the controversy over Thomas Cheney's book, *The Golden Legacy: A Folk History of J. Golden Kimball* (Provo, UT: Brigham Young University Press, 1973), which was withdrawn and destroyed right after publication due to stories concerning Heber J. Grant that were unacceptable to someone in the LDS Church.
39. Lowry Nelson, "Speaking Out: Mormons and Negroes," *Christian Century* 91 (October 16, 1975): 949–50.
40. An interview with Brooks by Davis Bitton and Maureen Ursenbach was published as "Riding Herd: A Conversation with Juanita Brooks."
41. Jeffrey Ogden Johnson (1944–) was manager of the reference bureau of the Utah State Archives and author of a number of articles.
42. Emma Lee.
43. Leonard John Nuttall (1834–1905) was the private secretary of LDS Church presidents John Taylor and Wilford Woodruff. His diaries are published as Jedediah S. Rogers, *In the President's Office: The Diaries of L. John Nuttall, 1879–1892* (Salt Lake City: Signature Books, 2007). John Willard Young

(1844–1924) was a counselor in the LDS Church First Presidency and a counselor to the Quorum of Twelve Apostles.

44. Brooks does not mention this letter or the $500 cash payment in her biography of Emma Lee. P. T. Reilly, in his book *Lee's Ferry: From Mormon Crossing to National Park* (Logan: Utah State University Press, 1999), 82n27, references a similar letter transmitting a $500 draft to L. John Nuttall dated May 11, 1879, written for Emma Lee in Warren Johnson's hand. Nuttall notes in his diary for July 11, 1879, that he sent the $500 cash payment with other freight with his son, Leonard, to Lee's Ferry. Rogers, *In the President's Office*, 11.
45. David Grow was a member of the Brigham Young University faculty.
46. Elizabeth L. Snow Beckstrom (1890–1985) mostly taught junior high school and then was librarian for Dixie College for fourteen years.
47. Brooks describes the first dedication of the St. George Temple on January 1, 1877, when Wilford Woodruff, Erastus Snow, and Brigham Young Jr. offered dedicatory prayers. The temple was dedicated again on April 6, 1877, during the LDS Church Conference held at the St. George Temple.
48. Charles Walker's description in his diary of the temple dedication is in Larson and Larson, *Diary of Charles Lowell Walker*, 440–43.
49. Charles Smith (1819–1905) emigrated from England in 1843, arrived in the Salt Lake Valley in 1848, and eventually settled in St. George in 1862.
50. Brigham Young Jr. (1836–1903) was a member of the LDS Church Quorum of Twelve Apostles from 1868 until his death.
51. Fort Cameron was a United States military installation located in Beaver, Utah, from 1872 to 1883.
52. Ruth Louise Partridge (1898–1981) was a Utah author and poet.
53. The book Brooks received was actually Ruth Louise Partridge, *Other Drums* (Provo, UT: Privately printed, 1974).
54. Andrew Jenson, "Plural Marriage," *Historical Record* 6, no. 5 (May 1887): 233–34.
55. Todd Compton has identified thirty-three well-documented wives of Joseph Smith. Todd Compton, *In Sacred Loneliness: The Plural Wives of Joseph Smith* (Salt Lake City: Signature Books, 1997).
56. Mary Lythgoe Bradford (1930–) is the former editor of *Dialogue* and is the author of books, essays, and poetry. Bradford requested some thoughts from Brooks on being a woman writer from Utah.
57. Brooks is referring to the meeting she had with Apostle Delbert Stapley in 1961 over the John D. Lee notice of his reinstatement.
58. Fawn Brodie's letter included a copy of Brodie's prepublication negative review of William Wise's *Massacre at Mountain Meadows: An American Legend and Monumental Crime.* Brodie praised Brooks's book on the Mountain Meadows Massacre and felt Wise had used much from her book verbatim in his.

59. Trudy Ann McMurrin (1945–2009) was the daughter of Sterling McMurrin, who served as developmental editor to help Brooks write the later portions of her biographical essays that was eventually published as *Quicksand and Cactus*.
60. Brooks was moved back to St. George in early 1977. She sold her house in Salt Lake City.
61. This is the last letter in her extant collections.

Bibliography

Manuscript Collections

Dale L. Morgan Papers. BANC MSS 71/161 c. The Bancroft Library, University of California, Berkeley.

Institutional Archives, Huntington Library.

Juanita Brooks Papers. MSS B103. Utah State Historical Society.

Levi Peterson's Collection of Juanita Brooks Papers. MSS B 1221. Utah State Historical Society.

Levi S. Peterson Collection. WSUS 05-02-001. Archives, Stewart Library, Weber State University.

Special Collections, J. Willard Marriott Library, University of Utah.

Other Sources

Alder, Douglas D. *Honoring Juanita Brooks: A Compilation of 30 Annual Presentations from the Juanita Brooks Lecture Series, Dixie State University.* St. George, UT: Dixie State University, 2014.

Alter, J. Cecil. "Journal of Captain Albert Tracy, 1858–1860." *Utah Historical Quarterly* (1945): 1–128.

Anderson, Nels. *Desert Saints: The Mormon Frontier in Utah.* Chicago: University of Chicago Press, 1942.

Anderson, Richard L. "Oliver Cowdery's Non-Mormon Reputation." *Improvement Era* 71, no. 8 (August 1968): 18–19, 22, 24, 26.

———. "Reuben Miller, Recorder of Oliver Cowdery's Reaffirmations." *BYU Studies* 8, no. 3 (Spring 1968): 277–93.

"Appraisal of the So-Called Brodie Book." Salt Lake City: *Church News*, May 11, 1946.

Arrington, Leonard. *Great Basin Kingdom: An Economic History of the Latter-Day Saints, 1830–1900.* Cambridge: Harvard University Press, 1958.

———. "Inland to Zion: Mormon Trade on the Colorado River, 1864–1867." *Arizona and the West* 8, no. 3 (Autumn 1966): 239–50.

———. "Planning an Iron Industry for Utah." *Huntington Library Quarterly* 21, no. 2 (May 1958): 237–60.

Ashby, Robert L. *Holden, Utah: Early History Compiled by Robert L. Ashby at the End of 100 Years, 1855–56–1955–56.* Privately printed, 1956.

Backus, Anna Jean. *Mountain Meadows Witness: The Life and Times of Bishop Philip Klingensmith.* Spokane: Arthur H. Clark, 1995.

Bagley, Will. *Blood of the Prophets: Brigham Young and the Massacre at Mountain Meadows.* Norman: University of Oklahoma Press, 2002.

———. *The Pioneer Camp of the Saints: The 1846 and 1847 Mormon Trail Journals of Thomas Bullock.* Spokane: Arthur H. Clark, 1997.

Bahr, Howard M. *Saints Observed: Studies of Mormon Village Life, 1850–2005.* Salt Lake City: University of Utah Press, 2014.

Bailey, Paul Dayton. *Jacob Hamblin: Buckskin Apostle.* Los Angeles: Westernlore Press, 1948.

Barney, Ronald O. *The Mormon Vanguard Brigade of 1847: Norton Jacob's Record.* Logan: Utah State University Press, 2005.

Beadle, J. H. *Western Wilds and the Men Who Redeem Them: An Authentic Narrative.* Cincinnati: Jones Brothers, 1877.

Beattie, George William, and Helen Pruitt Beattie. *Heritage of the Valley: San Bernardino's First Century.* Pasadena: San Pasqual Press, 1939.

Berry, James Henderson. *Speech of Hon. James H. Berry, of Arkansas, in the Senate of the United States: On the Question of Excluding Hon. Reed Smoot, of Utah, from the United States Senate, Monday, February 11, 1907.* Washington, DC: US Government Printing Office, 1907.

Bitton, Davis, and Leonard J. Arrington. *Mormons and Their Historians.* Salt Lake City: University of Utah Press, 1988.

Bitton, Davis, and Maureen Ursenbach. "Riding Herd: A Conversation with Juanita Brooks." *Dialogue* 9, no. 1 (Spring 1974): 11–33.

Bonney, Edward. *Banditti of the Prairies; or, The Murderer's Doom!!: A Tale of the Mississippi Valley.* Chicago: T. B. Peterson and Brothers, 1850.

Bradshaw, Hazel. *Under Dixie Sun: A History of Washington County by Those Who Loved Their Forebears.* St. George, UT: Washington County Chapter Daughters of Utah Pioneers, 1950.

Brimhall, George Washington. *The Workers of Utah.* Provo City, UT: Printed by Enquirer Co., 1889.

Brodie, Fawn. "A Lincoln Who Never Was." *Reporter* 20 (June 25, 1959): 25–26.

———. *No Man Knows My History: The Life of Joseph Smith.* New York: Alfred A. Knopf, 1945.

———. *Richard Burton's City of the Saints and across the Rocky Mountains to California.* New York: Alfred A. Knopf, 1963.

———. "Who Won the Civil War Anyway?" *New York Times Book Review,* August 5, 1962.

Brooks, Juanita. *The Christmas Tree.* Salt Lake City: Peregrine Smith, 1972.

———. "The Christmas Tree." In *A Dixie Christmas: Stories of Christmas Past,* edited by Lyman Hafen and Roland Lee, 34–44. St. George, UT: Publishers Place, 1988.

———. "The Cotton Mission." *Utah Historical Quarterly* 29, no. 3 (July 1961): 201–21.

———. *Dudley Leavitt: Pioneer to Southern Utah.* St. George, UT: Printed by author, 1942.
———. "Early Buildings." *Utah Historical Quarterly* 29, no. 3 (July 1961): 241–53.
———. *Emma Lee.* Logan: Utah State University Press, Western Text Society Series, 1975.
———. "The Face of the Land." *Utah Historical Quarterly* 29, no. 3 (July 1961): 193–97.
———. "The First One Hundred Years of Southern Utah History." *Proceedings of the Utah Academy of Sciences, Arts and Letters* 24 (1946–1947): 71–79.
———. "From the Journal of John Pulsipher." *Utah Humanities Review* 2, no. 4 (October 1948): 351–79.
———. "From the Journal of John Pulsipher." *Western Humanities Review* 3, no. 1 (January 1949): 38–55.
———. *Frontier Tales: True Stories of Real People.* Western Text Society Special Publication. Logan: Utah State University Press, 1972.
———. *George Brooks: Artist in Stone.* St. George, UT: By the author, 1965.
———. *History of the Jews in Utah and Idaho.* Salt Lake City: Western Epics, 1973.
———. "Home Reminiscences of Uncle Will Brooks." In *A Believing People: Literature of the Latter-day Saints,* edited by Richard H. Cracroft and Neal E. Lambert, 94–102. Provo, UT: Brigham Young University Press, 1974.
———. "I Married a Family." *Dialogue* 6, no. 2 (Summer 1971): 15–21.
———. "Indian Relations on the Mormon Frontier." *Utah Historical Quarterly* 12, nos. 1–2 (January–April 1944): 1–48.
———. "Jacob Hamblin: Apostle to the Indians." *Arizona Highways* 19, no. 4 (April 1943): 31–55.
———. "Jacob Hamblin: Apostle to the Indians." *Improvement Era* 47, no. 4 (April 1944): 210–11, 249, 251–55.
———. *Jacob Hamblin: Mormon Apostle to the Indians.* Salt Lake City: Westwater Press, 1980.
———. "Jest a Copyin'—Word f'r Word." *Utah Historical Quarterly* 37, no. 4 (Fall 1969): 375–95.
———. *John Doyle Lee: Zealot–Pioneer Builder–Scapegoat.* Glendale, CA: Arthur H. Clark Company, 1961.
———. *John Doyle Lee: Zealot–Pioneer Builder–Scapegoat.* Rev. ed. Glendale, CA: Arthur H. Clark, 1972.
———. "John D. Lee: Diary of the Mormon Battalion Mission." *New Mexico Historical Review* 62, nos. 3–4 (July and October 1967): 165–209 and 281–332.
———. *Journal of the Southern Indian Mission: Diary of Thomas D. Brown.* Logan: Utah State University Press, 1972.
———. "Journal of Thales H. Haskell." *Utah Historical Quarterly* 12, nos. 1–2 (January–April 1944): 70–98.
———. "The Land That God Forgot." *Utah Historical Quarterly* 26, no. 3 (July 1958): 207–19.

———. "The Land That God Forgot." In *A Zion Canyon Reader*, edited by Nathan N. Waite and Reid L. Neilson, 201–6. Salt Lake City: University of Utah Press, 2014.

———. "Letters." *Truth* 21 (March 1956): 310–13.

———. "Memories of a Mormon Girlhood." *Journal of American Folklore* 77, no. 305 (July–September 1964): 195–219.

———. "The Mormons in Carson County, Utah Territory." *Nevada Historical Society Quarterly* 8, no. 1 (Spring 1965): 3–23.

———. "The Mountain Meadows: Historic Stopping Place on the Spanish Trail." *Utah Historical Quarterly* 35, no. 2 (Spring 1967): 137–43.

———. *The Mountain Meadows Massacre*. Stanford: Stanford University Press, 1950.

———. *The Mountain Meadows Massacre*. 2nd ed. Norman: University of Oklahoma Press, 1962.

———. *The Mountain Meadows Massacre*. 2nd ed. Fourth Printing. Norman: University of Oklahoma Press, 1970.

———. *Not by Bread Alone: The Journal of Martha Spence Heywood, 1850–1856*. Salt Lake City: Utah State Historical Society, 1978.

———. *On the Mormon Frontier: The Diary of Hosea Stout, 1844–1861*. 2 vols. Salt Lake City: University of Utah Press, 1964.

———. *On the Ragged Edge: The Life and Times of Dudley Leavitt*. Salt Lake City: Utah State Historical Society, 1973.

———. "The Outsider." In *Great Western Short Stories*, edited by J. Golden Taylor, 393–404. Palo Alto: American West Publishing, 1967.

———. "The Outsider." In *Westward the Women: An Anthology of Western Stories by Women*, edited by Vicki Piekarski, 158–67. New York: Doubleday, 1984.

———. "A Place of Refuge." *Nevada Historical Society Quarterly* 14, no. 1 (Spring 1971): 13–14.

———. *Quicksand and Cactus: A Memoir of the Southern Mormon Frontier*. Salt Lake City: Howe Brothers, 1982.

———. "Silver Reef." *Utah Historical Quarterly* 29, no. 3 (July 1961): 281–87.

———. "The Southern Indian Mission." *Improvement Era* 48, nos. 4–6 (April, May, and June 1945): 188, 212–15, 262–63, 342, 368–69.

———. "Speech Given at the Dedication of a Monument Honoring the Victims of the Massacre at Mountain Meadows." *Utah Historical Quarterly* 24, no. 1 (January 1956): 72–77.

———. "St. George, Utah: A Community Portrait." *Symposium on Mormon Culture*, 1–8. Logan: Utah Academy of Sciences, Arts and Letters, 1952.

———. *Uncle Will Tells His Story*. Salt Lake City: Taggart, 1970.

———. "Vignettes." *Utah Historical Quarterly* 29, no. 3 (July 1961): 289–302.

———. "Ye Who Are Called to Labor." *Improvement Era* 51, nos. 8–9 (August–September 1948): 498–99, 532–33, 564–65, 593–94, 596–97.

Brooks, Karl F. *The Life of Amos Milton Musser.* Master's thesis, Brigham Young University, 1961.
Cardon, A. F. "Mountain Meadows Burial Detachment, 1859: Thomas Gordon's Diary." *Utah Historical Quarterly* 35, no. 2 (Spring 1967): 143–46.
Carter, Clarence Edwin. *The Territorial Papers of the United States.* Washington, DC: US Government Printing Office, 1934.
Carter, Kate. *Heart Throbs of the West: A Unique Volume Treating Definite Subjects of Western History*, vol. 12. Salt Lake City: Daughters of Utah Pioneers, 1951.
———. *The Mormon Battalion.* Salt Lake City: Daughters of Utah Pioneers, 1956.
Cheney, Thomas. *The Golden Legacy: A Folk History of J. Golden Kimball.* Provo, UT: Brigham Young University Press, 1973.
———. *Lore of Faith and Folly.* Salt Lake City: University of Utah Press, 1971.
Clark, Robert A., and Patrick J. Brunet. *The Arthur H. Clark Company: An American Century, 1902–2002.* Spokane, WA: Arthur H. Clark, 2002.
Clayton, William. "The Pioneer Journal of Heber C. Kimball." *Utah Genealogical and Historical Magazine* 30 and 31 (1939 and 1940).
———. *William Clayton's Journal.* Salt Lake City: Deseret News, 1921.
Cleland, Robert Glass, and Juanita Brooks. *A Mormon Chronicle: The Diaries of John D. Lee, 1848–1876.* 2 vols. San Marino, CA: The Huntington Library, 1955.
Compton, Todd M. *A Frontier Life: Jacob Hamblin, Explorer and Indian Missionary.* Salt Lake City: University of Utah Press, 2013.
———. *In Sacred Loneliness: The Plural Wives of Joseph Smith.* Salt Lake City: Signature Books, 1997.
Cooley, Everett L. *Diary of Brigham Young, 1857.* Salt Lake City: Tanner Trust Fund, University of Utah Library, 1980.
———. "Journals of the Legislative Assembly: Territory of Utah Seventh Annual Session, 1857–1858." *Utah Historical Quarterly* 24, nos. 2–4 (April, July, and October 1956): 107–22, 237–60, 339–57.
Corbett, Pearson H. *Hyrum Smith Patriarch.* Salt Lake City: Deseret Book, 1963.
———. *Jacob Hamblin, the Peacemaker.* Salt Lake City: Deseret Book Company, 1952.
Cowley, Matthias F. *Wilford Woodruff: History of His Life and Labors as Recorded in His Diary Journals.* Salt Lake City: Deseret News, 1909.
Cradlebaugh, John. *Utah and the Mormons: Speech of Hon. John Cradlebaugh.* Washington, DC: L. Towers, 1863.
D'Arc, James V. *When Hollywood Came to Town.* Layton, UT: Gibbs Smith, 2010.
DeVoto, Bernard. *The Year of Decision: 1846.* Boston: Little, Brown, 1943.
Egan, William M. *Pioneering the West, 1846 to 1878: Major Howard Egan's Diary.* Richmond, UT: Howard R. Egan Estate, 1917.
Esshom, Frank. *Pioneers and Prominent Men of Utah.* Salt Lake City: Utah Pioneers Book Publishing, 1913.
Ferris, Mrs. B. G. *The Mormons at Home.* New York: Dix & Edwards, 1856.

Fisher, Vardis. *Children of God.* New York: Harper & Brothers, 1939.

Gardner, Hamilton. "Report of Lieut. Col. P. St. George Cooke of His March from Santa Fe, New Mexico, to San Diego, Upper California." *Utah Historical Quarterly* 22, no. 1 (January 1954): 15–40.

Givens, Terryl L., and Matthew J. Grow. *Parley P. Pratt: The Apostle Paul of Mormonism.* Oxford: Oxford University Press, 2011.

Godfrey, Donald G., and Rebecca S. Martineau-McCarty. *An Uncommon Pioneer: The Journals of James Henry Martineau, 1828–1918.* Provo: Religious Study Center, Brigham Young University, 2008.

Gove, Jesse. *The Utah Expedition, 1857–1858.* Concord: New Hampshire Historical Society, 1928.

Grow, Matthew J., et al. *The Joseph Smith Papers, Administrative Records, Council of Fifty Minutes, March 1844–January 1846.* Salt Lake City: The Church Historian's Press, 2016.

Gunn, Stanley R. *Oliver Cowdery: Second Elder and Scribe.* Salt Lake City: Bookcraft, 1962.

Hafen, LeRoy R., and Ann W. Hafen. *Handcarts to Zion: The Story of a Unique Western Migration, 1856–1860.* Glendale, CA: Arthur H. Clark, 1960.

Hafen, LeRoy, et al. "Mountain Meadows Massacre by Juanita Brooks." *Western Humanities Review* 5, no. 2 (Spring 1951): 209–15.

Hale, Veda Tebbs. "In Memoriam, Maurine Whipple." *Sunstone* 88 (August 1992): 13–15.

———. *"Swell Suffering": A Biography of Maurine Whipple.* Salt Lake City: Greg Kofford Books, 2011.

Hansen, Klaus J. *Quest for Empire: The Political Kingdom of God and the Council of Fifty in Mormon History.* East Lansing: Michigan State University Press, 1967.

Hardy, Pansy. "The Influence of Southern Nevada and Southern Utah on the Writings of Dr. Juanita Brooks and Dr. LeRoy R. Hafen." Master's thesis, Brigham Young University, 1965.

Harmer, Mabel. *The story of the Mormon Pioneers.* Salt Lake City: Deseret News Press, 1944.

Heap, Gwinn Harris. *Central Route to the Pacific, from the Valley of the Mississippi to California: Journal of the Expedition of E. F. Beale, Superintendent of Indian Affairs in California, and Gwinn Harris Heap, from Missouri to California, in 1853.* Philadelphia: Lippincott, Grambo, 1854.

Henrie, Agatha Manetta Price. *Descendants of John Doyle Lee, 1812–1877.* Provo: Privately printed, 1960.

Hickman, William. *Brigham's Destroying Angel.* New York: Geo. A. Crofutt, 1872.

Horne, Dennis B. *Latter Leaves in the Life of Lorenzo Snow.* Springville, UT: CFI, 2012.

Hunter, B. H., C. A. Patrides, and J. H. Adamson. *Bright Essence: Studies in Milton's Theology.* Salt Lake City: University of Utah Press, 1971.

Hunter, Rodello H. *A Daughter of Zion.* New York: Alfred A. Knopf, 1972.

Hyde, John. *Mormonism: Its Leaders and Designs*. New York: W. P. Fetridge, 1857.
Hyde, Myrtle Stevens. *Orson Hyde: The Olive Branch of Israel*. Salt Lake City: Agreka Books, 2000.
Hymns: Church of Jesus Christ of Latter-day Saints. Salt Lake City: Church of Jesus Christ of Latter-day Saints, 1948.
Jenson, Andrew. *The Historical Record*, vol. 7. Salt Lake City: Andrew Jenson, 1888.
———. *Journal History of the Church of Jesus Christ of Latter-day Saints*. LDS Church Archives, Salt Lake City.
———. "Plural Marriage." *The Historical Record* 6, no. 5 (May 1887): 233–34.
Johnson, Melvin C. "Just a Housewife? Juanita Brooks." *Journal of Mormon History* 42, no. 2 (April 2016): 214–23.
"Justice at Last! Execution of John D. Lee for Complicity in the Mountain Meadows Massacre." *Supplement Frank Leslie's Illustrated* (April 14, 1877): 109–11.
Kelly, Charles. *Journals of John D. Lee, 1846–47 and 1859*. Salt Lake City: Western Printing Company, 1938.
———. "Lee's Lost Gold Mine." *Desert Magazine* 9, no. 10 (August 1946): 9–11.
Kelly, Charles, and Hoffman Birney. *Holy Murder: The Story of Porter Rockwell*. New York: Minton, Balch, 1934.
Kenney, Scott C. *Wilford Woodruff's Journal*, vol. 3, *1846–1850*. Midvale, UT: Signature Books, 1983.
Kimball, Stanley B. *Heber C. Kimball: Mormon Patriarch and Pioneer*. Urbana: University of Illinois Press, 1981.
King, David S. *Mountain Meadows Massacre: A Search for Perspective*. Washington, DC: Potomac Corral of the Westerners, 1970.
Korns, J. Roderick. "*West from Fort Bridger: The Pioneering of the Immigrant Trails Across Utah, 1846–50*, edited by Dale L. Morgan." *Utah Historical Quarterly* 19 (1951): ix–xx, 1–297.
Kraut, Ogden. *Jesus Was Married*. Dugway, UT: Pioneer Press, 1969.
———. *The Three Nephites*. Dugway, UT: Pioneer Press, 1969.
Krenkal, John H. *The Life and Times of Joseph Fish, Mormon Pioneer*. Danville, IL: Interstate Printers and Publishers, 1970.
Lange, Dorothea, and Ansel Adams. "Three Mormon Towns." *Life* 37, no. 10 (September 6, 1954): 91–100.
Larson, A. Karl, and Katharine Miles Larson. *Diary of Charles Lowell Walker*. 2 vols. Logan: Utah State University Press, 1980.
Lauritzen, Jonreed. *Arrows into the Sun*. New York: Alfred A. Knopf, 1943.
Leavitt, Francis Hale. "Steam Navigation on the Colorado River." *California Historical Society Quarterly* 22, nos. 1–2 (March and June 1943): 1–25, 151–74.
Lee, Hector. *The Three Nephites: The Substance and Significance of the Legend in Folklore*. Albuquerque: University of New Mexico Publications in Language and Literature 2, 1949.
Lee, John D. *Mormonism Unveiled; or, The Life and Confessions of the Late Mormon Bishop, John D. Lee, Written by Himself*. St. Louis: Bryan, Brand, 1877.

———. *Mormon Menace: Being the Confessions of John Doyle Lee Danite—An Official Assassin of the Mormon Church Under the Late Brigham Young.* New York: Home Protection Publishing, 1905.

Lee, Verne R. *The Early Journals of John D. Lee.* Privately printed by Verne Lee, n.d.

Leone, Mark. "Why the Coalville Tabernacle Had to Be Razed: Principles Governing Mormon Architecture." *Dialogue* 8, no. 2 (Summer 1973): 30–39.

Leon-Portilla, Miguel. *Aztec Thought and Culture.* Norman: University of Oklahoma Press, 1963.

Let Every Sluice of Knowledge be Open'd and Set a Flowing: A Tribute to Philip May Hamer on the Completion of Ten Years as Executive Director. New York: National Historical Publications Commission, 1960.

Lillard, Richard G. *Desert Challenge: An Interpretation of Nevada.* New York: Alfred A. Knopf, 1942.

Limerick, Patty. "Quicksand, Cactus, and the Power of History in Polarized Times: Bringing Juanita Brooks and Dale L. Morgan Back into the Conversation." Keynote Address, Utah State Historical Society Conference, Salt Lake City, September 30, 2016.

Little, James A. *Jacob Hamblin: A Narrative of His Personal Experience, as a Frontiersman, Missionary to the Indians and Explorer, Fifth Book of the Faith-Promoting Series.* Salt Lake City: Juvenile Instructor Office, 1881.

Luce, Ray. "The Mormon Battalion: A Historical Accident?" *Utah Historical Quarterly* 42, no. 1 (Winter 1974): 27–38.

———. "Samuel Brannan: Speculator in Mexican Lands." Master's thesis, Brigham Young University, 1968.

Lyford, C. P. *The Mormon Problem: An Appeal to the American People.* New York: Phillips & Hunt, 1886.

Lyman, Edward Leo. *Candid Insights of a Mormon Apostle: The Diaries of Abraham H. Cannon, 1889–1895.* Salt Lake City: Signature Books and Smith-Pettit Foundation, 2010.

Madsen, Brigham D. *Studies of the Book of Mormon.* Urbana: University of Illinois Press, 1985.

Mahoney, Tom. *The Story of George Romney: Builder, Salesman, Crusader.* New York: Harper, 1960.

Mark, Mary Ellen, Harry Reid, and Mark Hedengren. *Ansel Adams and Dorothea Lange's Three Mormon Towns.* Oakland: Oakland Museum of California, Utah Arts Council, 2012.

Marquardt, H. Michael. *Later Patriarchal Blessings of the Church of Jesus Christ of Latter-day Saints.* Salt Lake City: The Smith-Pettit Foundation, 2012.

Mathias, O. Boyd. *Mormon Church and Its Negro Doctrine.* Term paper for a graduate social science seminar, University of Kansas City, Missouri.

McQuarrie, L. M. *Half Angel.* Garden City, NY: Doubleday, 1946.

Miller, Albert E. *The Immortal Pioneers*. St. George, UT: Privately published, 1946.

Moore, Beth Shumway. *Bones in the Well: The Haun's Mill Massacre, 1838*. Norman, OK: Arthur H. Clark, 2006.

Morgan, Dale L. "The Changing Face of Salt Lake City." Special Issue, *The Valley of the Great Salt Lake. Utah Historical Quarterly* 27, no. 3 (Summer 1959): 209–32.

———. *The Great Salt Lake*. Indianapolis: Bobbs-Merrill Company, 1947.

———. *The Humboldt: Highland to the West*. New York: Farrar & Rinehart, 1943.

———. *Introduction to the Inventory of State Archives of Utah: The State of Deseret*. Salt Lake City: Utah Historical Record Survey, Work Projects Administration, 1940.

———. *Jedediah Smith*. Indianapolis: Bobbs-Merrill, 1953.

———. *Overland in 1846: Diaries and Letters of the California-Oregon Trail*. Georgetown, CA: Talisman Press, 1963.

———. "The Reminiscences of James Holt: A Narrative of the Emmett Company." *Utah Historical Quarterly* 23, no. 1 (January 1955): 1–33.

———. "Scenic Backdrop with People." *Saturday Review of Literature* 28, no. 45 (November 10, 1945): 17.

———. "They Happened to Be Mormons." *Saturday Review of Literature* 28, no. 33 (April 18, 1945): 16.

———. *The West of William H. Ashley: The International Struggle for the Fur Trade of the Missouri, the Rocky Mountains, and the Columbia, with Explorations Beyond the Continental Divide, Recorded in the Diaries and Letters of William H. Ashley and His Contemporaries, 1822–1832*. Denver: Fred A. Rosenstock, Old West Publishing, 1964.

Neff, Andrew Love. *History of Utah 1847–1869*. Salt Lake City: Deseret News Press, 1940.

Nelson, Lee. *Beyond the Veil*, vol. 3. Orem, UT: Cedar Fort, 1990.

Nelson, Lowry. "Speaking Out: Mormons and Negroes." *Christian Century* 91 (October 16, 1975): 949–50.

Nibley, Hugh. *No Ma'am That's Not History: A Brief Review of Mrs. Brodie's Reluctant Vindication of a Prophet She Seeks to Expose*. Salt Lake City: Bookcraft, 1946.

Nibley, Preston. *Presidents of the Church*. Salt Lake City: Deseret Book, 1968.

Nuggets of Truth and Gems from the Speeches and Letters of the Leading Minds of Utah (Past and Present). N.p.: 1895.

O'Dea, Thomas F. *The Mormons*. Chicago: University of Chicago Press, 1957.

———. "Mormon Values: The Significance of a Religious Outlook for Social Action." PhD diss., Harvard University, 1953.

Partridge, Ruth. *Other Drums*. Provo, UT: Privately printed, 1974.

Penrose, Charles W. *Blood Atonement as Taught by Leading Elders of the Church of Jesus Christ of Latter-Day Saints: An Address Delivered in the Twelfth*

Ward Assembly Hall, Salt Lake City, October 12, 1884. Salt Lake City: Juvenile Instructor Office, 1884.

———. *The Mountain Meadows Massacre: Who Were Guilty of the Crime?* Salt Lake City: Juvenile Instructor Office, 1884.

Perego, Ugo A., and Scott R. Woodward. "Mountain Meadows Survivor? A Mitochondrial DNA Examination." *Journal of Mormon History* 32, no. 2 (October 2009): 53–61.

Peterson, Levi S. "In Memoriam: Juanita Brooks." *Sunstone* 13, no. 5 (October 1989): 6–8.

———. *Juanita Brooks: Mormon Woman Historian*. Salt Lake City: University of Utah Press, 1988.

Pratt, Orson. "Interesting Items Concerning the Journeying of the Latter-day Saints from the City of Nauvoo, until Their Location in the Valley of the Great Salt Lake." *Millennial Star* 11 and 12 (1849–1850).

Prince, Gregory A., and Wm. Robert Wright. *David O. McKay and the Rise of Modern Mormonism*. Salt Lake City: University of Utah Press, 2005.

Quinn, Michael. "The Council of Fifty and Its Members, 1844 to 1945." *BYU Studies* 20, no. 2 (1980): 163–97.

Reid, Lorenzo H. "Early History of Utah's Dixie." Master's thesis, Brigham Young University, 1931.

Reilly, P. T. *Lee's Ferry: From Mormon Crossing to National Park*. Logan: Utah State University Press, 1999.

Ricketts, Norma Baldwin. *The Mormon Battalion: U.S. Army of the West, 1846–1848*. Logan: Utah State University Press, 1996.

Rigdon, Sidney. *Oration Delivered by Sidney Rigdon on the 4th of July, 1838 at Far West, Caldwell County, Missouri*. Far West, MO: Printed at the Journal Office, 1838.

Roberts, B. H. *B. H. Roberts Defense Before Congress*. Dugway, UT: Pioneer Press, n.d.

———. *A Comprehensive History of the Church of Jesus Christ of Latter-day Saints, Century I*. 6 volumes. Salt Lake City: Church of Jesus Christ of Latter-day Saints, 1930.

Robertson, Frank. *Fort Hall: Gateway to the Oregon Country*. New York: Hastings House, 1963.

Rogers, Jedediah S. *The Council of Fifty: A Documentary History*. Salt Lake City: Signature Books, 2014.

———. *In the President's Office: The Diaries of L. John Nuttall, 1879–1892*. Salt Lake City: Signature Books, 2007.

Romney, Thomas C. *Life Story of Miles Park Romney*. Independence, MO: Zion's Printing and Publishing, 1948.

Saunders, Richard L. *Dale Morgan on the Mormons Collected Works, Parts 1 and 2, Kingdom in the West, The Mormons and the American Frontier, Volumes 14 and 15*. Norman, OK: Arthur H. Clark, 2012 and 2013.

———. *Eloquence from a Silent World: A Descriptive Bibliography of the Published Writings of Dale L. Morgan.* Salt Lake City: Caramon Press, 1990.

Schindler, Harold. *Orrin Porter Rockwell: Man of God, Son of Thunder.* Salt Lake City: University of Utah, 1966.

Scowcoft, Richard. *Children of the Covenant.* Boston: Houghton Mifflin, 1945

Smart, William B., and Donna T. Smart. *Over the Rim: The Parley P. Pratt Exploring Expedition to Southern Utah, 1849–1850.* Logan: Utah State University Press, 1999.

Smith, Craig S. "The 1847 Mormon Pioneer Trek: A View from the Unpublished Journal of Albert Carrington Written for George A. Smith." *Overland Journal* 27, no. 1 (Spring 2009): 3–17.

Smith, Emma. *A Collection of Sacred Hymns for the Church of the Latter Day Saints.* Kirtland, OH: F. G. Williams, 1835.

Smith, Ethan. *View of the Hebrews.* Poultney, VT: Smith and Shute, 1825.

Snow, LeRoi C. "An Experience of My Father's." *Improvement Era* 36, no. 11 (September 1933): 677, 679.

Sonne, Conway B. *Knight of the Kingdom.* Salt Lake City: Deseret Book, 1949.

———. *World of Wakara.* San Antonio: Naylor, 1962.

Sorensen, Virginia. *The Evening and the Morning.* New York: Harcourt Brace & World, 1949.

———. *The House Next Door.* New York: Charles Scribner's Sons, 1954.

———. *Many Heavens.* New York: Harcourt Brace, 1954.

———. *On This Star.* New York: Reynal & Hitchcock, 1946.

———. *Where Nothing Is Long Ago: Memoirs of a Mormon Childhood.* New York: Harcourt, Brace, & World, 1963.

Stafford, Helen Cortez. *Sweet Love Remembered.* Salt Lake City: Deseret Book Company, 1946.

Stegner, Wallace. *The Gathering of Zion.* New York: McGraw Hill, 1964.

Stenhouse, Fanny. *Tell It All: The Story of a Life's Experience in Mormonism.* Hartford: A. D. Worthington, 1874.

Stevenson, Edward. *Reminiscences of Joseph the Prophet and the Coming Forth of the Book of Mormon.* Salt Lake City: Published by the author, 1893.

Stewart, Ora Pate. *Tender Apples: A Biography of Ettie Lee.* Salt Lake City: Deseret Book, 1965.

Stott, Clifford L. *Search for Sanctuary: Brigham Young and the White Mountain Expedition.* Salt Lake City: University of Utah Press, 1984.

Stout, Reed Albert. "Autobiography of Hosea Stout." Reprinted from *Utah Historical Quarterly* 30 (1962): 1–88.

Swartzell, William. *Mormonism Exposed: Being a Journal of a Residence in Missouri from the 28th of May to the 20th of August, 1838: Together with an Appendix, Containing the Revelation Concerning the Golden Bible, with Numerous Extracts from the "Book of Covenants."* Pekin, OH: Published by the author; Printed in Pittsburg, 1840.

Taylor, J. Golden. *Hawthorne's Ambivalence Toward Puritanism*. Monograph Series 12, no. 1. Logan: Utah State University Press, 1965.

Taylor, J. Lewis. "John Taylor: Family Man." In *Champion of Liberty: John Taylor*, edited by Mary Jane Woodger, 193–217. Provo: Religious Studies Program, Brigham Young University, and Salt Lake City: Deseret Book, 2009.

Taylor, Raymond W., and Samuel W. Taylor. *Uranium Fever*. New York: Macmillan, 1970.

Taylor, Samuel W. *Family Kingdom*. New York: McGraw-Hill, 1951.

———. *The Kingdom or Nothing: The Life of John Taylor, Militant Mormon*. New York: Macmillan, 1976.

———. *Nightfall at Nauvoo*. New York: Macmillan, 1971.

Telling, Irving. "New Mexico Frontiers: A Social History of the Gallup Area, 1881–1901." PhD diss., Harvard University, 1952.

Topping, Gary. *Utah Historians and the Reconstruction of Western History*. Norman: University of Oklahoma Press, 2003.

———. "Women of Letters, A Unique Literary Tradition." In *Women in Utah History*, edited by Patricia Lyn Scott and Linda Thatcher, 295–323. Logan: Utah State University Press, 2005.

Turley, Richard E., Jr. "Juanita Brooks: 'Ahead of Her Time.'" Speech delivered to Alta Club Forum, January 24, 2017. Salt Lake City: Alta Club, 2017.

Turley, Richard E., Jr., Janiece L. Johnson, and LaJean Purcell Carruth. *Mountain Meadows Massacre Collected Legal Papers*. 2 volumes. Norman: University of Oklahoma Press, 2017.

Turley, Richard E., Jr., and Ronald W. Walker. *Mountain Meadows Massacre: The Andrew Jenson and David H. Morris Collections*. Provo, UT: Brigham Young University Press, 2009.

Turner, Floy L. *While the Desert Blossomed*. Provo, UT: J. Grant Stevenson, 1962.

Udall, Stewart. *The Quiet Crisis*. New York: Holt, Rinehart and Winston, 1963.

U.S. Congress. *Message of the President of the United States, Communicating, in Compliance with a Resolution of the Senate, Information in Relation to the Massacre at Mountain Meadows in Utah Territory*. 36th Congress, 1st Session, Ex. Doc. 42. Washington, DC: US Government Printing Office, 1860.

Utah: A Guide to the State. New York: Hastings House, 1941.

von Grueningen, John Paul. *The Swiss in the United States*. Madison, WI: Swiss-American Historical Society, 1940.

Walker, John Phillip. *Dale Morgan on Early Mormonism: Correspondence and a New History*. Salt Lake City: Signature Books, 1986.

Walker, Ronald W., Richard E. Turley Jr., and Glen M. Leonard. *Massacre at Mountain Meadows: An American Tragedy*. Oxford: Oxford University Press, 2008.

Watson, Elden J. *The Orson Pratt Journals*. Salt Lake City: Privately published, 1975.

West, Ray B. *Rocky Mountain Reader*. New York: E. P. Dutton, 1946.

Whipple, Maurine. *The Giant Joshua*. Boston: Houghton Mifflin, 1941.
———. *This Is the Place: Utah*. New York: Alfred A. Knopf, 1945.
Wise, William. *Massacre at Mountain Meadows*. New York: Thomas Y. Crowell, 1976.
Wright, Evan P., et al. *Biographies: Federal Heights Ward*. Salt Lake City: Federal Heights Ward Genealogical Committee, 1963.
Young, Brigham. *Journal of Discourses by Brigham Young, His Counsellors, The Twelve Apostles, and Others, Reported by G. D. Watt*. Volume 2. Liverpool: F. D. Richards, 1855.
Young, Kimball. *Isn't One Wife Enough?* New York: Henry Holt, 1954.

Index